THE FLORENTINE GALLEYS
IN THE
FIFTEENTH CENTURY

Oxford University Press, Ely House, London W. 1

GLASGOW NEW YORK TORONTO MELBOURNE WELLINGTON
CAPE TOWN SALISBURY IBADAN NAIROBI LUSAKA ADDIS ABABA
BOMBAY CALCUTTA MADRAS KARACHI LAHORE DACCA
KUALA LUMPUR HONG KONG TOKYO

A Venetian galley of the late fifteenth century

THE FLORENTINE GALLEYS
IN THE
FIFTEENTH CENTURY

BY

MICHAEL E. MALLETT

———✦———

WITH

The Diary of
Luca di Maso degli Albizzi
Captain of the Galleys
1429–1430

OXFORD
AT THE CLARENDON PRESS
1967

TO
PATRICIA

PREFACE

THE idea of this book developed while I was working on my thesis for the degree of Doctor of Philosophy in the University of Oxford. The thesis itself had a rather wider scope, dealing with the economic importance of Pisa in the fifteenth century and the effects on the Florentine economy of the Pisan war. However, it soon became apparent that the economic position of Pisa under the first Florentine domination depended to a considerable extent on the communal galley system which Florence had started in order to exploit to the full the commercial advantages which she had gained from the possession of her own ports. This book is therefore an expansion and development of several chapters of that thesis.

My research on this subject has been spread over nearly ten years and in that time I have incurred innumerable obligations, for which a few words in a preface are a very inadequate acknowledgement. For financial support during the early stages of the research I am indebted to the Ministry of Education, and to the British Council and the Italian Government for a one-year exchange scholarship to the Scuola Normale Superiore at Pisa. However, I owe my greatest debt to the British School at Rome which gave me a two-year scholarship and also an additional grant to travel to archives round the coasts of the western Mediterranean. I am also indebted for later research grants to the trustees of the Arnold Historical Essay Fund, to the Canada Council, and to the University of Manitoba.

I must next express my gratitude to the numerous Italian archivists and librarians whose unfailing help and kindness have made my work in their collections both fruitful and pleasant. My particular thanks go to Dr. Sergio Camerani, the Director of the Florence archives, for permission to publish the diary of Luca di Maso degli Albizzi, to Dr. Gino Corti who has given me invaluable assistance with the transcription of this diary, and to Dr. Roberto Abbondanza, now Director of the archives in Perugia, who in my early years in Florence did much to smooth the path of my research. Similarly my thanks go to Dr. Bruno Casini and

Professor Emilio Cristiani who helped to guide my first hesitant steps into the archives in Pisa.

So many fellow scholars have assisted me with their ideas, suggestions, and encouragement that I cannot mention them all by name. However, I must express my deep gratitude to my thesis supervisor and friend, Professor John Hale, for his constant kindness and advice at every stage of this work, to Professor Nicolai Rubinstein whose profound knowledge of Florentine history and friendly interest in my work have been a constant source of stimulation and encouragement, and to Dr. Philip Jones who, when I first went to Florence, put me on the track of some of the main sources for this history of the galleys. My thanks are also due to Dr. R. C. Anderson who very kindly read and commented on my chapter on galley construction, and to Professor Jacques Heers who read the entire manuscript in its penultimate draft.

To my friends and colleagues, both in Winnipeg and in Rome, I owe much for their continual encouragement and interest, and in particular I must thank Signorina Luciana Valentini who typed the manuscript. Finally it is only fitting that this book should be dedicated to my wife without whose unfailing patience and constant inspiration it would never have been written.

M. E. M.

CONTENTS

PART TWO

The Diary of Luca di Maso degli Albizzi

1429–30

LIST OF PLATES

MAPS

ABBREVIATIONS

1. *Archives*

(*a*) ASF   Archivio di Stato, Florence

Balìe	Registri delle Balìe
Consoli del Mare	Archivio dei Consoli del Mare
Consulte	Registri delle Consulte e Pratiche
MAP	Archivio Mediceo avanti il Principato
Miss. I Canc.	Registri delle Lettere Missive della prima Cancelleria
Miss. II Canc.	Registri delle Lettere Missive della seconda Cancelleria
Provv.	Registri delle Provvisioni
Sig. X, VIII	Signoria, Dieci di Balìa e Otto di Pratica, legazioni e commissarie; missive e responsive
Strozziana	Carte Strozziane
Tratte	Registri delle Tratte

Albizzi Diary	Sig. X, VIII, 5, I
Cronaca di Benedetto Dei	ASF, Manoscritti 119

(*b*) ASP   Archivio di Stato, Pisa

Comune	Archivio del Comune
Contratti	Archivio della Gabella dei Contratti

(*c*) ASR   Archivio di Stato, Rome

(*d*) PRO   Public Record Office, London

LTR Customs	Exchequer Lord Treasurer's Remembrancer Enrolled Customs Accounts
KR Customs	Exchequer King's Remembrancer Customs Accounts
KR Memoranda	Exchequer King's Remembrancer Memoranda Roll

(*e*) SCC   Southampton Civic Centre, Southampton

SPCB	Southampton Petty Customs Books

(*f*) ACA   Archivo de la Corona de Aragón, Barcelona

Ancoratge	Real Patrimonio, Derecho del Ancoratge

(*g*) ARV   Archivo del Reino, Valencia

Guiatges	Archivo Real, Guiatges

(*h*) BNF	Biblioteca Nazionale, Florence

| Naz. | Manoscritti del Fondo Nazionale |
| Magliabechiana | Manoscritti del Fondo Magliabechiano |

| *Quadernuccio di Luigi Vettori* | Magliabechiana XIII, 79 |

2. *Periodicals and other works*

Annales	*Annales: économies, sociétés, civilisations*
ASI	*Archivio storico italiano*
ASLSP	*Archivio della Società ligure di storia patria*
ASRSP	*Archivio della Società romana di storia patria*
BSP	*Bollettino storico pisano*
EHR	*English Historical Review*
Muratori	Muratori, L. A. (ed.), *Rerum Italicarum Scriptores*, Milan, 1723–51
RBPH	*Revue belge de philologie et d'histoire*
RIS	*Rerum Italicarum Scriptores*, Nuova edizione, riveduta, ampliata e corretta con la direzione di G. Carducci, Città di Castello, 1900– .
RSI	*Rivista storica italiana*
Sapori, *Studi*	Sapori, Armando, *Studi di storia economica medievale*, 2 vols., Florence, 1955
Studi storici	*Studi storici*, periodico trimestrale diretto da Amedeo Crivellucci

N.B. All dates cited are New Style.

PART ONE

A History of the Florentine Galleys
1421–80

I

INTRODUCTION: FLORENCE AND PISA AT THE BEGINNING OF THE FIFTEENTH CENTURY

THE year 1406 was a time of great rejoicing in Florence. After a long siege Gino Capponi's troops had finally entered Pisa and brought the subdued and exhausted city under Florentine rule. Pisa surrendered on 9 October, and three days of celebrations marked the event which became for the chroniclers the greatest achievement of the Albizzi régime.[1] Even at the end of the century, after the Pisans had once more won their independence, 9 October was still celebrated with a solemn Mass in Sta. Maria del Fiore.[2] Following the occupation the Florentines took immediate steps to safeguard this new acquisition both against external assault and against internal revolution. Repairs to the outer walls were carried out with feverish haste, and the building of a new citadel on the eastern side of the city was begun and took the best part of the century to complete.[3] A garrison of 1,000 infantry and 500 lances was stationed in the city, and 300 of the wealthiest and most influential Pisan citizens were sent to Florence lest they should foment discontent.[4]

All this excitement and activity was not just because another Tuscan city had fallen under Florentine domination; the subjugation of Pisa was the realization of an ambition which had dominated Florentine policy for over a century. Ghibelline Pisa had been one of the traditional enemies of Guelph Florence, but anachronistic political disputes of this nature were not the real issues at stake.

[1] G. O. Corazzini, *Lettera dei casi quando i Fiorentini presero Pisa*, for Nozze Modena-Rosessi Tedesca, Florence, 1894, pp. 14–15; M. Palmieri, *De captivitate Pisarum liber*, ed. G. Scaramella, *RIS*, xix, pt. ii, Città di Castello, 1904; Neri Capponi, *Commentarii dell'acquisto di Pisa nel 1406*, in *Cronichette antiche di varii scrittori del buon secolo della lingua toscana*, raccolte da D. M. Manni, Milan, 1733.

[2] *Historia fiorentina di Piero di Marco Parenti*, f. 55 (BNF, Naz. II. II. 130).

[3] P. Silva, 'Pisa sotto Firenze dal 1406 al 1432', *Studi storici*, xviii, 1909–10, pp. 139–40.

[4] Ibid., pp. 141–4.

The rivalry between the two cities was primarily economic. Florence, situated 60 miles inland on the banks of the Arno, had to have a secure outlet to the sea if her commercial prosperity was to continue. Pisa, almost at the mouth of the Arno, represented a permanent threat not only as a commercial rival but as a physical barrier to Florence's commerce. The occupation of Pisa represented the climax of a 'tendenza al mare' which had been the key to Florentine foreign policy and commercial activity for over two centuries.[1]

In fact the fall of Pisa in 1406 was the completion of a dramatic reversal in the economic and political position of the two Tuscan cities. Up to the end of the twelfth century Pisa had been the larger town, and with her advantageous position at the mouth of the Arno had not only dominated Tuscan internal trade, but had also been in the forefront of Italian maritime powers whose merchants had followed the crusaders into the eastern Mediterranean. From 1016, when the Pisans had driven the Saracens from Sardinia, until the battle of Meloria in 1284, Pisa was able to maintain her commercial supremacy over her inland rival, although the latter had already outgrown her in size and industrial development.

Indeed commercial rivalry had only sprung up between the two in the thirteenth century. Throughout the twelfth century, from the time when Florence had willingly submitted to Pisan leadership in the crusade against Majorca in 1113, up to the commercial treaty of 1171, the Florentines were only too glad of Pisan friendship. In 1171 Pisa could afford to be magnanimous and allowed considerable commercial concessions to secure an ally in the Tuscan hinterland. At this time Florence was just beginning to expand commercially and the generous benefits which she derived from this treaty, including the right to load her goods on Pisan ships paying the same charges as Pisan goods, and paying only half the duties which Pisans paid in Porto Pisano, were very real factors in the rapid growth of Florentine commercial interests in the early years of the thirteenth century.[2]

However, throughout the twelfth and thirteenth centuries the Florentines had to rely on Pisan shipping and on sharing in the

---

[1] A. Doren, *Studien aus der florentiner Wirtschaftsgeschichte*, vol. i, *Die florentiner Wollentuchindustrie*, Stuttgart, 1901, pp. 115–16.

[2] This first commercial treaty was published by P. Santini (ed.), *Documenti dell'antica costituzione di Firenze*, Florence, 1895, p. 5.

concessions won by the Pisans in foreign ports. As the Pisans established themselves in Constantinople, Cyprus, Antioch, Tyre, Acre, Alexandria, and Tunis, the Florentines followed, trading as Pisans and enjoying the same privileges.[1] But from the beginning of the thirteenth century onwards the relations between the two cities began to deteriorate as each realized the danger to her own commercial position constituted by the other. In 1220 hostilities broke out between them with Lucca as the ally of Florence, and Siena aligned with Pisa as the Tuscan champions of Ghibellinism. The immediate cause of this war was the seizure of Florentine merchandise in Pisa by the Pisans as a reprisal for certain indignities suffered by Pisans in Rome at the hands of Florentines. Although it was not in fact the first war between Pisa and Florence, a similar alliance system having grown up in the second half of the twelfth century, it was the first which broke out over a specifically commercial matter.

In 1251 Florence obtained the right to use the port of Talamone from the counts Aldobrandeschi, and this effort to free themselves from commercial dependence on Pisa provoked another war. This indicated that Pisa was already herself becoming dependent on Florentine traffic through her port. Pisa was forced to submit in 1254 and the peace terms included the concession of passage for Florentine goods through the city completely free of customs duties. In fact it had not taken the Florentines long to realize that Talamone, owing to its size, its isolated position and its unhygienic living conditions, was not the answer to their problem.[2]

The supremacy established by the Florentines by virtue of this treaty became even more pronounced when, after the battle of Meloria, Pisa ceased to rank as one of Italy's major sea powers. Once Pisa's naval prestige had disappeared every advantage to be drawn from an alliance with her vanished also, and complete domination remained the only ultimate answer for Florence. But in the thirty years following Meloria Pisa was able to hold her own in the struggle with Florence by entrusting herself to a series of strong generals and tyrants. The treaty of 1293 did nothing to

[1] For a useful recent study of Florentine commercial expansion in the thirteenth and fourteenth centuries, see S. Borsari, 'L'espansione economica fiorentina nell'Oriente cristiano sino alla metà del Trecento', *RSI*, lxx, 1958.

[2] L. Banchi, 'I porti della Maremma senese durante la Repubblica', *ASI*, 3rd ser., x–xii, 1869–70. For particular references to the Florentine use of Talamone, see x, pt. 2, pp. 82–84; xi, pt. 2, pp. 76, 77, 80–88; xii, pt. 2, pp. 72–87.

extend Florentine commercial privileges in Pisa, but gave the Pisans considerable concessions in Florence, notably the right to sell Greek wine in Florence free of dues.

It was perhaps these increased benefits to be derived from an alliance with Florence, i.e. not only passively handling Florentine trade through Pisa, but actively exploiting the Florentine market, which encouraged the growth of a pro-Florentine party in Pisa. This party, known in fourteenth-century Pisan politics as the Bergolini, consisted of a new capitalist class which had sprung up largely in the latter half of the thirteenth century to seize control of the new woollen industry and a new and more limited commerce which was concerned primarily with the western Mediterranean. These men appreciated that with her reduced naval power a more limited field of commercial operations was a sensible policy for Pisa; at the same time the new concentration on wool turned their eyes particularly to Spain, one of the great wool exporters. Opposed to the Bergolini and any thought of a Florentine alliance were the Raspanti, the older Ghibelline families who had inherited the by now traditional enmity with Florence, and who had led Pisa in her moments of commercial greatness in the eastern Mediterranean. They preferred to fight Florence to the last, extracting profit from her trade by heavy duties, and trying to maintain Pisa's old superiority in the East.[1] It was the rise to power of the Raspanti, under Rinieri della Gherardesca, in 1322, and again in 1355, which touched off periods of discriminating taxes on Florentine goods, open hostility and the removal of Florentine trade to Talamone. On the other hand, the return to power of the Bergolini led to the commercial treaties of 1343 and 1369, and in these events the new capitalist families of the Gambacorta and Dell'Agnello took the lead.

The treaty of 1369, which renewed all Florentine commercial concessions in Pisa, was the last of the series, and from then until the end of the century an uneasy truce continued between the two States. The Bergolini had virtually sacrificed the woollen industry which was unable to compete on equal terms with that of Florence, but Pisa continued to hold an important place in the commerce of

[1] For a good analysis of the changes in Pisa's political, social, and economic structure in the second half of the thirteenth century which led to the rise of these two parties, see D. Herlihy, *Pisa in the Early Renaissance*, Yale, 1958. An older work but still of considerable value is P. Silva, 'Intorno all'industria e al commercio della lana in Pisa', *Studi storici*, xix, 1910.

the western Mediterranean. A flourishing Catalan colony existed in Pisa,[1] and although the Florentines were now admitted to Tunis on terms of equality with the Pisans, the latter maintained their warehouse there. In Provence also the Pisans continued to have considerable interests,[2] and the old enmity with Genoa had died down once Pisa had lost Sardinia and virtually abandoned the eastern Mediterranean.

However, by the end of the century Florence's innate distrust of the Pisans, and the generally unsatisfactory nature of Pisa as a trade outlet in the existing circumstances, had led her to use Genoa as the real market for her maritime commerce. Much of the wool from England was brought in Genoese ships, and the ports of Tuscany were merely used as points of entry and exit.[3] At the same time a good deal of Florence's trade with the East passed through Venice, as is illustrated in the famous death-bed oration of Doge Mocenigo.[4] Ancona also was increasing in importance as an outlet for Florentine trade in the second half of the fourteenth century. The land route to the port was not much longer although a good deal more difficult than that to Pisa, and once there the shipment to the East was much easier either direct or via the great road across the Balkans.[5] But the desire for an independent outlet to the sea had not died

---

[1] P. Silva, 'Sulle relazioni commerciali tra Pisa e l'Aragona', *Bollettino pisano d'arte e di storia*, 1913, pp. 121–34.

[2] E. Massart, 'Le relazioni commerciali fra Pisa e la Provenza', *BSP*, iii, pp. 7–31.

[3] R. Piattoli, 'Il problema portuale di Firenze dall'ultima lotta con Gian Galeazzo Visconti alle prime trattative per l'acquisto di Pisa (1402–1405)', *Rivista storica degli archivi toscani*, ii, 1930, p. 159.

[4] 'Voi sapete che i fiorentini danno ogni anno panni sedicimila li quali consumiamo nella Barberia, nell'Egitto, nella Soria, in Cipro, in Rodi, nella Romania, in Candia, nella Morea et nell'Istria et ogni mese fiorentini conducono settanta mile ducati di tutte sorte mercantie in questa città che sono all'anno ducati ottocentoquaranta mille e più, e cavano lane francese, catalanese, cremise, stame, sede, ori, argenti filadi e gioie con gran beneficio di questa città.' See S. Romanin, *Storia documentata di Venezia*, Venice, 1853–61, iv, pp. 94 sqq. For a discussion of the accuracy of these figures see G. Luzzatto, 'Sull'attendibilità di alcune statistiche economiche medievali, *Giornale degli economisti e rivista di statistica*, ser. iv, lxix, 1929.

[5] For the development of Florentine trade through Ancona, see G. Bonolis, 'Sul commercio delle città adriatiche nel Medioevo', *Rivista internazionale di scienze sociali*, lvi, 1911, p. 180; J. M. Pardessus, *Collection des lois maritimes antérieures au XVIIIᵉ siècle*, Paris, 1828, iii, p. lxvii; R. Ciasca, *L'arte dei medici e speziali nella storia e nel commercio fiorentino dal secolo XII al XV*, Florence, 1927, pp. 558–65; C. Ciavarini, *Statuti anconitani del mare, del terzenale, e delle dogane, e patti con diverse nazioni*, Ancona, 1896, pp. 238 sqq.; W. Heyd, *Storia del commercio del Levante nel Medio Evo*, Turin, 1913, p. 863.

in Florence, although it was temporarily submerged by the internal social conflict and by the late fourteenth-century decline in her trade. That the final urge towards the complete occupation of Pisa should have come when it did was due to two factors; first the new situation created by the appearance of the Visconti in Pisa, and secondly the expansionist policy of the oligarchic régime led by the Albizzi.[1]

The alliance between Jacopo d'Appiano, the tyrant of Pisa, and Gian Galeazzo Visconti in 1397 was the initial move in the final crisis. Within two years Gian Galeazzo was recognized as *Signore* of Pisa, and Milanese troops were garrisoning the city while Milanese merchants dominated the market. Although the peace of Venice in 1400 still gave Florence the right to transport her goods through Pisa,[2] this was only a temporary concession granted until such time as Gian Galeazzo had succeeded in his plan to isolate Florence and strangle her trade. For this was his aim, and it was implemented by terrorizing Siena and Jacopo d'Appiano into withholding the use of Talamone and Piombino from the Florentines, and by the accession to power in Lucca of Paolo Guinigi, who, as an ally of the Visconti, obstructed the Florentine use of Motrone.[3] In this way the coast could be sealed off completely, and it only remained to take Bologna and cut the Florentine trade route to Venice. This was achieved in 1402, and immediately Pisa was closed to Florentine goods. The blockade was made even more secure by the

---

[1] For the events which led up to the acquisition of Pisa in 1406, see G. Capponi, *Storia della Repubblica di Firenze*, Florence, 1875, book iv, pp. 408–32; C. de la Roncière, 'La domination française à Pise (1404–1406)', *Mélanges d'archéologie et d'histoire*, xv, 1895; G. Scaramella, 'La dominazione viscontea in Pisa (1399–1405)', *Studi storici*, iii, 1894, pp. 423–83; P. Silva, 'Ordinamento interno e contrasti politici e sociali in Pisa sotto il dominio visconteo', ibid. xxi, 1913; R. Piattoli, 'Firenze e Genova al tramonto della libertà di Pisa', *Giornale storico e letterario della Liguria*, vi, 1930; C. O. Corazzini, *L'assedio di Pisa (1405–6)*, Florence, 1885; P. Silva, 'Il governo di Piero Gambacorta e le sue relazioni col resto della Toscana e coi Visconti', *Annali della R. Scuola Normale Superiore di Pisa*, xxiii, 1912.

[2] H. Baron, *Humanistic and Political Literature in Florence and Venice at the Beginning of the Quattrocento*, Harvard, 1955, p. 43. Baron discusses the pamphlet controversy between Antonio da Loschi and Coluccio Salutati in which the question of Florentine traffic was raised. Loschi in his *Invectiva in Florentinos* asks: 'Answer me what place, what granaries you believe will save you from starvation? . . . Realise that you are stripped of that port by which you need to live and breathe.' Salutati's response may perhaps be regarded as optimistic propaganda for he says: 'Believe me the fields of the Arno valley will suffice . . . and don't object that we have lost the port which I admit is most convenient for us. After all we have fought many wars with the Pisans, and whenever we did not have the port, it hurt them more than it did us.'

[3] Piattoli, 'Il problema portuale', pp. 159–64.

posting of a galley off the mouth of the Magra to nullify the effect of any last-minute wavering on the part of Guinigi. In fact the road to the Adriatic coast was still open but it was a difficult one, and by August not only was there a threat of famine in the city but also all commerce was said to have come to a standstill.[1] This moment of extreme danger to her commerce showed Florence unequivocally that in a completely dependent and well-defended Pisa lay the only hope of commercial security, and fortunately the lesson was learnt without great cost as Gian Galeazzo died of plague in September of the same year and the Milanese dominions were divided amongst his sons.

Although Siena and Piombino quickly reversed their policies once the shadow of the Visconti was removed, and allowed Florence to use their ports, it was now the occupation of Pisa which mattered to the Florentines. It took two and a half years of alternate use of force and bribes to open the gates of Pisa to Florentine troops, but by October 1406 the Pisans, betrayed in turn by the Visconti, the French, and their own leaders, were forced to submit.

This in a sense was the end of a chapter both in the struggle between Florence and Pisa and in Florentine commercial policy, although, as we shall see, in the latter story at least there was to be an appendix to this chapter, a pause before the next chapter could begin. During the thirteenth and early fourteenth centuries Florence had achieved the unique feat of building a position of almost unequalled wealth and economic strength without the use of a port of her own and without a fleet of her own. The main explanation for this was that Florence's economic strength rested only partly on commerce; the real basis of the Florentine economy was industry, and primarily the woollen cloth industry. Unlike Venice and Genoa which as maritime cities drew their wealth largely from trade, Florence had built up her wealth on the manufacture, processing, and sale of a particular article. Trade, of course, was involved and hence the importance of Pisa; the wool had to be imported, and the cloths had to be exported to find the best markets. But the real core of economic strength lay in Florence itself, in the workshops of the wool guild and the Calimala

---

[1] 'Qui non si fa niente di merchatanzia perchè tutte le strade sono serrate' was the report in September 1402 (*Storia di Milano*, Fondazione Treccani degli Alfieri, Milan, 1955, vi, p. 66). For further reports on the seriousness of the crisis for Florence see *Commissioni di Rinaldo degli Albizzi*, ed. Cesare Guasti, Florence, 1867, i, pp. 10–19.

guild. Here the wealth was amassed and the capital built up which made the Florentines also the leading bankers in Europe. All this was achieved with hired ships and a borrowed port, and as long as the Florentine economy continued to expand, as it did until about 1340, there was no reason why the Florentines should worry unduly about this phenomenon. But on the other hand, once a decline had set in in the second half of the fourteenth century with the collapse of the Florentine bankers in England, the Black Death, the social and political unrest in Florence itself, and the unsolved problem of Pisa, it was only natural that Florentines should feel that the key not only to economic recovery but also to even greater expansion would be to have their own fleet and their own port.

In fact in 1406 the way to the sea was only half open for Florence as Boucicault, the French governor of Genoa, who had been called in by the Pisans to protect them in the final crisis, still held the Pisan ports of Leghorn and Porto Pisano. These were sold to Genoa in the next year, and although Florence enjoyed a form of condominion and full trade facilities in Porto Pisano, the hostility of the Genoese exercised at such close quarters was a crippling curb on Florentine hopes of quickly becoming a seafaring nation.[1] Furthermore, no fleet of any significance was inherited from the Pisans, and there is no evidence of the Florentines starting any shipbuilding programme immediately, although they did appoint Andrea Gargiolli da Settignano as Captain of the Galleys in 1406. Therefore it seems that in this period immediately after the occupation of Pisa they continued to rely on foreign or hired shipping.[2]

Finally, however, in 1421 the two ports were bought from Genoa for 100,000 florins. The question of a sale had been raised

[1] P. Vigo, *Le repubbliche di Genova e Firenze per il possesso di Livorno*, Leghorn, 1915, *passim*. In 1408 and again between 1411 and 1413, Porto Pisano was virtually blockaded by the Genoese.

[2] M. Baruchello, *Livorno e il suo porto; origini, caratteristiche e vicende dei traffici livornesi*, Leghorn, 1932, p. 45; R. Doeheard and C. Kerremans, *Les relations commerciales entre Gênes, la Belgique et l'Outremont, 1400–1440*, Brussels, 1952, list a number of notarial documents relating to Genoese and other shipping plying between Porto Pisano and Flanders between 1406 and 1421; L. Piattoli, 'Le leggi fiorentine sull'assicurazione nel medioevo', *ASI*, 1932, pp. 226–33, points out the special concessions given to Catalan shipping during this period. There were in fact one or two long galleys built before 1421 for the protection of the coast and shipping; see Provv. 110, ff. 64 (29 July 1420) and 175 (15 Nov. 1420).

A recent important article on the commercial expansion of Florence in the fourteenth century and shipping in Pisa in the Datini period is F. Melis, 'Werner Sombart e i problemi della navigazione nel Medio Evo', in *L'opera di Werner Sombart nel centenario della nascita*, Milan, 1964.

PLATE 1

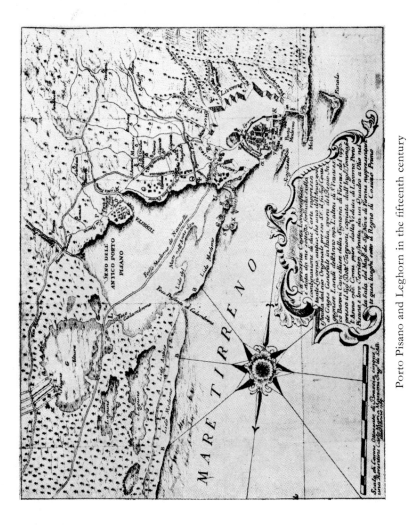

Porto Pisano and Leghorn in the fifteenth century

PLATE 2

Porto Pisano: the entrance to the harbour in the early fourteenth century

several times between 1406 and 1421 by both Genoa and Florence.
In Genoa the party of the Doge Tommaso Campofregoso regarded
Leghorn as an expensive liability particularly when the Republic
needed all her resources to defend herself from Milan. The first
price suggested by the Genoese was 160,000 florins but this was
refused by Florence, and it was only after the murder and cruci-
fixion of Luca Pinelli, the great Genoese opponent of the sale,
that the price of 100,000 florins was agreed.[1] In fact this is in itself
some indication of the value of Porto Pisano and Leghorn to
Florence as in 1405 she had paid only 200,000 florins to Gabriele
Maris Visconti for the title to Pisa and its whole *contado*. Now at
last the way to the sea was open and a state galley system could be
organized and ambassadors sent to the eastern Mediterranean to
seek trade concessions.

Certainly Pisa without its ports was not the great acquisition
that it appeared to be.[2] It had long since ceased to be a suitable
commercial port owing to the silting up of the mouth of the Arno,
which was itself frequently unnavigable. By the beginning of the
fifteenth century Pisa was 9 kilometres from the mouth of the river
having been only 3½ in the time of Strabo,[3] and the negotiation of
this stretch by seagoing vessels presented far greater difficulties
than its length warranted. Even in the thirteenth century the
Pisan fleet returning from the conquest of Majorca had to lighten
cargoes before going up the Arno to Pisa,[4] and in the fifteenth
century it sometimes took galleys two or three days to reach the
sea. Luca di Maso degli Albizzi's galleys in 1429 seem to have had
to resort to the use of capstans in getting to sea, presumably winch-
ing the galleys along the river with the aid of trees on the banks.[5]

[1] Vigo, *Genova e Firenze*, p. 80.

[2] 'Pisa senza Livorno non vale nulla, e che sia il vero e' Fiorentini ebbono la città
di Pisa l'anno 1406 ma mai non avevano navicato infino all'anno 1422 per amore di
Livorno.' *Cronaca di Benedetto Dei*, f. 9ʳ. 'Pisa senza essa (Livorno) era stata abban-
donata d'ogni commodità e emolumento'; F. Guicciardini, *Storia d'Italia*, ed. C.
Panigada, Bari, 1929, book ii, chap. i, p. 120.

[3] G. Merciai, *Mutamenti avvenuti nella configurazione del littorale fra Pisa e Orbetello dal
Pliocene in poi*, Pisa, 1910, p. 73. See also A. R. Toniolo, *Le variazioni storiche del
littorale toscano fra l'Arno e la Magra*, Milan, 1927; A. Main, *La costa del Tirreno
superiore e Porto Pisano*, Leghorn, 1888; F. Morozzi, *Dello stato antico e moderno del
fiume d'Arno*, Florence, 1762.

[4] P. Tronci, *Memorie istoriche della città di Pisa*, Leghorn, 1682, p. 5. Federigo
Visconti had similar difficulties on his way to and from Sardinia (Herlihy, *Pisa in
the Early Renaissance*, pp. 104–5).

[5] Albizzi Diary, f. 52ʳ. Albizzi experienced the same problems when on his way
to Spain in 1424, and on his return his galley was unable to get up the river at all

This situation was the result of a series of geographical factors which combined to decrease the value of the Arno as a water highway. In the first place the prevailing currents in the Tyrrhenian Sea move southwards along the coast and tend to deposit silt across the mouth of the rivers which debouch from it. Secondly, the downward slope of the Arno bed over the last 30 miles of the river's course is so gradual that in normal seasons the flow of the stream is unusually slow, and the sandy deposits carried along the bed tend to build up in the lower reaches. Moreover, the periods of drought in the summer reduce the flow of the river to a mere trickle, whilst in the autumn and spring with the seasonal rains and the melting of the snow in the Apennines, it becomes a torrent, known locally as the *piena*, which in the Middle Ages not only threatened Pisa with biannual flooding, but also prevented all navigation on the river.[1] Frequent attempts were made to alleviate the problem by dredging, and the banks of the Arno were protected from floods by a system of palisades. But the progress of sea-going ships between Pisa and the sea was at the best of times erratic.

This is not to say that such vessels were never seen in Pisa, for throughout the fifteenth century the shipbuilding yards remained in the old citadel at Pisa. The communal galleys were kept in the city 'between the bridges',[2] but were sent to Porto Pisano to load and unload their cargoes so that they could pass up and down the Arno empty. In 1477 a Neapolitan squadron with the Duke of Calabria and many Neapolitan noblemen on board, sailed up the Arno to Pisa to receive a festive welcome from many leading Florentines who had gone to meet them.[3] But this was an exception and usually the embarkation and disembarkation of both prominent travellers and merchandise took place in the ports.[4]

because of the shallow water (Sig. X, VIII, 5, ii, ff. 131 and 143). Giovanni Simone Tornabuoni reported that he had the greatest difficulty in getting his galley out of the Arno in 1473 (MAP XXIX, 314, 1 May 1473).

[1] L. Cantini, *Storia del commercio e navigazione dei Pisani*, Florence, 1797, ii, pp. 239–49; Targione Tozzetti, *Relazioni di alcuni viaggi*, Florence, 1768, ii, pp. 89–98.

[2] The bridge in Pisa at the western end of the city could be raised to permit ships to pass up river beyond it. The stretch of the Arno between this bridge, Ponte a Mare, and the next, Ponte Nuovo, ran alongside the commercial heart of the city, the Piazza S. Niccola, and here the galleys were moored. See Herlihy *Pisa in the Early Renaissance*, p. 92, and N. Toscanelli, 'Il Quartiere di Kinseca ed i ponti sull'Arno a Pisa nel Medioevo', *BSP*, 1934–5, p. 14.

[3] *La Istoria fiorentina di Piero Parenti*, ff. 4ᵛ–5ʳ (BNF, Naz. II. IV, 169).

[4] Eugenius IV in 1434 and Isabella of Aragon in 1488 both arrived in Leghorn,

This state of affairs had already existed throughout the period of the old Pisan republic, when Porto Pisano had been the port from which the Pisan trading and colonizing ventures had been launched. This was a large natural basin about 10 miles south of the mouth of the Arno, and it had at one time been linked to Pisa either by a southern arm of the Arno itself or by a canal. This link no longer existed in the Middle Ages and all water traffic had to go round by the mouth of the Arno.[1]

But even in the fourteenth century the suitability of Porto Pisano as a port was already in doubt, because of the interaction of the same geographical factors which had reduced the utility of Pisa itself. The mouth of the basin was constantly liable to silt up, and the threat had been increased by enemy action in 1259 and 1362 when the Florentines and Genoese had sunk blockships there. Also the basin itself was being reduced by the deposits brought down by the many small streams which emptied into it. The Pisans had foreseen the dangers, and besides making efforts to minimize them by dredging, etc., they had turned their attention to developing Leghorn.[2] Tax concessions had been granted to those who would settle there, a circuit of walls was built, and a new lighthouse begun in 1303.[3] The walls made the new port defensible from the land, an asset which Porto Pisano had never possessed. This development of Leghorn was continued by the Genoese during their brief domination, when it became the centre of the administration of both ports.

It is not possible to say when the change-over from Porto Pisano to Leghorn was complete, but it is probable that by the beginning of the sixteenth century the former was practically unusable, and the latter was ready to receive the full attention of the Grand Dukes. During the fifteenth century efforts were still made by the Florentines to rescue Porto Pisano from the creeping paralysis which threatened it. The mouth of the port was kept

and Lorenzo de' Medici departed from there in 1480. See G. Cambi, *Istorie fiorentine*, pub. by Ildefonso di Ser Luigi in *Delizie degli eruditi toscani*, Florence, 1785, i, p. 190 and ii, p. 39.

[1] Baruchello, *Livorno e il suo porto*, pp. 31–36; M. Rigobon, 'Per la storia delle sedi umane nel Valdarno inferiore', *Atti del R. Istituto veneto delle scienze, lettere ed arti*, 1920–1, p. 17.

[2] G. Bonaini, *Statuti inediti della città di Pisa*, Florence, 1870, vol. i *Breve Pisani Comunis*, p. 85.

[3] P. Vigo, *Porto Pisano; la sua difesa, il suo governo, la sua interna amministrazione*, Rome, 1898, pp. 24–25; Baruchello, *Livorno e il suo porto*, p. 47.

constantly dredged, and the new tower of the Marzocco was started in 1439.[1] It would appear from the records that the communal galleys used Porto Pisano as their base throughout their lifetime, that is up to 1480, but the indications are that other trade came to rely more and more upon Leghorn. Often the two names were interchangeable, and too much reliance cannot be placed on chance references to one or the other. Indeed they were so close to each other that confusion and a certain merging of functions was inevitable.[2]

Despite the money spent on the ports by first the Pisans and then the Florentines, and the tax concessions granted to the old inhabitants and to prospective settlers,[3] neither Leghorn nor Porto Pisano developed a substantial population before the end of the fifteenth century. The population of Leghorn in 1421 is estimated to have been 600–800,[4] and at the end of the century it was much the same. The merchants on the whole were not attracted to settle in the ports, and the meagre population was made up of port workers and fishermen, with a few reluctant Florentine officials. The warehouse and customs facilities were very limited. This reluctance to live in the ports was mainly the result of the notoriously unhealthy air of the surrounding marshes. The 'febbra livornina' was a recognized hazard and during the fifteenth century no less that six Florentine Captains of Leghorn died at their post, and at least two more were seriously ill.[5]

Therefore, although not in the true sense of the word a port

---

[1] E. Repetti, *Dizionario geografico, fisico, storico della Toscana*, Florence, 1841, iv, p. 617. For further examination of the construction work and repairs carried out by the Florentines in Porto Pisano during the fifteenth century, see G. Nudi, *Storia urbanistica di Livorno*, Venice, 1959, pp. 59–60.

[2] The papers of the Sea Consuls always refer to the galleys leaving Porto Pisano, whereas in the Missive della Signoria, where trade as a whole is treated, Leghorn is usually the port mentioned. Giovanni di Antonio da Uzzano in his *Practica della Mercatura* (see G. F. Pagnini, *Della decima e di varie altre gravezze imposte dal comune di Firenze*, Lucca, 1765, vol. iv) refers only to trade passing through Leghorn, and Heyd (*Commercio del Levante, passim*) cites Leghorn as the base for the galleys.

[3] The Florentine tax concessions to residents of Leghorn and Porto Pisano are published in full by P. Vigo, *Statuti e Provvisioni del Castello e Comune di Livorno*, Leghorn, 1892, pp. 1–63.

[4] Rigobon, *Valdarno inferiore*, p. 19.

[5] Reports of the deaths of officials in office can be found in the Tratte. Buonaccorso Pitti refused the post of Captain of Leghorn in 1423 to avoid the plague which was raging there (*Cronaca di Buonaccorso Pitti*, ed. Alberti Bacchi della Lega, Bologna, 1905, p. 244).

itself, Pisa continued to be the commercial centre for the trade of this part of the Tuscan coast. Within its walls there was some security from the 'malaria' which infested the whole Pisan plain, although in the summer months even Pisa became a very unhealthy spot. The customs house operated there, and all the merchants had their warehouses on the banks of the Arno. Under the Florentines Pisa continued to be the administrative centre of the area, and it was also the residence of the Sea Consuls who controlled trade, and an out-of-town resort for the Medici and other prominent Florentine families.[1]

All the merchandise passing between Florence (and the Tuscan interior) and the sea passed through Pisa, where all the merchants and the customs officials who were interested in it resided. Having been unloaded in the ports, the goods would be put on barges and sent round by the mouth of the Arno, or sent overland to Pisa.[2] This arrangement was not only a convenience to all concerned, but also enabled the traffic to make use of the natural route of the Arno. Although not the most direct route between Leghorn and Florence, the Arno valley was and still is the easiest both because of the value of the river itself for transporting goods and because of the good roads which ran along both banks.[3]

The value of the Arno for transporting goods inland from Pisa was very much affected by the seasonal variations in the flow of the river already mentioned. In the thirteenth century quite sizeable ships could reach Empoli under ideal conditions,[4] but by the fifteenth century the river was mainly used by flat-bottomed boats, and even these could not get further up than Signa. There goods had to be transferred to mule or cart for the last 10 miles into Florence. In fact it seems that despite its unsuitability for river traffic, the Arno was used for the transport of bulk goods such as grain,[5]

---

[1] The relationship between Pisa and Porto Pisano was very similar to that between Martigues and Port-de-Bouc, the former being the commercial centre for the port which enjoyed a notoriously unhealthy climate. See F. Reynaud, 'Le mouvement des navires et des marchandises à Port de Bouc à la fin du XVe siècle', *Révue d'histoire économique et sociale*, xxxiv, 2, 1956.

[2] Contratti, 280, ff. 120-4, *Statuti della dogana di Livorno*, published by P. Vigo, 'Statuto inedito della dogana di Livorno del secolo XV', *Miscellanea livornese*, ii, fasc. vii.

[3] The alternative to the Arno route was a poor road over the hills through Lari. This was the route which had to be used for much of the traffic during the Pisan war.

[4] Ciasca, *L'arte dei medici e speziali*, pp. 510-11.

[5] P. Vigo, *Porto Pisano*, p. 46.

salt,[1] iron,[2] and possibly wool.[3] Much has been written by economic historians on the enormous difference in cost between land and water transport in the Middle Ages, and a study of the costs of transport between Florence and Pisa along the thoroughly unsuitable Arno bears this out. In the fourteenth century the cost of taking grain from Pisa to Signa by boat was 2 *denari* a bushel, while to complete the journey by land to Florence, a distance of less than one-quarter of the other, cost 6 *denari* a bushel.[4] This disparity was to emerge as a considerable factor in the Florentine economy during the Pisan war (1494-1509), when the Arno was often unusable for river traffic. During this period transport costs of salt brought from Leghorn to Florence by the hill road were four or five times what they had been when the normal Arno route was in use.[5]

The importance of improving the value of the Arno as a means of carrying goods to and from the sea was fully appreciated by the Florentines, and in 1458 a commission of six Officials of the Canal was set up.[6] Their first instructions seem to have envisaged a canal which was to run all the way from Florence to Pisa, and which would enable large barges and even galleys to come right up river to Florence. However, very quickly this ambitious design was modified and attention was concentrated on the sections between Florence and Signa, and Pisa and Leghorn. The Canal Officials were empowered to buy up any land which was needed for the digging of these canals, and a special duty of 4 *denari* per *lira* of value was imposed on all imports through the Pisan customs to defray the costs of the canals. In fact even these projects did not get very far as the officials were soon burdened with a number of extraneous tasks which left them little time to think about canals.[7]

However, if these plans to facilitate trade between Florence and

[1] Balìe 30, f. 83ʳ (22 Dec. 1466); Provv. 178, f. 89ʳ (31 Aug. 1487); Provv. 180, f. 116ʳ (26 Jan. 1490).

[2] P. Ginori Conti, *Le magone della vena del ferro di Pisa e di Pietrasanta sotto la gestione di Piero de' Medici & Comp.*, Florence, 1939, pp. 60, 61.

[3] In 1572 there were still records of wool passing through the hands of the customs officials at Porto di Signa (ASF, Arte della Lana 160).

[4] P. Vigo, *Porto Pisano*, p. 46.   [5] Provv. 191, f. 3ʳ (13 Apr. 1500).

[6] Balìe 29, f. 17 (26 Aug. 1458). All the papers of these officials are collected in Balìe 32. The importance attached to this work is reflected by the fact that Cosimo de' Medici was one of the first six officials (Cambi, *Istorie*, i, p. 363).

[7] The Canal Officials were still in existence in the 1470's but by this time they were occupied with an inquiry into the state of Florentine trade, and with fortification and drainage works throughout the Pisan *contado* (see Balìe 32, ff. 26 sqq.).

Pisa never bore fruit in the fifteenth century, the plans for the expansion of trade outwards from Pisa were carried through with much more determination. Immediately after the purchase of Porto Pisano and Leghorn in 1421, a body of officials known as the Sea Consuls was set up to direct trade and launch a state galley system in imitation of that of the Venetians.

The Venetians had begun to employ the great galley as a commercial vehicle at the end of the thirteenth century, and very quickly devised a system of co-operation between the State and individual merchant entrepreneurs for their dispatch.[1] Up to the end of the thirteenth century large fleets of as many as twelve ships sailed at intervals to the eastern Mediterranean, but the extent to which these were subject to state control or were the results of specific contracts between the State and individual conductors is uncertain. However, by the first half of the fourteenth century the system of joint participation and regular voyages was established. The State built and equipped the galleys which were then hired to conductors for specific voyages. The schedules and routes were laid down by the State, and the conductor paid the hire price and made his profit out of the freight charges which he collected. During the fourteenth century the system gradually grew, with fleets operating to Cyprus, and Constantinople and the Black Sea from at least 1332 onwards, and thereafter voyages starting to Alexandria in 1346, to Flanders in 1347, to Syria in 1376, and to

---

[1] For a general picture of the Venetian galley system see R. Cessi, 'Le relazioni commerciali fra Venezia e le Fiandre nel secolo XIV', *Nuovo archivio veneto*, N.S. xxvii, 1914; J. Heers, 'Il commercio nel Mediterraneo alla fine del secolo XIV e nei primi anni del XV', *ASI*, cxiii, 1955; F. C. Lane, *Venetian Ships and Shipbuilders of the Renaissance*, Baltimore, 1934, pp. 133–7; A. Schaube, 'Die Anfänge der venezianischen Galeerenfahrten nach der Nordsee', *Historische Zeitschrift*, S. iii, ci, 1908; J. Sottas, *Les messageries maritimes de Venise au XIVe et au XVe siècles*, Paris, 1938; A. Tenenti and C. Vivanti, 'Les galères marchandes vénitiennes, XIV—XVIes siècles', *Annales*, 1961, 1; F. Thiriet, *La Romanie vénitienne au Moyen Age; le développement et l'exploitation du domaine colonial vénitien* (Bibliothèque des Écoles françaises d'Athènes et de Rome, 193), Paris, 1959; id., 'Quelques observations sur le trafic des galères vénitiennes depuis les chiffres des *incanti* (XIV—XVes siècles)', *Studi in onore di Amintore Fanfani*, Milan, 1962, ii; F. C. Lane, 'Venetian Merchant Galleys, 1300–1334; Private and Communal Operation', *Speculum*, xxxviii, 1963; A. Sacerdoti, 'Note sulle galere da mercato veneziane nel XV secolo', *Bollettino dell'Istituto di storia della società e stato veneziano*, iv, 1962.

A good description of the sources for a complete study of the Venetian galleys is to be found in F. C. Lane, 'La marine marchande et le trafic maritime de Venise à travers les siècles', *Les sources de l'histoire maritime: IVe Colloque d'histoire maritime*, Paris, 1962.

Aiguesmortes in 1402. The fleets were no longer so large as they had been in the thirteenth century, as the size of galleys had increased; four or five galleys was normal for most of the voyages. In the fifteenth century the system was still expanding, with the Aiguesmortes galleys extending their activities to the coasts of Catalonia, and the introduction of first a Barbary fleet in 1436 and later the *trafego* fleet which linked Alexandria and the Barbary coast. At the beginning of the fifteenth century about fourteen great galleys left Venice each year under this system, and during the century the number tended to increase so that in the second half it was usual for about twenty galleys to be dispatched. One of the main concerns in running the galley system was to ensure a rhythm of sailings which was most advantageous to the merchants. Thus it was important that the goods from the East should be in Venice in time for the great Christmas fairs when merchants from all over central Europe gathered there. It was equally important to ensure that the Flanders galleys and the Eastern galleys coincided so that goods could be passed as quickly as possible from Alexandria to London and vice versa. In conformity with these aims sailings for the East were timed for late July and August so that the galleys could be back by Christmas, while sailings for the West and Barbary usually took place in the spring and early summer with the Flanders galleys returning by the spring of the following year.[1]

The Venetian galleys at the beginning of the fifteenth century rarely carried more than 100 tons of valuable cargo but their size tended to increase during the century so that by 1490 great galleys capable of carrying 250 tons were not unusual. The galleys, particularly those to the eastern Mediterranean, tended to specialize to a much greater extent than Genoese, or later Florentine, shipping, and it was usual for galleys to Alexandria to load little else but pepper and ginger.

These state-organized Venetian galley fleets did not by any means carry the whole of Venetian commerce; in fact the great galleys made up only a small part of the total Venetian mercantile fleet. There was in addition not only the organized cotton fleet of sailing ships to Beirut and Cyprus, but also a vast fleet of privately owned and operated ships few of which were galleys.

---

[1] F. C. Lane, 'Ritmo e rapidità di giro d'affari nel commercio veneziano del quattrocento', *Studi in onore di Gino Luzzatto*, Milan, 1950, i.

However, it was the Venetian experience in organizing fleets of great galleys on which Florentines were able to draw in launching their own state-controlled galley system. The first galleys of the new venture sailed in the summer of 1422, and thereafter, until 1480 when the system was abandoned, Florentine galleys made more or less regular voyages to all parts of the Mediterranean and to Flanders and England. The only two modern economic historians who have devoted any space to considering this Florentine venture, Armando Sapori[1] and Gino Luzzatto,[2] have both written it off as a costly failure. A failure in a certain sense it was in that it failed to produce a permanent answer to Florence's economic problems; it failed to hold out in a world of growing individualism and rising capitalism. But the failure of the galley system was only relative. It had by no means virtually collapsed after a few years as both the above-mentioned historians maintain; in fact the height of galley activity was in the 1460's when as many as ten state galleys a year left Porto Pisano.[3] There does not seem to be any doubt that the communal galleys were a vital factor in fifteenth-century Florentine economic life; both Luzzatto and Sapori have drawn attention to the amount of wool which they brought in from England. They also did a great deal to increase Florentine prestige abroad. The possession of a reliable instrument of trade like the galleys was one of the factors which enabled the Florentines to oust the Venetians as the predominant trading colony in Constantinople after 1453.

Much of the neglect of this subject and many of the misconceptions about it are due to the absence of any continuous records for Florentine trade or shipping movements in the fifteenth century. There are no port books of Leghorn or Porto Pisano, and the records of the Sea Consuls contain actual details of voyages, cargoes, etc., only for a few years in the 1460's. So the picture which I have tried to build up of the working of the galley system resembles a mosaic from which many of the stones are missing. No doubt there were other galley voyages than those listed in

[1] A. Sapori, 'I primi viaggi di Levante e Ponente delle galere fiorentine', *ASI*, cxiv, 1956.
[2] G. Luzzatto, *Storia economica dell'età moderna e contemporanea*, Padua, 1955, i, pp. 98–99.
[3] Luzzatto in particular claims that, after the first few years of the system, the number of galleys sailing each year dropped to three (see *Storia economica d'Italia: il Medioevo*, Florence, 1963, p. 221).

Appendix A, although I venture to suggest that few can have escaped notice altogether; there are certainly plenty of names of galley officers missing, and, of course, the bulk of the cargo lists are lost. But I hope that I have been able to assemble sufficient material to fill in the main outline of a history of the galleys, and to justify this attempt to assess not only their importance to Florence and in fifteenth-century commerce as a whole, but also the real reasons for their suspension, and the bearing these factors may have had on late medieval shipping and particularly the Venetian galley system. I have also linked to this study the publication for the first time of the diary kept by Luca di Maso degli Albizzi during his voyage to Flanders and England as Captain of the Galleys in 1429. This diary is not only a valuable source from the point of view of the student of maritime history, but it also throws a good deal of light on the working of the Florentine galley system.

2

THE FLORENTINE GALLEYS

THE arrangements for the purchase of Leghorn and Porto Pisano from Genoa were concluded in June 1421, and by November proposals for the setting up of the office of the Sea Consuls were already being discussed by the Councils in Florence. The statute establishing the office finally received approval in December and with it a new group of government officials had joined the upper echelons of the Florentine administration.[1] The *Consoli del Mare*, or Sea Consuls, were not only given full authority in the supervision and direction of trade and commercial shipping, but they also received wide powers to provide for the development of the Florentine economy as a whole, and particularly to watch over the activities of the guilds. Although the name and to a certain extent the functions of the Consuls had been borrowed from the *Consoli del Mare* of the old Pisan Republic, these wide powers of overall supervision were a new departure. In fact they indicated a basic difference in structure and intention which the Florentines had introduced. The Pisan consuls had been representatives of the merchants; they had in fact been the consuls of the merchants' guild and as such the equivalents of the consuls of the wool guild, the notaries' guild, etc. They were not state-appointed and originally had no state responsibilities, but during the course of their history the Pisan government had tended to give them more

---

[1] Provv. 111, ff. 198ʳ–200ᵛ (13 Dec. 1421), published by G. Müller, *Documenti sulle relazioni delle città toscane coll'Oriente cristiano e coi Turchi*, Florence, 1879, pp. 279–81. For a more detailed study of the office of the Sea Consuls and its history during the fifteenth century see M. E. Mallett, 'The Sea Consuls of Florence in the Fifteenth Century', *Papers of the British School at Rome*, xxvii, 1959. Since I wrote this study my attention has been drawn by Prof. Marvin Becker to a group of officials known as the *Officiales maris* of Florence to whom there are some references in the 1360's. The exact functions of these officials I have not been able to determine, but it seems likely that they also should be considered as forerunners of the fifteenth-century Sea Consuls. For publication in French of parts of the archive of the Consuls relative to galley sailings to Flanders see A. Grunzweig, 'Les fonds du Consulat de la Mer aux archives de l'État de Florence', *Bulletin de l'Institut historique belge de Rome*, x, 1930.

and more official powers in connexion with the direction of trade.[1]
The Florentines, in order to increase the importance of the office
and to emphasize the vital nature of the affairs over which it pre-
sided, turned the Consuls into state officials appointed from a list
of candidates put forward by all the guilds. They became in a sense
a group of super-consuls with authority and jurisdiction over
the whole range of the Florentine economy. The creation of this
new office was a considerable blow to the prestige and authority
of the old-established *Sei della Mercanzia*, but the latter, whose main
function had been to deal with commercial litigation, had always
played a more passive role in the economic life of the city than that
which was now required of the Consuls. Florence was about to
launch a commercial offensive and this needed direction by a body
of leading merchants and citizens with the full authority of the
State behind them.

At first the headquarters of the Consuls, of whom there were six,
were in Florence; then in 1423 two were ordered to reside in Pisa,
and by 1426 three of them were permanently resident in Pisa while
the other three remained in Florence.[2] The two groups changed
round during their year in office, but they became in a sense two
separate departments. The Consuls in Pisa, as well as supervising
the day-to-day activity in the ports and building and dispatching
the communal galleys, took an ever-increasing part in the administration of Pisa and its *contado*, and particularly in the supervision
of the Pisan guilds.[3] The Consuls in Florence, on the other hand,
worked with the merchants in Florence; they hired out the galleys,
supervised the appointment of the galley officials, drew up the
regulations governing the conduct of the galleys, freight charges
to be levied, etc. They also acted as a commercial court and carried
out that part of the Consul's mandate which required them to
supervise the economic life of Florence. Finally they were responsible for the appointment and dispatch of trade embassies abroad.

The Sea Consuls were a group of officials who were to play a

---

[1] A. Schaube, *Das Konsulat des Meeres in Pisa*, Leipzig, 1888, pp. 216–17.

[2] 1426 is the date usually quoted for the division of the Sea Consuls into two
groups, but the 1423 statute has been generally ignored. It appears in Provv. 113,
f. 51^r (22 June 1423). For further discussion of this point, see Mallett, 'Sea Consuls',
p. 148.

[3] Strozziana II, 96, 18. This is an undated statement of the duties of the Consuls in
Pisa which brings out how much of the actual administration of Pisa and its *contado*
fell on their shoulders.

part in Florentine government for centuries to come, but the years of their greatest power and influence coincided with the life of the galley system, 1421–80. During this initial period the structure of the office of the Consuls, the number of Consuls, the methods of appointing them, and their peripheral duties were constantly changing in response to various political and economic pressures. For two brief periods they were dissolved and their duties were assumed by the Captains of the *Parte Guelfa*. But despite these vicissitudes, the Consuls maintained their importance and prestige, and during this period most of the leading merchants and citizens who were not openly hostile to the Medicean régime served in this capacity at least once.

The first six Consuls appointed from the lists presented by the guilds in 1421 were Niccolò di Giovanni da Uzzano, Gherardo di Jacopo Canigiani, Schiatta di Uberto Ridolfi, Agnolo di Ghezzo della Casa, Jacopo di Francesco Federighi, Banco di Sandro *coltriciaio*.[1] As these men were elected and not chosen by lot as the Consuls were to be in later years, it is of interest to see what qualifications and relevant experience they had to recommend them for this important new post. Niccolò da Uzzano is too well known as one of the more moderate leaders of the Albizzi oligarchy to need further introduction. He was obviously to lead the new enterprise, and his great wealth, his political and his mercantile experience eminently fitted him to do so. Canigiani had been an influential merchant in Pisa since the early years of the century. He had done business with Datini, and in 1419 was Florentine Captain of Pisa. In 1420 he had held the supreme post of Gonfalonier of Justice. Ridolfi, a scion of one of the great merchant families of Florence, was a wool merchant who had already twice been Prior and was to become Gonfalonier in 1425. Della Casa had also been Prior twice, and had experience of maritime affairs as he owned his own trading galley. In 1419 he had been one of the embassy sent to meet Martin V in the Romagna and escort him to Florence. Federighi had served as Prior on one occasion, and was in 1425 to be Captain of Leghorn. Finally Banco di Sandro was the most prominent minor guildsman of his day, serving with greater frequency than any of his fellows in official positions.

One of the first appointments made by the new Consuls was that of Taddeo di Piero di Cienni to be the first *provveditore* of the

[1] Cambi, *Istorie*, i, p. 155.

Consuls.[1] Cienni had worked as a factor in Venice for many years and was therefore fully familiar with the working of the Venetian galley system. For it was the Venetians whom the Florentines were preparing to imitate as by this time the Genoese relied almost entirely on carracks for their merchant shipping, and the State played little part in what was largely a private enterprise trade system.[2]

The Florentines were probably influenced in their choice of galleys rather than carracks by a variety of factors.[3] In the first place the galley was faster and more manœuvrable, particularly entering and leaving ports. This made it a more effective vehicle for a coastal carrying trade such as the Florentine galley trade very largely became. The great Genoese carracks on the other hand could not enter many of the smaller ports, and frequently experienced difficulty even in the larger ones. The galley also was far better able to defend itself against pirates, with its larger crew. Furthermore, the fact that galleys were generally held to be less seaworthy than sailing ships did not apply to the great merchant galleys which were quite capable of coping with Atlantic seas. On the other hand, the costs of using galleys were far higher because of the larger crews and smaller storage space; but then insurance rates were lower and in many cases merchants did not bother to insure goods which travelled on galleys. In many ways therefore the inherent advantages and disadvantages tended to cancel each other out; the galley remained the better vehicle for luxury goods which took up limited space and could pay the higher freight rates; while the carrack, or any type of sailing ship, held the advantage in carrying bulk goods of low value. The Venetians persevered

---

[1] Cambi, *Istorie*, i, p. 157. The Consuls normally had three *provveditori* who were their principal executive assistants. One worked with the Consuls in Florence, and two in Pisa, one as supervisor in the ports, and the other at the arsenal.

[2] Doeheard and Kerremans, *Relations commerciales*, *passim*, refer in their text and tables consistently to Genoese 'galleys', but the documents which they publish almost invariably use the term *navis*. Other sources seem to be agreed that by the fifteenth century the Genoese relied largely on carracks for their trade which dealt much more in bulk commodities than did the Venetian. See J. Heers, 'Commercio nel Mediterraneo', *passim*, and *Gênes au XVᵉ siècle*, Paris, 1961, pp. 267 sqq.; R. Lopez, 'Quattrocento genovese', *RSI*, lxxv, 1963.

[3] For analysis and comments on the part played by galleys in medieval trade, see particularly J. Heers, 'Types de navires et spécialisation des trafics en Méditerranée à la fin du Moyen Âge', *Le Navire et l'économie maritime du Moyen Âge au XVIIIᵉ siècle (IIᵉ Colloque d'histoire maritime)*, Paris, 1958. Another useful contribution to the subject is J. H. Parry, *The Age of Reconnaissance*, London, 1963, pp. 54–56.

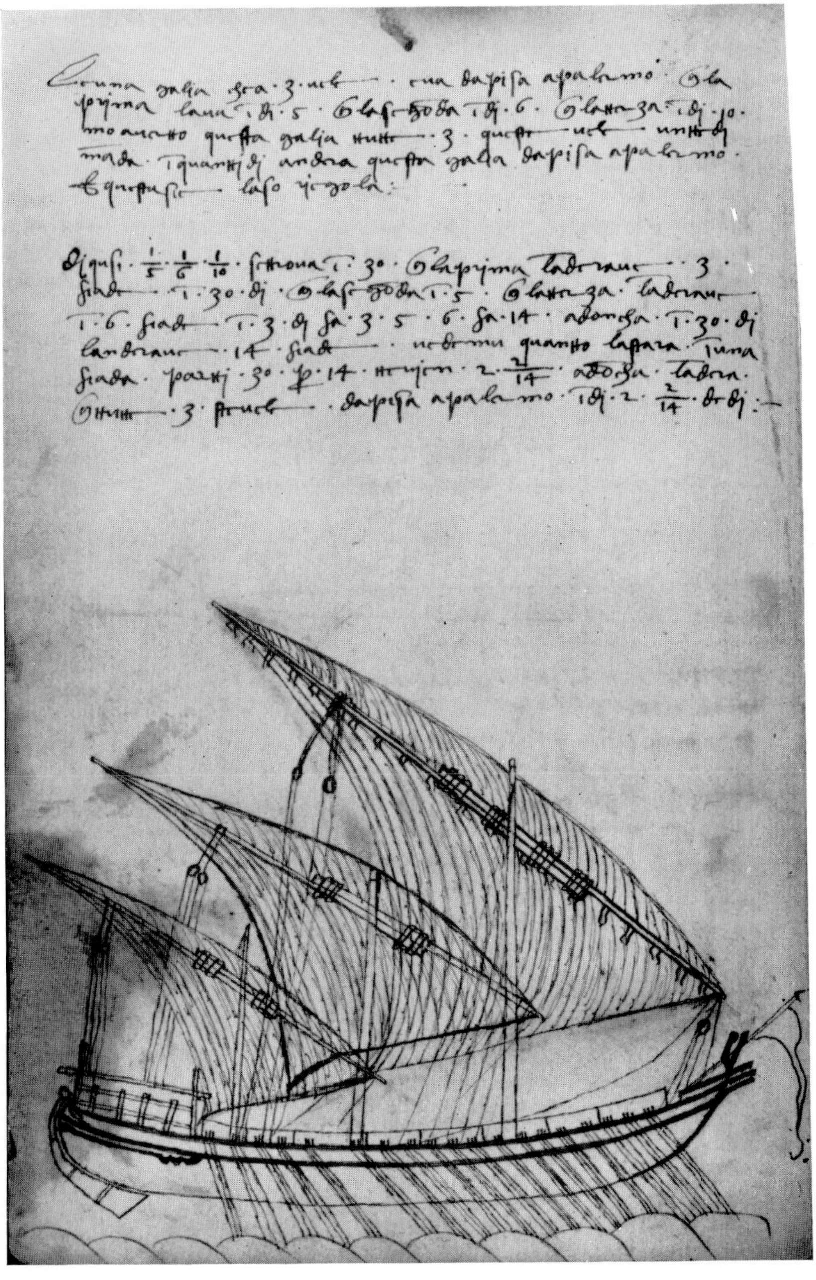

PLATE 3

A Venetian great galley: a drawing from Timbotta's treatise on galley construction

PLATE 4

A fifteenth-century merchant galley

with galleys because much of their trade was in spices; the Genoese used carracks because alum, wool, dyes, grain, etc., played a larger part in their trade. The Florentines probably chose galleys because they hoped to break into the spice trade, and because wool was for them a vitally important commodity and not just another item of bulk trade. In fact from this point of view the choice was probably a mistake because the Florentine galleys never did get a substantial share of the spice trade, and wool whatever its importance was basically a bulk commodity which could be carried more economically in carracks.

However the most important factor was that Florence, having decided to organize a shipping system partly run by the State like that of Venice, naturally also chose to service it with great galleys as did the Venetians. Galleys were more reliable in following set schedules, and the Venetians seemed to have found a profitable and effective system which was still expanding in the early fifteenth century. On the other hand the Genoese, relying by this time on privately owned carracks with an uncoordinated schedule of sailings, seemed to be losing ground particularly in the eastern Mediterranean.[1]

Finally, the shipbuilding yards in Pisa were geared to the building of galleys; galleys had always served the Pisan Republic, and any basic change of policy would have led to inevitable delays in getting the system launched.

So it was galleys on which the Consuls were to concentrate, and their first task was to build two great galleys and six long ones as quickly as possible.[2] To finance this work the *Studio Fiorentino* was to put up 1,200 florins a year, which was said to be sufficient to cover the cost of two long galleys, and the *Monte* was to provide 7,400 florins a year, a liability which was in 1425 taken over by the *Camera del Comune*.[3]

These first galleys which the Florentine Sea Consuls ordered were ready very quickly. The first long galley was able to leave

[1] Heers, *Gênes*, pp. 363–406, discusses the gradual decline of Genoese influence and trade in Alexandria, Syria, and Cyprus during the first half of the fifteenth century.

[2] Provv. 111, ff. 198^v–200^v (13 Dec. 1421).

[3] Ibid., f. 199^v. Mallett, 'Sea Consuls', p. 166. By 1441 it was reckoned that a great galley cost 2,800 florins to build (Provv. 132, f. 252^r, 5 Oct. 1441). At this stage the Venetian arsenal was receiving a subsidy of 9,600 ducats a year in addition to income from auctions. A ducat was approximately equivalent in value to a florin (Lane, *Venetian Ships and Shipbuilders*, p. 137).

on its trials in April 1422, and by September the two great galleys were ready to sail for Alexandria.[1] The speed with which the whole project got under way was partly because large numbers of experienced workmen and sailors were invited to come from Venice and Genoa, with offers of higher wages than usual.[2] It was also partly because the Consuls inherited the Pisan shipbuilding yards in the old citadel of Pisa, under the direction of master shipbuilder Guglielmo Novellino. A new shipbuilding yard had been constructed in Leghorn by the Genoese and some sources state that some of the communal galleys were built there. But if this is so it can only have been one or two of the long galleys, as the great galleys seem always to have been built in Pisa.[3]

Pisa had always been notable for its shipbuilding, and the Consuls were fortunate in having good supplies of the essential raw materials close at hand. Shortage of timber was one of the principal handicaps of the Venetian shipbuilding industry, but Pisa was well provided from the forests of the Alpi Apuane round Monte Pisano and Cerbaia. Timber was also floated down the Arno from the upper reaches.[4] The Consuls were given the monopoly of the use of this timber,[5] and were required to keep a stock in hand in the old citadel so that green wood would not have to be used for the galleys.[6] Oak was the principal timber employed in the building of the galleys, but quantities of larch and fir were also needed. There was also a flourishing iron industry in the same area around Buti and Calci which was able to provide the nails and other iron fittings needed. Finally the Consuls were permitted to import the materials necessary for galley building free of any customs duties.[7]

Nothing was laid down in the original statutes as to the actual

[1] See below, p. 37.

[2] *Cronache di Giovanni Sercambi, lucchese*, ed. Salvatore Bongi, in *Fonti per la storia d'Italia*, 1890–2, iii, p. 304.

[3] P. Vigo, *Statuti e Provvisioni*, pp. lxxi–lxxii, maintains that four of the first six galleys were built in Leghorn. But there are no references, in the Florentine statutes relative to galley-building, to any built outside Pisa (viz. Provv. 134, f. 190^v, 5 Feb. 1444, and Provv. 161, f. 147^v, 30 Oct. 1470). Vigo's authority is G. Vivoli, *Annali di Livorno*, Leghorn, 1843, ii, p. 190, whose account of the opening of the galley system is full of errors.

[4] Herlihy, *Pisa in the Early Renaissance*, pp. 23–24 and 167.

[5] Pagnini, *Della decima*, ii, p. 36; see also Provv. 160, f. 111^v (8 Aug. 1469).

[6] Provv. 164, f. 293^v (28 Feb. 1474).

[7] Provv. 113, f. 52^v (22 Jan. 1423).

size of the galleys to be built by the Consuls, but from other sources it is not difficult to arrive at some idea of what they must have been like. The long galley, or *galea sottile*, was the traditional warship of the Mediterranean in the Middle Ages, and was to continue as such until at least the end of the sixteenth century. Although the size of these long galleys varied considerably, by the fifteenth century it is possible to perceive some uniformity in the largest war galleys produced by the Mediterranean naval powers. These ran to between 132 and 138 feet in length, about 15 feet in the beam and with a depth amidships of about 6 feet. The particular characteristics of these galleys were their very slim build which gave them greater speed through the water and great manœuvrability, and their long pointed prows which could be used for ramming the enemy.

The following table sets out the dimensions of some late medieval galleys:

Type and period	Length		Beam		Depth	
Venetian	*ft.*	*in.*	*ft.*	*in.*	*ft.*	*in.*
Long galley—15th cent.	131	6	16	6	5	9[1]
„ „ „ „	133	4	15	10	6	3[2]
Great galley— „ „	134	6	19	10	9	0[1]
„ „ „ „	(139)		19	3	9	0[2]
Genoese						
Long galley—1383	124		14		5	9[3]
„ „ 15th cent.	135		15		5	9[4]
'Bastard galley' „	135		16	6	6	9[4]
Florentine						
Long galley— „ „	138		11	6	7	8[5]
Great Galley „ „	138		25		9	
„ „ „ „	143	9	19	2	9	6

[1] BNF, Magliabechiana XIX, 7, MS. entitled *Fabbrica delle Galere* published in part in French by A. Jal, *Archéologie navale*, Paris, 1840, ii, pp. 6 sqq. The manuscript measurements in Venetian feet have been converted at 1 Venetian foot = 1·135 English feet.

[2] British Museum, Cottonian MS., Titus A. 26. This is a similar handbook on galley construction written by the Venetian Giorgio Timbotta about 1445. See R. C. Anderson, 'Italian Naval Architecture about 1445', *Mariners' Mirror*, xi, 1925.

[3] R. di Tucci, 'Costruzione di galee genovesi durante il dogado di Leonardo Monvaldi', *Ad Alessandro Luzio; gli Archivi di Stato italiani*, i, Florence, 1933.

[4] Heers, *Gênes*, p. 270; E. A. D'Albertis, *Le costruzioni navali e la navigazione al tempo di Colombo*, Genoa, 1893, p. 28. The *bastard* galley was a large war galley used as admiral's flagship, etc.

[5] For further discussion of the dimensions of the Florentine galleys see below, p. 34.

All the full-sized galleys of this period were triremes in the sense that they were rowed by three men to a bench each with his own oar. This was the system known as *a sensile* which began to be replaced in the second decade of the sixteenth century by the system of more than one man to each oar, known as *a scaloccio*. In the galley *a sensile* the benches for the oarsmen had to be set at an angle, and the oars were naturally of different lengths. They varied between 29 and 32 feet long and weighed up to 120 lb. There were normally 25–28 benches on each side giving a total of 150–168 oarsmen and oars. However, in all galleys one bench on each side was taken out to make room for a minute cooking area on one side and for the galley's boat on the other.

In addition to oars as a source of power, all medieval galleys also used sail. The long galleys had one or very occasionally two masts, but the merchant galleys of the fifteenth century began to appear with three masts. The sails, of which each galley carried four or five of different sizes, were lateen sails, except for a small square storm sail.[1]

An additional mast and hence additional sail area was not the only difference between the great galley and the long galley. The great galley had been introduced by the Venetians at the end of the thirteenth century particularly for the Flanders voyage. It was first and foremost a merchant galley and therefore was designed with considerably more storage space than the long galley. It was also far more seaworthy and was able not only to operate throughout the winter but also to make the voyage to England with little risk. In fact for two centuries the great galleys of Venice, Genoa, Florence, and later Naples came to England and Flanders, often in the depth of winter, and suffered very few losses. The Florentines lost two galleys in sixty years as a result of shipwreck on this route, and one of these was in fact a long galley, which had been sent to escort the convoy. The Venetians lost one galley in 1437 and two in 1495 on the Flanders route, but the latter were reported to have been considerably overloaded.[2]

The great galley in order to fulfil its different functions was built much wider in the beam than the long galley. The dimensions of the average great galley were about 137 feet in length, 19 in the beam, and about 9 feet depth amidships. At the same time the

---

[1] For further details of the rig of medieval galleys see below, p. 208 n. 6.
[2] Lane, *Venetian Ships and Shipbuilders*, p. 25.

profile was more rounded, giving it some of the appearance of a carrack and providing greater storage space. As a result of these modifications the great galley was less manœuvrable and not so fast; it relied more on its sails than on its oars as the number of oarsmen was not increased in proportion to the additional weight.[1] The size of the crews in the two types of galley was in fact very similar. The great galley might require a few more sailors to handle its greater sail area, while the long galley would normally carry more fighting men. The Florentine great galleys carried between 200 and 220 men, of whom about 150 were oarsmen and ordinary sailors and the remaining 50–70 made up of officers, senior sailors, and marines.[2] Venetian galleys of the same period also carried a crew of about 210, while the Genoese long galleys carried 176.[3] Much of the fighting strength of a galley lay in its large crew, for in addition to the officers and marines, who were naturally armed, it was usual to provide arms for the sailors and sometimes for the oarsmen as well.[4] This was possible because the oarsmen of the fifteenth-century galleys were not slaves, except in pirate galleys where prisoners were frequently used. In the galleys of the Italian maritime States the oarsmen were paid freemen, sometimes conscripted, but nevertheless forming a professional class drawn largely from the families of fishermen and sailors living along the coasts. The pay by contemporary standards was good; a senior

[1] Venetian great galleys in the later years of the fifteenth century were sometimes known to leave two-thirds of their oars behind as they were used so rarely (Lane, op. cit., p. 16).

[2] *Consoli del Mare* IV, 4, *Capitoli dei conductori e patroni*, c. 1. In fact the figures stated here are 154 oarsmen and sailors and 50 officers and marines, but this did not include the patron nor, in cases where a Captain was sailing, the Captain's suite of ten persons. The Captain's galley sailing to Alexandria in 1445 carried a crew of 210 in addition to the Captain and his suite (*Quadernuccio di Luigi Vettori*). The first Florentine galley to go on trials in 1422 carried about 240, but this was a brief voyage and no doubt a number of non-essential spectators were on board. For further discussion of the crews of the Florentine galleys see below, pp. 201–2.

[3] Lane, *Venetian Ships and Shipbuilders*, p. 24; D'Albertis, *Costruzioni navali*, p. 27.

[4] Oarsmen on the Florentine galleys were armed with a long pike or *facchino* (*Consoli del Mare* IV, 4, *Capitoli dei conductori e patroni*, c. 1). On Venetian galleys they were sometimes trained as cross-bowmen. Luigi Vettori in his *Quadernuccio* includes an inventory of all the equipment on one of the 1445 Alexandria galleys and amongst the personal arms he includes 150 helmets (*choppi*), 60 large shields (*palvezi*), 60 dozen darts, 150 breast-plates, and 60 long pikes. This would suggest that although all the oarsmen were provided with armour, only the outer rank received pikes. For a similar description of the arms carried by a Genoese galley in the sixteenth century, see E. Pandiani, 'Il primo commando in mare di Andrea Doria con uno studio sulle galee genovesi', *ASLSP*, lxiv, 1935, p. 350.

oarsman in the Florentine galleys received 3½ florins a month, while the helmsmen and marines received 4½ or 5 florins a month.[1] At the same time the conditions although hard were not so grim as the traditional portraits of the galley slaves made out.[2] In fact in normal conditions on a merchant galley the oars were used very little; they were usually necessary for getting in and out of harbour, and when the wind dropped or turned against the galley. But even in these circumstances the oarsmen always rowed in shifts, one-third of the complement rowing at once. The full body of oarsmen was only put to work in an emergency, which in the case of a merchant galley would be to escape capture or to avoid going aground.

Even discipline was not so strict as one might expect, at least on the Venetian galleys. This was largely because the men were volunteers and could not be treated too hardly if the galleys were to be manned. Manfroni in his researches on this subject noted that this tendency towards comparatively lax discipline was particularly noticeable in offences judged and punishments pronounced after the voyage had ended.[3] It was an international maritime custom that swearing and games of chance were forbidden at sea, and offenders were punishable by fines.[4] Albizzi had

[1] Consoli del Mare IV, 6, *Capitoli dei conductori*, ff. 26ᵛ–27; Müller, *Documenti*, p. 287. These were the rates in 1459.

[2] The classic account of galley life is Jean Marteilhe, *Mémoires d'un protestant condamné aux galeres de France pour cause de religion*, published in translation by the Folio Society, London, 1957. However, the life of a galley slave at the end of the seventeenth century must have been rather different from that of a free oarsman in the fifteenth, although apart from the change in the method of rowing, the galleys themselves altered surprisingly little.

[3] C. Manfroni, 'La disciplina dei marinai veneziani nel XIV secolo', *Rivista marittima*, 1902.

[4] Consoli del Mare V, *Capitoli dei capitani*, c. 15. 'Ancora acciochè la riverentia dello omnipotente Iddio e di tutti i Suoi santi e Sante di Paradiso si mantenga et conservi, è ordinato che qualunche persona che sarà in su alchuna di dette galee bestemmiasse Iddio o la Sua Gloriosissima Madre sempre Vergine Maria caggia in pena per la prima volta che bestemmiasse di lira una, e per la seconda di lire due, e per la terza di lire tre e di due bastonate, e così ogni volta che bestemmiasse. Et chi bestemmiasse alcuno Santo o Santa di Paradiso per la prima volta caggia in pena di soldi dieci piccoli, per la seconda volta soldi venti piccoli. Et se dalle due volte in su bestemmiasse alcuno di detti Santi o Sante caggia in pena per ogni volta di soldi trenta piccoli e di due bastonate.

'Et perchè l'uso del giuocho è gran cagione di fare bestemmiare e anchora induce spesse volte scandalo, è ordinato che niuno, di che stato o conditione si sia, ardisca o presuma in su dette galee giuochare ad alcuno giuocho prohibito secondo gli ordini del comune di Firenze.'

The penalties which the Captain could impose on gamblers varied according to rank; an officer or marine could be fined one to two florins, and an ordinary sailor

to deal with a gambling school during the period in which his galleys were held up at Ribadeo on their way north; he fined the twelve offenders 1 florin each. On another occasion he had one of the marines flogged and put ashore for stealing a silver cup.[1]

Certainly living conditions on a galley must have been less pleasant than on a big carrack. The whole waist of the vessel where the oarsmen sat was open to the elements except for awnings which were rigged to protect the men from the sun and rain. The officers were housed in the stern-castle in reasonable comfort, while the marines were mostly stationed on a ramp over the bows of the galley where the artillery was mounted. Although bombards did not become standard equipment on Venetian galleys until 1461 Florentine galleys seem to have carried them from the start.[2] The 1445 Florentine galleys to Alexandria each mounted one large bombard and four smaller cannon.[3] Albizzi's galleys also carried bombards, as he fired one of them as a signal to the garrison of Gorgona on his return.

Because of the large crew carried and the comparatively narrow beam and shallow draft of a merchant galley, stowage space for merchandise was limited. The average fifteenth-century galley is usually thought to have been able to carry between 150 and 250 tons of merchandise, but the figures available for cargoes both of Florentine and Venetian galleys indicate that they rarely exceeded 150 tons and were often lower.[4] The cargo was mostly stowed in the hull beneath the oarsmen's benches, but a certain amount was also carried lashed down on the narrow gangway which ran down the centre of the galley. Lack of space also made it unusual to carry large supplies of provisions; a considerable amount of ship's biscuit was loaded as an emergency ration but as can be seen from the Albizzi diary the galleys relied very much for all other provisions on frequent visits to the shores which they passed. This practice of constantly taking on fresh supplies not only explains the absence of scurvy among the crews, but also goes some way to account for the habit of sailing close to land whenever possible.

or oarsman a half to one florin. Two-thirds of the proceeds from such fines went to the Sea Consuls, and one-third to the Hospital of Santa Maria Nuova in Florence.
[1] Albizzi Diary, f. 59ʳ.　　[2] Sacerdoti, 'Galere da mercato veneziane', p. 81.
[3] *Quadernuccio di Luigi Vettori*, f. 5ᵛ.
[4] See the discussion of the Florentine cargo lists in Chapter 5, and also cargo lists quoted in Heers, 'Commercio nel Mediterraneo'. H. Lapèyre and R. Carande, *Relaciones comerciales en el Mediterraneo durante el siglo XVI*, Cagliari, 1957, p. 15, assess the cargo capacity of the average galley at 80–100 tons.

It was the normal but by no means the invariable custom for merchant galleys to skirt the coasts of the Mediterranean. That this was partly due to limited navigational knowledge is well known; the fifteenth-century mariner would have had a compass, a lead and line, and possibly an astrolabe, but he lacked any reliable means of estimating distance covered and he would have had a very inexact knowledge of currents and tides.[1] At the same time what charts he might have had would have been very inaccurate, and by far his most reliable aid would have been his portolan or rutter. This was a mariner's handbook describing the coasts in the same manner as a modern motorist's handbook describes roads. The portolan led the mariner round the coast describing the physical features, the navigational hazards, giving the distances and bearings between each feature, describing the entrances to the ports and the winds needed to enter them, etc. Such a manual was designed entirely for coastal traffic, and for such traffic was almost the only aid needed. But the great galleys were never rigidly tied to the coast, and even when following a coastline from port to port they tended to head well out to sea to get the best of the wind. This was because they relied largely on their sails for propulsion, and was in contrast to the long galleys which tended whenever possible to keep close inshore in order to have the calmer water and use their oars. Similarly, whereas it was the custom for long galleys to heave to each night in a sheltered spot to rest the oarsmen, the great galleys were able to sail for several days and nights on end whenever shortage of provisions or the necessities of trade did not require them to put into port.[2]

The Florentine galleys relied a good deal on carrying trade for their cargoes, and it was their custom in the Mediterranean to go from port to port loading and unloading small quantities. The

---

[1] For a recent and very useful summary of fifteenth-century navigational knowledge and practice, see Parry, *The Age of Reconnaissance*, pp. 69–113.

[2] E. Fasano Guarini, 'Au XVIᵉ siècle: comment naviguent les galères', *Annales*, 1961, March–April. In this interesting study Mlle Fasano Guarini examines a group of sixteenth-century Venetian galley itineraries and makes some important points about the rhythm of the voyages, e.g. the amount of time spent in port, and the amount of time spent navigating with oars and with sails. The galleys she is studying were, however, long galleys or 'bastard' galleys, and her conclusions are not entirely valid for great galleys. The latter did not hug the coast or use their oars to anything like the extent which Mlle Guarini's galleys did. The table in Appendix C gives an idea of how the time was spent on Albizzi's two voyages in comparison with the voyages studied in the above-mentioned article.

PLATE 5

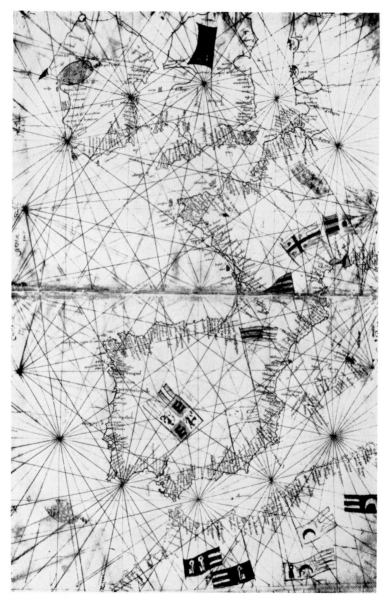

The Portolan of Petrus Vesconte, *c.* 1327

routes and ports of call were laid down in advance by the Sea Consuls, and they not only took account of what products would be available at certain times of the year and where there would be a market for them, but they also served to apportion certain stretches of coast to particular galleys. Thus at one stage the Flanders galleys were not allowed to call on the coast of Catalonia as this damaged the trade of the Catalonia galleys. Similarly on their return from England they did virtually no trading at all as they were filled with wool for Florence. On such occasions the galleys frequently ceased to follow the coasts at all and cut across the open seas to save time. They invariably chose the direct route across the Bay of Biscay rather than following the French coast, and on their return to the Mediterranean they sailed straight across from Alicante to Porto Pisano, touching only at Majorca.

It is therefore mistaken to think of medieval merchant galleys as tied to the coasts entirely through lack of navigational knowledge, or even through fear of being caught in the open by storms. Certainly storms were to be avoided if possible, but the great galleys proved themselves as seaworthy as any sailing-ship, and no vessel which was afraid of being caught in a storm would ever have risked the crossing of the Bay of Biscay in mid-winter. For just as it is wrong to think of all galleys as coastal vessels, so it is wrong to think that all galleys were laid up during the winter. Winter and summer were alike to the great galleys; in fact the Flanders and Levant galleys of Florence left port in the autumn of each year and sailed through the winter. The great galleys were therefore much more like sailing-ships than galleys in many respects; but because of their greater manœuvrability they were more adapted for use as coastal traders, and also because they carried limited provisions they were more dependent on frequent visits to port than were sailing-ships.

We have two chronicle reports on the first galleys built by the Florentines which confirm the impression that the Florentine galleys conformed fairly closely to the normal fifteenth-century pattern. Giuliano di Tommaso di Guccio Martini in his *Ricordi* quoted the measurements of the long galleys as being 72 *braccia* in length, 6 *braccia* in the beam, and 4 *braccia* deep amidships. At the same time he reports the dimensions of the great galleys which in 1423 were preparing to go to Flanders as being 75 *braccia* in length,

10 in the beam and 5 deep.[1] The size of the Florentine *braccia* is rather uncertain but it is generally thought to have been 23 inches. If we accept this, Martini's figures come very close to the averages which we have already arrived at, e.g. the long galleys 138 × 11½ × 7½ feet, and the great galleys 143¾ × 19 × 9½ feet. The only considerable difference between these galleys and those of other seafaring nations seems to be the comparative slimness of the long galleys. Our other chronicle source, the monk Pietriboni, gives the dimensions of the first galleys as 'di portata 400 botti, le quale io misurai lunghe il vano dentro braccia 72 e nel mezzo il tondo loro braccia 13, e alte braccia 4⅔ dal piano alla coverta'.[2] Pietriboni's beam measurement of 25 feet is unexpectedly wide, but this was probably the overall width including the out-riggers.[3]

Within a few years of 1422 Florence is said to have possessed eleven great galleys and fifteen long ones,[4] and Caggese assesses the Florentine fleet at its height as thirty galleys in all.[5] If anything these estimates are probably optimistic, particularly as the most likely sources for the first indicate that the eleven great galleys and the fifteen long galleys were not in commission at the same time. In fact in 1463 there were reported to be eleven great galleys available and the building programme was cut by half as this was said to be more than sufficient.[6] The average life of a galley was ten to twelve years, so that by 1468 when fifteen long galleys were ordered for the brief war against Colleoni and Venice, the number of great galleys in commission had probably fallen. The *Dieci di Balìa* took over the control of this war-galley building programme, but we do not know if they were ever finished.[7] Certainly judging by the programme of sailings there can never have been more than eleven great galleys in service and usually far fewer; and the rare displays of naval strength put on by Florence never involved more than four or five long galleys, so one must assume that the order

[1] Tozzetti, *Relazioni di alcuni viaggi*, ii, p. 230.
[2] Pietriboni's figures are quoted by Sapori, 'Primi viaggi', p. 79.
[3] In fact two other sources do quote an average beam measurement of 23 feet for great galleys, Jal, *Archéologie navale*, i, p. 387, and F. C. Lane, 'Venetian Naval Architecture about 1550', *Mariners' Mirror*, xx, 1934, p. 32, but both these also at other times quote a figure of about 17 feet.
[4] Pagnini, *Della decima*, ii, p. 35.
[5] R. Caggese, *Storia del commercio*, Florence, 1922, p. 116.
[6] Consoli del Mare III, f. 157ᵛ (31 Jan. 1463), and Provv. 153, f. 230ʳ.
[7] Provv. 158, f. 170ʳ (13 Jan. 1468).

for fifteen to be built was a very exceptional occasion. By 1473 there were only four great galleys in service and a new one was to be built immediately;[1] and when they were finally taken out of service in 1480 there were still only five.[2]

The evidence would suggest that all the galleys were built by the Florentines themselves, as there are no records of any purchases from elsewhere. Two long galleys were in fact sold to Genoa in 1441,[3] and a further one to Bernardo Castiglione in 1472,[4] but the only reference to a galley being acquired is in 1465 when the Pope presented one in Ancona.[5] It seems probable that this was in fact the return of the one that was promised to Pius II for his crusade the year before, together with two long galleys.[6] These galleys were to be manned by selected prisoners from the state prison in Florence at the request of the Papal Legate, Forteguerra.[7] It is a rather ironic fact that the only recorded time that prisoners were put to the oars in Florentine galleys in the fifteenth century was when those galleys were to serve the Pope. In 1481 a further five long galleys were promised to the Pope.[8]

But let us return to the year 1422 and the immediate use to which the new Florentine galleys were put. Contemporary chroniclers and subsequent historians have produced an extraordinary series of conflicting accounts of the first sailings of the Florentine galleys which official sources do nothing to clarify. The older authorities on Florentine fifteenth-century commerce, Tozzetti and Pagnini, describe the celebrations in Florence on 15 April 1422 for the launching of the first communal galley which left on 20 April for Alexandria.[9] Tozzetti's source for this is an anonymous *Diario di*

[1] Provv. 164, f. 159ᵛ (8 Oct. 1473).

[2] Consoli del Mare III, f. 235 (3 Aug. 1480), and Provv. 171, ff. 17ʳ–19ʳ. See also Grunzweig, 'Consulat', pp. 47–48.

[3] Provv. 132, f. 21ʳ (15 Apr. 1441). The two were to be sold for 1,000 florins.

[4] Miss. II Canc. 4, f. 27ᵛ (17 Apr. 1472). This galley was to be sold with no fittings or equipment for 500 florins.

[5] Provv. 155, f. 227ʳ (17 Feb. 1465).

[6] Provv. 155, f. 9ʳ (18 Apr. 1464). Much has been written about the reluctance of the Florentines to join the crusade against the Turks, and indeed it was against their economic interests to do so. But the evidence here does suggest that at least an effort was made to prepare some galleys, and even the names of some of the crews are mentioned. The return of the galley by the Pope in the next year, after the crusade had collapsed, seems to suggest that some part of the obligation was fulfilled.

[7] Provv. 155, f. 42ᵛ (7 June 1464).

[8] Provv. 172, f. 11ʳ (14 Apr. 1481).

[9] Tozzetti, *Relazioni*, ii, p. 329; Pagnini, *Della decima*, ii, p. 59.

Firenze,[1] and the account is supported by Bartolomeo Corazza in his diary,[2] who describes the galley as a long one called the *Santa Reparata*, and relates that the ambassadors to the Sultan (presumably Felice Brancacci and Carlo Federighi) were on board. Corazza then rather destroys our faith in his testimony by relating that the departure was followed on 1 July by the departure of the great galleys for Flanders. This statement is unsupported by any other writer and it is fairly well established that the first galleys did not go to Flanders until 1425. Tozzetti and Pagnini also state that the patron of this first galley to Alexandria was Zenobi Capponi, but they do not specifically mention that Brancacci and Federighi sailed in the galley. This general outline was followed by Capponi and Heyd,[3] the latter definitely stating that the two ambassadors sailed in the first single galley, and that two great galleys followed within a few days. On the other hand Felice Brancacci in his diary states that he and Federighi went with two galleys, leaving on 12 July and returning to Porto Pisano on 11 February 1423.[4] This is borne out to a certain extent by Pietriboni in his unpublished chronicle which provides the source for Sapori's article.[5] Pietriboni mentions the celebration on 15 April, and the departure on 20 April, but states that this galley was in fact going on its trials off the coast of Corsica. Then on 12 July two long galleys sailed for Alexandria with Brancacci and Federighi. These galleys were the *S. Giovanni Battista* and the *S. Antonio* and the patrons were Giuliano di Turpia and Bindo delle Brache. It would seem therefore that the *Sta. Reparata* with its patron Capponi did not go on this occasion.[6] These galleys carried 4,000 cloths and 56,000 ducats but returned on 12 October having done no trade in

---

[1] BNF, Magliabechiana, XXV, 50.

[2] 'Diario fiorentino di Bartolomeo di Michele Corazza', ed. G. O. Corazzini, *ASI*, 5th ser., xiv, 1894, p. 277. See also Vivoli, *Annali di Livorno*, ii, pp. 191–3.

[3] Capponi, *Storia di Firenze*, i, p. 451; Heyd, *Commercio del Levante*, p. 1045.

[4] *Diario di Felice Brancacci*, ed. D. Castellacci, *ASI*, 4th ser., viii, 1881, *passim*. For the instructions which were given to these ambassadors and the agreement signed with Sultan Abn Nasr Barsebai, see Pagnini, *Della decima*, ii, pp. 187–204.

[5] Sapori, 'Primi viaggi', *passim*. Pietriboni's chronicle is to be found in BNF, Convento di Santa Maria Novella, c. 4, 895.

[6] Ibid., p. 77. The word which became common in many of the Italian maritime states for the commander of a single galley was *padrone*. This is usually expressed in English as *patron*, although a more exact translation would be *master*. However, the term *master* implies ownership, and as the patrons of the Florentine galleys were not the owners, nor indeed permanent commanders, I have thought it best to adhere to the normal practice and retain the word *patron*.

Alexandria owing to the general hostility there. The two ambassadors stayed on, however, and eventually returned with the second pair of galleys, which were great galleys this time, commanded by Piero Guicciardini, which had left on 4 September and returned on 11 February 1423.[1]

It would seem that the most reliable of these accounts should be that of Brancacci, and if we accept his evidence of the ambassadors sailing on 12 July with two galleys, it would also be reasonable to believe that theirs were the first to sail to Alexandria, and that the one galley sailing alone on 20 April and commanded by Capponi did not in fact go there. One would imagine that in launching a venture as important as this, the ambassadors bearing the essential letters of introduction and with express authority to treat with the Sultan and ask for trade concessions would travel in the first galleys. It would also be logical to suppose that a galley launched on 15 April would hardly have been able to set out on a voyage to Alexandria on 20 April, and the statement that in fact it went on trials in neighbouring waters seems altogether more reasonable. The fact that Pietriboni supports Brancacci except for the piece of additional information, which the latter had no reason to mention, that the ambassadors did not in fact return on the same galleys as those on which they went, makes it clear that the older writers have been misled.

It is easy to see how some of the chroniclers came to make the mistakes which they did; the galley launched on 15 April was probably heralded as the one which would go to Alexandria with the ambassadors; it was almost certainly the first of the six long galleys ordered to be completed. Therefore when news that it had in fact sailed on 20 April came back to Florence, it would not be unnatural for some less well-informed observers to presume that it had gone to Alexandria.

Thus to recapitulate briefly the galley activities in the first year of the system, 1422, there were three departures from Porto Pisano. On 20 April one long galley commanded by Zenobio Capponi left

---

[1] Ibid., pp. 78–79. Sapori published the cargo list of these galleys in his appendix, p. 91, and a translation is to be found below, p. 115. Corazza in describing the return of the ambassadors from Egypt reports that all the bells in Florence were run 'dipoi andò un bando per parte de' Signori che si serrasseno tutte le botteghe, a pena di 4 fiorini, e così se fece. E ordinossi una processione il sabbato e la domenica mattina, solenne e bella; e cantossi la Messa in Santa Maria del Fiore; predicò il maestro Domenico da Fighine de' Frati Predicatori' (Corazza, p. 277).

for trials off Corsica. On 12 July two long galleys sailed for Alexandria with the two ambassadors to the Sultan, returning without the ambassadors on 12 October. Finally two great galleys loaded with merchandise and cash sailed on 4 September for Alexandria, and returned with the ambassadors in February of the next year.

Until 1424 Alexandria was the terminus of all the galley voyages. After the first two fleets of 1422 a further two galleys sailed on 26 July 1423, returning on 28 November, and two more returned to Porto Pisano in January 1425.[1] In 1424 the Consuls, with the number of galleys available rapidly increasing, began to extend their activities. Luca di Maso degli Albizzi, the author of the diary published below, appeared for the first time in his new role as sea captain when he commanded a great galley on its trials in the western Mediterranean early in this year.[2] The galley, which was probably one of those designed specifically for the voyage to England and Flanders with capacious holds for wool, went as far as Aiguesmortes before returning to Porto Pisano on 1 February 1424.

In April of the same year two galleys left for Barcelona and Valencia to inaugurate another route. The Captain of the fleet was Andrea Giugni, and his galleys were preceded by a few days by a special long galley carrying Luca degli Albizzi as ambassador to the King of Aragon.[3] Albizzi's galley returned on 1 June and the two great galleys were back in the Arno on 5 June.

Meanwhile as early as 1421 Bartolomeo della Galea had been sent to Tunis to open negotiations for trade concessions,[4] but there is no evidence yet of the galleys going to Barbary.

Finally on 6 May 1425 the first fleet of three galleys left for Flanders and England under the captaincy of Salomone di Carlo degli Strozzi.[5] This was the climax of the first stage of the history

---

[1] Sapori, 'Primi viaggi', pp. 81 and 86.

[2] Ibid., p. 81.

[3] Ibid., p. 81. Luca di Maso was a prolific writer of diaries, of which several remain. He kept a diary of this voyage to Spain which is to be found in Sig. X, VIII, 5, II, *passim*.

[4] L. de Mas Latrie, *Traités de paix et de commerce et documents concernant les relations des Chrétiens avec les Arabes de l'Afrique septentrionale au Moyen Âge*, Paris, 1866; M. Amari, *I diplomi arabi del R. Archivio Fiorentino*, Florence, 1863, pp. 151–64, and Appendix, p. 12.

[5] Sapori, 'Primi viaggi', p. 82. The Signoria had written ahead to ensure a good reception for these galleys in December 1424 (Miss. I Canc. 30, f. 86ᵛ).

of the galleys, not so much because it was the longest voyage to be attempted, but because it was the English wool which Florence needed before all else, and the unlimited acquisition of which was one of the prime functions of the galleys. These galleys arrived in Sluys on 8 July, were in London on 20 October, and finally returned to Porto Pisano on 25 February 1426.

During the absence of these galleys the Consuls had prepared and the Councils had approved a complete body of regulations to govern the operation of the galley system. In three short years three routes had been opened up, and before long Constantinople, the Barbary coast, and Sicily were to be added. The time had come for a more careful organization of the enterprise, and it is the lists of instructions and regulations which appeared in 1425 and at intervals thereafter which provide us with our best insight into the workings of the galley system.

3

THE ORGANIZATION OF THE GALLEY SYSTEM

THE principle upon which the Florentine galley system was to work was one of a blend of state and private enterprise. The State was to provide the galleys themselves and thus bear the major capital expense, while the actual trading to be done by the galleys was largely directed by private merchants. This was the theory in very simple terms, although of course in fact state control played by far the greater part and hedged the merchants round with a whole series of regulations which served in the end to choke the element of private enterprise.

The preparations for each voyage of the communal galleys, whether it was to be one galley or a fleet of two, three, or four galleys, began with the auction of the contract for the voyage. The aim was to find one merchant or a group of merchants who would be responsible for the overall direction of the venture, and would presumably draw the maximum commercial profit from it. The holding of the auction was one of the tasks of the Sea Consuls in Florence, and the method of conducting it was laid down in the general galley regulations passed by the Councils in 1425 and 1441.[1] These regulations also laid down the time of year at which each different galley fleet should sail, and the auctions were usually held five or six months ahead of that time. Thus the galleys for England and Flanders which sailed in mid-September were usually auctioned in February.

The auction was always preceded by an official proclamation by the heralds of the Consuls of the number of galleys to be auctioned,

---

[1] Consoli del Mare III, ff. 6^r–8^v (23 May 1425) and ff. 52^r–55^v (15 Apr. 1441). See also Provv. 115, ff. 58^v–61 and 132, f. 21^r. The latter of these sets of regulations is published by Grunzweig in French ('Consulat', pp. 15–20). Both sets deal with general aspects of the galley system, e.g. dates of auctions and sailings, method of auction, appointment of officials, etc., whereas the particular regulations for each voyage to be found in registers IV and V of the Archive of the Consoli del Mare contain precise instructions concerning ports of call, length of stay in each port, etc. The duties of each major officer are also laid down in these latter sets of regulations.

their destination and the conditions of the proposed contract.[1] The proclamation sometimes preceded the auction by as much as a month, although the official interval was fifteen days. The auctions during the first half of the century were held in the Loggia dei Lanzi under the personal supervision of the Consuls, and for each fleet of galleys four auction days were set aside. These were generally spread over a period of about twelve days, and the first three quickly became pure formalities, although presumably the intention was to give more men a chance to record a bid. In practice very few bids were received at the first three auctions, and all attention was concentrated on the fourth and final one. The auction lasted on each occasion for an hour and the time was estimated by a burning candle the last and highest bid received before the candle burnt out being the successful one.[2]

In times of crisis and particularly during the second half of the century, the sailings of the galleys became more irregular and auctions were frequently announced at short notice with sometimes only a matter of weeks between the auction and the sailing of the galleys.[3]

[1] 'Al nome sia dello omnipotente Iddio e della sua gloriosissima madre sempre virgine Madonna Santa Maria et di messer Santo Giovanni Battista, singulare patrono et protettore della magnifica et potente comune di Firenze, et di tutta la celestiale corte di paradiso che concedino prospero et buono viaggio nell'andare, stare et tornare a salvamento.

'E' Consoli del Mare del comune di Firenze fanno notificare a ciascuna persona che gli 'anno messo pel viaggio di Fiandra et d'Inghilterra colle scale usate due galee grosse di mercato, insieme et in conserva, bene armate, fornite et corredate, et in punto per partire et fare vela da Porto Pisano a dì xv del mese di settembre proximo che de'e venire et a quegli capitano et padroni che secondo gli ordini saranno electi.

'Et pertanto chi vuole, così cittadino comè forestiere, caricare in su dette galee alcuna mercatantia di qualunche ragione o conditione si sia pel detto viaggio et pe' porti et luoghi et distretti, la met[t]a in punto da carichare al detto tempo. Et anche al tornare d'Inghilterra et di Fiandra si possa in su dette galee caricare qualunche mercatantia et robe per conducere a Pisa et a qualunche altro porto usato pel detto viaggio a pregi et noli usati. Et se fusse alcuno cittadino sotto posto del comune di Firenze il quale volesse torre sopra se dette galee o alcuna d'esse pello detto viaggio a ogni sua spesa sub nome et segno del popolo et comune di Firenze, dandogli i detti Consoli le dette galee fornite et in ordine con tutti i corredi et fornimenti et sartie si richede, vengha a dì cinque del mese di febraio proximo che viene a proferire in che modo le vuole, che'l detto dì le incomincieranno incantare. Notificando che 'lle scale, noli, capitoli del capitano, padroni et di chi le volesse conducere sono ordinati pe' detti Consoli in uno libro che apresso ai Consoli in uficio gli puo vedere et pigliare copia.' (Consoli del Mare V, f. 10r).

[2] Details of individual auctions are to be found in Consoli del Mare V and VII, *passim*.

[3] Provv. 162, f. 45v (18 May 1471). On this occasion the auction of the galley for

In January 1461 the venue for the auctions was moved to the Mercato Nuovo, by then the centre of the city's commercial and financial life.[1] An added reason for this change was that the Loggia dei Lanzi was very draughty in winter as the winds whistled aross the Piazza della Signoria, and it was hoped that prospective bidders would be more forthcoming if they could bid in less uncomfortable circumstances. In August of the same year it was also decided to dispense with the candle as a means of deciding the end of the auction, as it was considered too easy to see when it was about to go out. This had led to all the bidders waiting until the last possible moment in order to secure the galleys at a low price; and then a few seconds of extreme confusion in which it was difficult to decide who in fact had made the highest bid.[2] In the future the clock of the Palazzo della Signoria was to be used. This could not be seen from the Mercato Nuovo, and the first strike of 22 hours was to be the signal for the end of the auction. In order to prevent enter-prising merchants altering the clock to gain an advantage in the bidding, the clock-keeper was paid a special wage to guard the clock during auctions, and he was accompanied in his vigil by a servant of the Consuls.[3] The Consuls themselves were not above bribing merchants to put up dummy bids in order to stimulate the auction and produce better offers.[4]

The amounts raised in these auctions varied considerably and much depended upon the international situation, the destination of the proposed voyage, the number of galleys to be sent, and the stopping-places which had been announced for the voyage. In the 1440's conductors (as the winners of the contracts were called) were paying up to 5,100 florins for the hire of two galleys going to England and Flanders,[5] but in 1460 interest had fallen to such an

Catalonia and Sicily was ordered to take place within fifteen days, and the galley was to sail fifteen days after that; but this was an unusual degree of haste.

[1] Provv. 151, f. 337ʳ (23 Jan. 1461), and Consoli del Mare III, ff. 139–40ʳ. At the same time the Consuls were excused from personally attending the first three auctions in each series, thus underlining the fact that these had become mere formalities.

[2] Provv. 152, f. 123ʳ (22 Aug. 1461), and Consoli del Mare III, f. 143ʳ.

[3] Consoli del Mare VII, f. 95ʳ (2 Mar. 1467).

[4] Ibid., f. 93ʳ (30 May 1466). During the auction of two Flanders galleys the bidding had stuck for half an hour at 5 florins! The Consuls therefore took Corrado Vecchietti aside and offered him 25 florins if he would make a bid of 200 florins. As a result of the manœuvre the final price reached 528 florins and the Consuls were well pleased.

[5] Provv. 136, f. 183ᵛ (30 Sept. 1445). This was an unusually high price as two years before the Flanders galleys had only fetched 910 florins (see below, p. 45).

extent that it became necessary for the Consuls to announce that bids of less than 100 florins would be ignored.[1] By the later 1460's a certain revival of interest is indicated by successful offers of 528 florins for two Flanders galleys in 1466,[2] 1,000 florins in 1467,[3] and 1,253 florins in 1473.[4]

We have no information about the Levant galleys until the late 1450's when they were more popular than those going to the West. In 1458 one Levant galley was auctioned for 1,418 florins,[5] and in 1460 two Constantinople-bound galleys fetched 1,540 florins.[6] In 1466, 3,015 florins were given for a double voyage;[7] in 1467, 1,031 florins for a single voyage by two galleys,[8] and in 1473, 1,701 florins.[9] The single galleys that went to Catalonia, West Barbary, and Sicily seem to have been the most consistently popular, with 875 florins as a successful bid in 1442,[10] 2,930 florins for a double voyage in the same year,[11] 1,705 florins in 1465,[12] 512 florins in 1467,[13] 817 florins in 1469,[14] and 900 florins in 1474.[15] The only Barbary auctions of which we have a record are those of 1460 when a single galley fetched 524 florins,[16] and 1466 when 300 florins was the price paid for a single galley.[17]

But the auctions were not always a matter of prospective conductors offering sums of money for galley contracts. Up to 1460 there was frequent mention of a loan which the Consuls made to the successful contractors, and sometimes the size of this loan would enter into the bidding, with the galleys going to the conductor who would accept the smallest loan. In 1441, 6,000 florins

[1] Provv. 150, f. 204ᵛ (4 Jan. 1460).

[2] Consoli del Mare VII, f. 64ʳ (2 May 1466), and Grunzweig, 'Consulat', p. 94.

[3] Ibid., f. 70ᵛ (12 Feb. 1467) and Grunzweig, 'Consulat', p. 96.

[4] Provv. 166, f. 67ᵛ (7 June 1475).   [5] Pagnini, *Della decima*, ii, p. 38.

[6] MAP XCVII, 129. For comparative figures of the auction prices paid for Venetian galleys to the eastern Mediterranean see Thiriet, *Romanie vénitienne*, pp. 421–3.

[7] Consoli del Mare VII, f. 62ᵛ.

[8] In fact the two sources for this auction differ as to the actual figure, owing to a notary's error. Consoli del Mare VII, f. 46ʳ records a successful bid of 1,031 florins, and Provv. 159, f. 109ᵛ a bid of 1,301 florins. In this case the Consoli del Mare report is probably the more reliable being a contemporary record, while the Provvisione dates from two years later.

[9] Provv. 166, f. 67ᵛ (7 June 1475).   [10] Provv. 132, f. 352ʳ (17 Feb. 1442).

[11] Consoli del Mare V, ff. 6–7 (23 Dec. 1442).

[12] Provv. 155, f. 250ᵛ (14 Mar. 1465).

[13] Consoli del Mare VII, f. 72ᵛ (28 Aug. 1467).

[14] Ibid., f. 74ʳ (25 Jan. 1469).   [15] Provv. 166, f. 69ᵛ (7 June 1475).

[16] MAP XCVII, 129.

[17] Consoli del Mare VII, f. 44ᵛ (14 June 1466).

were put aside as capital for each of the major voyages, those to Flanders and to Constantinople, and this was to be loaned to the conductors of each voyage and repaid on completion of the voyage. At the same time the Consuls were authorized to pay up to 1,500 florins subsidy to conductors to stimulate interest in the enterprise.[1] In 1443 a loan of 8,000 florins to the conductors of the Flanders galleys was authorized,[2] and in 1446 it was stated that only 4,000 was available for the loan in that year.[3] In subsequent records mention of the loan appears only once, in 1461 when it was decided to send an extra galley to Flanders and pay the conductor who had already contracted for the other two a subsidy of 425 florins a month, and a loan of 3,000 to cover his additional expenses.[4]

The period between 1461 and 1465 was a crucial one for the galleys in that every effort was made to stimulate interest in the galleys but at the same time trade conditions were very difficult. In the circumstances subsidies given by the Consuls became the principal object of bids at the auctions, instead of offers in the other direction. In 1462 the principle of subsidies was officially accepted for the Levant galleys and they were disposed of to the bidder who wanted least from the Consuls, which was 2,500 florins.[5] In 1463 it was announced that 2,500 florins would be given with the Flanders galleys for the next three years.[6] The reasons for and the consequences of this temporary crisis will be discussed later, but suffice it to say here that this reversal of the normal practice completely disorganized the finances of the Consuls and made it obvious once and for all that the system could not finance itself. Between 1465 and 1477 there was no further mention of subsidies, but in that year the situation arose again when no one would take the galleys to Constantinople without a subsidy, and this was virtually the end of the enterprise.[7] During the crisis in the 1460's the galleys had been kept going by the artificial method of subsidies because it

---

[1] Provv. 132, f. 21ʳ (15 Apr. 1441).

[2] Consoli del Mare V, f. 35ᵛ (5 Feb. 1443), and Grunzweig, 'Consulat', p. 83.

[3] Consoli del Mare III, f. 182 (24 Oct. 1446), and Grunzweig, 'Consulat', p. 43.

[4] Ibid., ff. 145ᵛ–146ʳ (22 Aug. 1461), and Grunzweig, 'Consulat', pp. 35–36.

[5] Provv. 152, f. 297ʳ (29 Mar. 1462); Consoli del Mare III, f. 149; Müller, *Documenti*, pp. 301–2.

[6] Consoli del Mare III, f. 156 (30 Jan. 1463); Provv. 153, f. 228ᵛ; Grunzweig, 'Consulat', pp. 38–39.

[7] Consoli del Mare III, ff. 230ᵛ–231ʳ (18 May 1477); Provv. 168, f. 57ᵛ; Müller, *Documenti*, pp. 311–12.

was apparent that the recession was only temporary;[1] but in 1480 the more drastic step was taken of removing the galleys altogether, at first only for four years, but in fact permanently.

The sort of juggling that went on at these auctions is well illustrated by the auction of 1443 for two Flanders galleys. The Consuls had offered a loan of 8,000 florins with these galleys and the first bid was an enterprising one from Neri Capponi for a loan of 6,000 florins and a subsidy of 1,000. Francesco Tosinghi bettered this by offering to accept a loan of 6,000 and a subsidy of 990 florins; alternatively he offered to take a loan of 8,000 and pay an auction price of 1 florin. The bidding continued along these two possible lines until the subsidies demanded with the 6,000-florin loan had dwindled to nil, at which stage the offers for the 8,000-florin loan had reached 500 florins. The auction then became simpler as the prices offered gradually crept up, although occasional bids for only one of the two galleys with half the loan continued to complicate the issue. Francesco Tosinghi, who had made the running, dropped out when the price reached 800 florins, leaving three men to fight it out: Ludovico Mattei, Giovenco della Stufa, and Niccolò Buti. Both the former were only interested in one galley, and Buti finally won the contract with a bid of 910 florins for the two galleys and a loan of 8,000 florins. It is interesting to note that Della Stufa and another of the early bidders in the auction, Giuliano Ridolfi, served as Buti's patrons on this voyage.[2]

The conductors who gained these contracts were usually Florentine merchants or bankers who regarded the galley voyages not only as possible profitable investments, but also as a means of securing favourable transit for their own merchandise. Often they were men with some maritime experience, having served as captains or patrons on the galleys, but it was not usual for a conductor to sail with his own galleys. His role was mainly one of financier although through his representatives, the patrons, who commanded the individual galleys, he could exert a good deal of influence over the whole enterprise. In fact it sometimes happened in the later years that a merchant or financier who hired the galleys would employ an experienced conductor to carry out the practical

[1] Due to the three-year ban on the export of wool from England in foreign shipping. See below, p. 109.
[2] Consoli del Mare V, ff. 36ᵛ–38ᵛ (14 Feb. 1443) and Grunzweig, 'Consulat', pp. 83–85.

side of his duties. This was particularly so when a group of merchants acting as a limited company took up the contract. In such cases, although the contract was formally allotted to a single merchant, he would then name his partners in the company or *magona* which had been formed for the direction and the financing of the voyage.

The most prominent among the galley conductors were the Martelli family, who were closely linked economically to the Medici, and whose name perhaps frequently served as a cover for their wealthier and more illustrious backers.[1] The two brothers Antonio and Bartolomeo Martelli shared the control of three fleets in the 1460's, two to the Levant and one to Catalonia. Bartolomeo Martelli was an experienced galley commander who had been Captain of the Galleys on two occasions, and had served in the Medici *accomanda* in Ancona. Antonio was purely a merchant, and besides these ventures which he shared with his brother, he was conductor of three other fleets. He had been assistant manager of the Venice branch of the Medici bank and then in 1448 joined the partnership in Pisa. No other individual came anywhere near Antonio Martelli's record, but other leading figures who hired the galleys on one or more occasions were Luca di Buonacorso Pitti, Jacopo d'Andrea Pazzi, Andrea di Lotteringo della Stufa, Antonio di Luca degli Albizzi, Ludovico Strozzi, Angelo Dietisalvi Nerone, Zenobio Biliotti, Pierfilippo Pandolfini, and Bongianno Gianfigliazzi.

Having been allotted the galleys, the first responsibility of the conductor was that of paying a prize of 24 florins towards the work of refacing the Palace of the Signoria.[2] He then had to present the names of his associates, his guarantors, and his possible galley patrons to the *Signoria* and the Councils. In the early years the conductor was expected to present a short list of not more than six nominees from which a special council of consuls of the guilds and the Sea Consuls would choose one patron for each galley; the

---

[1] Five of the sons of Niccolò d'Ugolino Martelli were either branch managers or senior factors of the Medici bank, and for many years Ugolino and Antonio Martelli were the active partners in the Medici branch in Pisa. See R. De Roover, *The Rise and Decline of the Medici Bank, 1397–1494*, Cambridge (Mass.), 1963, pp. 275–8 and 388.

[2] Balìe 26, f. 53 (18 Aug. 1444). For the best statement of the duties and responsibilities of the conductors see Consoli del Mare IV, 4, *Capitoli dei conductori e patroni, passim*, published by Grunzweig, 'Consulat', pp. 63–71.

successful patrons had to receive favourable votes from at least two-thirds of the consuls present.[1] In the later stages of the system the conductor would nominate his patrons, and his nominees would have to be approved by the *Consiglio del Cento* by a majority of two-thirds.[2] A conductor would usually nominate as his patrons young relatives or business connexions, or possibly the son of a wealthy business colleague. Antonio di Niccolò Martelli, being conductor of the Flanders galleys in 1469, nominated Ugolino and Bartolomeo, his brothers, among his associates, and Carlo d'Ugolino as one of his patrons. The other patron was Nerozzo di Piero del Nero, a member of a family often associated with the Martelli in business ventures. In the event Carlo Martelli was not approved by the Council and had to be replaced.[3] Similarly in 1462, when both the Levant and the Flanders fleets were controlled by Antonio Martelli, there was a younger member of the Martelli family acting as a patron in each fleet.[4] Here we see the sort of interlocking pattern of state control and private enterprise which produced the galley system. Although the patrons were the representatives of the conductor he was not allowed a free hand in their selection. They had to be approved by the State in some way or other, because this was first and foremost a state enterprise.

The patrons were therefore the representatives of the conductor and commanded the individual galleys.[5] They were responsible for paying the crews out of the conductor's money. They also attended to the loading and unloading of the cargo and saw that all charges due were entered in the books so that their employer was not being defrauded. Although the patrons had to be at least 30 years old,[6] they were often little more than that and were frequently young merchants getting first-hand experience of the markets of Europe. A patron had to furnish a list of ten guarantors for 5,000 florins each for his good behaviour and obedience to the regulations during the voyage.[7] In the event of the death of the

---

[1] Provv. 115, ff. 58ᵛ–61ʳ (23 May 1425). The special council was the same as that which was responsible for the initial stages of the election of the Captains of the Galleys. See below, pp. 48–49.

[2] Provv. 151, ff. 145ᵛ sqq. (30 July 1460) and Consoli del Mare III, ff. 132–7ᵛ.

[3] Consoli del Mare VII, ff. 123–6 (27 Feb. and 1 Apr. 1469).

[4] See Appendix A.

[5] For an account of the duties of a patron, see Consoli del Mare IV, 4, *Capitoli dei conductori e patroni, passim* (published by Grunzweig, 'Consulat', pp. 63–71).

[6] Provv. 134, f. 111ᵛ (31 Aug. 1443).

[7] Provv. 152 f. 152ᵛ (26 Sept. 1461).

Captain of the fleet during the voyage, one of the patrons would take over the command.

The commander of the fleet or the Captain was appointed by the State. The original intention was that he should be a man of some standing in the city, preferably with some experience of the sea. He was not only Captain of the fleet but also the official representative of Florence when the galleys touched at foreign ports. He was therefore appointed as a state official and was supposed to have no personal interest in the trading side of the voyage, and no connexions with the conductor. In fact in later years the social and political aspects of the appointment sometimes overrode the need for a man with maritime experience, and it became necessary on occasions to appoint an admiral as second-in-command and technical adviser to a Captain who had never been to sea.[1] However, the fact that the same man often captained two or three voyages indicates that they were usually men with some experience of the sea and command.

The original method of electing the Captain was for a special council of consuls of the guilds and the Sea Consuls to be set up as an electoral committee. The council was formed by resort to the *borse*, a method of choosing public officers by lot which was particularly popular with the Florentines due to its supposed impartiality. In this case a *borsa* was made up for each of the five major guilds[2] into which went the names of all the consuls and ex-consuls of the guild over a period of years. From each of these *borse* three names were drawn, thus giving fifteen electors from the major guilds. From the remainder of the guilds, fifteen in all, excluding the judges and notaries, five were chosen again by lot and a *borsa* made up for each of these five of consuls and ex-consuls. One name was then drawn from each of these *borse*, thus providing a further five electors from the minor guilds. The electoral council

---

[1] Müller, *Documenti*, p. 295. The only other reference in the documents to this post is in Provv. 163, f. 129ᵛ (30 Oct. 1472), when Antonio Calafati, a Genoese sailor, inhabitant of Pisa, who was admiral in Bernardo del Nero's Levant fleet of 1469, pleaded for the remission of penalties imposed upon him for insolence to the Captain during the voyage. The Venetians also used the term *admiral* in the sense of technical adviser, whereas in Genoa the admiral was the commander of a fleet (C. Manfroni, 'Cenni sugli ordinamenti delle marine italiane nel medio evo', *Rivista marittima*, 1898, fasc. xii).

[2] This method of appointing the Captain is described in Provv. 115, ff. 58ᵛ–61ʳ (23 May 1425). The five major guilds involved were the wool guild, the Calimala cloth guild, the money-changers, the silk guild, and the doctors and apothecaries.

was thus composed of twenty consuls of the guilds and the six or eight Sea Consuls. As this council was not only responsible for the first stage in the election of the Captains, but also for the final appointment of galley patrons and galley commissaries, it assumed a certain importance. Whether a new council was formed for each series of galley appointments is not clear, but it seems likely that the chosen guild consuls acted as advisers to the Sea Consuls on other aspects of the voyages besides the choice of officials.

Once the council was formed each member was called upon to nominate candidates for the post of Captain of the Galleys. Each of the consuls of the guilds could nominate two candidates, and each of the Sea Consuls three. The council then voted on each of the nominees in turn, and the names of the ten nominees with the most votes went forward to the *Signoria*, who together with their usual advisers made the final choice.[1] The Captain finally chosen was expected to give a prize of 10 florins to the consul who had nominated him, thus presumably encouraging the latter to take their responsibilities seriously.

This system was changed in 1465 and in keeping with the normal practice of the time all element of favouritism was supposedly ruled out by having a special *borsa* of Captains from which the names were drawn.[2] Although the names which went into the *borsa* were presumably screened for practical suitability for the post as well as political conformity, it was soon apparent that this system did not produce the best galley captains. In 1467 the system was therefore modified; twelve names were drawn from the *borsa* for each captaincy, and one elected from those twelve in the *Consiglio del Cento*.[3] It is significant that one of the effects of both

---

[1] In 1425 the council which was summoned by the *Signoria* for the purpose of electing the galley Captains consisted of, in addition to the Gonfalonier of Justice and the Priors, the twelve 'Good Men', the sixteen standard-bearers of the Companies, the Captains of the *Parte Guelfa*, the *Otto della Custodia*, and the *Sei della Mercanzia*. In 1441 (Provv. 132, f. 21ʳ) this group was enlarged by the addition of twenty-five selected guild consuls.

[2] Provv. 156, f. 218ʳ (12 Nov. 1465). The *borsa* system was not so impartial as it was believed because not only were the names which went into the *borsa* carefully screened, but also the frequent use of the right of refusal often resulted in less popular posts ending up with the people who really wanted them in the first place. Thus posts in Leghorn in particular, and to a certain extent in Pisa, tended to become monopolized by certain families who had built up possessions and commercial interests there, and who therefore found service in the unhealthy coastal atmosphere less onerous.

[3] Provv. 158, f. 109ʳ (16 July 1467).

these systems was to take any control over the appointments out of the hands of the guilds and thus to accentuate the political rather than the professional status of the Captain.

The Captains had to be at least 40 years old,[1] and were usually elected about three or four months before the galleys were due to sail. The usual rate of pay was 300 florins per voyage if only one galley was sent, 400 if two, and 500 if three, the salary to be paid by the conductor.[2] In practice a Captain was very rarely appointed if only one galley was sailing, and the patron filled the post instead. Out of his salary the Captain had to pay the wages and living expenses of four squires (one of whom had to be a notary) and two personal servants. The rest of his suite, consisting of a chaplain, a doctor, and two trumpeters, were paid by the conductor direct.[3]

During the voyage the Captain had complete judicial authority over all those sailing in the fleet and for capital offences he could either impose the death-penalty himself or hand the offenders over to the proper authorities on reaching a port within the Florentine jurisdiction. Once the voyage had started he was not allowed to leave his galley except at Southampton and Constantinople where the galleys made long stops.

A Captain had to furnish the Consuls with a list of six guarantors for 3,000 florins each,[4] and he usually travelled on the galley of the conductor who had offered less to the Comune.[5]

It is obvious from what has gone before that the post of Captain of the Galleys was one of the most significant if not one of the most popular in the rota of Florentine state appointments. The salary alone placed the Captain in the top income bracket of Florentine officials,[6] while his combined role of travelling ambassador and commander of the fleet gave him almost unequalled prestige during

[1] Provv. 134, f. 111ᵛ (31 Aug. 1443).

[2] Provv. 150, f. 159ᵛ (8 Dec. 1459), and 151, f. 41ᵛ (25 Apr. 1460).

[3] For these and other details regarding the duties and responsibilities of the Captains, see Consoli del Mare V, ff. 11–31ᵛ, *Capitoli dei capitani, passim* (Grunzweig, 'Consulat', pp. 50–63).

[4] Provv. 152, f. 152ᵛ (26 Sept. 1461).

[5] Balìe 26, f. 53 (18 Aug. 1444).

[6] In 1444 a Sea Consul in Pisa received 150 florins for his six-month tour of duty, while one in Florence received only 48 florins. The Captain of Pisa received 600 *lire* (120 florins) a month but he had a large staff to pay out of this. He was probably the best paid official in the hierarchy and in comparison with him the average galley captain with two galleys got 400 florins for seven months. See L. Martines, *The Social World of the Florentine Humanists*, London, 1963, pp. 143 and 148, for further information on Florentine salaries.

the term of his office. Luca di Maso degli Albizzi on his voyage had to negotiate with both the King of Portugal and the Duke of Burgundy, although the galley regulations prevented him from leaving his galley to meet them in person. Ludovico Acciaiuoli, Captain of the galleys to England and Flanders in 1466–7, obtained an audience in London with Edward IV;[1] and in 1460 the Sultan Muhammed II was entertained on board the galleys of Francesco Vettori in Constantinople.[2] Nevertheless, in the 1460's it seemed to be becoming increasingly hard to find leading Florentines who would accept the post of Captain. In 1466 twenty-two nominees refused the post before a Captain could be found.[3] But this reluctance is partly explainable on the ground that it was a highly specialized post demanding at least a liking for the sea and a willingness to put up with a certain amount of restriction and discomfort for long periods. The system of selection by lot which was in operation in 1466 inevitably led to a large number of refusals, and it is perhaps a bad time to try to assess the popularity of the post. Certainly, however, a glance at the list of those who did serve is sufficient to reveal some of the most powerful men in Florence.

A definite reluctance to serve was, however, even more noticeable amongst the nominees to the post of *rassegna* or *commissario* on the galleys in the later years. These officials were the immediate representatives of the Sea Consuls on the galleys. They were elected by the Consuls[4] and paid, 6 to 8 florins a month and keep, by the conductors.[5] There was one commissary appointed for each galley and they were the only men on the galleys who were outside the jurisdiction of the Captain. They had to report directly to the Consuls within four days of returning to Porto Pisano. They were obliged to make regular inspections of the galleys and the crews, to take note of all absentees and reductions of pay for any reason.[6]

---

[1] Consoli del Mare VII, f. 71 (22 May 1467), and Grunzweig, 'Consulat', p. 96.

[2] Pagnini, *Della decima*, ii, p. 253.

[3] Tratte 226, unpaginated (14 Feb.–1 Apr. 1466).

[4] In the electoral council of consuls of the guilds and Sea Consuls already referred to, each of the guild consuls could nominate one candidate for the post of commissary and each of the Sea Consuls two. The list of nominees was then voted on in this council and the man with the most votes got the post (Provv. 115, ff. 58ᵛ–61ʳ, 23 May 1425).

[5] Consoli del Mare IV, 3, *Capitoli dei rassegnatori*, c. 5. In 1444 the pay was reduced from 8 to 6 florins (Consoli del Mare III, f. 71, 19 Feb 1444).

[6] Consoli del Mare IV, 3, *Capitoli dei rassegnatori*, *passim*, and Grunzweig, 'Consulat', pp. 71–72.

They were required to keep an inventory of the equipment of the galley and a nominal roll of the crew for use on those inspections.[1] They were not only responsible for reporting breaches of the regulations to the Consuls, but also for seeing that the crews were not exploited in any way by the patrons. The commissaries were supposed to be at least 32 years of age, but this stipulation seems to have been frequently circumvented and younger men appointed by special dispensation.[2] In 1465 the *borsa* system was applied also to this post,[3] and in 1472 in order to avoid corruption born of experience, it was decided that only men who had not been to sea before were eligible.[4] The post of commissary was considered as a useful apprenticeship for sons of merchants and future state officials, and one finds amongst the names of those who held the post many of the best families in Florence.[5] It was repeatedly stressed that no relative of any of the Sea Consuls could hold any of these posts, nor yet could one of the Consuls have any share in the trading of the galleys.

The final state appointment on the galleys was that of notary or purser. One was appointed to each galley and was responsible for keeping a record of the merchandise loaded and the charges due.[6] The Captain had his own notary who was one of his suite and was responsible for registering all the decisions on policy made by the Captain and his advisers, and all the fines and punishments which he ordered. The notaries were in the later years drawn from a special *borsa* of notaries, used by the Consuls for the notarial posts under their control.

The instructions to the notaries of 1442 set out in detail the

---

[1] The *Quadernuccio di Luigi d'Andrea Vettori* of 1445 is the only one of such records which has survived, and its importance is such that I hope to be able to publish it shortly in its entirety. The Quadernuccio consists of an inventory of all the equipment and fittings of Vettori's galley, a nominal roll of the entire crew, and a very brief itinerary of the voyage.

[2] Provv. 150, f. 84ʳ (18 Aug. 1459). See Consoli del Mare VI, *passim*, for exceptions to this rule. In 1444 the age limit was only 25 (Consoli del Mare III, f. 71ʳ).

[3] Provv. 156, f. 218ᵛ (12 Nov. 1465).

[4] Provv. 164, f. 70ᵛ (4 June 1472).

[5] Amongst those who served as commissaries on the galleys in the 1450's and 1460's were Donato Capponi, Zanobi del Nero, Oddo Guicciardini, Niccolò Donati, Giovanni Buondelmonte, Francesco Strozzi, Castellano Frescobaldi, Domenico Giugni, Pieramadeo Macchiavelli, Jacopo Salviati, Simone Vespucci, Ruggiero Corbinelli, Guglielmo Altoviti, and Carlo Bartoli.

[6] See Consoli del Mare IV, 4, *Capitoli degli scrivani*, *passim*, and Grunzweig, 'Consulat', pp. 73–78.

freight charges to be levied on all goods using the communal galleys. There were different charges for every type of merchandise and for each stage in the galleys' voyages. As the charges were even laid down for goods likely to travel on intermediate stages, such as Barcelona to England, Marseilles to Sicily, Naples to Constantinople, etc., these lists provide a useful source of information on the circulation of commodities in fifteenth-century trade. In 1461 all freight charges were revised and while many of the charges on outgoing goods were reduced slightly, the charges on imports were in some cases reduced by half. The wider implications of this move and the light it casts on the history of the galley system will be discussed later; here it need only be noted that this decline in receipts from freight charges contributed greatly to the reluctance of conductors to take the galleys in the early 1460's without considerable subsidies to help them.

In addition to the freight the galleys also carried a few passengers, usually merchants travelling with their merchandise. It was laid down that a merchant who had paid more than 20 florins in freight charges on a particular voyage was entitled to free passage for himself. If he paid more than 40 florins he could also take a bona fide servant free of charge.[1] It was a long-standing tradition that merchants travelling with their goods should be consulted by the Captain before any decision affecting the trading prospects of the voyage was made.[2] On the Florentine galleys the practice was for the Captain to call a council of representatives of the merchants, the patrons, the mates, and other experienced sailors to advise him on any major problems which arose during the voyage.[3]

From what has gone before it must already be apparent that a conductor when he won a galley contract was letting himself in for a considerable capital outlay before he saw any of his money back. His assets were the freight charges and any personal commercial profit which he could draw from his own goods on the galleys. To set against this there were not only the wages and living expenses of the crews, but also a proportion of the commissioning and running costs of the galleys themselves. For if the responsibility for building and equipping the galleys lay largely with the Consuls,

---

[1] Consoli del Mare V, *Capitoli dei capitani*, c. 20.

[2] *Cambridge Economic History of Europe*, iii, Cambridge, 1963, p. 59.

[3] Albizzi consulted his council on such matters as the possible overloading of the galleys, means of evading pirates, choice of ports of call, etc.

the expenses of spare equipment which was carried were shared between the Consuls and the conductors. The Consuls provided spare spars and rigging, a spare tiller, blocks, forty extra oars, and a barrel of gunpowder. The conductors then had to furnish additional sail-cloth, and all the smaller accessories needed by a medieval ship, such as caulking oakum, pitch, nails, rope, etc.[1] He also had to arm the crew according to a set scale; the cross-bow marines had to have body armour and a cross-bow, and the senior sailors who manned the poop and the tiller had to have at least a cuirass. In addition the outer rank of oarsmen had to be armed with a long pike.[2] Amongst the conductor's responsibilities for victualling the galleys were regulations on the amount of biscuit and soap that had to be taken on board at Porto Pisano.[3] In 1462 it was reckoned that the conductor's outlay on commissioning and expenses of one galley on one of the long voyages was about 5,000 florins.[4] With the first system of freight charges the 1429/30 galleys of Luca di Maso degli Albizzi to Flanders brought back 16,000 florins in freights.[5] There were two galleys in the fleet so this left a considerable margin of profit against which, of course, had to be set the original sum paid for the contract. But in these circumstances contract bids of up to 5,000 florins were conceivable. After 1461, however, we find that 12,000–15,000 florins is the estimated taking in freights for a fleet of three galleys.[6] In this case the conductor needed to reckon on taking at least the maximum 15,000 before he could even offer a positive bid, let alone make any profit; hence the inevitability of subsidies.

In some cases the conductor was relieved of some of the extraordinary charges which could be incurred on a long voyage by a system of charging additional costs to the merchandise carried and thus levying an additional freight charge. Albizzi was ordered to do this to offset the wages of additional marines which he took on in England to protect his galleys against pirates. After some

[1] Consoli del Mare IV, 4, *Capitoli dei conductori e patroni*, c. 5.
[2] Ibid., c. 1.
[3] In the regulations of 1442 it was laid down that each galley should carry 46,000 lb. of biscuit on leaving Porto Pisano. 2,000 lb. of soap also had to be carried on each galley.
[4] Provv. 152, f. 297ʳ (29 Mar. 1462). Another source tells us that it was reckoned to cost 35 florins a day to keep a galley at sea (ASF, Legazioni e Commissarie della Signoria VII, ff. 74–76).
[5] Albizzi Diary, ff. 62ʳ and 106ʳ.
[6] Provv. 152, f. 297ʳ (29 Mar. 1462).

voyages an extensive audit was held to assess the additional costs and see how much could legitimately be paid by the owners of the goods transported. Such charges included bribes to customs officials, unexpected port dues, expenses incurred by the Captain in his diplomatic capacity, the costs of safe-conducts, additional pilots, presents to foreign potentates, etc. The records of such audits which have come down to us show that neither the Captain, nor the conductor and his patrons could expect to get away with unnecessary extravagance in these matters, but on the other hand the owners of the merchandise usually had to reckon on paying out rather more than the set freight charges before they had finished.[1]

The bulk of the work of preparing the galleys for sea was done at Pisa, 'between the bridges'. There the Consuls had to hand them over to the patrons, or the conductor himself if he went, a certain time before the appointed sailing date. In 1425 the time laid down was only three days before sailing, but in 1458 it became fifteen days.[2] The patrons then had to put at least 100 men aboard each galley to sail down the Arno and round to Porto Pisano for loading the cargo.[3] On return the process was reversed and when the cargo had been completely unloaded, the conductor and his patrons were responsible for bringing the galleys back up the Arno and handing them over to the Consuls with all issued equipment checked, and deficiencies made up or paid for. To avoid the frequent difficulties encountered as a result of loading galleys in shallow water, it was forbidden to load them in less than $3\frac{1}{2}$ *braccia*, or about 7 feet of water.[4]

The conductors were also responsible for finding the crews of the galleys, but the appointment of the senior sailors, the mates, navigators, and helmsmen, had to be approved by the Consuls, to whom all officers had to swear that they would observe the galley regulations. In times of crisis greater stress than usual was laid on the provision of experienced crews, and the number of marines and officers was increased. At least half the sailors who performed

---

[1] Consoli del Mare VII, ff. 66, 69, and 71; Grunzweig, 'Consulat', pp. 97–99, publishes the records of one of these audits which contained not only a list of the extra expenses involved, but also a list of the merchants whose goods were loaded on the galleys and the value of each individual consignment.

[2] Provv. 115, ff. 58ᵛ–61ʳ (23 May 1425), and Balìe 29, f. 70 (15 Nov. 1458).

[3] Consoli del Mare III, f. 128ᵛ (12 Nov. 1459).

[4] Provv. 133, f. 177ʳ (14 Sept. 1442).

responsible and specific duties on the galleys had to be Florentine subjects.

Restrictions were imposed on the amount of personal baggage that could be loaded by both officers and sailors. The former could not load baggage valued at more than two and a half times their salary, and similar restrictions on sailors' baggage indicate an attempt to restrain if not to deny the accepted maritime custom of the 'seaman's venture'.[1] The reason for these restrictions was obviously the limited space available for merchandise on a galley, but they did nothing to make service on the galleys any more popular.

The salaries to be paid to each category of sailor were laid down by the Consuls, as was also the number to be engaged for each galley.[2] The men of Leghorn were liable to be conscripted into the galleys and could only escape service by paying the salary of a substitute.[3] In 1430 the press gangs even followed them as far as the Florentine camp before Lucca, where many had gone to escape serving on the galleys.[4] However, the nominal roll of Vettori's galley in 1445 reveals that the majority of the senior sailors and marines in the galleys were not local men; they came from the Ligurian coast, from the Tuscan interior, and on this occasion from Rome, Venice, Hungary, and the Biscay ports.[5] Leonardo Spini when fitting out a brig for a voyage to Tunis manned it almost entirely with Corsicans, but this was not a communal venture and the men were all volunteers.[6]

It was not only the unpopularity of the service which often made it difficult to find crews for the galleys; in 1464 plague was responsible for decimating the crews of the Catalonia galleys, and creating a shortage of sailors for replacements in Pisa and Leghorn.[7] Furthermore, the problems of the conductor and patrons with

---

[1] Provv. 151, f. 22^v (7 Apr. 1460).

[2] Consoli del Mare IV, 4 *Capitoli dei conductori e patroni*, c. 2, and ibid. III, f. 140^v (29 Nov. 1459).

[3] Vigo, *Statuti e Provvisioni*, Statutes of 1477, ch. vi, p. 88.

[4] MAP IV, 30 (15 Aug. 1431). The Sea Consuls asked Averardo de' Medici and Neri Capponi, commissaries in the camp at Lucca, to send back certain local inhabitants who had fled to the army rather than serve on the galleys. It is true, however, that on this occasion the alternative was service on the armed galleys rather than on the merchant galleys.

[5] *Quadernuccio di Luigi Vettori*, ff. 6^r–13^r and 17^r–37^r.

[6] MAP LXXXIII, f. 66 (undated).

[7] Provv. 155, f. 106^r (8 Aug. 1464).

regard to the finding of a crew were by no means over when the galleys left Porto Pisano. Desertions were frequent at ports along the route, and sometimes galleys found themselves so undermanned by the time they reached their destinations that new men had to be hired.[1] The patrons were in fact obliged to fill gaps in their crews caused by sickness or desertion, and it was a part of the duties of the commissaries to make a note of such gaps and fine the patron the equivalent of the salary of the missing sailor as long as the gap remained unfilled. Although this regulation may have been effective against a deliberate and parsimonious policy of laying off of hands by the patrons, it did not take into account the difficulties of finding replacements outside Florentine ports. Albizzi tried to fill the gaps in his oarsmen in England in 1430, but could only get a few Germans and Flemings to sign on.

With these problems always in the front of their minds, patrons tended to be very reluctant to let their men go ashore in ports. This was particularly true if, having once got the crew on board in Porto Pisano, there should be any delay in sailing. The regulations imposed very strict fines on patrons whose galleys did not sail on the scheduled dates but nevertheless punctuality was not always possible. No merchandise could be loaded after the advertised departure date, even if there was a valid reason for delay, and indeed unfavourable winds could sometimes make it impossible to leave Porto Pisano for weeks.

Once they had left Porto Pisano, the Captain and the patrons had a further set of regulations to which they had to adhere. For each voyage the stopping-places were laid down in advance with the maximum number of days to be spent in each. The Florentine galleys relied a good deal on carrying-trade and the tight schedule laid down by the Consuls enabled them not only to cover a maximum number of ports, but also to gain a greater reputation for speed and efficiency than the Venetians.[2] Each of the major voyages had a turn-round point at which a longer stop was allowed. In Southampton a stop of forty days was permitted; within the first ten, lists of all the merchandise to be loaded had to be sent to the Captain by the merchants concerned, while the inbound cargo was

---

[1] Vettori's roll reveals that in 1445 the desertions and deaths amongst the crew of one Alexandria galley were over 16 per cent. of the total. Out of a crew of 210, thirty-three deserted and three died during the voyage.

[2] D. B. Quinn and A. A. Ruddock, *The Port Books or Local Customs Accounts of Southampton for the reign of Edward IV*, Southampton, 1937–8, ii, p. xxxii.

unloaded. In the next twenty days heavy goods were loaded with the capstan, and in the final ten days the light merchandise was put aboard by the merchants themselves. No goods could be loaded after the forty days had elapsed and if the galleys were filled before that period was up, the Captain could set sail immediately.[1] It was customary for merchants to give tips to the senior sailors at the end of loading, although no member of the galley crews was entitled to ask for any payment other than the authorized freight charge.

Although there were few restrictions on what commodities could be carried in the galleys, there were two which are of interest. The first was a ban on the loading of foreign silk cloths.[2] This was imposed at a very early stage and indicates that already in the 1420's the rising Florentine silk industry was coming in for its share of protection. Secondly there was a ban on galleys for Eastern destinations carrying female slaves or arms as merchandise.[3]

One of the greatest problems of the galleys when at sea was the large number of pirates which abounded particularly in Greek and Spanish waters. Frequently this piracy assumed a semi-official nature when the fleets of two nations at war with each other assumed the right to stop and search neutral shipping for goods belonging to their enemy. Such practices were very much open to abuse and it was often difficult to distinguish between the free-lance pirate who plundered any shipping, and accredited warships which were more discriminating but often just as dangerous.[4] Albizzi had constant worries on this score during his voyage as can be seen from his diary, and his solutions to the piracy problem were threefold. Firstly his own galleys, which were by that time committed and beyond the reach of help from Florence, should be allowed to take on additional cross-bowmen. A galley relied for

---

[1] Consoli del Mare V, *Capitoli dei Capitani*, c. 6.

[2] Consoli del Mare III, ff. 20–21ᵛ (3 Sept. 1426), and Grunzweig, 'Consulat', pp. 8–9.

[3] Provv. 151, f. 148ʳ (30 July 1460).

[4] In 1436 the Florentine *Signoria* protested to the Queen of Naples that goods of Antonio Pazzi and Francesco Tosinghi, Florentines living in Barcelona, had been seized off a Portuguese ship by a Genoese privateer. Furthermore, Bartolomeo Peruzzi, a young Florentine merchant travelling with the goods, had been tortured by the Genoese into stating that the goods were not Florentine but Catalan, and hence liable to seizure as the Genoese were at war with Aragon (Miss. I Canc. 34, f. 122ʳ, 3 Oct 1436).

protection very much on the size of its crew and so increasing numbers was the standard way to offset foreseeable threats. In the Captains' instructions laid down for the 1443 voyage it was specifically stated that the Captain could, if pirate activity warranted it and if the patrons and the Consul in England approved, take on extra marines in England without reference to the Sea Consuls. Judging by Albizzi's remarks it seems that this instruction already applied in 1429 but he was in any case forced to appeal to Florence for authority as he suspected that the Consul and the Florentine merchants in England would be unwilling to approve the extra expenses of more marines, which would inevitably fall on the merchandise. The position was set out fully by Albizzi in his letters to the Sea Consuls from Sluys and Southampton:

Therefore in this letter little remains to be said except to remind you that provision must be made for our return because, as I wrote before, in the spring many balingers, ships, and armed galleys which are being fitted out in Seville, will be at sea for the war with the Catalans; and the same one presumes will apply to the Catalans and their ships. And you know that these are two nations who are inclined to seize goods wherever they can find them. Furthermore these galleys are held to be richer than they are, and they each have the chance to say that they wish to check if we are carrying goods of their enemies. Therefore, wishing to save our honour and the galleys, it is absolutely necessary in my opinion to arm the galleys well on the return passage, because although the patrons have their full complement, the galleys are not properly manned, nor yet can one tell them to man them better. The reason for this being that those who were taken on in Pisa have proved themselves quite useless, both sailors and marines. Yet it was necessary to enrol them all whether the patrons wanted them or not. A good number of them were enrolled there for friendship and to please the patrons and at the request of many of the citizens; and all of them took an oath to return with the galleys. Therefore, when one reckons up, these galleys have about 130 oarsmen who really row, and about twenty-five officers and marines who are conscientious and useful; as for the rest, one cannot count on them at sea except to eat the biscuit, and they even do little of that when the sea gets up. So you can see how we are armed. These galleys each need fifty good marines and 160 oarsmen who can row. Therefore I would suggest with respect that it seems to me that one must increase the crews by at least twenty oarsmen and ten marines per galley in view of the dangers that there are, and charge it to the general average of the merchandise. This would be my intention if the merchants in London approve; but, however, because they have insurance and the insurers are not here, I believe that they will not want to incur the expense. And so, wishing to do my duty, I cannot do less than inform you once more and beg you, if it pleases you and seems useful to you, to send immediately a courier to order that this is done or such similar action as seems best to you: and the expense you can put to the merchandise and to the insurers and other parties who will benefit from it.[1]

Secondly Albizzi asked permission to be allowed to take the initiative against suspicious and unfriendly shipping, thus allowing his two powerful galleys to overwhelm a small hostile force before it was able to gather strength. This permission was refused, and indeed it was specifically stated in the regulations that galley captains who attacked other shipping would be severely punished. Finally Albizzi suggested that in the future the size of the fleets should be increased to three or four galleys of which one might well be an armed galley. He argued that Venetian fleets to Flanders usually consisted of four galleys and they never seemed to have any trouble. Little notice was taken of this suggestion at the time but in later years the Consuls did occasionally increase the size of fleets because of reports of pirate activity. On only one occasion did they adopt the idea of sending an escorting long galley and this was in 1458 when Alessandro del Vigna, the Captain of the fleet, sailed in a long galley. The experiment was a disaster as the long galley proved less seaworthy than her great consorts and sank with its Captain in the Bay of Biscay.

Occasionally two or three long galleys were sent out to meet returning great galleys if there were particular threats in local waters, but this was the nearest the Florentines ever came to providing escorts again.

Once the galleys had surmounted all these hazards and returned to port safely, there remained one final regulation which the conductor and patrons had to observe. Every galley which went to the eastern Mediterranean had to bring back a carpet bought by the patron out of the conductor's money, and similarly every Flanders galley had to bring back a tapestry. These had to be presented to the Sea Consuls at the end of the voyage for the furnishing of their offices in Florence, and other public palaces.[2] In 1461 conductors were told that in future they should give cash presents

---

[1] Albizzi Diary, f. 86ʳ⁻ᵛ. Letter written on 12 Dec. from Sluys to the Sea Consuls.
[2] Provv. 126, f. 135ᵛ (30 July 1435).

of 12 florins instead of a carpet, and 20 florins instead of a tapestry.[1] One might imagine that perhaps the Consuls were becoming overwhelmed with carpets and tapestries in their offices; but in fact the avowed reason for the change was that conductors had been presenting inferior articles which did not have anything like the cash value intended when the regulation was passed.

The return of the galleys was always a matter for some rejoicing in Florence. The messengers who brought the news received a present from the *Signoria*, and fireworks were let off in honour of the occasion.[2] Indeed it is not surprising that the return of the galleys despite all the hazards which they faced was a cause for jubilation; what is perhaps surprising is that the galleys almost invariably did return safely. It was perhaps the very reliability of the galleys which made their comings and goings of declining interest to the chroniclers, rather than any falling-off in their economic importance.[3]

---

[1] Provv. 152, f. 123ʳ (22 Aug. 1461), and Consoli del Mare III, f. 143ᵛ.

[2] Miss. II Canc. 6, f. 59ʳ (26 Jan. 1474), and Consoli del Mare VII, ff. 95ᵛ and 98ʳ.

[3] Sapori assumes rather the opposite in describing the way in which the chronicler Pietriboni quickly ceases to take any interest in the galleys (Sapori, 'Primi viaggi', pp. 82–83).

4

THE VOYAGES OF THE GALLEYS

So far we have followed the history of the galleys up to the voyages of 1425 and the regulations issued in that year for the overall co-ordination of the system. From then until 1480 single galleys and fleets of galleys sailed at more or less frequent intervals for most parts of the Mediterranean, and for Flanders and England. For purposes of simplification I have divided the voyages geographically, following the history of each set of voyages to a particular area through to its chronological conclusion before embarking on a different set. This method has one great disadvantage, besides that of making comparative chronology rather more difficult, and that is that frequently voyages to different parts of the Mediterranean were linked not only by the timing of arrivals and departures in Porto Pisano, but by actually using the same fleet. Much of the trade of the Florentine galleys was a carrying trade, and although they had to call as frequently as possible at Porto Pisano, they often in fact only passed through on their way from one part of the Mediterranean to another. The best example of this was the voyage which covered both Catalonia and Sicily. The galleys on this route, almost throughout their history, went first to Barcelona, Valencia, and Majorca, and then back through Porto Pisano to Sicily, or vice versa. Sometimes this route was extended as far as the Barbary coast, thus impinging upon what was usually a separate sphere of operations. Sometimes the Barbary galleys extended their activities as far as Alexandria, while on occasions the galleys on voyages to Constantinople and Syria were allowed to pay preliminary or concluding visits to Spain.

These extended voyages tend to blur the pattern of series of voyages to particular geographical areas; but nevertheless it is possible to divide the activities of the Florentine galleys roughly into several spheres. In the eastern Mediterranean the galleys went at various times to Alexandria, Constantinople and the Black Sea, and Syria. In the western Mediterranean they served Catalonia, Provence, the west coast of Italy, and Sicily on one run; and the

Barbary coast from the Straits of Gibraltar to Tunis, and sometimes as far as Alexandria on the other. Outside the Mediterranean they went to Flanders and England, sometimes also calling at Lisbon and Cadiz. There is a reference to a Florentine fleet in the Baltic in 1445 led by Bartolomeo Martelli,[1] but there are no details to be found about this in the official sources. An examination in detail of these sets of voyages will enable us to get a clearer picture of the ramifications of the Florentine galley system, the rhythm of departures and arrivals and interruptions in it, and also of the Florentine families and merchants who played a large part in the enterprise as a whole.

Although there were frequent regulations establishing standard time-tables for the departure of the galleys, it is not possible to rely on these as evidence of actual sailings. For most of the period under examination too many factors militated against regular sailings being maintained for more than two or three years. Thus all the voyages which I shall describe are documented by something more than general regulations; e.g. specific regulations ordering the preparation of a particular fleet, letters, port records, lists of official appointments, diaries, cargo lists, etc.[2]

The eastern Mediterranean

One of the difficulties in piecing together the story of Florentine voyages to the eastern Mediterranean is the frequent use of the word 'Levant' as the only indication of the destination of many of the voyages. The majority of the voyages so described were certainly to Constantinople, but there are a few about which it is impossible to be sure of the exact destination and one suspects that some may have been to Alexandria. Certainly after 1425 news of the Alexandria galleys becomes sparse. After the first three years of the galley system in which Alexandria was the principal destination of all the eastern galley fleets, interest in this run seems to have declined. Perhaps the Florentines realized at this stage that they were going to have little success in breaking into the spice market. Heyd claims that between 1425 and 1444 there was a complete suspension of sailings to Alexandria, and the immediate reason for this was Florence's war with Milan which occupied all her

---

[1] P. Litta, *Famiglie celebri italiane*, Milan, 1819–67, s.v. Martelli, table ii.
[2] Full lists of all the documentary sources for the galley voyages described below are to be found in Appendix A. Only the more important and immediately relevant references will be quoted in the footnotes of this chapter.

resources.[1] However, this war does not seem to have impeded the western voyages, and so long a suspension of voyages to Alexandria seems unlikely, as in 1427 Roberto Martelli was asking the Sultan of Tunis for a continuation of the safe conduct extended to the Florentine galleys stopping at Sousse and Tunis on their way to Alexandria.[2] Furthermore, in 1435 Francesco Mannelli was sent to Alexandria to apologize for a temporary suspension in the sailings of the galleys which was the result of wars in which Florence had become involved. The tone of the Signoria's letter to the Sultan on this occasion did not suggest that the suspension had already lasted ten years.[3]

It would seem likely then that after the initial series of direct voyages to Alexandria, it became the practice for galleys visiting the Barbary coast to extend their run as far as Alexandria on occasions.[4] The Venetians also used this route along the north coast of Africa for their galleys in 1442 and at intervals thereafter. However, in 1444 preparations were made for a definite Alexandria fleet which was to be an annual enterprise; the Consuls were authorized to send two galleys a year to be auctioned in June and to sail before mid-April of the following year.[5] These galleys in fact sailed on 12 June 1445 with Giovenco della Stufa as their Captain. Giovenco carried letters of introduction to the Sultans both of Egypt and of Tunis,[6] and as this is one of the few voyages of which we have a complete itinerary, it is worth following in some detail.[7] The two galleys after leaving Porto Pisano headed southwards calling at Porto Ercole, Gaeta, Naples, and Palermo. They then sailed round the western coast of Sicily to Trapani and thence to Tunis. Tunis was obviously one of the major ports of call as the fleet remained there over three weeks. During this period Francesco di Lorenzo della Stufa, a young relative and squire of the Captain, disappeared and in the following years two successive ambassadors were sent from Florence to

---

[1] Heyd, *Commercio del Levante*, pp. 1046, 1052.

[2] Amari, *Diplomi arabi*, appendix, pp. 12–14.

[3] Miss. I Canc. 34, ff. 128–9 (15 Jan. 1435), and Amari, op. cit., appendix, pp. 15–16.

[4] Consoli del Mare V, f. 4ᵛ (21 Dec. 1442). The regulations laid down for the voyage to Catalonia and Sicily at this time permitted the galley to go on from Sicily to Tunis and Alexandria at the discretion of the conductor.

[5] Balìe 26, f. 53 (18 Aug. 1444) and Consoli del Mare III, f. 72ʳ.

[6] Miss. I Canc. 36, ff. 101–2, and Amari, op. cit., appendix, pp. 17–18.

[7] *Quadernuccio di Luigi Vettori, passim.*

negotiate for his release from the Sultan's prison.[1] From Tunis the galleys sailed along the coast of North Africa to Tripoli and ultimately to Alexandria where they arrived on 17 September. Here they spent two and a half months before sailing northwards and westwards to Rhodes, Crete, Modon, and Syracuse. Thus on the return journey they were following the more usual route between Italy and Alexandria. But at Syracuse the fleet diverged from this route and instead of heading for home through the straits of Messina, it set off southwards for another visit to North Africa. The galleys called once more at Tripoli, and then spent a further month at Tunis before returning to Porto Pisano via Palermo. They re-entered harbour on 4 April 1446 after nearly ten months away and after a voyage which must have been almost unique, because in the next year the itinerary of the Alexandria galleys was established along a far more direct route.

In 1447 lists of authorized ports of call were published for all the voyages and on the Alexandria run they were to be: Talamone, Gaeta, Naples, Salerno, Castello a Mare, Palermo, Messina, Syracuse, Modon, Rhodes, Alexandria, Beirut, and Jaffa; thence the galleys could return by way of Cyprus, Chios, and Crete.[2] This marked a definite break with the Barbary voyage, although there is no direct evidence of voyages following this route in the years immediately after 1447. The years 1449–54 were in fact bad ones for the galleys owing to the wars with the Aragonese, and the wars in Italy which ended with the Peace of Lodi, so it is not perhaps surprising that the next reference to an Alexandria fleet is in 1456.[3] In April of that year two galleys were preparing to sail to Alexandria with Angelo Dietisalvi as one of the patrons. These galleys returned on 9 September so their route must have been a very direct one.[4]

In 1458 the Consuls reverted to the device of sending the Barbary galleys from Tunis to Alexandria.[5] One galley was serving the

---

[1] Amari, *Diplomi arabi*, appendix, pp. 20–24. In Aug. 1446 Tommaso Velluti was sent, and in July 1449 Angelo Petrocchi went on the same errand.

[2] Consoli del Mare III, ff. 78ᵛ–79ᵛ (27 Mar. 1447); see also Müller, *Documenti*, pp. 291–2.

[3] Early in 1453 it was announced that 'consideratis temporibus adversis que currunt respectu guerre et insuper quod Consules maris non possunt facere exercitium maris pro quo fuerunt deputati . . .', the number of employees of the Consuls was reduced for the duration of the war (Consoli del Mare III, f. 105ʳ⁻ᵛ, 30 Jan. 1453, and Grunzweig, 'Consulat', p. 28). [4] Tratte 81, f. 124.

[5] Balie 29, f. 70ᵛ (15 Nov. 1458), and Consoli del Mare III, ff. 121ʳ–3ʳ.

Barbary coast at this time, and the decision as to whether or not to go on to Alexandria was left to the conductor. In 1460 two galleys were put on the route and in 1461 these also were authorized to go on to Alexandria at the discretion of the conductor.[1]

Bernardo Corsi, the Captain of the three galleys which were sent in 1465 to Syria to open up new trade routes, was authorized to call at Alexandria, and took with him letters of credence and instructions which indicated that there had been a temporary lapse of trade relations between Florence and Egypt.[2]

Finally in 1471, owing to a severe outbreak of plague in Constantinople and the subsequent disruption of trade, Alexandria came into the picture once more as a port of call for the galleys. In October of that year the two Medici Burgundian galleys, whose activities will be discussed in more detail later, were in Chios preparing to go on to Alexandria.[3] However, by the next year Constantinople was once more open to trade and in the remaining few years of the galley system there are no further references to visits to Alexandria.

The pattern of voyages to Constantinople is rather less erratic than that of those to Alexandria, but nevertheless obscurity surrounds the opening up of the route. In May 1429 the *Signoria* decided to send one galley to Constantinople; they chose one that had recently been to Catalonia as being in the best condition, and proposed to hire it out for eighteen months commencing 1 July. During this time the galley was to go to Constantinople at least twice, and could operate through Porto Pisano to southern France and Catalonia to secure extra trade. It could not, however, pick up goods in Porto Pisano for Catalonia as this would have been damaging to the trade of the ordinary Catalonia galleys.[4] This is the first official record of a voyage to Constantinople; ambassadors had been sent there to negotiate for trade concessions in 1422, but apparently without success, and it was not until 1439 on the occasion of the Council of Florence that the Emperor granted the required trade concessions.[5] Indeed there is no evidence of the *Signoria*'s plan being carried out in 1429, and it is usually thought

[1] Provv. 151, f. 335ʳ (23 Jan. 1461).

[2] For full details of this voyage see below, p. 70.

[3] MAP XXV, 109 (10 Oct. 1471).

[4] Provv. 120, f. 159ᵛ (27 May 1429), and Müller, *Documenti*, p. 283.

[5] W. Heyd, *Le colonie commerciali degli Italiani in Oriente nel Medioevo*, Venice, 1866–8, i, pp. 458–9; P. Bonfante, *Storia del commercio*, Turin, 1946, p. 235.

that an effective service of Florentine galleys to Constantinople did not start until 1436.[1] However, one must accept the possibility of a voyage in 1429–30, although there seems to have been no attempt to follow it up until 1436. The 1436 venture was presumably the first voyage of the galley of the *Magona Vecchia* which had in 1435 received a five-year contract for voyages to Constantinople and beyond.[2] In 1437 the Consuls planned to send two galleys but in the end only one sailed in August of that year with Francesco Mannelli as patron. This galley was unloading in Constantinople by the end of October.[3]

In 1439 the *Magona* contract was prematurely terminated although in that year two galleys were offered to the Byzantine Emperor to bring him to Italy for the Council.[4] It was not until 1444 that there is any evidence of renewed communal voyages to Constantinople. In that year one galley was to be auctioned for the voyage in January and it was to be permitted to go to Catalonia first.[5] In fact it was in 1444 that Neri di Stefano Cambi is reported to have been on board a galley commanded by Giovanni Tosinghi which was wrecked in the eastern Mediterranean.[6] It seems likely that this was the first casualty amongst the galleys although we have no news of how serious the disaster was.

The ports of call for the Constantinople run were fixed along with the rest in 1447 and they were Talamone, Civitavecchia, Gaeta, Naples, Castello a Mare, Salerno, Palermo, Messina, Modon, Negroponte, Gallipoli, and Constantinople. On the return voyage the galleys could call at Chios and Rhodes.[7] However, the general lull in Florentine trade in the early 1450's and the fall of Constantinople to the Turks brought operations to a halt

---

[1] Heyd, *Commercio del Levante*, p. 866, states that in 1436 a number of Florentine ships left for Constantinople. These carried letters which described this initiative as the *beginning* of trade (see also Müller, *Documenti*, p. 162). Bonfante (op. cit., p. 235) places the opening of the galley service between Porto Pisano and Constantinople in 1426.

[2] See below, pp. 86–87.

[3] Provv. 128, f. 120ʳ (11 July 1437); U. Dorini and T. Bertele, *Libro dei conti di Giacomo Badoer*, Rome, 1956, i, pp. 203, 236, 248.

[4] Bonfante, *Storia del Commercio*, p. 235. Presumably this offer was not taken up as four papal galleys were sent on the same mission under Antonio Condulmiero (A. Guglielmotti, *Storia della marina pontificia nel Medioevo*, Rome, 1886, ii, pp. 147–8).

[5] Provv. 134, f. 164ʳ (30 Dec. 1443); Consoli del Mare III, f. 69ᵛ; Müller, *Documenti*, pp. 284–5.

[6] S. Ammirato, *Delle famiglie nobili fiorentine*, Florence, 1615, pp. 71 and 74.

[7] Consoli del Mare III, ff. 78ᵛ–79ᵛ.

until 1456 when a single galley was hired to the wool guild for the distribution of cloth in the East.[1] Two galleys were then prepared by the Consuls in spring 1457 but despite efforts throughout the summer, safe-conducts for these could not be obtained from the King of Naples, and it was felt to be too dangerous to send them without.[2]

In 1458 another effort to dispatch a fleet was made. The Captain, Francesco Vettori, and patrons were appointed, but departure was delayed as it was decided rather late to send two galleys instead of one for greater security. There was then some doubt as to whether there would be enough cloth available to fill two galleys, but they were ordered to sail regardless in August.[3] In October there was a report of Florentine eastern galleys being harassed by hostile shipping off Gaeta,[4] but otherwise we know nothing about the voyage of this fleet.

The two galleys of 1459 also ran into difficulties, this time on their return. Filippo di Filippo Tornabuoni was Captain, and he had with him Paolo di Piero degli Albizzi and Bartolomeo Pucci as patrons, and Baldassare di Giovacchino Ricci as a Medici agent travelling on Pucci's galley. The fleet had a good voyage out, leaving in mid-August and arriving at Constantinople on 28 September.[5] From there Pucci's galley went into the Black Sea, which was the first recorded occasion on which a Florentine galley did so. The experiment seems to have been a success for in the next year trade concessions were obtained from the Emperor of Trebizond, and the visits to the Black Sea became a permanent feature of the galley itineraries.[6] On their return in June 1460 these galleys were met at Piombino by a letter from the *Signoria* warning them of Neapolitan and Genoese fleets lurking off Porto Pisano. Tornabuoni was advised to wait at Piombino until the danger had passed.[7]

Before the return of this fleet two more galleys had left for Constantinople with Francesco Vettori once again in command. They arrived at their destination in May 1460, and Benedetto Dei

---

[1] ASF, Arte della Lana 53, f. 96 (26 Sept. 1456).

[2] Tratte 81, f. 124, and Miss. I Canc. 41, ff. 20 and 53.

[3] Provv. 149, f. 126 (15 July 1458), and Consoli del Mare III, f. 115ʳ.

[4] Miss. I Canc. 42, f. 58ᵛ (14 Oct. 1458).

[5] MAP VI, 374. Ricci wrote a series of letters describing the outward part of this voyage to Giovanni di Cosimo de' Medici (MAP VI, 372, 374, 377, and 399).

[6] Müller, *Documenti*, pp. 186–9. Pucci's galley picked up 700 ducats' worth of freights in the Black Sea (MAP VI, 377).

[7] Miss. I Canc. 43, f. 43ʳ (3 June 1460).

PLATE 6

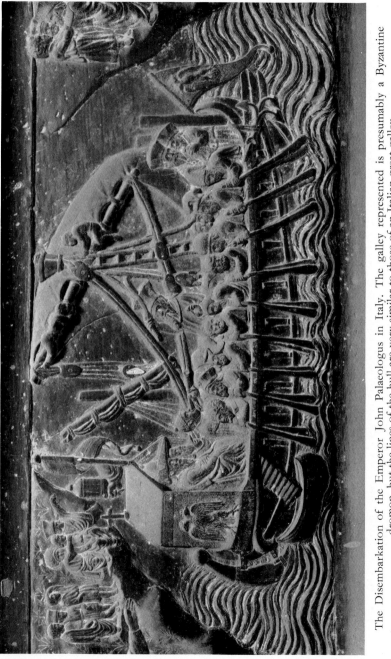

The Disembarkation of the Emperor John Palaeologus in Italy. The galley represented is presumably a Byzantine dromon, but the lines of the hull are very similar to those of an Italian great galley

PLATE 7

The Disembarkation of Pope Eugenius IV in Leghorn, 1434. (*See p.* 106)

who accompanied this fleet reported that Muhammed II was entertained on board the galleys by Vettori and his patrons.[1]

Two more galleys were being prepared in the summer of 1460 with Jacopo Sacchetti as Captain, but further details concerning this fleet are lacking. However, for the next few years our information is more complete as the Sea Consuls' record of galley sailings has come down to us. In 1461 three galleys were supposed to sail, but in the end only two went under Filippo di Francesco Tornabuoni, leaving early in September. Three galleys had originally been planned because of the reported activity of pirates; in fact this danger did materialize on the return voyage of the galleys in the spring and early summer of 1462, and Tornabuoni was instructed to take on extra marines in Modon.[2] Two long galleys were then sent to meet the fleet at Messina and escort it home.[3]

Giuliano Ridolfi was the Captain of the 1462 fleet, which consisted of three galleys and left Porto Pisano in August, returning on 5 February 1463. One or two of these galleys went into the Black Sea and traded in Trebizond and Caffa. Vanni Strozzi, one of the patrons, reported that the outward cargoes for this fleet were good, but Ridolfi on his return bewailed the difficulties of getting return cargoes in the disturbed East, and the galleys had in fact brought home 200 Genoese refugees from Chios.[4]

By the time the 1463 fleet was ready to sail considerable pressure was being brought to bear by the Venetians to prevent the Florentines trading with the Turks with whom they were now at war. The departure of the galleys was definitely postponed, but the indications are that they did eventually sail under Luigi di Buonaccorso Pitti, returning in April 1464.[5] It is possible that the galleys went

[1] Pagnini, *Della decima*, ii, p. 253, and C. Manfroni, *Storia della marina italiana*, Leghorn, 1897–1902, iii, p. 40. Francesco Vettori captained three major galley fleets, and died during his final voyage in Lisbon in 1465.

[2] Miss. I Canc. 43, f. 174ʳ (18 Nov. 1461).

[3] Provv. 152, f. 198ᵛ (7 Dec. 1461). Filippo di Giovanni Bonsignori was Captain of these two long galleys, and with him as patron went Paolo di Giovanni Machiavelli, who was to become one of the leading Florentine galley commanders.

[4] Benedetto Dei accompanied this fleet and makes no mention of Vanni Strozzi (*Cronaca*, ff. 54ᵛ–55ʳ). But Strozzi is recorded as a patron in the Tratte, and was writing from the galleys at about this time (MAP X, 351). Ridolfi's report is to be found in MAP X, 290.

[5] Provv. 154, f. 335ʳ (25 Feb. 1464). Filippo Rinuccini reported that Venetian ambassadors came to Florence to try to prevent the sailing of the Levant galleys, but were told 'che per questo anno non si poteva fare di manco che le galee non andassino, conciosiacosachè si fussino lavorati molti panni e fatte molte incette per

to Phocaea instead of Constantinople, and certainly Benedetto Dei who seems to have gone on this voyage only mentions going as far as Rhodes.[1]

There is no evidence of a fleet sailing in 1464; by this time pirate activity and the hostilities between Venice and the Turks made trade conditions almost impossible. This was also the year in which Pius II was organizing his crusade, and the Florentines were not perhaps as oblivious to his pleas for co-operation as has sometimes been thought.[2] However, in 1465, recognizing that Constantinople was temporarily closed to trade, the Consuls organized an alternative fleet to Syria. Three galleys were prepared and they were authorized to go to Catalonia both before and after their run to the eastern Mediterranean. The official Captain was Bernardo Corsi, but in fact Ruggiero di Tommaso Minerbetti captained the first voyage to Catalonia, and then Corsi took over when the galleys returned to Porto Pisano on 12 July 1465. They left for Syria on 29 August, also calling at Chios, Rhodes, Cyprus, and Alexandria, and returned on 28 January. The final run to Catalonia was completed in the spring of 1466, and it was not until 6 May that the galleys finally returned to Porto Pisano after a year of intensive activity. This was one of the most extensive and apparently successful trading operations conducted by the Florentine galleys in the Mediterranean, and it is significant that it occurs in the mid-1460's, over forty years after the opening of the galley system.[3]

The years 1466–9 were taken up with a complicated and not entirely successful double voyage to the East which suffered endless delays. Two galleys were auctioned to Antonio Altoviti and Domenico Fagiuoli for two successive voyages to Constantinople. The original intention was that the turn-round in Porto Pisano between the voyages should be a rapid one so that the whole venture could be completed within a year. However, after completing the first voyage during the summer of 1466, the conductors, who had also acted as patrons, fell to wrangling over who should

là, e oltre a questo si ritrovassino di là molte nostre robe e uomini, che non vi andando le galee, rimarrebbero male . . .' (*Ricordi storici di Filippo di Cino Rinuccini*, ed. G. Aiazzi, Florence, 1840, p. xci).

  [1] Dei mentions Bernardo Peruzzi, Piero Borromei, Istoldo Altoviti, and Bartolomeo Parete as being with these galleys (M. Pisani, *Un Avventuriero del Quattrocento; la vita e le opere di Benedetto Dei*, Naples, 1923, p. 95).

  [2] See above, p. 35 n. 6.

  [3] Once again Benedetto Dei was with the fleet but he gives no details of any value in his chronicle.

pay for the refit of the galleys between the voyages. They felt that this was the duty of the Consuls, whereas the latter, who had probably devised the whole scheme so that they could avoid the expense of the refit, refused to accept this responsibility.[1] As a result of this difference of opinion the galleys lay idle in Porto Pisano for nearly two years. The Captain, Bernardo del Nero, pleaded to be released from his post so that he could take other jobs, and was allowed a temporary release until the galleys were ready to sail.[2] Furthermore, the 1467 fleet of galleys which had been auctioned in February of that year, according to the regulations, had to be held up until Altoviti and Fagiuoli had settled their differences with the Consuls and completed their contract. In fact the departure date of these 1467 galleys was finally settled for May 1469.[3] There was in fact one galley operating in the eastern Mediterranean in the latter half of 1467 with Piero Vespucci as patron, but this was the illusive *galea Ferrandina*, the activities of which will be discussed later.[4]

Altoviti and Fagiuoli finally got their galleys off again on 27 December 1468, but even once under way the voyage was a very slow one and in June 1469 the fleet was still in Rhodes.[5] The difficulties attending this double voyage and the lack of enthusiasm for it were already some indication of an impending crisis for the galley system. Giovanni Benizi, the conductor of the postponed 1467 galleys, succeeded in getting a captain appointed for his galleys in 1469,[6] and Benedetto Dei reported that there were three Florentine galleys in Negroponte in 1470 with good cargoes of cloth; so it may be that this fleet did eventually sail.[7]

As we have already seen, the Medici galleys in 1471, destined for Constantinople, went to Alexandria instead; but in 1472 two galleys made the voyage, returning, however, with a very

[1] Provv. 158, f. 27ʳ (27 Apr. 1467) and f. 88ʳ (20 June 1467); Consoli del Mare III, f. 195ᵛ (15 Sept. 1468). [2] Provv. 158, f. 70ᵛ (10 June 1467).

[3] Provv. 159, f. 109ᵛ (30 July 1468); Consoli del Mare III, f. 192; Müller, *Documenti*, pp. 307–9.

[4] See below, pp. 102–3.

[5] Provv. 163, f. 129ᵛ (30 Oct. 1472). The Genoese, Calafati, was admiral of this fleet and had a serious quarrel with Del Nero in Rhodes.

[6] Lorenzo Davanzati (Tratte 81, f. 117).

[7] *Cronaca di Benedetto Dei*, f. 84ʳ. Heyd, *Commercio del Levante*, pp. 906–7, suggests that between 1467 and 1472 Florence bowed to public opinion and suspended sailings to the Levant, but this does not seem to be the case. Although there was a move to withdraw the heads of Florentine firms in Pera during this period, in fact the number of firms and merchants increased.

disappointing cargo.[1] Further galleys were prepared in 1473, and
Dei reported the return of one galley in 1474,[2] but evidence for the
sailings in the 1470's becomes more and more sparse. It is certain
that the fleet auctioned for the 1474 voyage never sailed, as the
conductors sued the Consuls for their contract money back. We
know that galleys were auctioned and prepared in 1475 but beyond
that, nothing. Throughout this period the *Ferrandina* was going
backwards and forwards to the eastern Mediterranean, and it may
be that this took care of much of the available trade on the route.

However, a fleet of two galleys captained by Lorenzo Carducci
left in September 1477 for Constantinople,[3] and the final fleet of the
series was being prepared for departure in 1478. By this time more
and more of the trade between Florence and Constantinople was
using the overland route via Ragusa, and for the short crossing of
the Adriatic which this route involved ships were hired in Ancona.[4]
There is evidence of only one state-inspired venture actually to
Ragusa and that was in 1429, when one galley was hired to Domenico Dolfini for five years. During this period he had to make two
voyages in the first year and three in subsequent years between
Porto Pisano and Ragusa, loading at least 1,000 Florentine cloths
for each voyage.[5]

The western Mediterranean

A voyage that had a close connexion with that of Alexandria
was the one to the Barbary coast. Bartolomeo della Galea in 1421
and Roberto Martelli had already prepared the way for the dispatch of galleys to Barbary, and had won trade concessions for

---

[1] *Cronaca di Benedetto Dei*, ff. 40ᵛ–41ʳ. The captain of these galleys had an audience
with the Grand Turk in Constantinople (Domenico Malipiero, 'Annali veneti
dall'anno 1457 al 1500', *ASI*, ser. i, vii, 1843, p. 86).

[2] Ibid., f. 41ᵛ. This galley was commanded by Piero Attavanti and was still waiting
to leave Porto Pisano on 6 Mar. 1474 (MAP XXX, 125).

[3] There is no evidence for including Lorenzo Carducci in the list of Florentine
consuls in Pera (cf. F. Babinger, 'Lorenzo de' Medici e la corte ottomana', *ASI*,
cxxi, 1963, p. 315). He was Captain of the Galleys and his letter of credence (published by Müller, *Documenti*, pp. 222–3) referred to him as such and as *orator*, not as
consul. It was stated that his stay in Constantinople was only expected to be brief,
and indeed it would have been most unusual for a Captain of the Galleys to have
travelled only one way with his fleet.

[4] Richards, *Florentine Merchants in the Age of the Medici*, Cambridge (Mass.), 1932,
passim. The Selfridge Medici papers in the Baker Library at Harvard also contain
many references to the use of the overland route in the 1480's and 1490's.

[5] Provv. 120, f. 350ᵛ (20 Oct. 1429), and Consoli del Mare III, f. 31ʳ.

Florence from the Sultan of Tunis. Martelli had in fact asked for a *continuation* of concessions to the galleys stopping at Tunis on the way to Alexandria. This would indicate that Florentine galleys were visiting the Barbary coast some time before the Venetians, who sent their first galleys in 1436. However, we have no specific details for these early years although as galleys going to Barbary went either via Catalonia or via Sicily, it is possible that some of those for which we have evidence in those areas were in fact on their way to or from Barbary.

In 1442 conductors of galleys on the Catalonia–Sicily route were authorized to extend their voyages from Sicily to the Barbary coast if they wished.[1] Then in 1445 Giovenco della Stufa's Alexandria galleys visited Tunis and Tripoli both on their outward and return voyages.

However, it is not until 1447 when the ports of call were laid down that we get any clear idea of what the Barbary voyages involved. In fact from these lists it appears that there were two distinct Barbary routes. The Barbary coast galleys went southwards, via Naples and Sicily, to Tunis and Tripoli, and on occasions to Alexandria. Meanwhile the west Barbary galleys followed the northerly route along the coast of France, calling at Marseilles and Port-de-Bouc, then Barcelona, Majorca, Bone, Algiers, and Oran. Giovenco della Stufa was probably sailing on this latter route when he entered Barcelona in August 1455 bound for Almeria.[2] Catalonia galleys were not allowed beyond Valencia so it seems likely that this galley, whose next stop was to be in southern Spain, was going on to west Barbary.

Bartolomeo Pucci took a galley to west Barbary in 1456 and in 1457 the west Barbary galley of Jacopo Nasi was scheduled to go on to Sicily after returning from its Barbary run.[3] In 1458 Benedetto Dei boarded a Florentine galley bound for Tunis in Genoa and this was probably the galley of Bongianno Gianfigliazzi which passed through that port on its way to Tunis and the Barbary coast;[4]

---

[1] Provv. 133, f. 251 (14 Dec. 1442).

[2] ARV, Guiatges 705, unpaginated (18 Aug. 1455).

[3] This galley passed through Valencia on its way to Almeria on 30 June (ARV, Guiatges 705, unpaginated). The probable regulations for this voyage were published by Pardessus, *Lois maritimes*, iv, p. 594.

[4] C. Mazzi, 'Le carte di Benedetto Dei nella Medicea Laurenziana', *Rivista delle biblioteche e degli archivi*, xxv, 1914, p. 137; J. Heers, *Les Livres de comptes de Giovanni Piccamiglio, homme d'affaires génois, 1456–9*, Paris, 1959, pp. 185 and 232. The Genoese record actually refers to 'Giovanni Bonfigliazzi', but as Gianfigliazzi was at this time

and it was in November of that same year that these galleys were once more authorized to go to Alexandria.[1]

Late in 1459 two galleys were put on the Barbary run and the scope of the voyage was once again changed. These galleys were to leave in the first week of April of each year, and, sailing via Genoa and Marseilles, were to call at Tunis, Bone, Bougie, Algiers, Oran, Almeria, Malaga, and Cadiz. At this stage they were not permitted to call either in Catalonia or Sicily.[2] However, before this new regulation came into force in April 1460, a Florentine galley called at Valencia in December 1459 on its way to Tunis.

Giuliano Ridolfi captained the first two-galley fleet on the new Barbary run and with him went Angelo Spini as special envoy to the Sultan of Tunis to seek a renewal of trade concessions.[3] Angelo Spini was himself Captain of the next fleet which sailed in April 1461. These galleys were held up by pirate activity off Seville for a fortnight in July, and eventually returned on 3 October. In 1462 pirate activity in the western Mediterranean was causing considerable anxiety and it was decided not to send the Barbary galleys.[4] But at the end of the year as the threat had diminished and galleys and crews were lying idle, it was agreed to send one galley as quickly as possible. Piero di Giuliano Vespucci went as patron and the voyage was a direct one through Sicily to Tunis and back in March and April 1463.[5]

No other galleys were dispatched to Barbary in 1463, but in 1464 the Catalonia–Sicily galleys captained by Bernardo Vespucci were due to go on from Sicily to Tunis. However, they were forced to turn back in December as they were leaking, and a special galley was sent to Tunis in March 1465.[6] This galley was to go and return via Cagliari so as not to damage the trade of the

---

carrying letters from the *Signoria* to the Sultan of Tunis, it seems likely that it was he (Amari, *Diplomi arabi*, appendix, pp. 24–25).

[1] Balìe 29, f. 70ᵛ (15 Nov. 1458).

[2] Provv. 150, f. 159ᵛ (8 Dec. 1459).

[3] The departure of these galleys was delayed as it was necessary to use the Flanders galleys which did not return until late February (Provv. 151, f. 1, 1 Apr. 1460). This is an indication of the sudden and rapid expansion of the system in the early 1460's; in 1460 there were insufficient galleys to go round whilst by 1463 there were eleven available. See also Amari, *Diplomi arabi*, appendix, pp. 28–30.

[4] Provv. 153, f. 181ᵛ (26 Nov. 1462), and Consoli del Mare III, f. 155ʳ.

[5] The escort of the Aragonese fleet under Villamarina was requested for this galley, but it is not known whether the request was granted (Miss. I Canc. 44, f. 63ᵛ).

[6] Provv. 155, f. 218ᵛ (8 Feb. 1465), and Consoli del Mare III, f. 168ᵛ.

next Sicily galleys in Palermo.[1] Finally in March 1466 Amerigo Benci took a galley to Tunis, returning in June.

Thereafter until 1478 references to the Barbary voyages disappear completely; it may well be that some of the Catalonia–Sicily galleys called on the Barbary coast but the idea of independent voyages seems to have been dropped. Finally in 1478 a two-galley fleet was auctioned for two successive voyages to Catalonia and Barbary; this was part of a final effort to keep the galley system going which involved three major fleets in this one year. Zenobio Biliotti was captain and the galleys completed the first voyage by May, and passed through Valencia on their way to Almeria and Barbary for the second time on 27 July 1478. They finally returned in company with the Flanders galleys in February 1479 after an eventful passage along the south coast of France.

Much has already been said in passing about the other western Mediterranean route which the Florentine galleys used, the Catalonia–Sicily run. This was at one time described as the most profitable voyage of all[2] and it certainly seems to have been the least erratic, partly perhaps because the shorter distances involved made the galleys less vulnerable to molestation from pirates. The first voyage, that of 1424, has already been described, and at this time there is no indication that the Catalonia and Sicily runs were to be combined. However in 1427 regulations were laid down for a voyage serving Sicily and Catalonia.[3] At this time the Flanders galleys were allowed to stop at Barcelona and Valencia on their way out, and between July 1428 and December 1429 there are records of eight Florentine galleys calling at Barcelona.[4] Of these seven seem to have been on the Flanders route but one, supposedly commanded by Nicolò de' Mari, called twice at Barcelona within a month, which would indicate that it only went as far as Valencia

---

[1] In fact the conductor of this galley had to pay 200 ducats compensation to the conductor of the next Sicily galleys, in addition to this restriction on his route.

[2] Provv. 155, f. 60ᵛ (14 June 1464), and Consoli del Mare III, f. 166ʳ.

[3] Consoli del Mare III, ff. 12ᵛ–13ʳ (16 Jan. 1427).

[4] M. Del Treppo, 'Assicurazioni e commercio internazionale a Barcellona nel 1428–9', *RIS*, 1957–8, i, p. 522. Del Treppo in fact mentions seven galleys, including Carnesecchi's Flanders galley, but for some reason he found no references to Vespucci's Flanders galley which accompanied Carnesecchi's. This omission is perhaps an indication that Del Treppo's estimates which are drawn from insurance records may not be complete.

or Majorca.[1] Furthermore, a galley of Piero Zampini was said to have been on the Catalonia run at this time although there is no evidence of its appearance in Barcelona.[2]

For ten years after this there is a complete absence of news about these galleys. There was no mention of Catalonia or Sicily in the contract of the *Magona Vecchia* in 1435, although it is highly probable that the galleys which these contractors sent to England and Flanders did call at Barcelona and Valencia. However, by 1439 when the next reference appears it is accepted that the same galley should serve both Catalonia and Sicily.[3] It sailed in May of that year first to Catalonia, and then on return to Porto Pisano it was to be sent on to Sicily. In the same year it was decided to send one of the returned Flanders galleys on to Sicily, perhaps because at some stage it had picked up sufficient cargo destined for Sicily to justify sending the galley on rather than unloading the goods to wait for the next regular voyage to Sicily. This sort of flexibility was essential if the galleys were to make profits, but on the other hand it played havoc with the set time-tables which were another essential feature of galley policy.

In December and January 1439–40 two more galleys captained by Francesco Tosinghi were in Barcelona, and for the next few years the valuable series of Aragonese anchorage accounts for this port furnish a number of reports of Florentine galleys.[4] On 5 March 1440 Lorenzo Moro arrived in Barcelona from Pisa, and left again for Valencia on 1 April. He was back five days later after what must have been a very brief stop in Valencia, and on 8 April he departed once more for Pisa. In the same month Giovanni Ventura arrived with another Florentine galley, and in July 1440 a galley commanded by Giovanni '*Badi Baruxel*' arrived in Barcelona from

[1] Del Treppo, 'Assicurazioni e commercio', i, pp. 526 and 532, ii, p. 73. Nicolò de' Mari was a wealthy Genoese merchant and insurance magnate, and it seems unlikely that such a man would have been patron of a Florentine galley. He was certainly interested in trade with Catalonia, but it is more probable that he had heavy financial investments in the galley and its cargo than that he was actually in command of it.

[2] Provv. 120, f. 159ᵛ (27 May 1429). On its return from Catalonia this galley was to be sent to Constantinople. See also Müller, *Documenti*, pp. 283–4.

[3] Provv. 130, f. 77ᵛ (22 May 1439).

[4] ACA, Ancoratge 2–64 (June 1439–Oct. 1447). The series is not continuous in that the records for Dec. 1441 and June 1443–Oct. 1445 are missing. For a discussion of the general importance of these records for this period, see C. Carrère, 'Le droit d'ancrage et le mouvement du port de Barcelone au milieu du XVᵉ siècle', *Estudios de historia moderna*, iii, 1953.

Pisa. This may well have been the Florentine Giovanni Bandini de' Baroncelli who served as a patron on the galleys on other occasions. Finally in December yet another galley returned from Catalonia having sailed some time in the autumn. It is perhaps significant that the moment a reliable and continuous source for shipping movements in Barcelona becomes available, it reveals considerable Florentine traffic. One suspects that a similar record for the years 1435–9 might well tell the same story.

In 1441 it was laid down that there should be two voyages a year on the route, each by one galley going first to Catalonia and then, after ten days stop in Porto Pisano, on to Sicily. These galleys were to sail in February and July.[1] Even before these regulations were passed a spring galley had sailed for Catalonia, arriving in Barcelona on 26 March. This time the patron was Leonardo Mannelli and again the visit to Valencia was an abbreviated one. There is no evidence of the scheduled autumn voyage in 1441, but in view of the regularity of the sailings on the route at this time, it seems likely that there was one.[2]

The spring galley of 1442 was delayed owing to repairs and was then sent to Sicily first in order to catch the sugar crop.[3] It was also used to pick up a cargo of grain in Corneto.[4] It finally got to Barcelona on 30 June, and this time went on to Majorca. The autumn galley, of which Giovanni Bandini de' Baroncelli was patron, did the voyage in the normal order, arriving in Barcelona on 16 October, and then going to Majorca. By December it was back in Porto Pisano preparing to go to Sicily, and both the *Signoria* and the Consuls made great efforts to hurry Bandini on his way. It was in this same month that it was decided to permit galleys going to Sicily to go on to the Barbary coast.[5] In 1443 it was decided to send two galleys in the spring as the voyage was proving so profitable. Niccolò Cerretani and Ludovico Gucci were the patrons and they left for Catalonia at the end of April. By June they had returned and were on their way to Sicily with the intention of making yet another complete voyage to Catalonia and Sicily on their return. This more elaborate spring voyage does not

---

[1] Provv. 132, f. 21ʳ (15 Apr. 1441).
[2] The anchorage account for Dec. 1441 is missing from the series, which gives added justification for supposing a lost voyage.
[3] Provv. 132, f. 352ᵛ (17 Feb. 1442).
[4] Miss. II Canc. 1, f. 75ʳ (27 Mar. 1442).
[5] Provv. 133, f. 251ʳ (14 Dec. 1442).

seem to have affected the autumn galley of which Antonio di Lorenzo della Stufa was patron, and which was about to sail for Sicily in December.

Leonardo Mannelli was patron again for the spring galley of 1444, and although the patron of the autumn galley is not known, there is evidence that it did make the voyage. In 1445 the first reference is to a galley under Giuliano Ridolfi sailing in July. Whether it had already been to Catalonia or whether on this voyage the normal order was reversed is not clear, but the same galley did go on to Catalonia in October, calling at Barcelona and Valencia.

In 1446 too the regular pattern of spring and autumn sailings established in the early 1440's seems to have broken down. A galley commanded by Antonio della Stufa returned to Barcelona from Majorca on 5 August which would imply departure from Porto Pisano in midsummer. The same was true of the only recorded voyage in 1447, when Niccolò di Giovanni Nasi brought a galley into Barcelona from Valencia on 13 July.[1]

At this time the ports of call for the voyage were laid down as Nice, Marseilles, Port-de-Bouc, Aiguesmortes, Collioure, Barcelona, Majorca, and Valencia; and the same on return. Then the galleys could call at Talamone, Civitavecchia, Gaeta, Naples, Salerno, Castello a Mare, Palermo, Messina, and Syracuse.

By 1448 relations with Aragon had deteriorated sharply and there were no sailings for Catalonia or Sicily. This was the end until the mid-1450's and even then with the reopening of normal trade in the western Mediterranean, the galleys to west Barbary handled the Catalonia trade in 1456 and 1457. Two Florentine galleys arrived in Savona with cargoes of Sicilian sugar in 1458 and it is probable that these were operating on the Sicily–Catalonia run.[2] In March 1459 Cosimo Masi was preparing to depart with another galley on this run.[3] This was to be a double voyage in

---

[1] Nasi had in fact been one of the conductors, with Benintendi Pucci, of the Flanders galleys of 1445-6, and had been promised a free contract for a Catalonia voyage as compensation for unexpected losses incurred on that voyage (Provv. 136, f. 183ᵛ, 30 Sept. 1445).

[2] J. Heers, 'Le Royaume de Grenade et la politique marchande de Gênes en Occident, XVᵉ siècle', *Moyen Age*, lxiii, 1957, pp. 110–11. It may be that one of these galleys was Gianfigliazzi's Barbary galley which had made a preliminary voyage to Sicily.

[3] By this time the valuable series of anchorage records had ceased and so we have no further readily accessible information on shipping in Barcelona.

each direction, a device which saved unnecessary auctions and administrative expenses as well as giving more scope to the merchants.[1] In 1460 the Consuls tried to auction two galleys for the voyage, adding Savona as an additional port of call; but there was little enthusiasm and no takers at the auction, and it was admitted that two galleys were excessive for the trade available.[2] In fact there is no evidence of a galley going at all this year, although Catalonia was probably served by the Barbary galleys and possibly by an extension of the Constantinople voyage.[3]

When the next fleet did sail in May 1461 under Luigi Pitti there were in fact two galleys as a last-minute report of increased pirate activity and the presence of a fleet of six French galleys off Corsica had forced the Consuls to send an extra galley after all. In 1462 pirates once more interfered with plans for the dispatch of the galleys, and there is no clear evidence of a sailing in this year. However, two galleys sailed in the spring of 1463 to Catalonia with Giovanni dell'Antella as captain. Conditions were still rather hazardous and trade poor; the galleys were in Valencia 20–27 April and then returned via Majorca and Collioure, apparently avoiding Barcelona. They got back to Porto Pisano on 9 May, and sailed for Sicily on 26 May, but were forced to turn back because of pirates. The Aragonese admiral Villmarina offered to escort them but this offer was regarded with some scepticism. The idea of sending a long galley with them was then considered, and eventually Dell'Antella was ordered to leave for Sicily before the end of July.[4] Reports of Florentine galleys in Palermo in mid-August would seem to indicate that Dell'Antella obeyed his instructions and finally completed the voyage.[5]

Two galleys were again dispatched in 1464 under Bernardo Vespucci. They called at Marseilles on their way back from Catalonia

[1] Balie 29, f. 70ᵛ (15 Nov. 1458).

[2] Provv. 150, f. 161ᵛ (8 Dec. 1459) and f. 204ᵛ (4 Jan. 1460); 151, f. 350ᵛ (9 Feb. 1461).

[3] Benedetto Dei, who travelled with Francesco Vettori's galleys to Constantinople in 1459–60, also records a visit to Sardinia with the galleys in 1460. Whether this was a separate venture, or whether Vettori's sailed westwards after returning to Porto Pisano, is uncertain (Pisani, *Avventuriero del Quattrocento*, p. 95).

[4] Zenobio Biliotti and Piero Neretti, the conductors, were authorized to make another complete voyage because of the delays and subsequent losses which the galleys had suffered, but there is no evidence that they did so (Provv. 154, f. 96ᵛ, 30 June 1463).

[5] Archivio di Stato di Palermo, notaio Giacomo Comito (1462–3).

on 19 June. But having returned they found plague raging in Leghorn which delayed their departure for Sicily. They finally got away again at the end of October but were unable to go to Tunis as planned as the galleys were found to be leaking; so they returned in January 1465.

As has been seen, the Syria galleys of 1465 were in Catalonia in June of that year, and they were followed by a fleet of two galleys captained by Ruggiero Minerbetti sailing in July. This fleet had been waiting to depart for some time, having been auctioned in the previous year, but its departure had been postponed in order to avoid clashing with the Syria galleys.[1]

The 1466 galleys were auctioned for two voyages in each direction and were captained by Piero Nasi. They sailed first for Sicily on 16 June, returning to Porto Pisano on 13 July. They then left for Catalonia, returning on 24 September. One of the galleys suffered damage in Marseilles, but both galleys managed to complete the next stage of the voyage to Sicily by the end of January 1467. At this stage the damaged galley had to give up as the Consuls claimed that they could not afford to repair it.[2] Nasi and his patrons were released from their responsibilities and Agostino Biliotti took over the command of the single remaining galley for further voyages to Catalonia in April and May, and to Sicily in June 1467. This voyage had been so protracted that no further galleys were prepared for the route in the spring of 1467.

One galley only was sent in the spring of 1468 with Piero Corsellini as conductor and patron. This galley returned from Catalonia on 14 June and from Sicily on 1 August. The policy at this time was once again for single galleys to sail in the spring and autumn, covering the whole route once only. The complex quadruple voyages of the two-galley fleets had resulted in inevitable delays and complications, and a return to the simpler system of the early 1440's was a great improvement. The pirate menace apart, it was obviously felt that the regularity achieved by the single-galley voyages was of more importance than the greater commercial flexibility produced by the two-galley quadruple voyages.

However, no galley sailed in the autumn of 1468 as the auction

---

[1] The unscheduled voyage of Strozza Strozzi's galley to Barbary probably also served to delay the departure of this fleet. Zenobio Biliotti, who was to become one of the most experienced of the galley commanders, was sent as patron in this fleet by express orders of the *Signoria* (Provv. 155, f. 144ʳ, 25 Oct. 1464).

[2] Provv. 157, f. 201ʳ (27 Jan. 1467).

had failed to produce an offer.[1] The next galley to sail was in the spring of 1469. Agostino Biliotti was again the patron, and the galley passed through Port-de-Bouc on its outward journey on 10 April.[2] It returned from Catalonia on 12 May, and from Sicily on 19 July. Once again no galley seems to have sailed in the autumn of this year.

However, in the spring of 1470 two galleys were on the route, captained by Niccolò Cerretani. They passed through Port-de-Bouc on their way to Catalonia on 16 April, and returned through the same port on 21 May. In 1471 one or two galleys sailed early in the year calling at Port-de-Bouc on 15 February and again on 16 April. The fact that these galleys took two months to complete their trading beyond Port-de-Bouc indicates perhaps that they went further than Catalonia, e.g. west Barbary. This possibility is reinforced by the fact that another galley sailed in June for Sicily, commanded by Alberto Villani. This galley returned to Porto Pisano on 27 July, and then went on to Catalonia, returning on 10 November.

By the next year it seemed to be established that one galley a year went to Catalonia in the spring, sometimes for a double voyage. The galley which left in the spring of 1472 passed through Port-de-Bouc on 8 May and 1 July, and by 9 July was back in Porto Pisano waiting to go on to Sicily. The 1473 galley commanded by Giovanni Simone Tornabuoni had a very similar time-table. It was in Port-de-Bouc from 18 to 22 May, and back again in the same port on 2 July. In between it had called at Valencia on 3 June. On 16 July Tornabuoni was back in Porto Pisano and on 3 September he returned again from Sicily.[3] This galley was then due to repeat the whole voyage, and in fact another Catalonia voyage did take place in the autumn. The indications are, however, that Tornabuoni was no longer patron but was replaced by Giovanni d'Antonio Pazzi.[4] This

---

[1] Consoli del Mare VII, f. 73ᵛ (30 Aug. 1468).

[2] At this stage a new outside source becomes available for the story of the galleys, the port books of Port-de-Bouc (or the Italian *Boccholi*). See F. Reynaud, 'Le mouvement des navires', *passim*.

[3] The series of Tornabuoni letters which cover this voyage (MAP XXIX, 314, 366, 509, 709 and XXI, 396) report satisfactory cargoes on the way to Catalonia, but poor trading conditions there. Tornabuoni was offered a cargo for Barbary in Valencia, but refused it, perhaps because his instructions did not allow him so much flexibility in his schedule.

[4] Litta, *Famiglie celebri*, s.v. Pazzi, table vii. The theory that Pazzi replaced Tornabuoni for the second voyage is reinforced by the fact that Tornabuoni's letters from his galley to Lorenzo de' Medici cease abruptly after 3 Sept.

time the galley passed through Port-de-Bouc on the way out on 16 October, and finally returned to Porto Pisano in mid-January.

In 1474 the patron was Leonardo Spini and the conductor Francesco Sassetti, a combination which would indicate a largely Medici enterprise.[1] This galley completed the Catalonia half of its voyage in April and May. It then took on extra marines in Porto Pisano to confront the danger of Piombinese pirates on the way to Sicily, and returned to Porto Pisano after this run on 5 September. Like its predecessor of the year before this galley then covered the route again in the autumn, calling at Port-de-Bouc on 21 October.[2]

The patron in 1475 was Agostino Mannelli, and 7 April and 23 May the dates of appearance in Port-de-Bouc.[3] But in 1476 Pierfrancesco Tosinghi who was patron in that year, having completed the run to Catalonia with an outward stop at Port-de-Bouc on 6 May, was unable to go to Sicily as plague was raging in Leghorn and no ships could enter Sicilian ports which had come from a plague area.[4]

In 1477 two galleys which had previously been commissioned as escorts for the *Ferrandina* on its return from the East, and then used to carry salt to Sarzana, were finally sent to Catalonia in August. They were followed by the two galleys of 1478 which were sent to Barbary and Catalonia under Zenobio Biliotti. This seems to have been the last communal fleet on the route.

Flanders and England

Now we turn to the most fully documented and in some ways the most important of all the galley routes, that to Flanders and England; important because it was these galleys which brought back much of the wool so vital to the Florentine economy. The initial voyage of the series, that of 1425, has already been discussed, and it is usually thought that the enterprise was not repeated until 1428 owing to a dispute with the Genoese over the rights of trade

---

[1] Spini was for some time Medici factor in Pisa, and Sassetti was, of course, general manager of the Medici group of companies. Other Medici employees who served as galley commanders were Bartolomeo Martelli, Giovenco di Lorenzo della Stufa, Agostino di Sandro Biliotti, and Ludovico Masi.

[2] It does appear that an auction was in fact held to reallocate the galley after the first voyage; but presumably Sassetti and the Medici felt that it was worth continuing. See Provv. 165, f. 92^v (22 July 1474).

[3] This galley seems to have sailed later than planned as it was first used to bring in a cargo of grain (Provv. 166, f. 12^v, 3 Apr. 1475).

[4] Provv. 167, f. 86^v (31 July 1476).

between England and Tuscan ports.[1] One of the conditions attached to the sale of Leghorn in 1421 was that all Florentines who wished to bring goods from England and Flanders to Tuscany had to do so in Genoese ships. This monopoly was rescinded, however, in a treaty signed in 1426 between Florence and Milan, the new overlord of Genoa,[2] and in fact on 11 May 1427 a new fleet sailed for the north. The patrons initially were Niccolò Corbinelli and Luigi di Buonaccorso Pitti; but Pitti was taken ill in Bruges and returned by land, his place being taken by Jacopo Benizi. These galleys left London on 4 November and finally returned to Porto Pisano in mid-March.[3]

The evidence on the galley activities on this route in 1428 and 1429 is somewhat confused, as in addition to two fleets of communal galleys there seem to have been at least two privately owned Florentine galleys on the route.[4] First there was a galley of Francesco Ventura which passed through Barcelona in summer 1428 on its way to the north. This galley called at Southampton, the first Florentine galley recorded as doing so, and left that port on 19 November. After the completion of its voyage it also went on to Naples presumably to unload goods picked up during its travels. This galley was almost certainly a private venture, both because it appears to have been sailing alone which Florentine communal galleys to Flanders never did, and also because there is no reference to it in official sources.[5] But at the same time that it was leaving Southampton, a new communal fleet commanded by Frosino da Verazzano and consisting of three galleys left Porto Pisano. They passed through Aiguesmortes, Collioure, and Barcelona on their way north. The original intention was for the galleys to go to Southampton rather than London, which had been the terminal of the two previous fleets. All the merchants in England were

[1] Pagnini, *Della decima*, ii, p. 30.

[2] Baruchello, *Livorno ed il suo porto*, p. 47. However, there is some indication that the Genoese themselves had not accepted the loss of the monopoly in 1429 (MAP LXXXVIII, cc. 99–107).

[3] Luigi Pitti got back by land before the galleys having left his son Doffo also sick in Bruges. He went to Porto Pisano to meet the returning galleys on 10 Mar. (*Cronica di Buonaccorso Pitti*, pp. 253–4).

[4] Del Treppo, 'Assicurazioni e commercio', i, p. 527.

[5] There is evidence for the appearance of this galley in Barcelona (Del Treppo, 'Assicurazioni e commercio', i, p. 522 and ii, pp. 46 and 68), Valencia (ARV, Guiatges 706, unp.), and Southampton (PRO, KR Memoranda 205, recorda, Trinity, rot. 10, and 209, recorda, Hilary, rot. 54).

advised to prepare their wool at Southampton for shipment to Italy, and then for some reason Da Verazzano went to London after all, arriving on 14 January. This caused considerable dismay amongst the merchants who, rather than move all their wool to London, loaded it on a Genoese ship of Francesco Vivaldi and claimed exemption from the extra duties incurred in Porto Pisano by shipping on non-communal vessels.[1] This exemption was granted as the fault had not been theirs, and meanwhile Da Verazzano did eventually send one of his galleys commanded by Filippo Guadagni to Southampton in April. The whole fleet set off homewards in that month, arriving in Porto Pisano in the summer.[2]

In the early summer of 1429 another privately owned galley set out on the route. This galley was known as the galley of Priore di Marioto, but its patron on this voyage was a certain Matteo di Ser Antonio. It called at Aiguesmortes, La Nouvelle, Collioure, Barcelona, Valencia, Malaga, Cadiz, and was reported off Lisbon on 24 November. The English customs accounts reported its presence in Southampton in December, and it then passed on to Sluys, leaving that port on the same day as Albizzi's fleet, 6 January 1430.[3] It seems that this galley was built in Narbonne and was part-owned by Galvano Salviati and Giovanni Ventura who were Florentine merchants in Valencia,[4] but Albizzi's interest in it and reference to it in his letters home suggest that it was operating out of Porto Pisano and was under the eye of the Consuls. On its way home it ran into trouble from pirates off the coast of Portugal, and got so delayed that Albizzi's fleet caught up with it.

For the story of the 1429 communal galleys we have all the

---

[1] Provv. 120, f. 89ᵛ (23 Apr. 1429).

[2] There is some uncertainty regarding the dates of the visit of these three galleys to London. W. B. Watson, 'The Structure of the Florentine Galley Trade with England and Flanders in the Fifteenth Century', *RBPH*, xxxix–xl, 1961–2, pt. ii, p. 328, quotes 14 Jan.–25 Mar. as the dates; whereas PRO, KR Memoranda 206, rot. 24 implies that the galleys were still in London on 13 Apr. One of Da Verazzano's mates on this voyage was Petruccio Guerra who was later chosen, on Da Verazzano's recommendation, to patron a galliot during the Lucchese war in 1430; see Guasti, *Commissioni di Rinaldo degli Albizzi*, iii, p. 340.

[3] For reports of the voyage of this galley see Albizzi Diary, ff. 76ᵛ and 105ʳ; Del Treppo, 'Assicurazioni e commercio', i, pp. 526 and 528–9, ii, p. 46; P. Studer (ed.), *The Port Books of Southampton, 1427–30*, Southampton Record Society, 1913, pp. 107–8, Quinn and Ruddock (*Port Books*, ii, p. xxiii) in fact place this as one of the three 1428 communal galleys, but the dates do not fit and we already have the names of the three patrons of these galleys.

[4] Del Treppo, op. cit., i, pp. 528–9.

information we need in the diary of the Captain, Luca di Maso degli Albizzi. In this year the programme of sailing for the Flanders route had been changed from three galleys sailing once a year to two fleets of two galleys sailing in February and September.[1] Luca's fleet was the first to sail under the new system and was also the first communal fleet not to go to London. After a varied and at times hazardous voyage the galleys arrived in Sluys on 6 December. On the way they had called at Lisbon, apparently the first Florentine galleys to do so, and had opened trade negotiations with the King of Portugal. Relations with Portugal became even closer when Luca's galleys were held up for a month in Ribadeo together with the fleet which was taking the Infanta Isabella to Burgundy to marry Philip the Good. The combined fleets crossed the Bay of Biscay together and it is noticeable that the galleys seemed to suffer far less from the bad weather than the Portuguese ships, of which nine became detached from the main fleet and at least one wrecked. Even having parted company at the mouth of the Channel, Luca had not heard the last of the Infanta. Once in Sluys, which he had been able to reach with the galleys while the Infanta's ships would not venture out of Southampton, he was in danger of having his galleys requisitioned by the Duke of Burgundy to go to England and fetch the stranded bride. Here surely is decisive evidence of the seaworthiness of the great galleys. In a stormy December the Duke of Burgundy was proposing that Florentine galleys should make the crossing to England and back because a fleet of Portuguese ships, presumably among the largest they had, was unable to do so. Fortunately on Christmas Day the Infanta finally arrived in a lull in the bad weather, and Luca was able to depart on his way. From 7 January until 23 February the galleys were in Southampton, and here Luca's diary gives details of the excursions which he made in England, as well as of his struggle to get his galleys properly equipped to face the pirates on the way home. In fact the homeward run was comparatively uneventful and very fast; thirty-two days sufficed to bring the galleys back from Southampton to Porto Pisano, including several days wasted on the coast of Portugal owing to adverse winds.

Probably partly as a result of Luca's warnings about pirate activity off the Atlantic coast of Spain, and partly because of the

---

[1] Consoli del Mare III, f. 26ʳ ⁻ᵛ (24 May 1429); Provv. 120, f. 155ʳ; Grunzweig, 'Consulat', pp. 11-13.

war with Lucca, the fleet planned for February 1430 did not sail. In fact there is no definite evidence of a fleet sailing between 1430 and 1436, which is perhaps strange when one considers the initial enthusiasm for the project and constant references to the importance of maintaining the good reputation of the galleys. Early in 1432 there was a report that four ships had just left England for the Mediterranean loaded with wool and so one assumes that no galley fleet can have been on the route during this winter.[1] Furthermore, in the winter of 1433–4 there were reports that the Venetian galleys were picking up wool for Florence, which makes it seem likely that no Florentine galleys were available this year either.[2] Nevertheless one of these reports did imply that for the Florentine galleys not to sail in autumn 1433 would be exceptional and perhaps an unfortunate precedent.[3] However, when one remembers that the war with Lucca did not end until the Peace of Ferrara of 1433, and then there followed the internal political crisis of the expulsion and restoration of the Medici, it is perhaps not altogether surprising that there was little enthusiasm for galley ventures in these years.

However, in 1435 an entirely new system was initiated with the founding of the *Magona Vecchia*. A *magona* in the usual sense of the word was a company formed for the furtherance of shipping ventures,[4] and in 1435 the Consuls leased three galleys to a group of private conductors for five years.[5] Two of these galleys were to make voyages to England and Flanders, and one to Constantinople. The contractors were to receive a loan of 15,000 florins in the first three years to help them in the initial stages of the enterprise, and this was to be raised by the imposition of additional customs duties in Florence and Pisa.[6] The contractors were expected to start paying back the money as soon as the five years had elapsed. It has

---

[1] Strozziana III, 112, f. 98 (4 Feb. 1432).

[2] Ibid., ff. 121 (29 Aug. 1433), 135 (11 Oct. 1433), and 158 (24 Jan. 1434).

[3] Ibid., f. 121.

[4] Heyd, *Le colonie italiane*, i, p. 388, gives a full bibliography of the word *magona* which is of Arabic origin. See also F. C. Lane, *Andrea Barbarigo, Merchant of Venice, 1418–1449*, Baltimore, 1944, p. 92.

[5] Provv. 126, f. 135ᵛ (30 July 1435); Consoli del Mare III, ff. 41–42; Grunzweig, 'Consulat', pp. 13–14. See also G. Bonolis, 'Sulle maone genovesi e su una maona fiorentina sconosciuta', *Diritto commerciale*, xxv, 1907, and R. Cessi, 'Studi sulle maone genovesi', *ASI*, lxxvii, 1919, pp. 49–53.

[6] Provv. 126, ff. 137ʳ–138ᵛ (30 July 1435), 151ʳ (5 Aug. 1435), and 158ʳ (13 Aug. 1435).

not yet been possible to trace the names of any of the participants in the Magona, but it is more than likely that the Medici had a large hand in it, and one imagines that the Martelli would not have been idle when such a venture was launched in their favourite commercial field. Certainly an account was opened with the Medici bank in the name of the 'maionieri delle galee di Firenze' in 1436.[1]

The Magona dispatched the first two galleys in October 1436 and a Florentine fleet arrived in Southampton on 27 December.[2] Whether these were the Magona galleys or a fleet which had left earlier is not clear. Certainly it would have been a very quick passage for the Magona galleys, but they may have been calling at Southampton before going on to Sluys. In that case the galleys of Bernardo Ventura which were reported in England in 1437 could have been the same fleet on its way back.[3] One thing that is certain is that there was only one Magona fleet operating in this period, and if there were in fact two fleets the second must have been a separate communal venture either in the summer of 1436 or the spring of 1437.

The Magona dispatched a second fleet in 1438 which arrived in Southampton early in 1439. Again there were two galleys of which the patrons were Jacopo Tedaldi and Bartolomeo Capponi.[4] By the time this second pair of Magona galleys left in September 1438, the contractors had received 10,000 florins in loans from the State, instead of the 15,000 florins promised in the first three years of the contract. Perhaps as a result of this the sailings of the galleys had not been so regular as had been hoped. At this stage, therefore, the Magona contract was terminated by consent of both parties, and new dates were laid down for the repayment of the loan.[5] This was the one major attempt by Florence to contract the galleys out on a long-term basis, and it would seem that the cause of its failure was largely financial. The new customs duties had only yielded 8,530 florins by October 1438, while the Consuls had already paid

---

[1] MAP CXXXIV, 1, f. 8ʳ.

[2] G. Biscaro, 'Il Banco Filippo Borromei e compagni di Londra, 1436–39', *Archivio storico lombardo*, 4th ser., xix, 1913, p. 80.

[3] Ibid., p. 80.

[4] Jacopo, sometimes called Papi, Tedaldi had been patron of one of the Florentine galleys at the Battle of Rapallo in 1431 (see below, p. 105), and was also to make another voyage to Flanders and England in 1441.

[5] Provv. 130, f. 77ᵛ (22 May 1439).

out 10,000 of the loan and were due to pay another 5,000 as soon as possible. It was typical of Florentine financial policy that when the authorized sources of income proved insufficient for a project, little constructive effort was made to fill the gap and the project was instead abandoned.

The experiences of the Magona contractors made potential contractors rather wary at the auctions of the 1439 galleys and no acceptable bids were received. The Consuls were determined to keep up the supply of wool and so in December the wool guild was authorized to take over the direction of the voyage.[1] As the galleys were sailing so late, and as the need for wool was urgent, it was decided to send the fleet direct to England stopping only at Majorca and Cadiz, and to forbid casual trading on the way.

For the next few years until the outbreak of the war with Aragon, two galleys sailed regularly in the autumn to Flanders and England. In 1440 the two galleys commanded by Andrea Pazzi and Bartolomeo Martelli were in Barcelona by 5 November. They were in England in the spring, leaving Southampton on 13 June and returning to Porto Pisano in August. The Captain of the next galleys, which left in mid-October 1441, was Benedetto Mannelli, and these galleys were in Southampton from 6 February to 19 April 1442. One of Mannelli's patrons was Giuliano Ridolfi who now appeared amongst the senior galley men for the first time, and who after commanding more fleets than any other Florentine was twenty years later to lose his life in the wreck of his galley in the Channel.[2]

In 1442 the Captain, according to the English records, was an improbable figure called 'Simone Venisa'. The Florentine records report that Giovanni Bandini de' Baroncelli was preparing to go as Captain in August but as he in fact seems to have captained the Sicily galleys in December, he must have been prevented from going on the longer voyage at the last moment.[3] The galleys arrived in Southampton on 7 March having been held up in Sluys where the Duchess of Burgundy (the Portuguese Infanta Isabella of Albizzi's diary) had attempted to hold them as hostages for the

---

[1] Provv. 130, f. 286^v (30 Dec. 1439); Consoli del Mare III, f. 46^{r-v}; Grunzweig, 'Consulat', p. 15.

[2] Giuliano di Niccolò Ridolfi held positions of command in seven galley fleets; he sailed four times as Captain and three times as patron.

[3] Consoli del Mare V, f. 2^{r-v} (11 Dec. 1442), and Miss. II Canc. 1, f. 114^v (22 Aug. 1442).

payment by the Florentine Republic of overdue interest on *Monte* shares held by her brother Don Pedro.[1] The galleys were eventually released after the Captain and patrons had given their guarantee that the money would be paid. The fleet eventually left Southampton on 20 April.[2]

We have more details than usual of the 1443–4 voyage as Giovenco della Stufa, one of the patrons, had been at one time a Medici factor and was a correspondent of Giovanni di Cosimo de' Medici, and some of his letters have survived in the Medici archives.[3] The two galleys passed through Aiguesmortes on 20 November, and left Cadiz on 14 December for their voyage northwards. They then seem to have swung well out into the Atlantic, not sighting land for nine days, and eventually touching at Bayonne before setting off across the Bay of Biscay. The crossing from Bayonne to Dartmouth, 900 miles, was made in three days, which is a striking indication of what the galleys could do under favourable conditions.[4] At Dartmouth, Giovenco reported, they were received with great honour; it was unusual for Florentine galleys to put in there and this may have contributed to the warmth of their reception. However, in Sluys, which they eventually entered on 3 January, they once more ran into trouble from the Duchess of Burgundy as the *Signoria* had still done nothing about paying her brother's *Monte* interest.[5] It was thus over a month before they were once more on their way, and they entered Southampton on 16 February. On the homeward voyage which started on 9 April there were again delays as the galleys were held up for twenty-five days by bad weather in Brest. However, despite this they arrived back in Porto Pisano on 4 June, which

---

[1] MAP V, 131 (5 Feb. 1443), a letter from Antonio della Stufa in Bruges. For further details of Don Pedro's *Monte* holding which had been bequeathed to him by his father, John I, see F. M. Rogers, *The Travels of the Infante Dom Pedro of Portugal*, Harvard, 1961, pp. 25–28.

[2] In Southampton the patrons, Bartolomeo Martelli and Leonardo Mannelli, were entertained by William Soper and Nicholas Bilot (PRO, Accounts various, Foreign merchants, 128/31, m. 32ʳ). Also travelling with these galleys either in some official capacity or as merchants were Antonio di Lorenzo della Stufa, Jacopo Guicciardini, and Jacopo Pazzi (MAP V, 431).

[3] MAP V, 469 and 525, VII, 445.

[4] Albizzi's time for the run from Ribadeo to Mousehole Bay was four days but he claimed that his galleys were held up by the Portuguese ships which he had agreed to accompany.

[5] Consoli del Mare III, f. 74ʳ⁻ᵛ (1 Oct. 1444), and Grunzweig, 'Consulat' pp. 22–23.

indicates a sailing time of thirty-two days, taking into account the lost twenty-five days. This was exactly the same as the time taken by Albizzi in 1430.[1]

The efforts of the Duchess of Burgundy to force Florence to pay its debts to her brother by harassing the galleys seems to have borne fruit in 1444–5, as the conductors of the fleet for this year were instructed to pay Don Pedro 2,800 florins, and were relieved of paying a corresponding amount of the Sea Consuls.[2] We have no information on the itinerary of this fleet nor indeed very much on that of the next which was captained by Francesco di Cambi Orlandi and sailed in the autumn of 1445. Both fleets took letters of recommendation to the Duke and Duchess of Burgundy and the Mayor and Aldermen of Southampton to smoothe their passage, and that of 1445–6 returned to Porto Pisano on 31 July 1446.[3] Giuliano Ridolfi sailed again with the 1446/7 fleet, this time as Captain, but no details of the itinerary of these galleys have survived.

The ports of call laid down in 1447 for the Flanders voyage were Port-de-Bouc, St. Felix de Guixols, Majorca, Valencia, Javea, Villajoyosa, Denia, Alicante, Almeria, Malaga, Cadiz, Lisbon, Corunna, Sluys, Sandwich, and Southampton. It is notable that Aiguesmortes and Barcelona were deliberately omitted to protect the trade of the Catalonia galleys, and this explains why mention of the Florentine Flanders galleys rarely appears in the Barcelona anchorage accounts at this time.[4] Another interesting feature of the itinerary of these galleys was their reluctance to touch at ports on the west coast of France. It has been suggested that this was the result of French trade monopolies of which we have lost all record, but of which there is occasional evidence in the trade of the French Mediterranean ports.[5] Nevertheless such monopolies could not have affected the coast of Gascony and Bordeaux until after 1453. However, there are two other possible reasons for this

[1] Lane, *Venetian Ships and Shipbuilders*, p. 16. Venetian galleys in 1509 sailed from Southampton to Otranto (2,500 miles) in thirty-one days, a time generally considered to have been a record.

[2] Consoli del Mare III, f. 74ʳ⁻ᵛ (1 Oct. 1444).

[3] For the letters of introduction see Miss. I Canc. 36, ff. 56 and 137.

[4] Consoli del Mare III, ff. 78ᵛ–79ᵛ (27 Mar. 1447), and Grunzweig, 'Consulat', pp. 24–25. Barcelona was restored as a port of call for the Flanders galleys in 1460 (Consoli del Mare III, ff. 132ʳ–137ᵛ, 24 July 1460).

[5] Y. Renouard, 'Les hommes d'affaires italiens à La Rochelle au moyen âge', *Studi in onore di Armando Sapori*, Milan, 1958, i.

tendency of the Florentine galleys; first it is apparent that the galleys by the time they left the Mediterranean were usually fully loaded with cargoes for which there were good markets in northern Europe. Just as they tended to return from England with as few stops as possible because their cargoes were destined for Florence, so after Gibraltar they called at a minimum number of ports in order to save time on their way to the markets of Flanders and England. Coastal trade was in fact a means to an end for the Florentine galleys and not the end itself. It was quicker to go straight across the Bay of Biscay, and even the hazards of such a crossing were not sufficient to oblige the galleys to run round the coasts of western France. The second factor was the English fear that the Italians would attempt to encroach on the lucrative Gascon trade. In 1439 the House of Commons asked that the Italian galleys should not be allowed to bring goods from any port west of Gibraltar,[1] and although this plea does not seem to have become a matter for legislation, nevertheless the Florentines probably made a point of avoiding the French west coast ports in order to maintain good relations in England.

The 1447–8 fleet was running very late by the time it reached England as a result of being detained in Sluys during January at the petition of certain Portuguese merchants. The dispute concerned forty-five casks of sugar which were part of the cargo of the galleys, and the galleys were only released when two Florentine merchants in Bruges, Bernardo Cambi and Antonio di Francesco, went surety for the patrons.[2] The very short visit to Southampton from 18 April to 8 May indicates that for some reason trade was poor. It may have been that the bulk of the wool available had already been taken owing to the lateness of the season, or perhaps news of impending trouble with Aragon had already reached Bartolomeo Martelli, the Captain, and he hurried home with half-empty galleys. Whatever the reason he was back in Porto Pisano by 16 June after another rapid return voyage.[3]

[1] R. Flenley, 'London and Foreign Merchants in the Reign of Henry VI', *EHR*, 5th ser., xxv, 1910, p. 646.

[2] L. Gilliodts van Severen, *Cartulaire de l'ancienne estaple de Bruges; receuil de documents concernant le commerce intérieur et maritime, les relations internationales et l'histoire économique de cette ville*, Bruges, 1904–6, i, pp. 683 and 692.

[3] These galleys were expected to run into trouble on their return and 200 marines were prepared in Leghorn ready to board the armed galleys and go out to escort them home (Consoli del Mare III, ff. 80ᵛ–81, 23 Apr. 1448).

As we have seen from our examination of the other routes the
years 1448–55 saw an almost complete cessation of galley sailings.
In fact a further fleet was auctioned and prepared to go to the
north in 1448, but it almost certainly never sailed.[1] Furthermore,
both in 1451 and 1453 Captains of the Flanders galleys were
nominated.[2] As Captains were always appointed after the galleys
had been auctioned one can only assume that serious attempts were
made to dispatch fleets in these years, but there is no other evidence
available about these enterprises. In fact we cannot be sure of
another fleet until the autumn of 1455 when Bartolomeo Martelli,
one of the most experienced galley commanders, was Captain of
a fleet which was in Southampton from 5 to 25 April 1456. Once
again this was an unusually short visit, about half the time allotted
for the loading of the wool; but Giovanni degli Albizzi had reported from England before the galleys arrived that cargoes would
be bad that year.[3]

Two galleys were again to sail in September 1456 with Alessandro del Vigna as Captain, but there is no definite evidence that
this fleet sailed.[4] As there is no indication of a fleet at all in 1457 and
as Del Vigna was also Captain in 1458, it is possible that for two
years there were no fleets and Del Vigna who had been appointed
in 1456 finally went in 1458.[5] However, it is equally not impossible
that he went twice in three years, although the very short stop of
the galleys in Southampton in the spring of 1456 suggests a certain
recession in the wool trade which might have discouraged sailings
in the next two years. It was in fact in 1457 that anti-alien feeling
caused the Italian merchants to withdraw from London, and this
no doubt affected the decision not to send galleys in that year.[6]

[1] Provv. 139, f. 126ᵛ (8 Oct. 1448).
[2] Tratte 225 (*bis*), f. 39. In fact Neapolitan galleys made their first voyage to
England and Flanders in 1451–2 (C. Marinescu, 'Les affaires commerciales en
Flandres d'Alphonse V d'Aragon, roi de Naples, 1416–58', *Revue historique*, ccxxi,
1959, pp. 35–36).   [3] MAP V, 969 (3 June 1455).
[4] There was a Florentine galley in Genoa in Oct. 1456 on its way at least as far as
Cadiz, but this could well have been a west Barbary galley; see Heers, *Piccamiglio*,
p. 137.
[5] A galley was being built for the Flanders run in July 1457, but beyond this
there is complete silence about the route in this year (Consoli del Mare III, f. 114,
8 July 1457). However, in Feb. 1458 wool bought by the London branch of the
Medici was being shipped across to Calais, which would suggest that there were no
galleys available at that time (MAP XII, 219).
[6] J. Heers, 'Les Génois en Angleterre: la crise de 1458–1466', *Studi in onore di
Armando Sapori*, ii, p. 812.

Whatever may have happened in the intervening years, certainly Del Vigna's 1458-9 voyage was something of a disaster. For the only recorded time in the galley history a long galley was sent with the two great galleys as escort, and Del Vigna sailed on this.[1] The fleet was late in leaving, passing through Genoa in December and Valencia on 24 January 1459. Simone Nori, who accompanied these galleys as far as Marseilles before setting off overland to Flanders, reported that the galleys only just escaped capture at the hands of four French galleys off the coast of Provence.[2] The lateness of the galleys perhaps had a direct bearing on the disaster which overtook them, because it seems to have been considerably more hazardous to cross the Bay of Biscay going northwards after the turn of the year than it was before.[3] Del Vigna's long galley, less seaworthy than its two great consorts, was overwhelmed by the elements and sank, Del Vigna going down with it. Perhaps as a result of this disaster, or for some other reason, the remaining two galleys were much delayed and did not enter Southampton until 4 September.[4] The two patrons were Francesco Tedaldi and Niccolò Bembi, and one of these must have taken over the captaincy.[5] These galleys left Southampton on 3 November and seem to have also had a long journey back as they were still being refitted for their next voyage on 31 March 1460.[6] This was a hurried refit and one must assume that they cannot have returned before the beginning of March, after a voyage of at least fifteen months.

The next fleet did not wait for the return of its predecessors, although it also seems to have been delayed. As a result of anti-alien feeling in Southampton, the galleys went to London, calling only briefly at Cowes on their way back to the Mediterranean in

---

[1] Miss. I Canc. 42, f. 110ʳ (4 May 1459). This is a letter of the *Signoria* to the new Captain deploring the loss of Del Vigna in the armed galley.

[2] MAP IX, 341.

[3] H. Lapèyre, *Une Famille de marchands, les Ruiz*, Paris, 1955, pp. 187-9.

[4] MAP XCIX, 33.

[5] This was probably Francesco di Papi Tedaldi, the humanist and Latin writer (see P. O. Kristeller, 'Una novella latina e il suo autore; Francesco Tedaldi, mercante fiorentino del Quattrocento', *Miscellanea in onore di Emilio Santini*, Palermo, 1955). He was also nominated as a patron of one of the Flanders galleys in 1462, but on that occasion he did not in fact make the voyage (Provv. 153, f. 148).

[6] Provv. 151, f. 1ʳ (1 Apr. 1460). Cino di Filippo Rinuccini was purser on Tedaldi's galley and recorded that the brother-in-law of the painter Benozzo Gozzoli was a trumpeter on the galley and died on the voyage (*Ricordi storici di Filippo di Cino Rinuccini*, p. 251).

August 1460.[1] The delays suffered by these two galley fleets were probably in part due to increased pirate activity, as in 1460 it was decided to send three galleys to strengthen the fleet against such interference.[2] In fact only two eventually sailed as it had been impossible to prepare a third in time. There are indications that these galleys may have been in Southampton in April and May 1461, and they passed through Cadiz on their way home on 2 July.[3]

In 1461 three galleys were again ordered with Bongianno Gianfigliazzi as Captain. It seems that three did in fact sail, one staying at Sluys while the other two visited England.[4] London was the port of call again owing to the continued high feeling against the Italians in Southampton. These galleys had not returned to Porto Pisano by 29 March 1462, but nevertheless preparations for the next fleet were right up to time. This fleet again consisted of three galleys captained by Jacopo Guicciardini, and it had reached Valencia by 6 November. There was then a long delay somewhere round the coast of Spain and the galleys did not arrive in Sluys until 18 February 1463. From there they went to Southampton in March and did not get back to Porto Pisano until late summer.[5]

The 1463 fleet was captained by Giuliano Ridolfi and it was to be the last service which this experienced galley commander was to render to the Republic. This fleet was sent out via Civitavecchia in order to pick up cargoes of alum from the Tolfa mines opened the year before, and for the next few years the Western galleys probably followed the same practice.[6] The three galleys passed

[1] For further information on the state of anti-alien feeling in England at this time, see A. A. Ruddock, *Italian Merchants and Shipping in Southampton, 1270–1600*, Southampton, 1951, pp. 162–86, and Heers, 'Les Génois en Angleterre', *passim*.

[2] Consoli del Mare III, f. 131 (25 Apr. 1460), and Grunzweig, 'Consulat', p. 31.

[3] Quinn and Ruddock, *Port Books*, ii, pp. xxx and xxxviii–xxxix, think that the two galleys which left Southampton on 5 May 1461 commanded by 'Michel George' and 'Rogerus dit Thomas' were these Florentine galleys. Ruggiero di Tommaso Minerbetti was in fact one of the patrons, but the other was supposed to be Jacopo Acciaiuoli. If these were in fact the Florentine galleys, then the very small cargoes which they loaded in Southampton would suggest that they had also called at London to load the bulk of their cargo.

[4] Provv. 152, f. 119 (22 Aug. 1461); Consoli del Mare III, ff. 145ᵛ–146ʳ; Grunzweig, 'Consulat', pp. 35–36.

[5] Quinn and Ruddock, *Port Books*, ii, p. xxx, suggest that the two galleys in London commanded by Francesco Bembo and Marcke Dalage in May 1463 might have been Florentine. However both the names of the patrons and the evidence of Guicciardini's fleet would seem to rule out this possibility.

[6] Consoli del Mare III, ff. 162ᵛ–163ʳ (31 Aug. 1463), and Grunzweig, 'Consulat', pp. 39–40. The anchorage books of Civitavecchia, some of which have survived from

through Valencia on 29 November, and once again had to sail north in the stormy early months of the year. Ridolfi's galley loaded with Medici alum went down with all hands off the Isle of Wight,[1] and Angelo Dietisalvi Nerone, the conductor and senior patron, took over the command. The two remaining galleys were in Southampton from 1 May to 11 June, and finally returned in August 1464 when they had to be unloaded in Portovenere owing to pirate activity along the coast.[2]

The Flanders voyage was also fatal for the next Captain, Francesco di Paolo Vettori, but this time the cause was not shipwreck. The fleet of three galleys sailed very late as plague had been raging in Leghorn, and rumours about the civil wars in England had made trade prospects seem uncertain. In fact it was the spring of 1465 before the galleys finally left Porto Pisano, although they had previously visited Civitavecchia to pick up cargoes of alum.[3] They passed through Valencia on 4 April, and then in Lisbon both Vettori and one of the patrons died. Niccolò Bini, the senior remaining patron, took over the command and the galleys reached Sluys on 27 October.[4] By this time Bini was also fatally ill, and he died in Bruges in November.[5] The violence of the epidemic which seems to have hit the galleys suggests the plague. It is possible that they carried it with them from Leghorn, but more probably sailing in the height of the summer and calling at port after port during the plague season was the cause of the outbreak. It may well be that the Consuls in scheduling their voyages for the autumn and winter months had this danger in mind.

The death of Bini left this fleet in serious difficulties as Agostino

this period (see ASR, Camerale III, Civitavecchia 867), give no information on Florentine galleys using the port. But in fact it seems that the bulk of the shipping which carried the Tolfa alum did not appear in the anchorage accounts, and the Tolfa records themselves do reveal the presence of Florentine galleys amongst other large alum ships which presumably were exempt from anchorage dues. For further discussion of Tolfa alum and its impact on the history of the galleys see below, pp. 136–7.

[1] *Ricordi storici di Filippo di Cino Rinuccini*, p. xciii.

[2] Provv. 156, f. 12ᵛ (24 Apr. 1465).

[3] Tommaso Portinari had particularly asked that these galleys should bring alum, as the market in the north looked promising. At the end of Jan. 1465 Giovanni Tornabuoni, Medici manager in Rome, reported that the galleys had loaded alum. See De Roover, *Medici Bank*, p. 161.

[4] MAP XVI, 184 and XII, 371. Vettori's heirs were given the right to use the crest of the Sea Consuls in his honour (Consoli del Mare VII, f. 41ᵛ, 12 Aug. 1465).

[5] MAP XII, 376.

Biliotti was now the only one of the four original commanders left. After some consultation between Tommaso Portinari, the Medici manager in Bruges, and the *Signoria*, it was decided to appoint Biliotti as Captain despite his comparative youth and inexperience. Agnolo Buondelmonte was promoted from purser to be patron, and Simone Nori, a Medici factor already resident in the north, went aboard the fleet to command the third galley.[1]

The galleys finally went to England in February after a long delay, perhaps to fill gaps in the crews caused by the epidemic, and called at Sandwich.[2] They then seem to have returned to Sluys before finally sailing for the Mediterranean on 28 April 1466. Biliotti, despite the original doubts about him, seems to have carried out his duties satisfactorily and brought the galleys back to Porto Pisano on 16 June.[3]

As a result partly of the long delays suffered on this voyage, and partly of the temporary dislocation of the wool trade caused by the 1463 ban on the export of English wool, no galleys sailed for the north in the autumn of 1465. The next fleet sailed punctually in September 1466 captained by Ludovico Acciaiuoli, and arrived in Southampton at the end of January 1467.[4] These galleys did not go to Sluys at all and returned to Porto Pisano on 7 May after a trouble-free voyage. Troubles and delays did, however, beset the fleet which sailed in October 1467 under Giorgio Ridolfi. The outward voyage was unusually slow, with first a long delay in Marseilles which made it 19 December before the fleet reached Valencia,[5] then a further delay somewhere along the south coast of Spain so that it was 28 February 1468 before they left Cadiz.[6] There were still delays to come as these galleys did not reach Sluys until nearly the end of April, and spent a further month there. We have no information as to the causes of this slow progress, but it is apparent that

---

[1] MAP XII, 376.

[2] *Calendar of Patent Rolls, 1416–1467*, pp. 517–18.

[3] Consoli del Mare VII, f. 65ʳ (16 June 1466).

[4] MAP XX, 177. The published index of the *Archivio Mediceo avanti il Principato*, Rome, 1951, i, p. 352, cites this letter of Girolamo Strozzi as being written in *Ancona*. A close study of the letter reveals however that it was written in *Antona* (Southampton).

[5] Consoli del Mare III, f. 190 (13 Jan. 1468); ARV, Guiatges, 707, unpaginated.

[6] Girolamo Strozzi was also travelling with these galleys. See MAP XX, 394 and F. Edler de Roover, 'Le Voyage de Girolame Strozzi de Pisa à Bruges et retour à bord de la galère bourguignonne *S. Giorgio*', *Handelingen van het genootschap 'Société d'émulation' te Brugge*, xci, 1954, pp. 118–19.

a voyage in which the outward run alone took six months, only a little less than the time allotted for the whole voyage, must inevitably have been uneconomic for its conductors. The galleys in fact returned on 10 September 1468, eleven months after sailing.

It is at this stage that one senses a real crisis facing the Sea Consuls with regard to the Flanders voyages. It was becoming harder and harder to find conductors to take the responsibility for them and so for the next few years after 1469 we find the communal galleys virtually replaced by the privately owned and more enterprising Medici galleys. There were attempts to dispatch communal galley fleets as well during this period, but information about them is imprecise and it seems that the Consuls were on the whole content to allow the Medici galleys a virtual monopoly of the route as long as they sailed regularly.

These Medici galleys, of which more will be said at the end of this chapter, were in England early in 1469, in 1470, and in 1473, in addition to their voyages to the eastern Mediterranean, and given this regularity and knowing the limited trade available on the run, it is not surprising that we hear little about the communal galleys during this period. But in 1469 a fleet was prepared to sail and we have rather more details than usual of the preparations. The Consuls sought the advice of some of the more experienced merchants as to when the galleys should sail, and they decided that the date of departure should be moved forward to July rather than September.[1] However, at the end of August Nerozzo del Nero, one of the patrons, was petitioning to be allowed to give up his post as there was no prospect of departure, and in October the galleys had still not left.[2] Finally in February 1470 all hope of sending these galleys was abandoned.[3]

The indications regarding the galleys prepared in 1470 are also vague, but there is a good possibility that these did in fact sail. A galley went through Valencia on 29 October on its way to Almeria, and it could not have been one of the Medici galleys;[4] furthermore, Priore Pandolfini, who was one of the patrons nominated for this voyage, does in fact appear to have commanded

[1] Consoli del Mare VII, f. 152ᵛ (14 Mar. 1469), and Grunzweig, 'Consulat', p. 102.
[2] Provv. 160, ff. 131ʳ (30 Aug. 1469) and 146ʳ (4 Oct. 1469); Consoli del Mare III, ff. 221ᵛ–222ʳ; Grunzweig, 'Consulat', pp. 44–45.
[3] Consoli del Mare III, f. 223ʳ and Grunzweig, 'Consulat', p. 45.
[4] ARV, Guiatges 707, unpaginated. The Medici galleys were in England in the autumn of 1470 and so could not have been going this way in October.

a galley to the north at this time.[1] Finally the galleys to which Benedetto Dei refers as returning richly laden from the West in 1472 must have been communal galleys as the Medici galleys were fully engaged in a voyage to the eastern Mediterranean in this year.[2]

The auctions in 1472 were definitely postponed because of lack of funds,[3] and in 1473 there was no reference at all to the galleys. In 1474, after the demise of the Medici fleet, a determined effort was made by the Consuls to get a communal fleet out. But when it was about to depart three foreign galleys arrived laden with wool and so the departure of the communal fleet was indefinitely postponed.[4] Another effort was made in 1476 but plague interfered this time and made it impossible to find crews.[5] Finally a fleet was got away in 1477 and it was to be the last of the series. Piero Nasi was Captain, and the galleys after a delayed departure, due to persistent bad weather, had a long and eventful voyage. They were in Southampton from 19 June to 17 August 1478, and on their return voyage were held up for a long period in Marseilles by pirates. They were also so overloaded that they had to hire a Biscayan ship to take the extra cargo.[6] They were finally joined in Marseilles by Zenobio Biliotti's Barbary galleys and the combined fleet successfully ran the gauntlet to Porto Pisano in February 1479.[7]

The Medici Galleys

Several references have already been made to the two galleys known as the *S. Giorgio* and the *S. Matteo*, which were controlled by the Medici and operated on the galley routes between 1468 and 1473.[8] These galleys were originally built in Pisa for Philip the

---

[1] Balìe 33, f. 98 (23 Mar. 1472). [2] *Cronaca di Benedetto Dei*, f. 40ᵛ.

[3] Balìe 33, f. 71 (29 Jan. 1472).

[4] Consoli del Mare III, f. 231ʳ (27 Apr. 1475), and Grunzweig, 'Consulat', pp. 46–47. See also Ruddock, *Southampton*, p. 211. The Venetian galleys from Flanders called at Porto Pisano this year, a very rare occurrence.

[5] Provv. 167, f. 85ᵛ (31 July 1476).

[6] E. Baratier and F. Reynaud, *Histoire de commerce de Marseille*, ii, Paris, 1951, p. 469.

[7] Alberto Villani, who had already commanded one of the Florentine galleys in 1471, was also patron of an alum galley going to Flanders in about 1477. This was probably not a communal galley, but may have been a Medici venture. (See Justo Fernández Alonso, *Legaciones y nunciatures en España de 1466 a 1521*, Rome, 1963, i, p. 406. I am grateful to Mr. A. Antonovics for drawing my attention to this reference.)

[8] For the Medici galleys see: F. Edler De Roover, 'Voyage de Girolame Strozzi';

Good in 1464, and were intended as his contribution to Pius II's crusade.[1] They seem to have been rather larger than the average Florentine galley as in 1469 the *S. Matteo* loaded 300 tons of alum in Civitavecchia. After the breakdown of the crusade and the death of Philip, Charles the Bold was persuaded to lease them to the Medici branch in Bruges for trading ventures, but they continued to sail under the Burgundian flag. It has been suggested that they did this to evade the regulations of the Sea Consuls, which discouraged trade in private shipping.[2] But the fact that already in 1465 the relevant trade monopolies had been abolished, and that these galleys seemed to enjoy a semi-official status anyway, makes this unlikely. It is more probable that the Burgundian flag was maintained as an indication of the ultimate ownership of the galleys, a sovereignty which was abundantly proved when Charles requisitioned them in 1470 for his war with Louis XI. The lease and use of the galleys was very much an enterprise of Tommaso Portinari, and Piero de' Medici always disapproved of them. In fact Portinari had been forced to agree to dispose of them in 1469 when the contract for the Bruges branch was renewed; but Piero's death later in the year enabled Portinari to continue to operate the galleys. He was, however, forced to sell the bulk of the shares in the ownership of them.[3]

The galleys were commanded for most of their active service by Antonio Popoleschi and Francesco Sermattei, although at first one of the patrons, or possibly the Captain, seems to have been Francesco Tedaldi.[4] The two galleys made their first recorded

id., 'A Prize of War', *Bulletin of the Business Historical Society*, xix. 3; R. De Roover, 'Le balance commerciale entre les Pays-Bas et l'Italie au quinzième siècle', *RBPH*, xxxvii, 1959; id, *Medici Bank*, pp. 341–8; A. Von Reumont, 'Di alcune relazioni dei fiorentini con la città di Danziga', *ASI*, 2nd ser., xiii, 1861; A. Grunzweig, *La correspondance de la filiale de Bruges des Medici,* Brussels, 1931, introduction pp. xx–xxi and p. 114; A. Sapori, 'La Banca Medici', Sapori, *studi,* ii.

[1] MAP X, 571 (25 May 1464) and MAP LXXII, 444. Jeoffrey de Thoisi, who was well known in the Mediterranean as a leader of Burgundian expeditions against the infidel, was in charge of the building of the galleys and was due to command them.

[2] Sapori, 'La Banca Medici', p. 1016.

[3] De Roover, *Medici Bank*, p. 343. The fact that the Medici were able to sell their interest in the galleys indicated that the ownership had in some fashion passed to them. But how this was achieved remains obscure.

[4] It has frequently been maintained that Francesco Tedaldi and Francesco Sermattei were one and the same man, e.g. Francesco di Ser Matteo Tedaldi (see the cited articles of Florence Edler). However, not only is there no evidence of the existence of this composite character in other Florentine records, but also the letters written by Francesco Tedaldi from the galleys in Leghorn in 1469 (MAP XX, 503

voyage to Flanders and England in the winter of 1468–9. They were probably in London in January and returned, via Tunis and Sicily, to Porto Pisano on 31 May 1469.[1] They then prepared for another voyage westwards and were loading alum in Civitavecchia on 17 October. The two galleys passed through Port-de-Bouc on 24 November.[2] On their arrival in Sluys early in 1470 they were temporarily requisitioned by Charles the Bold, and it was not until June that Sermattei's galley appeared in Southampton for its first visit.[3] The galleys remained in northern waters for the rest of the year and Sermattei's galley paid another visit to Southampton in December when it loaded its return cargo for the Mediterranean.

and 508) and those written by Francesco Sermattei in the summer of 1472 before the last voyage of the galleys (MAP XXVIII, 346, 356, and 498) are in entirely different hands. Tedaldi was still in command of one of the galleys when they were loading alum in Civitavecchia in 1469, but by the time this galley reached England in 1470 the patron was Sermattei. As Tedaldi was asking to be released from his post in the summer of 1469 (MAP XX, 508), one must assume that his request was granted. On the other hand Girolamo Strozzi referred to Tedaldi as still being with the galleys in 1472–3, but in what capacity is not clear (Strozziana III, 127, ff. 81–90).

[1] The date of return is documented by letters of Francesco Tedaldi and Antonio de' Medici reporting their arrival with 'your galleys' (MAP XX, 503 and XXIII, 252). For evidence of the galleys' visit to London in Jan. 1469 we have two letters of Tommaso Portinari which have been misdated in the published catalogue of the Medici Archive (MAP XII, 307 and 308, 9, 17, and 31 Jan. 1465 ?). These two letters in fact each contain a copy of the previous letter. Thus 307 contains a copy of the letter of 9 Jan., followed by the new letter of 17 Jan.; similarly 308 contains a copy of the letter of 17 Jan., and then the new letter of 31 Jan. In this way they are definitely linked and must be successive letters. Neither carries the number of the year, and both have been attributed to Jan. 1465/6. However, the original of the letter of 9 Jan. in fact exists at MAP XVII, 607 and bears the date 1468/9, and this immediately indicates that letters 307 and 308 must also be dated to this year. It is in fact in the letter of 31 Jan. that Portinari describes the loading of the galleys in London.

[2] Reynaud, 'Port-de-Bouc', pp. 156–7. There is no direct indication that these were the Medici galleys, but the fact that they did arrive in the north early in 1470 makes it likely. In fact a further misdated letter of Portinari probably refers to this voyage (MAP XVII, 465, 7 Dec. 1465 ?). This letter again lacks the year and has been tentatively dated to 1465 in the published catalogue. In the letter Portinari reports his return from Milan and also reports that the galleys are due to arrive imminently. Now in 1465 Portinari was in Milan but had already reported his return in a letter of 28 Oct. (XII, 371 and 372); in the same letter he also announced that the galleys had arrived on 27 Oct. These were in fact the ill-starred galleys of Vettori and Bini, which after the deaths of three out of four of their commanders were delayed in Sluys until Feb. 1466. Thus letter 465 cannot refer to this year and 1469 seems to be the best alternative. In this year Portinari was still in Milan on 27 Oct. (XXII, 227), and the Medici galleys were expected early in the New Year.

[3] Quinn and Ruddock, *Port Books*, i, pp. 60–61 and 96–99.

It is not known when Popoleschi and Sermattei got back to Porto Pisano from this voyage, but certainly by May they had returned and were loading for a voyage to the eastern Mediterranean. The galleys received special loading monopolies for this voyage, no other ships being allowed to load for the eastern Mediterranean while they were still in port.[1] Such monopolies were frequently given to the communal galleys, and the fact that they were now awarded to the Medici galleys indicates their special status. In this case the monopolies do not seem to have helped much as in mid-July the two galleys were still almost empty.[2] However, they did finally sail on 5 August with Paolo Machiavelli as Captain. They stopped at Rhodes on 5 September and reached Chios on 6 October.[3] From there they went to Alexandria rather than Constantinople due to the plague raging in the latter city, and Benedetto Dei reported their return to Porto Pisano in 1472. Either on the way back from this voyage or on a subsequent short voyage in the summer of 1472, the Medici galleys called at Naples, and then by August were in port preparing for what was to be their last voyage to northern waters.[4] They sailed on 26 September so heavily laden that 1,100 sacks of alum had to be left behind, and more alum was unloaded on to a Portuguese ship in Cadiz.[5] It was in the spring of 1473 that the two galleys were caught by the Hansa pirate Paul Beneke off Gravelines when on their way from Sluys to Southampton. Popoleschi's *S. Giorgio* escaped and entered Southampton on 29 April, but Sermattei's *S. Matteo* was taken with 30,000 florins' worth of alum and other merchandise, and Hans Memling's *Last Judgement* on board. The *S. Giorgio* left Southampton on 27 July and returned to the Mediterranean alone, but the eventual fate of the *S. Matteo* is rather uncertain. Benedetto Dei stated that the galley was restored and the English took everything; he also reports the capture of the galley by the vice-admiral of France, Coulon, in 1473, but this was a rumour which proved to be false as it was the Neapolitan galleys which had fallen foul of Coulon.[6] At the same time there is evidence of negotiations and reprisals

---

[1] MAP XXVII, 297.   [2] MAP XXVII, 405 (18 July 1471).

[3] MAP XXVII, 435, 441, 478, 485. These are all letters of Paolo Machiavelli to Lorenzo de' Medici. Francesco Scarfa was one of the Medici factors travelling with the galleys (MAP XXVII, 479).

[4] MAP XXVIII, 346 (2 Aug. 1472), 356 (5 Aug. 1472), and 498 (8 Sept. 1472).

[5] MAP XXI, 387.

[6] *Cronaca di Benedetto Dei*, f. 41ʳ and Grunzweig, *Correspondance*, p. xxxi.

in connexion with the loss of the cargo of the *S. Matteo* dragging on for years, and certainly the painting was never recovered.[1] Finally in 1474 the *S. Giorgio* is said to have appeared in Leghorn flying a Perpignan flag and with a Perpignan patron,[2] and in the same year there was also a report that she had been wrecked in a storm.[3] Whatever the final fate of these two galleys may have been, it seems that after 1473 they were no longer considered as Medici galleys, and they played no further part in the history of the Florentine galleys.

However, while on the subject of Medici-controlled galleys operating on the communal routes, it might be as well to try to trace the history of the galley *Ferrandina*. This galley was, during the late 1460's and 1470's, controlled and manned by Florentines. The Consuls took a considerable interest in it, sending out escorts for it and granting it monopolies, and yet it always seemed to operate alone, which would indicate that it was never a communal galley in the true sense of the word. The example of the Medici Burgundian galleys, which received very much the same treatment, leads one to suspect that the *Ferrandina* was also a galley hired by the Medici and their associates from the King of Naples.

The first reference to the galley is in 1467 when Piero Vespucci returned from the eastern Mediterranean as patron of a single galley which had called at Chios, Rhodes, Constantinople, and Messina.[4] The cargo list is recorded in the book of the Consuls, but Benedetto Dei who was on board the galley described it as the *Ferrandina*.[5] Following this voyage to the eastern Mediterranean, the *Ferrandina* went on to Savona and Marseilles.[6] In July and August 1468 she was loading alum in Civitavecchia for Flanders,[7] and early in 1469 a letter of Tommaso Portinari reported her imminent arrival in Sluys.[8] In July 1471 she was leaving Porto Pisano for a voyage to the eastern Mediterranean,[9] and in October Paolo Machiavelli, Captain of the Medici galleys, wrote to Lorenzo

[1] Edler De Roover, 'Prize of War', *passim*.
[2] Miss. II Canc. 6, f. 65ʳ (8 Feb. 1474).
[3] De Roover, *Medici Bank*, pp. 347–8.
[4] Consoli del Mare VII, f. 73ʳ (7 Dec. 1467), and MAP XX, 351.
[5] Mazzi, 'Carte di Benedetto Dei', p. 140.
[6] MAP CXXXVII, 234.
[7] ASR, Camerale III, Tolfa 2378, *Allumiere*, f. 19A; see also E. Zippel, 'L'allume di Tolfa e il suo commercio', *ASRSP*, XXX, p. 394, where he attributes this voyage to 1471.
[8] MAP XVII, 607 (9 Jan. 1469).   [9] MAP XXVII, 405.

de' Medici that the *Ferrandina* was in Candia with her patron, Francesco Benci, dying of dropsy.[1] According to Machiavelli a certain Neapolitan ambassador had been made patron in Benci's place. There were further reports, again from Medici sources, that the *Ferrandina* was in both Alexandria and Constantinople in the spring of 1472, and returned to Porto Pisano in July of that year.[2]

It is again Dei who gives us the next report on the movements of this galley, and this is in itself significant as Dei was a Medici agent. He mentions its return from an unspecified voyage in 1473,[3] and certainly in November 1473 she was loading in Porto Pisano.[4] In 1475 the galley was reported in Port-de-Bouc,[5] and finally in March 1477 there was a considerable stir in official circles over the safety of the galley when it was returning from another voyage to the eastern Mediterranean. The *Signoria* ordered two armed galleys to be prepared to go out and escort the *Ferrandina* as the threat from pirates had increased.[6] In April, however, it was reported that she had arrived in port before the intended escorts were ready to sail,[7] and indeed on 14 April she was preparing to sail again with Paolo Machiavelli and Bartolomeo Pucci, both experienced galley commanders, in charge of her.[8]

In the next year it was reported to the *Dieci di Balìa* that the *Ferrandina* had sunk in Porto Pisano and was causing considerable inconvenience to traffic; they gave orders to remove her.[9] This was presumably the end of this particular *Ferrandina*, but it had had a long and eventful career which deserves to be studied in greater detail.

The Long Galleys

The story of the Florentine galleys would not be complete without some consideration of the activity and importance of the long galleys which were built for the Republic. Whether the Florentines ever intended to establish a navy for aggressive purposes is uncertain, although the ratio of six long to two merchant galleys in the initial building programme might suggest that they

[1] MAP XXVII, 485 (6 Oct. 1471).
[2] Miss. II Canc. 4, f. 67ᵛ (3 July 1472); Selfridge 495c, ff. 96 and 121.
[3] *Cronaca di Benedetto Dei*, f. 41ʳ.
[4] MAP XXIX, 1002.   [5] Reynaud, 'Port de Bouc', pp. 157-8.
[6] Provv. 168, f. 10ᵛ (29 Mar. 1477).
[7] Provv. 168, f. 51ᵛ (30 Apr. 1477).   [8] MAP XXXV, 408.
[9] ASF, Missive X Balìa dentro il dominio VI, f. 55.

did. Also the order to build fifteen long galleys in 1468 indicates an attempt to build something more than a trade-protection squadron. However, whatever their original intentions or occasional visions of grandeur may have been, the Florentines in fact used the long galleys almost entirely for the protection of commerce and as guardships for the ports. If there was a threat of a naval war on a large scale, they usually resorted to hiring French or Catalan ships.[1]

Preoccupation with the protection of Porto Pisano and Leghorn can be seen in many of the orders issued to and by the Consuls, and the fact that shipping was not safe even in these ports is indicative of the difficulties which faced merchants and sailors, and of the weakness of Florence as a naval power. On several occasions ships were attacked and seized actually in the ports,[2] and in 1460 the returning galleys were stopped at Piombino as it was feared that the Aragonese and Genoese fleets which were revictualling in Porto Pisano would seize them the moment they appeared in their own port.[3] To counter these threats armed galleys and extra marines were kept constantly alerted in the ports, and occasionally something like a full-scale mobilization of all available shipping was ordered.[4]

The other principal task of the long galleys was escorting the great galleys, which they did on occasions when the threats from pirates and hostile shipping were particularly pressing. The effects of pirate activity on the galley schedules have already been noted in some detail, and although the shores of the Peloponnese in the East, and Castile in the West, were frequently danger spots, the most constant threat was along the Tuscan coast itself.[5] This partly explains why although it was very rare for escorts to be provided for a whole voyage, it was comparatively frequent for

[1] Manfroni, *Storia della marina italiana*, iii, p. 108. The Aragonese fleet was employed by Florence in 1425 in her war with Genoa (Sig. X, VIII, 60, II, f. 69), and again under its admiral Bernardo Villamarina in 1463 (Miss. I Canc. 44, f. 79ʳ).

[2] Miss. II Canc. 1, f. 160ᵛ (23 Feb. 1443); 7, f. 40ᵛ (27 Oct. 1475); 9, f. 47ʳ (15 May 1480).

[3] Miss. I Canc. 43, f. 43ʳ (3 June 1460).

[4] Miss. II Canc. 2, f. 93ᵛ (24 May 1444). On this occasion a galley commanded by Giovanni Bandini had been captured by hostile shipping, and one long galley commanded by Giovanni Vespucci, and several smaller ships were sent out to rescue it. See also Miss. II Canc. 3, f. 139ᵛ (19 Oct. 1470) for a similar mobilization in emergency.

[5] Provv. 110, f. 64ʳ (29 July 1420); Miss. I Canc. 42, f. 58ᵛ (14 Oct. 1458), and 43, f. 174ᵛ (18 Nov. 1461); Provv. 161, f. 147ʳ (30 Oct. 1470).

long galleys to be sent out to escort fleets home over the last perilous stretch. When this was done the merchants whose goods had received the additional protection were called upon to contribute towards the expenses of sending out the escorts.

For the tasks of guarding the ports and escorting merchant galleys, three or four long galleys in commission were probably sufficient. But for any real displays of naval strength such a fleet was absurdly inadequate as the Florentines soon realized. In 1425 two Florentine great galleys joined the Aragonese fleet which was blockading the Genoese coast. Matteo Castellani and Veri Guadagni were described as commissaries with this fleet and may have been the commanders of these galleys.[1] Luca degli Albizzi was also a commissary with the Aragonese fleet, and in his 1429 diary he refers to the long galleys of Agnolo Acciaiuoli which were also engaged in this campaign.[2]

However, the only naval success achieved by the Florentines, or to be more exact in which the Florentines participated, was the battle of Portofino or Rapallo in 1431. After failing rather ignominiously to get a blockading fleet to sea during the opening stages of the Lucchese war in 1430,[3] the Consuls managed to fit out three galleys and a number of smaller ships to join the powerful Venetian fleet under Pietro Loredano against the Genoese in the following year.[4] Paolo di Vanni Rucellai was Captain of the Florentine squadron, and it seems that at the critical moment of the battle only two of the Florentine galleys were actually present. The

[1] *Le commissioni di Rinaldo degli Albizzi*, ii, pp. 354–5, 357, 381.

[2] Sig. X, VIII, 5, II, ff. 159–245, and Albizzi Diary, f. 70ʳ.

[3] For the internal disputes and family rivalries which surrounded this project and the appointment of Ormanno di Rinaldo degli Albizzi to command the galley, see *Le commissioni di Rinaldo degli Albizzi*, iii, pp. 326–444.

[4] For further details of the battle of Rapallo see: Giovanni Rucellai, *Zibaldone Quaresimale*, ed. A. Perosa, Studies of Warburg Institute, No. 24, London, 1960, p. 47; S. Ammirato, *Istorie fiorentine*, Florence, 1824–7, vii, pp. 163–4; C. Guasti, 'Raimondo Mannelli alla battaglia di Rapallo', *Archivio veneto*, x, 1875, pp. 54–70; 'Lettera di Raimondo d'Amaretto Mannelli', ed. F. Polidori, *ASI*, appendix vi, 1844, pp. 138–67; M. Sanudo, *Vite dei dogi*, in *Muratori*, xxii, Milan, 1873, pp. 1018–21; G. Pelli, *Ritratti ed elogi degli uomini illustri toscani*, Lucca, 1771, i, p. 187; Papi (Jacopo) Tedaldi was the patron of the other Florentine galley which took part in the battle. Benedetto Strozzi, patron of the third galley which was prepared, was left behind to guard Porto Pisano (MAP V, 20, 120, 127). The problem of finding experienced crews for these galleys was brought out by both Rucellai and Strozzi in their correspondence (see source bibliography of the enterprise in Appendix A). The principal difficulty was to find bombardiers as all the available men were in the army besieging Lucca.

combined Venetian and Florentine fleet was blockading the Ligurian coast when it encountered the Genoese under Francesco Spinola. The result was a victory for the combined fleet, but the Florentine contribution would not have been a noteworthy one were it not for the fact that Raimondo Mannelli, patron of one of the Florentine galleys, captured the Genoese flagship and admiral. It is related that Mannelli had to stand over his helmsman with an axe to make him close with the Genoese galley, and he certainly continued to display great spirit and stubbornness after the battle when he refused to surrender his prisoner and the captured Genoese standard to the Venetians. He was eventually forced to give way by the *Signoria* who were anxious to see the Venetian fleet depart from Florentine waters. However, in his written justification of his actions he was able to make some pertinent remarks about the weak-willed naval policy of the Florentines, and how useless it was to possess ports if one did not seek to dominate the seas in front of them.[1] Here perhaps Mannelli put his finger on one of the principal defects of the whole Florentine maritime venture, the failure to appreciate that naval strength and the resulting prestige were important factors in medieval commerce. As long as her ships had to slink in and out of their own ports for fear of pirates, as long as even the threat of war meant suspension of trade, Florence could never hope to become a maritime power.

In 1434 it was a Florentine armed galley commanded by Giovanni Vitelleschi da Corneto, Bishop of Recanati and Macerata, which picked up Eugenius IV at Civitavecchia after his flight from Rome. Bartolomeo da Montegonzi was the commissary for the *Signoria* on this enterprise, and the Pope was brought safely to Leghorn, and thence to Florence.[2]

In 1448 came Florence's most ambitious display of strength, which ended in disaster. Two armed galleys were sent under Bernardo Ventura to help Piombino against the King of Naples. When the Sienese imposed a land blockade on the port, four more

---

[1] Guasti, 'Raimondo Mannelli', p. 67.

[2] Cambi, *Istorie*, i, pp. 189–90, and Guglielmotti, *Storia della marina pontificia*, ii, pp. 138–43. The Florentine galley did in fact go up the Tiber as far as S. Paolo but at that time the Pope was not yet ready to flee, and Vitelleschi withdrew in order to avoid provoking an incident. Eugenius IV was eventually brought down the Tiber in a small boat, from which he transferred to the galley of Vitelli d'Ischia at Ostia. The final transfer to the more luxurious Florentine galley was made at Civitavecchia.

galleys were sent to victual the garrison. However, they met a considerably larger Neapolitan fleet and were soundly defeated at the battle of San Vincenzo, two of the Florentine galleys being captured.[1] In fact at least four of the galleys used in this expedition were converted merchant galleys which were lying idle as a result of the suspension of trade, so even this enterprise gives a false impression of Florence's naval strength. Apart from this action little is known of Florence's naval activities during the Aragonese war. But in 1454 Pierozzo de' Pazzi, a noted naval *condottiere*, who at that time at least was fighting under the flag of his native city, was finally captured in a naval encounter off the Dragonata of Majorca, and later executed in Barcelona.[2]

Finally the Pazzi war in 1478 produced a further small Florentine contribution to the history of naval warfare. A certain Giovanni Fiorentino invented a kind of gunboat called an *albatrotte* which was designed to carry bombards with a range of nearly 200 yards. This vessel was built in Porto Pisano but there is no indication of to what use it was put.[3]

Thus the naval record of the Florentine galleys was not an impressive one and indeed one would hardly have expected it to have been. Florence lacked any maritime tradition and few of her citizens had any experience of naval warfare. It seemed sufficient for her purpose to establish a merchant fleet, and to entrust defence if necessary to hired shipping and naval mercenaries, just as the defence of her frontiers was in the hands of *condottieri*.

---

[1] Cambi, i, p. 263; Matteo Palmieri, *Annales, RIS*, xxvi, i, p. 157, Baruchello, *Livorno e il suo porto*, p. 62. See also Miss. I Canc. 37, ff. 120ᵛ (19 June 1448), 122ᵛ (22 June 1448), 125ʳ (29 June 1448), 128ʳ (5 July 1448), and 133ʳ (11 July 1448). The cost of fitting out this naval expedition was 6,500 florins, a serious drain on the resources of the Sea Consuls.

[2] J. Nuria Coll, 'Aspectos del corso catalan y del comercio internacional en el siglo XV', *Estudios de historia moderna*, iv, 1954, p. 179.

[3] P. Vigo, 'Porto Pisano', *Rivista marittima*, 1896.

5

THE TRADE OF THE GALLEYS

The Monopolies of the Galleys

THE picture of the ramifications of the Florentine galley system built up in the preceding pages, although revealing far greater communal maritime activity than had been suspected, does not lead one to believe that such a comparatively limited enterprise could possibly support the Florentine economy on its own. It would be reasonable to suppose that the communal galleys formed only a small part of the shipping which frequented Porto Pisano and Leghorn and carried Florence's maritime trade. Yet some historians have maintained that one of the most important features of the communal galley system was its monopoly of Florentine trade, and that when this monopoly was abandoned the galley system was doomed to collapse.[1] To show that discontinuance of any monopolies was by no means the only cause of the ultimate breakdown of the system is one of the aims of this study; but at the same time it is important to assess the exact nature of the monopolies enjoyed by the galleys if one is to perceive the true importance of the system as a whole.

Some have considered one of the aspects of the monopoly to have been a ban on private shipbuilding and private trading ventures by Florentines.[2] Others have described Pisa and its ports prior to 1465 as closed to foreign shipping in the most complete sense of the word.[3] Others still have felt that the monopoly was upheld by discriminating duties on goods not using communal shipping, and a ban on Florentines loading goods on foreign ships for ports served by the galleys.[4]

That some form of monopoly did exist is abundantly clear from

[1] Grunzweig, 'Consulat', p. 61; Sapori, *'Primi viaggi'*, p. 73; Luzzatto, *Storia economica dell'età moderna e contemporanea*, pp. 97–99.

[2] Baruchello, *Livorno e il suo porto*, p. 48.

[3] R. Caggese, *Firenze dalla decadenza di Roma al Risorgimento d'Italia*, Florence, 1917, ii, p. 401. 'Impossibile, inoltre, trasportare merci su navi che non siano fiorentine; il porto di Pisa prima e quello di Livorno poco più tardi, non sono aperti che ai sudditi di Firenze.'

[4] Grunzweig, 'Consulat', p. 6; Pagnini, *Della decima*, ii, p. 36.

the important derestricting decrees of 1465 and 1480. In November 1465 the Councils passed a decree permitting the import of goods from any part of the world, under any ownership and in any ships on the same terms and subject to the same duties as had previously covered the communal galleys.[1] The two curious aspects of this decree are, first the preamble which definitely suggests that before 1465 the galleys had a complete monopoly, and no goods could enter or leave the Florentine dominions by sea except on the galleys;[2] and secondly the fact that the decree refers only to freedom of import and makes no mention of exports. Whether both these can be attributed to loose phrasing and therefore disregarded as evidence remains to be seen.

This 1465 decree has usually been described as the opening of the Florentine ports to foreign shipping, and it is often felt that it was the result of the English ban on the export of wool in foreign shipping which was imposed in 1463 and which for at least one year deprived the galleys of their wool cargoes.[3] But that it did not finally break the monopoly of the galleys is apparent from the fact that a further derestricting decree was necessary in 1480. In the latter, much was made of the decline in imports into the Florentine dominions, and the galleys were taken out of service thus enabling once and for all both Florentine and foreign merchants to use what shipping they chose.[4] Why was this second decree necessary? Was it that the 1465 decree had been circumvented by the Consuls who had still been able to enforce a degree of monopoly for the galleys? Or was it that the 1465 decree had not been intended to abolish *all* the restrictions on non-communal shipping? In either case it was the suspension of the galley system rather than the theoretical abolition of monopolies which finally released Florentine citizens from any obligation to use the galleys, and encouraged them to embark on private trading ventures.[5]

Certainly one of the objects of the 1480 decree may have been to

[1] Provv. 156, f. 239ʳ (30 Nov. 1465); Consoli del Mare III, ff. 177ᵛ–178; Grunzweig, 'Consulat', pp. 41–42.

[2] Ibid. 'Considerato che egli è lunghissimo tempo che la nostra città ha fatto molte leggi et prohibito et sbandito tutte le mercantie che sono di bisogno, utili et necessarie universalmente alla città, contado et distretto di Firenze che non ci si possi conducere ne mandare robe se non per le nostre galee di che è seguitato et seguira grandissima incommodità . . . .'

[3] Ruddock, *Southampton*, pp. 208–9.

[4] Provv. 171, ff. 17ʳ–19ʳ (3 Aug. 1480).

[5] Richards, *Florentine Merchants*, pp. 47–48.

encourage free trade and nascent capitalism, but it cannot be true
to say that it permitted private Florentine trade and shipbuilding
for the first time. There is plenty of evidence of private Florentine
shipping throughout the galley period, sometimes encouraged by
the Consuls themselves. In the 1427 statutes of the Florentine
colony at Bruges the only Florentine shipping referred to were the
merchant galleys of the Commune. But by 1461 it had become
necessary to add clauses governing the handling of private
Florentine shipping; such ships had to pay a toll to the Florentine
Consul and were obviously by this time, before the 1465 decree,
not infrequent visitors to Sluys.[1] We have already noted the galleys
of Francesco Ventura and Priore di Marioto in England in the
late 1420's. It is possible that both these were controlled by
Florentines resident in Spain, and never in fact used Porto Pisano.
But this seems an unlikely thesis in view of the close links which
Florentine houses abroad usually maintained with Florence itself.
There were Florentine ships in Constantinople in 1436,[2] and the
Martelli in 1439,[3] Bartolomeo da Rabatta in 1453,[4] and Ludovico
Strozzi & Co. in the same year[5] all hired foreign shipping for their
trade from Porto Pisano. In the early 1460's there is evidence of the
Albizzi,[6] Bartolomeo Pucci,[7] and the Ferrantini[8] all owning or
hiring ships for their own trading ventures. In 1464 a Medici-
controlled galley, prior to the famous Burgundian galleys, was
operating between Flanders and the Mediterranean.[9]

The monopoly of the galleys was not then one which excluded
all private enterprise on the part of Florentines; to what extent was
it one which closed the ports completely to foreign shipping? Here

---

[1] G. Masi, *Gli statuti delle colonie fiorentine all'estero, secc. XV–XVI*, Milan,
1941, Capitoli della nazione fiorentina in Bruggia, c. 30; Grunzweig, 'Consulat',
pp. 104–15.

[2] Heyd, *Commercio del Levante*, p. 866.

[3] Strozziana V, 1461, ff. 23ᵛ–26. The Martelli were using a ship known as the
Contarina for bringing hides and wool from Spain to Porto Pisano.

[4] Miss. I Canc. 38, ff. 39ʳ (5 Feb. 1453) and 51ᵛ (19 Mar. 1453). Da Rabatta hired
the Genoese galley of Ludovico Campofregoso.

[5] Strozziana III, 116, f. 71 (25 Oct. 1453), and Cambi, *Istorie*, i, p. 294. In this case
the vessel was the Genoese carrack *Sta. Maria e S. Raffaelo*, sometimes known as the
Doria after its patron Marchionne Doria. She was described by Cambi as the largest
ship seen in Pisan waters for some time.

[6] Litta, *Famiglie celebri*, Albizzi, tables xiii and xviii.

[7] Ibid., Pucci, table xiv.

[8] Provv. 151, f. 100ᵛ (20 June 1460). This ship was the *Querina* hired by the
Ferrantini in 1460.

[9] MAP LXXII, 563.

again there is plenty of evidence of foreign shipping in Porto Pisano and Leghorn, and of Florentine goods travelling on such shipping during the galley period, which would seem to contradict the preamble of the 1465 decree.[1] In 1439 new anchorage charges were imposed upon all ships and galleys loading or unloading in the ports.[2]

The principal visitors to Porto Pisano in the period before 1465 were Catalan, French, and Genoese ships, either on their way to and from the East, or on local voyages. Porto Pisano was one of the principal ports of call for Catalan vessels visiting Italy, but ships from Barcelona bound for the eastern Mediterranean usually used the more direct route via Sicily. At least thirteen Catalan ships appeared in Porto Pisano in 1428-9, and some of them made two visits during that period.[3] Catalan ships were also frequently used by Florentine merchants for transporting their goods from England.[4] Furthermore, Venetian galleys on their way to and from Aiguesmortes frequently called at Porto Pisano.

Information on shipping other than communal shipping usually only appears in the Florentine archives when it is a question of a Florentine ship, or Florentine goods on a foreign ship, being seized by hostile vessels, and yet there is on average at least one reference a year in the first half of the century to such events. All the ships which passed in and out of the Florentine ports without incident never appear in the records.[5]

Thus the monopolies which were granted to the communal galleys were in no sense complete, and their real nature is stated best in the statutes of the Florentine colony in Bruges. Here it was

---

[1] Vigo, *Statuti e Provvisioni*, p. 109. Both the statutes of 1423 and 1477 refer to the considerable amount of foreign shipping which used Leghorn and Porto Pisano, and which only Livornese boatmen could unload.

[2] Consoli del Mare III, ff. 44ᵛ-45ʳ (17 June 1439). 'Item che ogni nave, ghalea o altro fuste che veranno in Porto Pisano o Livorno o nella foce d'Arno per charicare o scharicare alcuna ragione di merchantantia o vettovaglia o simili cose, debbino paghare per ancorraggio oltra al ancorraggio usato l'enfrascripta quantità di denari....'

[3] Del Treppo, 'Assicurazioni e commercio', i, pp. 523-37.

[4] Ruddock, *Southampton*, pp. 63-64. This was particularly true during the periods when the communal galleys were not sailing.

[5] Particularly fruitful sources for information on shipping in Porto Pisano and Leghorn are the Missive delle Prime e Seconde Cancellerie. In the former are frequent protests to foreign rulers about the molestation of Florentine shipping and trade by foreign shipping, and the latter contains many instructions to Florentine port officials and Sea Consuls regarding the treatment of specific vessels in the Florentine ports.

laid down that foreign goods could be loaded on the galleys when all Florentine goods had been loaded, and that Florentine goods could be loaded on other ships when there were no communal galleys sailing.[1] In England the embargo on the loading of Florentine goods on foreign ships extended for a period of two months on either side of the sailing date of the galleys.[2] This was a principle which was accepted before 1465, but afterwards it had to be restated for every voyage. On occasions between 1465 and 1480 the proclamation of a voyage contained the order that *no one* could load goods for the ports to be visited by the forthcoming galleys on any other vessels within two months of the sailing dates of those galleys.[3] This would seem to be a direct reversal of the 1465 decree unless that in fact only referred to imports. On other occasions it was only stated that no Florentine could use foreign shipping within such a period.[4] In 1472 the Captain of Leghorn was instructed to 'persuade' merchants to use the communal galleys soon to leave for Sicily.[5]

The other aspect of the galley monopolies was a discriminating import duty on goods arriving in foreign shipping. This took the form of an extra duty of 8 per cent. on all goods from the west, and particularly wool, not imported in the communal galleys.[6] This was first imposed in 1429, although extra duties of a less fixed nature seem to have been imposed previously. On occasions, particularly between 1448 and 1456, and again in 1464, the additional duties on wool were lifted because the galleys were not sailing and wool was in short supply.

It would seem both from the wording of the 1465 decree and from the state of affairs which appears to have existed between 1465 and 1480, that it was the additional import duty which was abandoned as a result of that decree. One feature of the galley monopolies was swept away allowing greater freedom of import, but the restrictions on loading on non-communal ships largely remained until 1480, although the gradually decreasing rhythm

---

[1] Masi, *Statuti*, Capitoli della nazione fiorentina in Bruggia, cc. 14 and 23.

[2] Consoli del Mare IV, 4, *Capitoli dei conductori e patroni*, c. 18.

[3] Provv. 156, f. 26ʳ (29 Apr. 1465); 159, f. 109ᵛ (30 July 1468); 163, f. 32ʳ (16 May 1472); Miss. II Canc. 5, f. 97 (24 June 1473). The Neapolitans, when they instituted state-controlled galley fleets to Flanders in the 1450's, introduced very similar monopolies (Marinescu, 'Affaires commerciales', pp. 35–36).

[4] Provv. 163, f. 182ᵛ (11 Feb. 1473), and 164, f. 159ᵛ (8 Oct. 1473).

[5] Miss. II Canc. 4, f. 115ʳ (24 Sept. 1472).

[6] Consoli del Mare IV, 4, *Capitoli dei conductori e patroni*, c. 26.

of galley sailings after 1470 tended to nullify their restrictive effect on trade.

Thus it appears that the galley monopolies were not so pernicious nor so far reaching as some have thought. Florentine ports were never closed to foreign shipping, in fact Florence relied for a large part of her trade on such shipping. Few of the bulk commodities such as grain, salt, iron ore, foodstuffs, etc., were carried by the galleys, nor yet was their service sufficiently frequent or sufficiently extensive to satisfy the commitments and ambitions of Florentine merchants. Hence there were large numbers of private ventures both in Florentine-owned ships and in hired shipping. The galleys were in fact intended to ensure a vehicle for certain essential items of Florentine trade and to serve as a prestige symbol to enhance the international standing of Florence and her merchants.

For some idea of what part of Florentine trade was handled by the galleys, and hence their importance in fifteenth-century Mediterranean commerce, we must turn to the few remaining cargo lists, the lists of freight charges and other pieces of evidence which have a bearing on the trade carried by the galleys, rather than on their movements and schedules which have already been discussed. Here once again it will facilitate the inquiry to consider each geographical sphere of galley operations separately, with the same reservations concerning interlocking voyages which have already been mentioned.

Trade with the eastern Mediterranean

The three principal trading areas in the eastern Mediterranean were Greece, Constantinople and the Black Sea, and the basin from Beirut round to Alexandria. It was the latter area which was the principal market for the spice trade with the two great emporia of Damascus and Alexandria. Spices in the Middle Ages included a vast variety of commodities ranging from pepper and ginger, which were exported in large quantities, to spikenard, galangal, and camphor, of which little circulated. Furthermore, as well as being the market for Eastern spices, the Levant itself produced a number of semi-luxury bulk goods such as fine Alexandria linen, cotton, and sugar, the last two of which were produced in large quantities in Cyprus.

Between Cyprus and Constantinople, on the galley routes, lay the islands of Rhodes and Chios. Rhodes was a favourite port of call not only as a Christian outpost in the eastern Mediterranean, but also as a famous market for all the commodities of the area. A flourishing colony of Florentine merchants was settled there, and great care was taken to maintain good relations with the Grand Master. Chios, on the other hand, was very much a Genoese centre and although Florentine galleys called there, the control of the valuable alum trade which centred on the island was largely in the hands of the Genoese. Chios was also, however, the exclusive source of mastic, and in addition furnished wine, oil, figs, marble, silk, and clay to the ships from the West.[1]

Constantinople was less well known as a spice market than Alexandria or Damascus, and of the better known spices only wormwood, rhubarb, and orpiment were found regularly there.[2] However, there were occasional supplies of pepper and indigo to draw on and in addition silk, brocades, wool, hides, wax, brazil-wood, and carpets.[3] Gallipoli was included in the galley itineraries as the outlet for Turkish cotton, and the Black Sea area was also one of the principal sources of domestic slaves which were in considerable demand in the households of Renaissance Florence.[4] Although the galleys were officially not allowed to carry female slaves, there were fairly frequent references in the Pisan customs accounts to the import of slaves on which a custom was levied as on all other merchandise.[5] But probably the bulk of the slave trade passed along the overland route through Ancona where several Florentine slave-merchants had their headquarters.[6]

---

[1] Müller, *Documenti*, p. 481. For an excellent recent discussion of the Levant trade area, see Heers, *Gênes*, pp. 363–406.

[2] *Calendar of State Papers Venetian*, i, pp. cxxxvi–cxxxvii.

[3] Heers, 'Commercio nel Mediterraneo', pp. 170 and 173.

[4] A. Zanelli, *Le schiave orientali a Firenze nei secoli XIV e XV*, Florence, 1885. One of the effects of the capture of Pisa and the opening up of direct communications with the East was that the Florentines were able to import their own slaves and not take the remains from the Venetian and Genoese trade. The result was a notable rise in the standards of beauty of the slaves in Florence, and also in the prices (see Zanelli, p. 46).

[5] The set duty for the import and export of slaves was 4 *lire* per head in the first half of the century, and later 6 *lire*. It is probable that the bans on the transport of slaves applied primarily to the outward voyages, as it had been the earlier custom of shipping Christian slave girls to the slave markets of the eastern Mediterranean which had led to the first bans in the thirteenth century. The fact that it was female slaves in particular which were forbidden adds weight to this idea.

[6] Zanelli, *Le schiave orientali*, pp. 36–38. For further information on slaves in Tuscany, see I. Origo, 'The Domestic Enemy: Eastern Slaves in Tuscany in the 14th and 15th Centuries', *Speculum*, xxx, 1955.

Florentine trade with Greece was facilitated by concessions granted by the Florentine prince of Corinth, Antonio Acciaiuoli, in 1422 and by Demetri Palaeologo in 1450.[1] Florentines had always been welcomed in the Greek ports, particularly Patras and Chiarentza, and after 1439 they enjoyed considerable commercial concessions in these ports.[2] Perhaps the principal attraction of the Greek market was the fine cochineal available there which was in great demand in the Florentine woollen industry. But malmsey was also a great attraction as it was much prized in England and could help to provide cargoes for the galleys to the north.

To see what use the Florentine galleys made of these trading opportunities in the eastern Mediterranean, we must turn to the lists of freight charges, the remaining cargo lists, and the Pisan customs accounts for our information. The freight charges do not in fact take account of any geographical divisions in this area, but merely give a list of the possible imports and exports of the Levant as a whole. The goods which the galleys were expected to carry to the eastern Mediterranean included woollen and silk cloths of all types, almonds, saxon green mineral dye, saffron, tin, lead, coral, brass, paper, apples, gossamer, soap, and violet. The return cargoes included all the items mentioned above in discussing the markets of the eastern Mediterranean, without any differentiation in provenance. In this case therefore the freight charges are not of great value.[3]

On the other hand, the full cargo lists which have survived, and brief indications of cargo and freight takings which can be gleaned from the sources, are of considerable interest. The first two merchant galleys to return from Alexandria under Piero Guicciardini brought back the following cargo from the East:

Cargo loaded in Rhodes for Sicily

216 bales pepper	2 bales incense powder
296 bales ginger	1 bale incense
27 bales cloves	2 bales indigo
52 bales lac	4 bales linen cloth
14 bales brazilwood	1 bale bocassins
10 bales cinnamon	5 bales myrrh

[1] Müller, *Documenti*, pp. 152 and 177.
[2] Heyd, *Commercio del Levante*, p. 868; D. A. Zakythinos, *Le Despotat grec de Morée*, Athens, 1953, ii, p. 262.
[3] Consoli del Mare IV, 4, *Capitoli degli scrivani*. Sections of these charges relating to the Levant trade are published by Müller, *Documenti*, pp. 357-9.

2 bales gum ammoniac
5 bales gall nuts
1 bale borax
1 bale galbanum
1 bale *borghi*
1 bale clove stalks
8 boxes *follori*
1 case cedar
44 bales linen and canvas
7 barrels gum
1 bale summach
6 bales raw cotton

1 case sugar
2 barrels silicate of magnesia
2 bundles bow staves
2 bales fish glue
9 bales deer-skins
2 bales silk
24 miscellaneous packages
5 cases manna
96 bales copper and other goods
1 bale candied sugar
6 bundles cassia
3 bales green ginger

Loaded in Alexandria and Rhodes for Gaeta

29 bales pepper
5 bales ginger
2 bundles brazil wood

1 barrel sweetmeats
5 large bales cotton
11 bales rabbit skins

Loaded in Alexandria, Rhodes, and Sicily for Porto Pisano

223 bales pepper
93 bales ginger
7 bales cloves
1 bale of aloe of Socotra
8 cases incense
7 cases mace
1 case myrrh
1 case cardamom
15 jars green ginger
8 bundles gum arabic
105 bales sugar
26 bales oxhides
1 bale lantern black

8 cases long cinnamon
1 bale red sandalwood
3 cases orpiment
1 box camphor
1 bale elephants' tusks
3 bales bocassins
2 bales linen
4 bales sponges
13 bales sweetmeats
11 bales saltpetre
6 barrels malmsey
10 packages dates
1 bale botargo

---

5 bales metal utensils
1 bale minivers
2 bales ham
1 case silk cloth
279 barrels tuna fish

788 strings of cheese
50 crates capers
8 crates cassia
7 bundles brazilwood[1]

[1] The last group of items were probably those loaded in Sicily. This cargo list was published by Sapori, 'Primi viaggi', p. 91. Also in a footnote on p. 80 Sapori discusses some of the spices named in the list. Heyd, *Commercio del Levante*, pp. 1121 sqq., provides considerable additional information on the nature and uses of these spices. The problem involved in using these cargo lists for statistical analysis of

From this list it appears that a very large proportion of the spices loaded were loaded in Rhodes and not in Alexandria. This would fit with the information previously given in the same source that trade conditions were not easy in Alexandria at this time. It is also significant to note that rather more than half the original cargo never reached Pisa at all, large amounts being unloaded in Sicily and Gaeta and replaced with bulk food commodities such as tuna fish and cheese. Whether the goods unloaded in Sicily belonged to Florentine merchants who thus made two sets of profits in one return voyage, or whether these goods were in fact loaded by Sicilian or other non-Florentine merchants is not clear. If one adopts the scale of measurements proposed in Appendix B, the total cargo of these two galleys on leaving the East was in the region of 145 tons. Of this cargo rather more than half was pepper and ginger. Another fact which emerges is that less than half the goods unloaded in Sicily were replaced, and the galleys arrived in Porto Pisano carrying considerably less cargo than when they left the East. The discrepancy in the value of the cargo was even greater as the goods in Sicily were of comparatively low value.

Of the amount of freight charges collected we have no indication for this voyage, nor would it be wise to attempt to assess the figure based on the 1442 freight charge lists, both because the same rates may not have been in force in 1422, and because those lists do not give the separate rates for shipment from the Levant as far as Sicily.

After this first trading voyage we have no indications of the cargoes of the eastern Mediterranean galleys until the 1460's, except for the very brief mentions of the galley in Constantinople in 1437 which Giacomo Badoer's accounts recorded as unloading gilded leather, and loading carpets, copper, and pepper for shipment to Messina.[1] In 1462 the galleys of Giuliano Ridolfi carried

---

trade is that the quantities quoted are quite indefinite. A number of generic terms are used such as *collo, sporta, farda, cassa*, etc., all meaning various types of package; but there is little indication of the exact weight or quantity involved. In translating these terms I have frequently had to use the same English word for a number of Italian terms. As will be seen from Appendix B (Weights and Measures), the types of package divide very roughly into two groups, those weighing 75–90 kg. and those weighing 145–70 kg.; those in the latter group are always described as large in the cargo lists which follow.

[1] *Libri di conti di Giacomo Badoer*, i, pp. 203 and 236.

an outward cargo worth 4,500–5,000 florins in freight charges to the conductors.[1]

The Syria galleys of Bernardo Corsi returned from their voyage on 26 January 1466 with the following cargo :[2]

106 bundles silk	9 casks orpiment
27 bundles brazilwood	7 bales cumin seeds
20 boxes crimson	4 bales wormwood seeds
1 bale cochineal	518 sacks Syrian cotton
8 barrels indigo	102 bales wax
134 bales gall nuts	41 bales rice
149 bales pepper	61 sacks soda
168 bales ginger	8 bales carpets
28 bales cloves	4 casks green ginger
7 bales larkspur	11 bales tragacanth
2 bales nutmeg	2 bales bocassins
10 bales cassia	10 bales Alexandria linen
15 bales cinnamon	2 bales spikenard
17 cases mastic	1 case lac

300 sacks Gaetan soap

It was also reported that 1,200 florins worth of freights were unloaded on the way home. How much cargo this represented in bulk is not known but when the galleys reached Porto Pisano they carried about 160 tons of cargo, worth about 4,500–5,000 florins in freights to the conductors.[3] The total value of the cargo landed in Porto Pisano was reported to be 23,480 florins.[4] It is strange that on this occasion no cargo seems to have been picked up in Sicily; it is possible that for some reason our cargo list is not complete, or perhaps the galleys had been expressly forbidden to load in Sicily to avoid damaging the trade of the Sicily galleys. It is also significant that pepper and ginger made up only about 20 per cent. of this cargo, although we are not to know how much of the 1,200 florins' worth unloaded were these commodities. At the same time, if the freight charge values are any

[1] MAP X, 351. The freight charge for a Florentine cloth at this time was 1 florin.
[2] Consoli del Mare VII, f. 61ᵛ.
[3] This figure has been assessed on the basis of the estimated quantities set out in the table in Appendix B, and the freight charge lists of 1461 (see Müller, *Documenti*, pp. 358–9).
[4] Consoli del Mare VII, ff. 65ᵛ–67ᵛ. This was the estimate produced at the audit of the expenses of the voyage.

guide, only about one-fifth of the total cargo was unloaded in Sicily.

Bernardo del Nero's two galleys which were the next to return from the East, and which probably called at Constantinople, brought back the following cargo :[1]

139 bundles silk	3 bales miscellaneous spices
75 sacks raw cotton	3 bales lac
24 sacks spun cotton	3 bales mustard seed
64 sacks wool	3 vases green ginger
11 bales cochineal	1 bale rhubarb
25 bales crimson	1 bale borage
34 bales brazilwood	1 case indigo
66 baskets wax	7 bales carpets
119 bales pepper	99 bales gall
21 cases cinnamon	1 piece camlet
5 bales nutmeg	12 large crates potash
6 bales cloves	3 bales cordovan leather
4 bales ginger	

Loaded in Sicily

526 cases sugar	2 bronze mortars
437 kegs tuna fish	6 bales of household goods and
473 strings cheese	books
1 box feathers	40,000 ducats in cash and jewels
10 bales woollen cloth	40 soldiers (*armati*)
3 bales fox skins	

On this occasion the spice proportion of the cargo fell even more appreciably, which would fit in with the theory that these galleys went to Constantinople where spices were not so common. Once again one must presume that a considerable part of the cargo from the East was unloaded in Sicily to make space for the large consignments of Sicilian products brought. In fact over half the cargo which arrived in Porto Pisano was of Sicilian origin. The value of the cargo unloaded in Porto Pisano according to the audit of the voyage expenses was 29,014 florins.[2]

The final complete cargo list which we have for the Eastern galleys is that of the single galley, probably the *Ferrandina*, of Piero

---

[1] Consoli del Mare VII, f. 67ᵛ.
[2] Consoli del Mare VII, ff. 68ᵛ–69ʳ.

Vespucci returned from Chios, Rhodes, Sicily, and Naples on 7 December 1467:[1]

46 bundles and 1 case silk	91 sacks Syrian cotton
2 boxes and 3 bales crimson	4 boxes tannin
43 barrels and 25 bales wax	1 bundle beaver fur
39 bales cinnamon	1 bundle Alexandria linen
142 bales ginger	2 bales camlets
139 bales pepper	6 bales carpets
39 bales cloves	180 bales Syrian soda
32 bales brazilwood	3 cases metal utensils
7 cases mace	21 bales woolfells
12 cases mastic	795 oxhides
6 cases miscellaneous spices	4 sacks wool
5 bales lac	40 baskets sulphur
1 bale nutmeg	1 box gum
1 bale wormwood seed	600 cantars alum
1 bale tow	2,745 Syrian sturgeon
2 boxes opoponax	20 boxes *calina*
3 cases fine Cypriot sugar	

This galley also loaded in Sicily and thereafter:

135 cases and 32 barrels sugar	24 bales Neapolitan linen
13 barrels saltpetre	1 case coral
364 kegs tuna fish	12,000 ducats
48 barrels butter	6 white slaves[2]
228 barrels alum	1 horse
26 barrels soap	1 *serpente*

The cargo of major spices was somewhat improved this time, indeed as a whole the galley seems to have been very well loaded, but there was still a marked preponderance of non-luxury commodities.[3] Particularly noteworthy was the 600 cwt. of alum brought from Chios or some other eastern source despite papal bans on the import of Turkish alum, and despite the fact that the Medici were already controlling the distribution of the Tolfa alum.

[1] Consoli del Mare VII, f. 73ʳ.

[2] Grunzweig ('Consulat', p. 96) has translated *teste* as terra-cotta vases, but the position of this item in the cargo lists, e.g. always at the end and sometimes with various livestock, makes it seem likely that the entries refer to slaves. For other examples of the use of *testa(e)* in this sense see G. Luzzatto, *Storia economica di Venezia dall'XI al XVI secolo*, Venice, 1961, p. 148, and Del Treppo, 'Assicurazioni e commercio', ii, p. 63.

[3] In fact the quantities loaded on this galley are so much larger than on any state galley throughout the century (*c.* 200 tons total cargo), that one must presume that the *Ferrandina* was a much larger vessel than the average Florentine merchant galley.

From this limited information one can perhaps draw some tentative conclusions. First, spices, and in particular pepper and ginger, did not play anything like the part in Florentine trade that they did in that of Venice, particularly in the later years. Heers reported Venetian galley cargoes for the early years of the century as follows:[1]

> 3 galleys in 1394: 2,190 bales pepper and 138 bales ginger
> 3 galleys in 1395: 2,100 bales pepper and 190 bales ginger
> 3 galleys in 1396: 1,573 bales pepper and 221 bales ginger
> 3 galleys in 1399: 2,100 bales pepper and 130 bales ginger
> 3 galleys in 1405: 844 bales pepper and 823 bales ginger

On these galleys these two items alone accounted for about 90 per cent. of the total cargo. The Florentines, on the other hand, loaded large quantities of cotton, linen, soda, hides, and silk which frequently outweighed the spices in the cargoes. Thus the Venetian fleets from the Levant sometimes brought back cargoes to the value of 200,000 ducats or more, seven or eight times the value of some of those recorded by the Florentines.

Secondly, apart from pepper and ginger, the Florentines concentrated on dye and tanning products in the range of spices.[2] This bears out the conclusion that support of home industries was one of the prime functions of the galleys and not just trade for its own sake.

Thirdly, frequently as much as half the more valuable Eastern cargoes of the galleys was off-loaded in Sicily, and replaced by bulk foodstuffs. This in itself emphasizes the very general nature of the commerce of the galleys, and at the same time would imply a basic misunderstanding of the true commercial value of the galley.

These conclusions are confirmed by the Pisan customs accounts which show the relatively small quantities of spices imported, compared to other products of the eastern Mediterranean.[3]

[1] Heers, 'Commercio nel Mediterraneo', pp. 166–8.

[2] Lac, brazilwood, indigo, gall, cochineal, crimson, tragacanth, mastic, orpiment, summach, soda, tannin, and alum were all used largely or entirely in the wool or leather industries.

[3] The Pisan customs accounts for the fifteenth century are to be found in ASP, Archivio del Comune Div. B, Nos. 23 *bis*–52. Eighteen books survive each covering a six-month period. Owing to the incomplete coverage, to the exemptions which were conferred on certain articles, and the unsystematic methods of recording the entries, these accounts cannot be used to provide a complete picture of the movements of goods through Pisa. They can, however, be used to throw light on some

Before we leave the trade of the eastern Mediterranean, a word must be said about the Florentine exports to the area. It is generally thought that in trade with the Levant the balance of trade tended to be against the Western merchants. On the whole there was a very limited range of valuable goods for which there was a demand in the eastern Mediterranean and which Western merchants could supply. But one commodity which did sell well was fine woollen cloth and this was what the Florentines had to offer in large quantities. The eastern Mediterranean was the principal market for the Florentine cloth industry, and during the fifteenth century it also became the principal market for the Florentine silk industry. Whereas at the beginning of the century the traffic in taffetas, brocades, fine silks, etc., was from East to West; by the end of the century the Florentines were exporting large quantities of these materials to the East. The galleys of 1474 carried 60,000 florins' worth of silk cloth to Constantinople; add to this the 3,300 woollen cloths which they also carried, valued at approximately 50 florins each, and one gets an outward cargo of at least the value of the return cargo of the same galleys which was estimated at an optimistic 150,000 florins.[1] This is a somewhat startling conclusion which is borne out by the few other figures of exports of cloth to the East which remain to us. In 1471 the galleys took 2,500 cloths,[2]

branches of the traffic, particularly the import trade. For example, the imports of pepper recorded in these accounts are as follows:

Oct. 1466–Apr. 1467	5,328 lb.
Oct. 1467–Apr. 1468	3,455 lb.
Oct. 1468–Apr. 1469	4,182 lb.
Apr.–Oct. 1469	11,279 lb.
Apr.–Oct. 1470	3,542 lb.
Apr.–Oct. 1473	14,840 lb.
Oct. 1476–Apr. 1477	—
Apr.–Oct. 1477	50,019 lb.
Apr.–Oct. 1478	4,268 lb.
Oct. 1482–Apr. 1483	4,039 lb.

(The Florentine lb. equals 339·5 grammes.) These are insignificant figures when compared with the imports of the Venetian galleys which reached 400,000 lb. per fleet.

[1] *Cronaca di Benedetto Dei*, f. 41ᵛ. This figure must include goods unloaded in Sicily but even so it is very much at variance with the values of the 1466 and 1467 fleets already quoted from official sources. One suspects that the latter may be rather low estimates but Dei's is almost certainly high.

[2] MAP XXVII, 441. The freight-charge value of the outward cargo of these galleys was estimated at 3,600 florins. The 1462–3 galleys loaded goods worth 4,500–5,000 florins in freights, and the 1461 galleys carried goods to the value of 6,000 florins in freights to the East. Benedetto Dei stated that 7,500 cloths were sent to the East in 1471 (*Cronaca*, f. 40ʳ).

in 1472 8,000 cloths[1] were sent, and in 1476 3,000 cloths.[2] The very rough estimates of the values of the return cargoes which I have already attempted compare unfavourably with these high-value outward cargoes, and one is forced to the conclusion that for the Florentines at least the trade balance with the East was not by any means unfavourable.[3]

Trade with the western Mediterranean

A good deal has already been said about the Sicilian market and the commodities which the Florentine galleys from the East picked up there. But it is now necessary to examine it more carefully, particularly in conjunction with the markets of Catalonia and Provence, with which it was so closely linked that it was felt to be advantageous for Florentine galleys to run from one to the other.

Sicily was a natural focus for Florentine trade, both as a stopping-place on the way to the Levant and to Barbary, as a producer of vital foodstuffs, particularly grain, and finally not least because of the large numbers of Pisans who had settled there both before and after the Florentine occupation of Pisa. In the early part of the

[1] *Cronaca di Benedetto Dei*, ff. 39^v and 40^v.

[2] Ibid., f. 42^v. The Pisan customs accounts record the following figures for the export of Florentine cloth. Cloths brought through Pisa for export by sea did not pay duty on leaving the city and therefore only appear in the import records with a note to the effect that they were to benefit from the special export concessions. The first column of figures in this list are therefore imports declared for export by sea, whereas the second column are the recorded exports which were presumably cloths which for some reason or other were not declared for export on their arrival.

Apr.–Oct. 1455	788	+	330	=	1,118
Oct. 1466–Apr. 1467	71	+	51	=	122
Oct. 1467–Apr. 1468	1,942	+	235	=	2,177
Oct. 1468–Apr. 1469	2,269	+	409	=	2,678
Apr.–Oct. 1469	1,763	+	1,141	=	2,904
Apr.–Oct. 1470	2,073	+	250	=	2,323
Apr.–Oct. 1473	156	+	86	=	242
Oct. 1476–Apr. 1477	750	+	50	=	800
Apr.–Oct. 1477	2,789	+	293	=	3,082
Apr.–Oct. 1478	373	+	34	=	407
Oct. 1482–Apr. 1483	856	+	27	=	883

Once again it must be remembered that these figures can only be a very rough guide. They do not cover consecutive years, nor is the destination of the goods ever mentioned. However, we can be fairly sure that the bulk of Florentine cloth exported did go to the East, although of course by no means all the cloth sent to the East went by sea.

[3] Del Treppo ('Assicurazioni e commercio', ii, pp. 54–57) came to the same conclusion with regard to the Catalan trade with the Levant.

century it was said that nearly all the bankers in Palermo were Pisans.[1]

The Florentine galleys rarely carried grain, but they did as we have already seen load considerable quantities of the other Sicilian exports, tuna fish, cheese, sugar, cotton, and some silk and saltpetre. In addition to the Levant galley cargoes there are records of four other cargoes from Sicily preserved. On 13 July 1466 Piero Nasi returned with two galleys loaded with:[2]

300 cases and 68 baskets sugar	1 case cinnamon
300 kegs tuna fish	40 cantars cheese

There are no surprises here except perhaps the very small load for two galleys. Bernardo del Nero's Levant galleys passing through two months later picked up much more than this in Sicily to add to their Eastern cargoes. However, it may be that this was only the part of the cargo unloaded in Porto Pisano and that a considerable quantity remained on board for Provence and Catalonia.

The comparative inferiority of the cargo quoted above is emphasized by the next one which is recorded, that of the single galley of Agostino Biliotti which returned from Sicily on 7 July 1467 with:[3]

52 bales alum	4 bales woolfells
265 cases and 125 barrels sugar	4 barrels saltpetre
45 jars butter	2 horses[4]
400 cantars cheese	

The alum was probably loaded in Civitavecchia which had by this time been established as the outlet for the Medici-controlled alum from the papal alum mines at Tolfa.[5] According to the next cargo list sugar was one of the commodities unloaded in Civitavecchia

---

[1] C. Traselli, 'Mercato dei panni a Palermo nella prima metà del secolo XV', *Economia e storia*, 1957, p. 163.

[2] Consoli del Mare VII, f. 65.   [3] Consoli del Mare VII, f. 72[v].

[4] Although a good deal of cheese was exported from Sicily, there was also the Neapolitan *cacio cavallo* of which large quantities appeared on the Pisan market. For remarks on the importance of Sicily as a producer of sugar in the Middle Ages see C. Trasselli, 'La produzione e commercio dello zucchero in Sicilia dal XIII al XIX secolo', *Economia e storia*, 1955.

[5] There were also smaller alum deposits on Ischia and the Lipari islands which may have been the sources of some of these shipments. See Heyd, *Commercio del Levante*, pp. 1128-9, and J. Delumeau, *L'Alun de Rome, XV–XIX siècles*, Paris, 1962, p. 19.

and this would have left space for alum. Piero Corsellini returned from Sicily on 1 August 1468 with the following cargo:[1]

301 cases and 105 half-cases sugar	3 bales black skins
25 barrels unrefined sugar	12 sacks sesame
983 Barbary hides	1 case mastic
67 bales alum	1 case cinnamon
76 jars butter	2 bales cloth
9 sacks cotton	4,000 ducats
2 boxes linen	

29 cases and 99 half-cases sugar were unloaded in Civitavecchia.

The final Sicilian cargo is that of Agostino Biliotti's galley which returned on 19 July 1469 with:[2]

106 cases sugar ⎫	
350 hides ⎬ unloaded in Naples and Civitavecchia	
442 cases sugar	4 sacks and 5 boxes linen
46 bales sheepskins	10 cases household goods
200 cantars cheese	13 sacks soap
6 bales madder	1 horse
7 bales wax	1 mule
74 jars butter	5 'men' (*uomini*)
383 bales alum	

Whether *men* on this occasion implies slaves or just passengers is not clear. It is the only time the entry appears on any cargo list, although slaves appear in others under different headings. It seems more likely that it refers to slaves as they were certainly considered a part of the cargo whereas passengers were an entirely different matter.

It is known that a good deal of the sugar which was brought from Sicily in the galleys was in fact destined for the coast of Provence, particularly Aiguesmortes;[3] at the same time cargoes of cloths for Sicily were picked up in Catalonia and Provence. The extent of the trade which went through Porto Pisano on this run is borne out by the cargo which the 1465 Syria galleys brought back from their first visit to Catalonia and which was destined for Sicily:[4]

521 bales woollen cloth (4,246 pieces)	34 bales linen cloth
61 cases coral	7 cases silk cloth
55 bales tanned leather	53 bales household goods

[1] Consoli del Mare VII, f. 73ᵛ.   [2] MAP XVII, 698.
[3] Balìe 29, f. 70ᵛ (15 Nov. 1458).   [4] Consoli del Mare VII, f. 61ʳ.

Imported cloths were in fact an important commodity on the Sicilian market, and in the first half of the fifteenth century a considerable number of Florentine cloths were exported there.[1] The galleys also brought in considerable quantities of non-Florentine cloths, and silks, iron, paper, and canvas.

Between Sicily and Porto Pisano lay the important intermediate ports of Salerno, Naples, Gaeta, and Civitavecchia. At the fairs of Salerno both Florentine merchants and Florentine goods were common,[2] while in Naples there was a large permanent colony of Florentine merchants encouraged to settle there by the benevolent policy of the Aragonese kings.[3] There are several references to Gaeta soap being loaded on the galleys, while Civitavecchia after 1462 became an important port of call for the alum, much of which was taken to northern Europe.

Alum, which once was described as 'no less necessary to the dyer than bread is to man', was one of the most important commodities in medieval trade. Up to 1462 the largest source of alum had been the mines of Phocaea in western Turkey which were controlled in the latter half of the fourteenth and the fifteenth centuries by the Genoese from Chios. With the capture of Phocaea by the Turks and the high tributes levied on the Genoese at Chios by the Sultan, the supply of alum to the West dried up after 1458. This led to an intensive search for alum and the discovery in 1462 of the rich deposits at Tolfa, which, being sited in the Patrimony of St. Peter, were exploited by the Papacy. Pius II and his successors quickly forbade the use of Turkish alum in the West and set aside the proceeds from the sale of Tolfa alum for crusading purposes. Furthermore, the contract for the distribution of Tolfa alum was given to the Medici, who, by 1466, had bought 91,270 cantars out of 125,185 produced up to then. It was natural that the Florentine and the Medici Burgundian galleys should become involved in the

---

[1] Trasselli, 'Mercato dei panni', *passim*; id., '*Frumento e panni inglesi nella Sicilia nel secolo XV*', Palermo, 1955, *passim*. Trasselli perceives a marked decline in the number of Florentine cloths on the Sicilian market after 1450, but nevertheless it was the Florentines who continued to import to Sicily large quantities of English, Catalan, and Provençal cloth.

[2] A. Silvestri, *Il commercio a Salerno nella seconda metà del Quattrocento*, Salerno, 1952, pp. 51–56; A. Sapori, 'Una fiera in Italia alla fine del Quattrocento', Sapori, *Studi*, i, pp. 443–74.

[3] Baruchello, *Livorno e il suo porto*, p. 54; Sapori, 'Fiera in Italia', p. 447; G. Coniglio, 'Mercanti fiorentini a Napoli attraverso gli anni del notaio Petruccio Pisano, 1465–6', *Samnium*, 1955, *passim*.

distribution of this alum, and indeed the possibility of handling almost unlimited quantities of this commodity had a considerable effect on the history of the galleys.[1]

On the other side of Porto Pisano lay the coasts of Provence and Catalonia, and for the Florentine galley trade with these areas we have a good deal of information. From Catalonia to Porto Pisano the galleys were expected to carry raw silk, woollen cloths, hides, alum, wool, cochineal, rice, and wax; from Aiguesmortes to Porto Pisano cloths, canvas, verdigris, almonds, and Burgundian linen were among the traditional items of trade.[2] Leaving aside for the moment the cargoes picked up on these coasts by the Flanders galleys on their way north, let us see what the cargo lists of the Catalonia galleys can add to the picture. In summer 1465 the three Syria galleys returned from their first voyage to Catalonia with:[3]

51 bundles silk	1 bale Perpignan cloth
18 bales cochineal	6 cases combs
402 sacks wool	8 cases books
27 cases sugar	51 bales spices
15 bales Languedoc cloth	2 bales leather
15 bales unspecified cloth	6 bales hats
25 bales linen cloth	7 white and black slaves (*teste*)

To have some idea of the total cargo of these galleys on this voyage one must also add the goods which were in transit to Sicily and which have already been described.[4] After their voyage to Syria these galleys again went to Catalonia, returning on 6 May 1466 with:[5]

18 bundles silk	304 Majorca cloths
3 bales cochineal	514 Perpignan cloths
2 cases silk cloth	1,625 Languedoc cloths
10 large bales rice	52 bales other cloths
501 sacks wool	162 bales linen cloth
5 bales woollen thread	22 cases combs
16 bales hats	13 bales metal utensils

[1] Delumeau, *L'Alun de Rome*, pp. 13–54 and 79–96; Zippel, 'L'allume di Tolfa', *passim*; M. L. Heers, 'Les Génois et le commerce de l'alun à la fin du moyen âge', *Revue d'Histoire économique et sociale*, xxxii, 1954; L. Liagre, 'Le commerce de l'alun en Flandres au moyen âge', *Moyen Âge*, lxi, 1955.
[2] Consoli del Mare IV, 4, *Capitoli degli scrivani*.
[3] Consoli del Mare VII, f. 61ʳ.   [4] See above, p. 125.
[5] Consoli del Mare VII, f. 64ᵛ.

6 cases books
11 cases and 20 bales household
goods
44 bales leather
12 large bales sheepskins

190 Spanish hides
1 bale woolfells
8 crates majolica
8 white and black slaves (*teste*)

At first sight it is surprising to find so considerable an import of Catalan and Provençal cloth into Pisa and Florence, and perhaps this phenomenon, which also applied to English cloths which were being imported in large quantities, has contributed to the theory of the rapid decline of the Florentine woollen industry in the fifteenth century. But two things must be borne in mind when considering this problem: first it is probable that a good part of this imported cloth was destined for Sicily and Southern Italy. On the previous voyage of these galleys, the cargoes were distinguished as the same galleys were going on to Sicily, and at that time relatively little Catalan and Provençal cloth was left in Porto Pisano. On this occasion the galleys were terminating their voyage in Porto Pisano and so the entire cargo had to be unloaded; the goods destined for Sicily would then have had to wait for the next galleys bound in that direction. The second point is that the Florentine wool industry concentrated on good quality cloth of which the bulk was for export. The practice of dyeing and refining foreign cloths and then re-exporting them, which had been so profitable a business for the Calimala guild in the fourteenth century, was in decline by this time, and the demand for Flemish cloths for this industry had fallen off almost completely. But there was still a considerable demand for the cheaper foreign cloths on the Florentine home market. A good deal of cheap cloth was made in Tuscany outside Florence but this was often of very inferior quality and did not satisfy the market. In fact by 1472 40,000 florins' worth of Perpignan cloths alone were being imported each year, and it was decided to ban the import and produce an identical article in Florence.[1]

However, to return to the cargo lists; on 24 September 1466 two galleys returned from Catalonia with:[2]

13 bales cochineal
1 bundle silk

75 bales Barcelona cloth
25 bales rough cloth

[1] Provv. 163, f. 154ʳ (22 Dec. 1472).   [2] Consoli del Mare VII, f. 68ʳ.

20 bales Languedoc cloth
9 bales corded cloth
1 bale doublet linings
4 bales hats
50 bales linen cloth
21 bales coral
13 cases knives

3 bales leather
14 cases household goods
4 cases books
4 cases medicines
119 kegs Spanish tuna fish
4 slaves (*schiave*)

One must presume from the appearance of slaves on so many of these Catalonia galleys that West African slaves captured by the Portuguese were beginning to filter through to Florence. Before, the chief source of slaves had been the Black Sea and the Genoese slave market at Caffa. Another interesting feature of all these cargo lists is the references to the import of books; these were the only galleys which participated in the book trade and one wonders whether these were Catalan or Provençal items.

In May 1467 Agostino Biliotti brought his galley in with:[1]

12 bales cochineal
5 bales ground cochineal
4 bundles silk
19 bales Catalan cloth
7 bales leather
2 sacks sugar
33 large bales rice
67 bales linen and canvas

5 bales wool
12 bales rough leather
46 bales Languedoc cloths
6 bales hats
13 bales other cloths
7 cases books
4 bales metal utensils
1 bale clothing

The final list which has been preserved is that of Piero Corsellini's galley which returned in June 1468 with:[2]

20 bales cochineal
12 cases sugar
204 bales wool
12 large bales rice
5 bales corded cloth
422 Barbary hides
6 bales leather
142 bales cloth

21 bales linen cloth
5 bales hats
3 bales metal utensils
20 bales canvas
25 sacks wool
2 bales serge
2 cases books
3 slaves (*schiave*)

These few lists bring out very clearly the constant items which Florence imported from Catalonia and Provence: wool, cloth, leather, and cochineal. The wool was mainly the *lana S. Matteo* from Spain which at this time ranked second only to English wool; and

---

[1] Consoli del Mare VII, f. 72ʳ. [2] Ibid., f. 72ᵛ.

was much used in the Florentine wool industry. In the early part of the century much of the importing of Spanish wool was in the hands of Catalan merchants,[1] but by the 1460's references to Catalan merchants in Pisa become rarer. It seems from the Pisan customs accounts that in the fifteenth century the amount of wool imported from Spain was rather less than that imported from England. Small quantities of wool were also imported from Provence, but it was of inferior quality.[2]

The importation of Spanish and French cloth has already been discussed, but the large imports of Spanish, Irish, and Barbary hides for the Pisan and Florentine tanning and leather industries are worthy of note. The activity of the Pisan tanning industry in the fifteenth century throws some new light on the state of Pisa under the domination of Florence and this will be discussed in more detail elsewhere.[3] But a significant fact from the point of view of the movement of trade is that of the very considerable quantities of raw hides imported into Pisa which are recorded in the customs accounts, the bulk emerged on its way to be distributed all round Tuscany as tanned leather.[4] The Spanish hides were held to be the best available, better even than the Irish skins which also appeared in large quantities on the Pisan market.

Finally Spain was the most prolific source of the prized dye cochineal or *grana* which was used considerably for the luxury cloths produced by the Florentine wool industry. The cochineal from Greece was of better quality but very limited quantities of it were available. Not only the Catalonia galleys but also the Florentine Flanders galleys brought back bales of cochineal to Porto Pisano.

As in the other spheres of Florentine trade, our information on Florentine exports to Catalonia and Provence is far more limited

[1] See Del Treppo, 'Assicurazioni e commercio', ii, p. 72, and ASP, Archivio del Comune, Div. B, n. 28 for the activities of Catalan wool merchants in 1415.

[2] For a table of the wool imports into Pisa in the fifteenth century see M. E. Mallett, 'Anglo-Florentine Commercial Relations, 1465-91', *Economic History Review*, 2nd ser., xv, 1962, appendix ii, p. 265.

[3] See M. E. Mallett, 'Florence and Pisa in the Fifteenth Century', in *Studies in Florentine History* to be published shortly by Faber & Faber. For a full description of the Pisan leather industry in the thirteenth century see Herlihy, *Pisa in the Early Renaissance*, pp. 137–45. On this topic see also F. Melis, *Note di storia della banca pisana nel Trecento*, Pisa, 1955, p. 24, and C. J. Singer, *The Earliest Chemical Industry*, London, 1948, pp. 84–87.

[4] In the six-month period Oct. 1466 to Apr. 1467 57,793 hides were recorded as entering Pisa by sea (ASP, Comune B, 39, *passim*).

than that on imports. We have no cargo lists and the information on exports in the Pisan customs accounts is not precise. One can say with some certainty, however, that Florence suffered a definite adverse trade balance in her trade with these areas. There does not seem to have been any great demand for the luxury Florentine cloths, particularly after 1422 when a ban on the import of foreign cloth into Catalonia was imposed.[1] Indeed in the period 1428–9 Catalan exports to Tuscany were valued at 9,770 Catalan pounds, and imports from that area at only 2,775 Catalan pounds.[2] Commodities which were exported by Florence on this route were silk cloths and brocades, corn, linen, spices, sulphur, and woad. Products both from the East and Sicily formed a good part of this trade, and in the later years large quantities of the Tolfa alum was exported to Provence.[3] Periodic bans on the import of spices in foreign shipping into France in the 1460's hit the Venetian trade to Aiguesmortes, but probably did not affect the Florentine galleys which carried relatively few spices.[4]

Thanks to the researches of De Mas Latrie and Amari[5] we are very fully informed about the commercial treaties between Florence and the Sultan of Tunis in the fifteenth century, but for the commodities of the trade we have little data. Barbary did not provide the luxury articles of the Levant, and at the same time remained a good market for Florentine cloth throughout the century. The principal exports from the Barbary coast were hides, wool, wax, cochineal, alum, silk, sugar, dates, tuna fish, and cotton; but the quality of nearly all these commodities was inferior to those of Catalonia and Sicily. The only cargo list which

---

[1] J. V. Vives, *La economía de los paeses de la Corona de Aragon en la Baja Edad Media*, Cagliari, 1957, p. 27.

[2] Del Treppo, 'Assicurazioni e commercio', ii, p. 72. It must be remembered, however, that Del Treppo was using only Catalan insurance contract figures and these would tend to reflect exports rather than imports, thus perhaps exaggerating the disparity between the two.

[3] Baratier and Reynaud, *Commerce de Marseilles*, pp. 459 and 467; Reynaud, *Port de Bouc*, p. 165. Nearly 1,500 tons of Tolfa alum reached southern France between 1462 and 1478 (Delumeau, *L'Alun de Rome*, p. 48).

[4] Reynaud, *Port de Bouc*, p. 155.

[5] L. de Mas Latrie, 'Relations commerciales de Florence et de la Sicile avec l'Afrique au Moyen Âge', *Bibliothèque de l'École des Chartes*, ser. iv, vol. v, 1859; id., *Relations et commerce de l'Afrique septentrionale ou Magreb avec les nations chrétiennes au moyen âge*, Paris, 1886; id., *Traites de paix et de commerce*, Paris, 1866; Amari, *Diplomi arabi*.

has been preserved is that of the galley which returned on 23 June 1465 with:[1]

70 cantars wax	28 bales hides
2,000 cantars cheese	3 bales wool
55 bales woolfells	11,000 gold doubloons

Cheese was not normally thought of as an export of Barbary and it may be that this was loaded in Sicily. If this was so we know even less than ever about Barbary trade as the cargo was made up of little else. It is always tempting to think that when a galley returned with large sums of cash on board that the balance of trade, for that particular voyage at least, had been favourable and that the value of exports had exceeded imports; and with Barbary this might be a true assumption. But the possibility always remains that the cash brought back was only an unspent portion of an even larger sum sent out to redress an expected unfavourable balance.

Trade with England and Flanders

For this sphere of the Florentine galley trade the surviving statistical information is considerably greater than for any other. This in itself has led to greater discussion of the problems by recent historians, and two articles in particular in recent years have considered the structure of the Florentine galley trade in northern Europe.[2] It is necessary to emphasize immediately the point that this trade in northern Europe must be regarded as one sphere of trade; the galleys, as both Professor De Roover and Professor Watson have pointed out, unloaded in Sluys and loaded in Southampton, and this cannot really be described as representing a favourable balance of trade with Flanders and an unfavourable one with England. This would be like saying that the Florentines enjoyed a favourable trade balance in Gallipoli and an unfavourable one in Constantinople. Just as one thinks of Florentine trade with the Levant as a whole, so one must think of the trade with northern Europe as a whole. As Watson has so rightly pointed out the exchange and credit links between London and Bruges were very close; in fact most of the Florentine merchants in the two cities belonged to branches of the same companies, and in many cases the branch in London was a subsidiary of the branch in Bruges. The

---

[1] Consoli del Mare VII, f. 61r.

[2] De Roover, 'La balance commerciale', and Watson, 'Structure of the Florentine Galley Trade'.

merchants on the galleys were either connected with these companies, or freelance merchants selling in Bruges and buying in
Southampton. In either case the two markets were closely linked.
No deep study of credit and exchange transactions, and trade
balances is needed to explain why the Medici, for example, with
associated branches in Bruges and London, should choose to sell
the Mediterranean cargoes quickly in the continental market of
Bruges and buy the return cargo of wool as near its source as
possible, particularly when only a two-day voyage separated the
two ports. The Florentines could have bought the wool from the
Staplers in Calais but they would have paid more for it; equally
well they could have sold the Mediterranean goods in England,
but I suspect less easily.[1] However, they chose to carry out the
operations separately because this caused little inconvenience and
brought maximum advantage.

The Florentine galleys to England and Flanders relied very much
for their north-bound cargoes on goods picked up in Provence
and Spain. Florence itself as we have seen had little to offer but the
luxury wool and silk cloths for which she was famous, and for
these there was a limited market in the north, particularly in
England where there was a tendency to restrict the import of such
cloths. She could in addition offer luxury goods brought from the
East by her galleys but the quantities involved were not great and
again as we have seen much of these goods was drawn off by her
trade with Sicily and Catalonia. Furthermore, the Venetians were
already flooding the northern markets with these commodities.
Thus the galleys left Porto Pisano probably not much more than a
quarter full and travelled round the western Mediterranean basin
picking up cargoes of madder, almonds, dates, raisins, rice, wax,
silk, cochineal, saffron, etc., from Port-de-Bouc, Aiguesmortes,
sometimes Barcelona, Majorca and Valencia, Javea, Denia,
Alicante, Malaga, and Cadiz.[2]

[1] Watson, op. cit. ii, p. 318, argues that 'the Florentines could just as easily have
sold their goods in Southampton and London as in Bruges'. He cites a letter of
Portinari of 1465 reporting that the King of England was angry that the galleys were
not unloading in Southampton because he was losing customs revenues, but this is
hardly direct evidence that the market for Mediterranean goods was as favourable in
England as in Flanders. One would imagine that the proximity of the Burgundian
court, and its more accessible relationship to the markets of northern Europe, would
have made Bruges a more favourable market than London or Southampton, which
were already well supplied by Venetian and Genoese merchants.

[2] Morosini, the Venetian chronicler, commented on the poor cargoes carried by

This progress round the Mediterranean coastline of the galleys in 1429 is fully described by Albizzi in his diary, and one of the most important points brought out by his narrative is the extent to which cargoes were picked up in these ports. Albizzi in his letter to the Sea Consuls from Aiguesmortes reported that they had so far picked up 200 bales of goods in Marseilles, Port-de-Bouc, and Aiguesmortes.[1] The galleys then stayed for a further two days in Aiguesmortes loading cargo but the total amount loaded in the port is left blank in the diary. The next port of call was Barcelona where the galleys parted company briefly, one going to Majorca and the other to Valencia. Albizzi's own galley which went to Majorca loaded dates, cardamom, cinnamon, cochineal, steel, and copper to a freight value of 400 florins.[2] As none of these articles are mentioned in the lists of freight charges for this particular route, we cannot assess the bulk of this consignment. But 400 florins' worth on an intermediate stage such as this probably represents about one-twelfth of the whole cargo of the two galleys. Meanwhile the Carnesecchi galley had loaded completely in Valencia and Denia.[3] The two galleys joined up again at Javea, and at the next stop, Benidorm, Albizzi's galley loaded a further 400 cantars of raisins.[4] From Villajoyosa, the next stop, Albizzi reported to the Consuls:[5]

On the 29th of last month, I wrote to Your Magnificence from Barcelona concerning all that had occurred on our voyage worthy of note up to then. After that the same night I departed with the Vespucci galley, on which I am sailing, leaving the consort to take on cargo at Barcelona and Valencia. I went to Majorca, and from there returned to Javea, by the Grace of God, on the 7th of this month at dawn. And there I heard that the other galley was at Denia, and had not yet come to Javea as we had arranged, as it had not completed loading. I sent a messenger immediately and that evening the galley arrived having loaded in Valencia and Denia, and it was laden up to the deck supports in such a way that it could take on no more. We have so far about half a cargo from all our stops and here today I hope that we shall fill up the rest as much as the galley can hold. Thus, thanks be to God, the galleys will have done their duty on the outward journey, and they have had

the first Florentine galleys when they left Porto Pisano for Flanders in 1425. He reported that their value was 20,000–25,000 ducats, which would indeed have seemed poor to a Venetian who was accustomed to galleys leaving for the north laden with spices (A. Morosini, *Chronique*, ed. L. Dorez and G. Lefevre–Portalis, Paris, 1898–1902, ii, pp. 302–3).   [1] Albizzi Diary, f. 54ʳ.   [2] Ibid., f. 58ʳ.
[3] Ibid., f. 52ᵛ.   [4] Ibid., f. 59ʳ.   [5] Ibid., ff. 58ᵛ–60ʳ.

good cargoes. However because they expected to find here about 3,000 cantars of their fruit,[1] they did not want to load other cargo at Barcelona; then having arrived here we found not more than two-thirds of the fruit ready so that it has therefore been necessary to take that of others, and nevertheless at a freight rate for Flanders of 3½ *soldi* per cantar. I hope to load here all today as much as we can and as much as the galleys can carry if time allows, and then we shall be on our way if it pleases God. I think it would be advisable for us to call at Alicante and at Cartagena, because there there is some cochineal which would pay a good freight. If cargo is lacking we shall load that, so that you can rest assured that the galleys will be well and reasonably loaded and with freight takings equivalent to other voyages in this direction. . . .

Besides stating the fact that Carnesecchi's galley was by this time very heavily laden, the letter brings out two further points. First, that despite the goods already loaded *en route* Albizzi's galley was still only half full; secondly, that while at Barcelona Albizzi reckoned on loading at least a further 3,000 cantars (200 tons), so that at that juncture the galleys can only have been about one-third full. At Villajoyosa Albizzi did indeed get the rest of his cargo, loading for an entire day, and even loading a further 440 cantars after all his advisers had declared the galley full. In fact the galleys were now so heavily laden on leaving Villajoyosa that a further consignment of forty bales of cochineal waiting at Alicante, which would have brought in a high freight, had to be left behind.[2]

All this was achieved before the galleys even touched at Alicante, Malaga, and Cadiz, and it indicates quite clearly, first that the galleys had no difficulty getting full cargoes on their way north, and secondly that they left Porto Pisano no more than one-quarter full and probably less.

By the time the galleys reached Southampton very little of this great cargo remained; in fact we know that Paolo Morelli, the Florentine resident factor in Southampton, unloaded:[3]

22 bales dates	2 boxes preserved fruit
33 bales aniseed	98 small baskets raisins
6 bales cochineal	9 barrels sweetmeats
9 barrels oil	4 cases silk cloth

In addition Gregorio Cataneo unloaded two bales of cochineal, Luca of Ancona four barrels of oil, and Antonio di 'Lorente' eight

---

[1] Presumably raisins, dates, etc., rather than fresh fruit.
[2] Albizzi Diary, f. 61ʳ.   [3] Studer, *Port Books*, p. 108.

quarters of figs. This small relic of the cargo could not have equalled more than 20 tons, thus equating closely with the minute cargoes observed by Watson. In fact the Albizzi galleys are the only ones of which we have any considerable record of the total north-bound cargo, and this data entirely confirms the theory that the bulk of the cargoes were unloaded in Sluys, and furthermore suggests that there is no reason to suppose that the galleys had any difficulty in getting full cargoes for the journey northwards.

As the English customs accounts throw very little light on the size and value of the north-bound cargoes of the Florentine galleys due to the fact that so little of these cargoes ever got to England, I shall not examine them in detail here. The picture is already quite clear and details of a number of the voyages have already been published in other places.[1] The one major change in the pattern came in the early 1460's with the opening of the Tolfa alum mines, when the Florentine galleys began to bring large cargoes of alum to northern waters, and rather more of this got to England than had been the case with earlier cargoes. The 1466-7 galleys carried nearly 200 tons of alum destined for England, and did not go to Sluys at all.[2] The Medici galley in 1470 loaded 300 tons of alum for England although the English customs accounts indicate that only 100 tons were unloaded in Southampton.[3] The same galley was also carrying a large cargo of alum when it was captured in 1473,[1] and Popoleschi's galley at the same time unloaded 250

---

[1] Watson, 'Structure of the Florentine Galley Trade', pp. 335–47, for the voyages of 1438–9, 1442–3, 1443–4, 1447–8, and 1463–4; Quinn and Ruddock, *Port Books*, i. pp. 60–61 and 96–99 for 1469–70 Medici voyage, and ii, p. xii for 1463–4 voyage and pp. 129–36 for 1477–8. Watson devotes a good deal of space to analysing these remnants of cargo, arriving at conclusions regarding the ownerships of the goods involved which he then, by implication at least, applies to the other nine-tenths of the cargoes about which we know in fact nothing. For instance, the fact that 53 per cent. of the total value of the cargo unloaded in England by the 1444 galleys was Catalan investment is a significant point; but one must at the same time remember that only about 20 tons out of a total cargo of over 200 tons has been analysed, and the proportion of Catalan investment in the whole cargo could be completely different. Similarly to assess 'the investment of Florentine merchants in the cargoes of their own galleys going to England' as 'only one-third of the investment made by other merchants and only one-quarter of the *total cargo value*', on the basis of the last tenth of the cargoes after the remainder had been unloaded 50 miles away on the European market, is rather misleading.

[2] ASR, Camerale III, Tolfa 2378, *Allumiere*, f. 14; MAP XII, 312.

[3] Quinn and Ruddock, *Port Books*, i, pp. 60–61 and 96–99.

[4] De Roover, 'Balance commerciale', pp. 381–2. The value of the cargo of this single galley which was destined for England was 37,500 florins.

bales of alum in Southampton.[1] These are the recorded figures and they take no account of the other galley fleets which are known to have carried alum and may have unloaded some in England.[2] This indicates a considerable alteration in the pattern of trade of the galleys in the North, with, at least on one occasion, Flanders left out altogether.

There must also have been an even more marked change in the pattern of trade along the first part of the voyage in the western Mediterranean. With the galleys loaded with alum from Civita-vecchia there would have been little space for the commodities of Provence and Catalonia. What effect this may have had on the delicate balance of Florentine international commercial and exchange transactions is rather beyond the scope of this study. However, it is quite possible that this simplification of operations was an ultimate disadvantage in that, once the Catalonia–England trade was relinquished and all hopes concentrated on alum, Florentine galley trade in the West was very susceptible to fluctuations in the supply of alum. If for some reason the supply of alum was not forthcoming, the Florentine galleys would be left without the bulk of their north-bound cargoes and it would take some time to rebuild the system of a wide-flung circle of markets round the western Mediterranean. The fact that in 1476 the Medici temporarily lost the Tolfa alum contract, and therefore the alum supply was cut off for some years, may have been a factor in disrupting the Florentine trade system and in the suspension of the galleys.[3]

So far it is only the north-bound cargoes of the Flanders and England galleys which have been discussed. Now we must turn to the return cargoes about which there is also a good deal of information available. Here in the return cargoes from England lay one of

[1] Quinn and Ruddock, op. cit. ii, pp. 220-1.

[2] Between 1462 and 1478 at least 7,075 tons of alum were exported from Civita-vecchia to the West beyond the straits of Gibraltar. Of this 4,504 tons went to Flanders, 1,531 tons to England, and 1,034 tons to uncertain destinations (Delumeau, *L'Alun de Rome*, pp. 214-15). In fact these figures are almost certainly too low as Delumeau takes no account of the alum carried by the 1463 and 1464-5 fleets. He quotes a figure of 9,183 cantars exported to Flanders in or before 1466 (op. cit., p. 34) but this was accounted for in one shipload in 1466 (ASR, Camerale III, Tolfa 2378, *Allumiere*, f. 14). Delumeau himself agrees that a considerable quantity of Medici alum is unaccounted for in his lists.

[3] For a discussion of the causes and effects of the rift between Florence and the Papacy, and the loss of the alum contract, see Delumeau, op. cit., pp. 88-96. It is significant that the 1477 galley fleet to England carried practically no alum.

the prime functions of the galleys, the maintenance of the supply of wool to the Florentine wool industry. The days when Flemish cloths were of value to the Calimala guild had largely passed; there was little now that Flanders could offer which could attract the Florentine merchants whose whole upbringing and training was centred on wool. English cloths on the other hand were sought after not for finishing in Florence, but because they enjoyed a growing popularity throughout the Mediterranean, and served to clothe the Tuscans and sell to everybody else.[1] The other main constituents of these return cargoes were metals, mainly lead and tin, which served as ballast and were also sought after in the Mediterranean markets. Having loaded their cargoes in England the galleys made for home as quickly as possible. Small quantities were unloaded in southern Spanish ports where stops had to be made for provisions, and the space was filled with wool, silk, and cochineal of which Florence could never have enough.

The Flanders fleet which returned in 1426 was said to have brought back 160,000 florins' worth of cargo in its three galleys,[2] but the first returning fleet of Florentine galleys of which we have a good idea of the cargo was that of Albizzi. The accounts given by Albizzi in his diary and by the English customs are very closely in agreement as to this cargo, i.e. :[3]

1,026 pokes wool (Albizzi—1,028)
63 large bales cloth, containing 670 Guildford cloths and 630 others

130 pieces tin ⎫
120 pieces lead ⎭ (Albizzi quotes 281 pieces in all weighing 160,000 lbs.)

7 beds ⎫
5 pieces worsted ⎬ (Albizzi computes the miscellaneous items at
5 dozen hairy caps ⎭ 17 large bales)

Albizzi also adds six large bales of cloth which were loaded by Genoese merchants for Cadiz and Malaga, and twenty-four large bales of goods from Flanders. He further reports that the galleys were thus fully laden and he expected the return freights to amount to about 10,000 florins.

---

[1] De Roover, 'Balance commerciale', p. 380, describes the Mediterranean market for northern cloths as having collapsed at the end of the fourteenth century, but although this applied to Flemish cloth, the figures give the impression that there was a considerable and growing market for English cloth.

[2] Sapori, 'Primi viaggi', p. 82.

[3] Albizzi Diary, f. 106ʳ, and Studer, *Port Books*, pp. 108–9.

In 1439 the galleys brought back :[1]

1,283 pokes wool	3,323 lbs. tin vessels
873 cloths	some woolfells
30 fothers lead	

This is slightly smaller cargo but does not take account of goods loaded in Flanders. In both these cases the vast bulk of the goods were owned by Florentines; but in 1443 there were signs of growing English interest in loading wool, in this case to the extent of 400 pokes. The cargo recorded in the English customs was :[2]

1,557 pokes wool	8 fothers lead
1,144½ cloths	1,034 lbs. tin vessels
61 pieces tin	36 calf-hides

For the galleys which returned in 1444 we are fortunate in having two records; that of the English customs account and also the cargo list sent by Giovenco della Stufa to the Medici on his arrival in Porto Pisano.[3] The comparison is an interesting one not only because it illustrates how little margin of error there seems to have been in English customs accounting, but also because we get an idea of the whole cargo and not just that part loaded in England.

KR Customs	*Cargo list*
1,389 pokes wool	1,399 pokes wool
1,190 cloths	26 large bales and
	52 small bales cloth
20 pieces tin	20 pieces tin
1,910 lbs. tin vessels	11 baskets worked tin
1,000 brooches	5 *tonelli* ⎫
Hides, fells, tallow, cheese	3 cases ⎬ metal utensils
	1 *cresta* ⎪
	1 bale ⎭
	62 pieces lead
	1 bale hats ⎫
	3 basket cloth ⎬ loaded in
	5 bales Arras cloths ⎬ Flanders
	2 bales feathers ⎭

---

[1] PRO, KR Customs, 141/25, ff. 25ʳ–27ʳ and 67ʳ–69ʳ, and Watson, op. cit. ii, p. 343.

[2] PRO, KR Customs, 141/23, ff. 32ᵛ–35ʳ and 41ᵛ–43ʳ, and Watson, op. cit. ii, p. 341.

[3] MAP VII, f. 445, and Watson, op. cit. ii, pp. 338–9. See also N. S. B. Gras, *The Early English Customs System*, Cambridge (Mass.), 1918, pp. 642–8. Giovenco della Stufa was at one time a Medici factor and may still have been in their employ, which would account for his sending a copy of the cargo list to the Medici.

200 hides	
32 bales cochineal	Loaded in
48 bundles Spanish silk	Spain
46 bales wax	

How room was made for this Spanish cargo is not clear; it would have been unusual for the galleys to leave England with space to spare, yet there is no record of anything unloaded in Spain. Another curious feature is the lead, which must have been loaded in England and yet seems to have escaped the eye of the customs officials. This may not have been the only time that large quantities of metals used as ballast were missed in the customs accounts, and this may account for one or two of the smaller cargoes recorded in these accounts.

The 1448 cargoes showed a marked drop in the amount of wool loaded, but it has already been noted that these galleys may well have had to cut short their stay in Southampton in order to hurry home. The cargo was:[1]

681 pokes wool	9 fothers and 2,289 lbs. lead
2,021 cloths	950 lbs. tin vessels
28 pieces and 2,000 lbs. tin	2,738 lamb-skins

In fact the total value of the cargo was not much below usual as the increase in the number of cloths loaded offset the loss in wool, cloth having a considerably greater value for weight. The value was assessed by the monk Pietriboni to have been 100,000 florins, and Sapori comparing this with the 160,000 florins worth brought back by the 1425/6 galleys, sees definite evidence of an immediate decline in the trade of the galleys.[2] But the fleet in 1448 consisted of only two galleys and not three as in 1425/6, and in addition 1448 was recognized to be a bad year.

Incomplete reports of the cargoes of the next two fleets are recorded in the Southampton port books. The 1455/6 galleys loaded 1160 pokes of wool and 1607 cloths, and those of 1459/60 at least 907 pokes and 908 cloths.[3] On the other hand the two galleys which returned in 1464 brought no wool due to the temporary export ban, and as cloths also were limited, the value of the cargo fell considerably:[4]

---

[1] PRO, KR Customs, 141/29, ff. 36ᵛ–40ʳ and 59ʳ–61ʳ, and Watson, 'Structure of the Florentine Galley Trade', ii, p. 345.   [2] Sapori, 'Primi viaggi', p. 85.

[3] SPCB 1455–56, ff. 39ʳ–43ᵛ and 1459–60, ff. 1–2.

[4] Quinn and Ruddock, *Port Books*, ii, pp. 210–11, and Watson, op. cit., p. 347.

843 cloths	3,500 lamb-skins
36 fothers lead	240 calf-skins
20 pieces tin	

By the autumn 1465, before the three-year ban on the export of wools by aliens was over, Gherardo Canigiani, the Medici manager in London, was able to report that good cargoes of wool awaited the next galley fleet.[1] When the galleys arrived in England in February 1466 they loaded:[2]

2,253 pokes wool	200 baskets lead
84 large bales cloth	26 baskets tin
30 bales metal utensils	20 crates worked tin
26 bales feathers	

In addition they loaded in Spain:

72 bundles Spanish silk	583 oxhides
2 bales cochineal	4 bales tanned calf-skins
26 large bales wax	

They also brought 40,000 ducats worth of gold and 15,000 ducats worth of miscellaneous merchandise on the deck. This was the largest recorded cargo ever brought back by the Florentine galleys from the north, but it was, of course, a three-galley fleet.[3] However, the value of the English cargo alone was over £13,000 or about 80,000 ducats. The two following fleets were not so successful although their cargoes were well in line with those of the earlier part of the century. The galleys which returned in 1467 brought:[4]

	From Spain
608 pokes wool	53 sacks Spanish wool
109 large bales cloth	33 bales cochineal
32 small bundles cloth	4 bundles silk
1 bale tanned calf-skin	3 bales serge
24 barrels tin vessels	1 sack Moroccan lace
31 baskets tin	1,263 large Spanish hides
36 baskets lead	12 slaves [*teste*]

The fact that forty bales of goods were unloaded in Cadiz and Malaga, while ninety bales plus an uncertain number of bales of

---

[1] MAP XVI, 182 (21 Aug. 1465).

[2] Consoli del Mare VII, f. 65ᵛ, and Grunzweig, 'Consulat', p. 95.

[3] Portinari also described this as the best cargo ever loaded by the galleys (MAP XII, 393).

[4] Consoli del Mare VII, f. 67ʳ, and Grunzweig, 'Consulat', p. 96.

hides were loaded in Spain, indicates that the galleys were not full when they left England. This was a very different story from Albizzi's day, although it had certainly happened at other times, particularly times of crisis. When the accounts of this voyage were audited, it was reckoned that the value of the cargo was 58,836 florins of which more than half was credited to two owners, Agnolo Tani and Jacopo Paganelli.[1] This was more than twice the value of the cargoes brought from the Levant in the same period.

The next year brought a rather better cargo :[2]

1,273 pokes wool	*From Spain*
67 large bales English cloth	4 casks mercury
40 small bales English cloth	2 bales *gioma*
23 bales spices	4 large bales wax
7 bales feathers	4 bales serge
416 baskets lead	54 bales Spanish cochineal
40 barrels tin vessels	10,000 ducats worth of gold
2 cases books	

Certainly this cargo, which was a good average, gives little impression of impending crisis. Furthermore, Francesco Sermattei with his Medici galley in 1470 picked up a useful cargo in Southampton :[3]

465 pokes wool	2 pipes tallow
2,173 English cloths	50 dozen lined caps
22 kerseys	800 lamb-skins
43 pieces worsted	7 barrels tin vessels
372 pieces lead (124 fothers)	

The last communal galley fleet also left a record of its English cargo in the customs accounts. The year was 1478 and this was the first communal fleet that had sailed for some years. Its cargo was :[4]

582 pokes wool	30 barrels tins
579 cloths	9 barrels tin vessels
46 pieces kersey	9,432 calf-skins
109 pieces lead	104 tanned hides

The striking feature of this list is the quite unprecedented quantity

---

[1] Consoli del Mare VII, f. 71^{r-v} (22 May 1467), and Grunzweig, 'Consulat', pp. 97–99. Agnolo Tani was the lifelong employee of the Medici who was at this time trying to reorganize the affairs of the Medici branch in London.

[2] Consoli del Mare VII, f. 74^v, and Grunzweig, 'Consulat', pp. 99–100.

[3] Quinn and Ruddock, *Port Books*, i, pp. 98–99.

[4] Ibid., ii, pp. 129–36,

of hides which appear. Previously hides had figured at the very bottom of the cargo lists both in terms of value and bulk; in 1439 none had been loaded, in 1443 three-dozen valued at 10*s.*; in 1444, £13. 16*s.* 8*d.* worh of hides, fells, cheese, and tallow; in 1448, 2,738 lambskins valued at £47. 6*s.* 8*d.*, and in 1464, 3,500 lambskins and 240 calfskins valued at £26. 13*s.* 4*d.* in all. In 1478, 786 dozen calfskins and some tanned hide were loaded with an approximate value of £131. The value of this part of the cargo was still negligible, but the bulk must have been at least a third of the total cargo of the two galleys. At the same time the amount of wool and cloths loaded had fallen dramatically and hence the need to fill the holds with hides which although useful to Florence were no substitute for the wool. If this was to be the trade trend it is not surprising that the Florentines felt that it was hardly worth while to send galleys all the way to England for cargoes largely made up of hides.

Whether the poor rewards for the 1478 fleet were the result of a long disruption in the rhythm of the galleys' sailings, and whether persistence might have succeeded in recovering the vital wool cargoes is a debatable matter. The English wool imports into Pisa in the summer of 1478 had been the highest on record in the Pisan customs and this might have accounted for a temporary dearth at the end of the year.[1] On the other hand, it also indicated that the trade had become reorganized in the temporary absence of the Florentine galleys. The fact that the wool was still coming in large quantities without the help of the galleys, and that direct English contacts with the Mediterranean were increasing yearly must, together with the comparative failure of the 1478 galleys, have made up conclusive arguments for suspending the galleys.

[1] ASP, Comune B, n. 47, *passim.* The total for the six months was in fact 527,855 lb., a figure rather more than double that for any other recorded six-month period.

6

CONCLUSION

THE pattern which has emerged in the history of the Florentine galleys is a very fluctuating one. Periods of intense activity were followed by lulls, enthusiasm by disinterest. Many of these fluctuations are easily explained by the rapid changes in Florentine internal and external affairs, but it is also in the story of the galleys themselves that we must seek the economic advantages which stimulated the periods of activity, and the economic and practical difficulties which seemed overwhelming during the periods of crisis.

There were three periods of activity and expansion in the history of the galleys; the opening years of the 1420's, the middle period of 1436–47, and a vigorous revival in the 1460's. The opening years were naturally a period of expansion; new routes were being opened up, trade concessions won, galleys built amidst considerable public interest and enthusiasm. Then came the Lucchese war and the internal political crisis involved in the overthrow of the oligarchy and the establishment of the Medici régime. One of the first moves of the latter was the setting up of the Magona Vacchia and a new impulse towards trade expansion. By the 1440's the galleys had settled into a rhythmic pattern which was only broken by the Aragonese wars. The final period of growth got under way shortly after the Peace of Lodi; the late 1450's were difficult years for the Medici and it was not until 1458 with the establishment of the Balia that Medici government was once more secure and able to advance. Then came the most determined effort of all to stimulate Florentine trade through the medium of the communal galleys; galley regulations were revised, the freight tariffs were replanned to encourage merchants to use the galleys, subsidies were offered to the conductors, the appointment of officers was more tightly controlled, and the lessons to be learnt from each voyage were studied minutely in *viva voce* examinations of the returned captains and patrons. Many of the stimulants offered were purely artificial and it is improbable that they could have succeeded in turning the galley system into an economically self-sufficient operation, but economic self-sufficiency was not the aim of the galleys. By the 1460's economic conditions were far more difficult than they had been in the 1420's for a state-inspired venture of this type. Competition for trade, particularly from new seafaring nations, was increasing annually; commercial conditions for the Italians both in England and in the eastern Mediterranean were deteriorating, and piracy seemed to be on the increase. Despite all this the galley system became for a few years a really active enterprise almost approaching in scope that of Venice. As many as ten magnificently equipped galleys flying the Florentine lilies were leaving Porto Pisano each year. But it could not last; once again wars were distracting Florence and diverting her wealth. The 1470 reform of the *Monte* postponed payments on *Monte* credits to the Sea Consuls amongst others, and the whole decade of the 1470's was one of growing financial difficulties for Florence.[1] The control of virtually unlimited supplies of alum, which had done much to stimulate the activity of the galleys in the 1460's, was lost, and the final blow came with the Pazzi conspiracy and the resulting war with Naples and the Papacy.

However, although it is easy to explain the fluctuations of the galley system in terms of Florence's current international and internal problems, these cannot be the whole story nor indeed the most significant part of it. The most urgent reason for the final decline of the galleys in the 1470's and their abandonment in 1480 was that they had outlived their usefulness. It cannot really be said that they had failed, because it had probably never been feasible for them to succeed as a profit-making enterprise or even a self-supporting one. The system had been created to serve a specific purpose and this periodically it had succeeded in doing; by 1480 there was no longer a need for it.

The purpose which the Florentine galleys had served was to provide an independent and reliable vehicle for the raw materials and products of Florentine industry. The wool and silk industries were the mainstays of the Florentine economy; to provide an independent supply of wool, silk, and dyes and to distribute the cloths were the functions of the galleys. They were not required to

---

[1] Balìe 31, ff. 79ᵛ–80ʳ (29 Jan. 1472). See also L. F. Marks, 'The Financial Oligarchy in Florence under Lorenzo', *Italian Renaissance Studies* (ed. E. F. Jacob), London, 1960.

bring back rich cargoes of spices to put money into the pockets
of the merchants; they were not called upon to import the food
necessary to feed the population of Florence; they were not even
expected to make great trading profits for the conductors who ran
them. Naturally incidental trading opportunities were taken when
the main functions of the galleys were not at stake. An elaborate
system of coastal trading was worked out to provide outward
cargoes for the wool galleys and return cargoes for the cloth
galleys. But the outward cargoes of the wool galleys were on the
whole not from Florence, nor were they luxury articles brought
from the East by the cloth galleys. They were picked up incidentally
in order to make best use of shipping which had to follow that
route anyway, and in order to make the enterprise more attractive
and more profitable to the private conductors who were expected
to bear a large share of the costs. Similarly much of the return
cargoes of the cloth galleys was not destined for Florence; some
was unloaded in Sicily, some went through to Catalonia. Florence
was not interested in establishing a market in spices; she was
interested as far as the eastern Mediterranean was concerned in
selling cloth. Whereas the wool galleys came straight back with
their cargoes of wool, putting into as few ports as possible, the
cloth galleys stopped wherever there was a market for Florentine
cloth; e.g. Naples, Salerno, and Sicily as well as the Levant. Thus
although the Catalonia voyage was recognized to be the most
profitable one in normal economic terms, it was the Flanders and
Levant galleys which were always the more important. But even
Catalonia provided wool, and Sicily and Barbary were markets for
cloths, so these voyages were also justified in Florentine terms.
When it was proposed to send a galley to Ragusa it was specifically
stated that it was primarily to take and sell cloth; it did not matter
what it did on the return run.[1]

Given these specific functions of the galleys, it would be natural
to expect that, if these functions ceased to be so important or were
fulfilled by other means, then the need for the galleys would pass.
By the 1470's it was not just the Venetians and the Genoese who
were carrying the trade between the northern seas and the Mediter-

---

[1] It is an indication of the extent to which cloth exports were deliberately chan-
nelled eastwards that the freight charge on a cloth sent to the Levant was $\frac{1}{2}$–1 florin,
while to England it was 2–2$\frac{1}{4}$ florins (Consoli del Mare IV, 4, *Capitoli degli
scrivani*).

ranean. Florence needed no longer to depend for wool supplies on the fleets of possible economic rivals and political enemies, if her own galleys were abandoned. French, Neapolitan, Basque, Catalan, and even English shipping were now available for hire, and were bringing in the wool on better commercial terms than the costly communal galleys could manage. At the same time the flow of cloths to the East was being directed more and more along the overland routes across the Balkans. Indeed the fact that this trade was not in the least affected by the suspension of the galleys is amply proved by the intense and apparently growing activity of the Florentine colony in Pera in the last years of the century.

It would probably be true to say that the Florentines had never envisaged that the galleys would become a profitmaking enterprise from the point of view of the State; the Venetians were still making considerable grants to the Arsenal although their galley system had been in operation for over a century and was generally considered a success. The individual conductors were naturally attracted by immediate profits, but the Sea Consuls and the Councils who directed them were concerned with the Florentine economy as a whole. But nevertheless the time was passing when a rigidly controlled state galley system of this type could serve the interests both of individual merchants and of the State. Many merchants were by the fifteenth century wealthy enough and sufficiently organized to bear the capital expenses of international maritime trade themselves, either as individuals or in partnerships. What real assistance could the State offer in exchange for the restrictions that it imposed on commercial freedom? It could organize convoys for greater protection; but the Florentines never sent more than three galleys together, unlike the Venetian *mude* which sometimes numbered ten or twelve ships. It could lend state support and prestige in the negotiations for trade concessions. This was useful at first, but it was an assistance which was quickly forgotten. It could offer continuity of administrative experience in the direction of the galleys, but this was largely discounted by the administrative inefficiency and peculation so often inherent in government departments. Furthermore, one of the defects of the whole Florentine administration was that continuity was discouraged; the constant changes in the Sea Consuls resulted in the deliberate wastage of any relevant administrative experience. So we come back to the main factor of relieving the merchants of heavy capital outlay; but the merchants were increasingly reluctant to accept this assistance when it meant losing much of their freedom of action, and when other alternatives were readily available. Furthermore, for the individual merchant using the galleys meant paying what was often an unduly high freight rate. For the bulk of goods which were carried on the galleys the freight rates were uneconomic.[1] But when in 1461 many of the rates were reduced to give added encouragement to the merchants, it was the turn of the conductors to suffer. They were unable to make any profit out of running the galleys without government subsidies, and the Florentine government was only prepared to pay subsidies as long as it felt that the galleys were important and as long as economic conditions held out some hope that subsidies would be only a temporary arrangement. But this situation did not last, the subsidies were withdrawn and the conductors gradually lost interest.

Finance was in fact a crucial factor in the history of the galleys; it was not only a question of providing subsidies when necessary, but of building and equipping sufficient galleys to satisfy the needs of the merchants, to keep up the size of the fleets so that safety was ensured, and generally to expand the scope of the system. But once again the divergence of aim between the government and the merchants was apparent. As far as the government was concerned the galleys were to be vehicles for wool and cloth, and to fulfil these functions comparatively few galleys were needed. However, many of the merchants were not particularly interested in wool and cloth and they resented the obligation to use the expensive and strictly routed galleys for the shipment of other goods. Had there been cotton and spice fleets to the East with interlocking time-tables to facilitate the shipment of the goods straight to northern Europe; had there been galleys available for local coastal traffic; had the fleets been four or more galleys with escorts, so that delays as a result of pirate activity could be avoided; then the merchants would have been more enthusiastic. The Venetians had all these refinements and yet even their galleys were encountering difficulties in the fifteenth century. As it was, the Florentine Sea Consuls were constantly short of money and could not afford to expand the

---

[1] On the Levant galleys the return freight charge for spices was $1\frac{1}{2}$ florins per cwt., while for cotton it was $1\frac{1}{4}$ florins. This difference bore little relationship to the difference in value.

system; voyages were delayed because no galleys were available until another voyage had been completed; they were delayed or even abandoned because there was no money to refit the galleys. For the merchants these delays meant financial losses and they resented being subject to these through no fault of their own.

In fact one of the secrets of success for a shipping system was and is a dependable rhythm of sailing; this the Florentines only rarely achieved due partly to events beyond their control such as the uncertain political state of Italy, but largely to circumstances which could perhaps have been controlled such as meagre financing, poor administration, and the piracy problem. Albizzi had some harsh things to say about the administration of the galleys and the state of the equipment which he had been given;[1] but much of the trouble lay with the Florentine system of constantly rotating officials. In some departments of the administration such as the government of the subject towns, this rotation was not a great disadvantage in that most of the Florentine upper class had this type of administrative experience. But the direction of a shipping line was an altogether different matter, and although there were a number of junior posts connected with the system both on the galleys and as *provveditori* in Pisa which could serve as apprenticeships for the Sea Consulate, the opportunities were too limited for it to be possible for more than a few of the Sea Consuls to have had any previous experience of the problems of the galley enterprise. Admittedly the Consuls relied a good deal on the advice of selected and experienced Florentine merchants in their administration of the system, but here again the problem arose of the difference between the merchant and the government point of view. Albizzi found the merchants very reluctant to authorize the hiring of additional marines to protect his galleys, on the grounds that they were already paying insurance and were not worried if the galleys were lost. The government, however, was not only loath to risk the capital value of the galleys themselves, but also the wool cargoes which had a value for the Florentine economy quite apart from the actual cash value of the wool.

The other factor which threatened and disrupted the rhythm of galley sailings was the pirate menace. Certainly the activities of the pirates seemed to increase in the fifteenth century, and to assess the causes of this would require a detailed study of its own.

[1] Albizzi Diary, ff. 57ʳ and 84ʳ.

It has been argued that an increase in trade and in shipping leads automatically to an increase in piracy; the more ships there are about the greater the temptation to turn to piracy. This may be true to a certain extent but it implies no corresponding increase in shipping protection methods. It has also been argued that the fall of Constantinople led to an increasing rift between Moslem and Christian, and that at the same time there was general decline in moral standards and in central authority within the Moslem states. Both these factors led to a rapid increase in the activities of Moslem pirates.[1] Again this may to a certain extent be true but most of the recorded acts and threats of piracy which affected the Florentine galleys were Christian in origin. The famous pirates of the fifteenth century, Coulon, Gattilusio, Suordinave, etc., were not Barbary pirates but European sea *condottieri* created by the same political and economic circumstances which gave birth to their better known land counterparts. To deal with such threats fleets had to be sufficiently powerful to command respect and inviolability; sea *condottieri* were no more anxious to risk their limited strength in a full-scale battle than were those on land. But the Florentines could never afford to send more than three galleys in a fleet, and single galleys and often pairs of galleys were sometimes held up for months, or even cancelled altogether, if pirates were reported to be active.

Thus, although by 1480 the galleys had outlived their usefulness, the system might have continued, had it been popular and almost self-supporting. But the system was too limited in scope, too inflexible in its regulations, and at the same time too erratic in its schedules to attract the support and confidence of the merchants. The Sea Consuls and the Florentine government were not entirely to blame for this although more money invested and better administration would have helped. But general political and economic conditions were against them and even the better organized and more experienced Venetians were undergoing difficulties by the end of the fifteenth century. They also had had to resort to offering subsidies to conductors.[2] Their galley schedules although less erratic than those of Florence show many of the same trends. The years 1431–4 were crisis years with an almost complete suspension of sailings in 1432; 1448–1450 saw a breakdown of

---

[1] E. Marengo, 'Genova e Tunisi, 1388–1505', *ASLSP*, xxxii, 1901, p. 71.
[2] Luzzatto, *Storia economica di Venezia*, pp. 75–76.

schedules in the western Mediterranean, and during the 1450's there were frequent breaks in the rhythm of sailings to England and Flanders. The fall of Constantinople in 1453 excluded the Venetian galleys from this area for over twenty-five years. By the end of the century the Aiguesmortes galleys had disappeared and the sailings of the Flanders galleys had become very erratic.[1] Finally in 1514 the galleys lost their monopoly of the spice trade and the end of their usefulness as merchant vessels was in sight.[2] Improvements in design and in rig had made the sailing-ships as easy to handle as the galleys, while improvements in fighting techniques and armament had made them almost as defensible.

The Florentines were not alone in their difficulties, and it is interesting to note that the periods of crisis and suspension of sailings, e.g. the early 1430's and 1448–55, also left their mark on the activities of the Venetian galleys. These were moments of international crisis and confusion which had their effect on international trade as a whole; they were not the result of inherent defects in the Florentine galley system or the administration of it. It was not a particular failure of the Florentines that they failed to dispatch fleets during these two periods. It is true that these periods of crisis affected the Florentine system more than the Venetian, but this is hardly surprising, bearing in mind the relative im-maturity of the former.

The whole galley enterprise had in fact rendered valuable service to Florence. It had played a major part in revitalizing the flagging wool industry and launching the new silk industry. It had won for Florence commercial and to a certain extent political prestige in all parts of Europe and the Levant. It had provided a fund of experience and maritime tradition to which the names of Amerigo Vespucci and Giovanni da Verazzano are abundant testimony, and which in the next century was to produce the more famous mari-time enterprises of the Grand Dukes and the Knights of San Stefano, and was to make Florentine galleys admired throughout Italy for their beauty and design. It need no longer surprise us that two of the leading figures in the quest for the New World were Florentines. At least three members of the Da Verazzano family had held responsible positions on the galleys, and another had served

[1] Tenenti and Vivanti, 'Les galères marchandes vénitiennes', *passim*.
[2] Lane, 'La marine marchande et le trafic maritime de Venise', p. 9.

as Sea Consul.[1] Frosino di Cecco da Verazzano had been one of the first Captains of the galleys in the 1420's. The Vespucci family had played an even more significant part in the history of the galleys. No less than six galley fleets had included a Vespucci as either Captain or patron; and besides the actual sailors of the family, Giuliano di Lapo Vespucci served twice as Sea Consul in the 1440's. Giovanni da Verazzano was far too young to have served in the communal galleys but Amerigo Vespucci might have occupied one of the junior posts in the galley fleets open to young men of good family. Certainly the evidence for the growth of family maritime traditions in both cases in the fifteenth century is now clear.

Finally perhaps it is not too much to imagine that memories of the events of the fifteenth century, of the capture of the Genoese flagship at Rapallo by Raimondo Mannelli, of the splendid welcomes accorded to Florentine Captains from Constantinople to Southampton, helped to inspire the Knights of San Stefano, and the twelve Florentine galleys which fought under the papal banners at Lepanto.

---

[1] Francesco di Donato da Verazzano was commissary on a Catalonia galley in 1447 (Tratte 80, f. 338) and Niccolò di Amerigo da Verazzano was Sea Consul in 1435.

APPENDIX A

Details of the Florentine Galley Fleets during the Fifteenth Century

Date	Details of fleet and known ports of call	Officers	Sources
1422			
20 Apr.	One long galley sailed for trials off Corsica	*Patron:* Zenobio Capponi	Sapori, 'Primi viaggi', p. 76
12 July	Two long galleys sailed for Alexandria; returned 12 Oct. Rhodes (13 Aug.) Alexandria (19 Aug.)	*Patrons:* Giuliano di Turpia Bindo di Bartolomeo delle Brache *Ambassadors:* Carlo di Francesco Federighi Felice di Michele Brancacci (outward voyage only)	Consulte 45, ff. 28ʳ-29ᵛ Sapori, op. cit., pp. 76-77 Brancacci, 'Diario' (For other sources see above, pp. 35-37)
4 Sept.	Two great galleys sailed for Alexandria: returned 11 Feb. 1423 Alexandria (18 Oct.) Messina (29 Dec.)	*Captain:* Piero di Luigi Guicciardini *Patrons:* Michele di Naddo Pagnini Francesco d'Arnaldo Mannelli (the above mentioned ambassadors returned with these galleys)	Sapori, op. cit., pp. 78, 79 and 91 Brancacci, 'Diario'
1423 26 July	Two great galleys sailed for Alexandria; returned 28 Nov.	*Patron:* Luca di Maso degli Albizzi	Sapori, op. cit., p. 81
1423-4	One great galley sailed for trials to Aiguesmortes; returned 1 Feb. 1424		Sapori, op. cit., p. 81
1424 8 Apr.	One long galley sailed for Catalonia; returned 1 June Port-de-Bouc (20 Apr.) Barcelona (25 Apr.) Tortosa (28 Apr.-10 May) Barcelona (12-27 May)	*Ambassador and patron:* Luca di Maso degli Albizzi	Sig. X, VIII, 5, II, *passim*

Date	Details of fleet and known ports of call	Officers	Sources
12 Apr.	Two great galleys sailed for Catalonia; returned 5 June Port-de-Bouc (20 Apr.) Aiguesmortes Valencia Barcelona (18–19 May) Collioure	*Captain:* Andrea di Niccolò Giugni *Conductors and patrons:* Luigi d'Antonio Covoni Piero d'Antonio Zampini	Sig. X, VIII, 5, II, *passim* Sapori, op. cit., p. 81
?	Two great galleys sailed for Alexandria; returned Jan 1425		Sapori, op. cit., p. 86
1425 6 May	Three great galleys sailed for Flanders and England; returned 25 Feb. 1426 Sluys (8 July) London (?–20 Oct.)	*Captain:* Salamone di Carlo degli Strozzi *Patrons:* Antonio di Lorenzo degli Albizzi Giovanni di Guccio Gucci Latino di Jacopo Pigli	Miss. I Canc. 30, f. 86^v PRO, KR Customs 76/13 PRO, KR Memoranda 209, recorda, Hilary, r. 4 Selfridge, *Letters*, n. 80 ——— Sapori, op. cit., p. 82 Morosini, *Chronique*, ii, pp. 302–3 Watson, 'Structure of Florentine Galley Trade', i, p. 1076
1425–6	Two great galleys joined Aragonese fleet in 1425, and one long galley in 1426	*Commissaries:* Luca di Maso degli Albizzi Matteo Castellani Veri Guadagni Averardo di Francesco de' Medici (Agnolo Acciaiuoli)	Albizzi Diary, f. 70^r. Sig. X, VIII, 5, II MAP I, 81 and VII, 83 ——— *Commissioni di Rinaldo*, ii, pp. 354–5, 377, and 381
1427 11 May	Two great galleys sailed for Flanders and England; returned *c.* 12 Mar. 1428 Sluys London (?–4 Nov.)	*Patrons:* Luigi di Buonaccorso Pitti (replaced by Jacopo Benizi at Sluys) Niccolò Corbinelli	PRO, KR Memoranda 209, recorda, Hilary, r. 4 ——— Cronica di Buonaccorso Pitti, pp. 253–4

Date	Voyage	Officers	References
1428 15 Nov.	Three great galleys sailed for Flanders and England Collioure Barcelona Sluys London (14 Jan.–25 Mar. 1429) Southampton (one galley) Barcelona (May 1429)	*Conductor:* Pinaccio Strozzi *Captain:* Frosino da Verazzano *Patrons:* Antonio Serragli Antonio degli Albizzi Filippo Guadagni	Provv. 120, f. 89[r] Consoli del Mare III, ff. 27[v]–28[r] Miss. I Canc. 32, f. 30[r] PRO, KR Customs 74/11 PRO, KR Memoranda 206, recorda, Michaelmas, r. 24 Del Treppo, op. cit. i, pp. 526, 532–3
1428–9	One great galley sailed for Catalonia	*Patrons:* Piero Zampini Jacopo Tedaldi	Provv. 120, f. 159[v] Müller, Documenti, p. 283
1429 ?	One great galley sailed for Catalonia Barcelona Valencia	*Patron:* Niccolò de' Mari[1]	Del Treppo, op. cit. i, p. 526, and ii, p. 73
14 Sept.	Two great galleys sailed for Flanders and England; returned 27 Mar, 1430 Southampton (7 Jan.–23 Feb.) For other details see Albizzi Diary	*Captain:* Luca di Maso degli Albizzi *Patrons:* Piero di Simone Vespucci Bernardo di Cristofano Carnesecchi	Albizzi Diary; PRO, KR Memoranda 209, recorda, Hilary, r. 4 SPCB 1429–30, ff. 68–69 Del Treppo, op. cit. i, p. 522 Studer, *Port Books*, pp. 108–9
?	One great galley prepared for voyage to Constantinople		Provv. 120, f. 159[v]
?	One great galley hired for voyages to Ragusa	*Conductor:* Domenico Dolfini	Müller, *Documenti*, p. 283 Provv. 120, f. 350[v]
1430			

[1] See above, p. 78.

Date	Details of fleet and known ports of call	Officers	Sources
1431 Aug.	Three galleys, two galliots, and one brigantine attached to Venetian fleet	*Captain:* Paolo di Vanni Rucellai *Patrons:* Raimondo d'Amaretto Mannelli, Jacopo (Papi) Tedaldi, Benedetto di Marco Strozzi *Patrons of galliots:* Guccio de' Medici, Gaddo da Livorno	See above, pp. 105–6, and MAP IV, 35, 245, and 248; MAP V, 20, 120, and 127
1432 ?	One long galley sent to Portovenere	*Patron:* Ludovico da Verazzano	MAP LXXXI, ff. 1–4
1433			
1434	One long galley sailed to pick up Eugenius IV Civitavecchia	*Patron and commissary:* Bartolomeo da Montegonzi	Cambi, *Istorie*, i, pp. 189–90; Rucellai, *Zibaldone*, p. 46; Guglielmotti, *Marina Pontificia*, ii, pp. 138–43
1435			
1436 Oct.	Two great galleys sailed for Flanders and England[1] Southampton	*Conductor:* Magona Vecchia *Captain:* Bernardo Ventura	Provv. 130, f. 77ᵛ Biscaro, 'Banco Filippo Borromei', p. 80; Heyd, *Commercio del Levante*, p. 866
?	One or more great galleys sailed for Constantinople		
1437 6 Aug.	One great galley sailed for Constantinople	*Conductor:* Magona Vecchia *Patron:* Francesco Mannelli	Provv. 128, f. 120ʳ; Responsive 7, f. 76; *Libro di conti di Badoer*, i, pp. 203 and 248

1 See above, p. 87, for discussion of the voyage to England and Flanders at this time.

Date	Sailing		Reference
1438 Oct.	Two great galleys sailed for Flanders and England Southampton (4 Jan; 7 Feb.–13 Apr. 1439)	*Conductor:* Magona Vecchia *Patrons:* Jacopo Tedaldi, Bartolomeo Capponi	Provv. 130, f. 77^v PRO, KR Customs 141/23 PRO, L'TR Enrolled Customs 19 SPCB 1438–9, ff. 52^r–53^v. Watson, op. cit. ii, pp. 340–1 Biscaro, op. cit, p. 80
1439 May	One great galley sailed for Catalonia and Sicily		Provv. 130, f. 77^v
Nov.	Two great galleys sailed for Catalonia Barcelona (5 Dec.) Valencia Barcelona (23 Dec.–20 Jan. 1440)	*Captain:* Francesco Tosinghi	ACA, Ancoratge 8, f. 10^r, and 8, ii, unp.
Dec.	Two great galleys sailed for Flanders and England		Provv. 130, ff. 192^v and 286^v Consoli del Mare III, f. 46
1440 Feb.	One great galley sailed for Catalonia Barcelona (5 Mar.–1 Apr.) Valencia Barcelona (6–8 Apr.)	*Patron:* Lorenzo Moro	ACA, Ancoratge 11, ii, unp. and 12, ii, unp.
Apr.	One great galley sailed for Catalonia Barcelona (25 Apr.–2 May)	*Patron:* Giovanni Ventura	ACA, Ancoratge 12, f. 11^v, and 12, ii, unp.
July	One great galley sailed for Catalonia Barcelona (31 July)	*Patron:* Giovanni Bandini Baroncelli	ACA, Ancoratge 15, f. 18
Oct.	Two great galleys sailed for Flanders and England	*Patrons:* Bartolomeo di Niccolò Martelli	Miss. II Canc. I, f. 9^r MAP LXXXIII, f. 178

Date	Details of fleet and known ports of call	Officers	Sources
1440 Oct.	Barcelona (5 Nov.) Valencia Sluys Southampton (?–13 June 1441)	Antonio Pazzi	MAP CXXXIV, 2, f. 246 PRO, LTR Enrolled Customs 19 ACA, Ancoratge 17, f. 2^v
?	One great galley sailed for Catalonia; returned 9 Dec.		Sig. X, VIII, 5, III, f. 416 Consoli del Mare IV, f. 1
1441 Mar.	One great galley sailed for Catalonia Barcelona (26 Mar.) Valencia Barcelona (3 Apr.)	*Patron*: Leonardo Mannelli	ACA, Ancoratge 21, f. 11^r and 22, f. 2^v
Oct./Nov.	Two great galleys sailed for Flanders and England Valencia Sluys Southampton (16 Feb.–19 Apr. 1442)	*Conductor*: Niccolò di Matteo Cerretani *Captain*: Benedetto Mannelli *Patrons*: Jacopo Tedaldi Giuliano di Niccolò Ridolfi	Miss. II Canc. 1, ff. 26^r and 29^{r-v} Consoli del Mare V, f. 33^v MAP V, 430 MAP CXXXIV, 2, f. 246 PRO, Accounts various Foreign merchants, 128/31, m. 28 PRO, LTR Enrolled Customs 19 ——— De Roover, *Medici Bank*, p. 145
1442 Mar./Apr.	One great galley sailed for Sicily and Catalonia Sicily Porto Pisano Barcelona (30 June) Majorca Barcelona (18 July)	*Patron*: Andrea di Trinca della Stufa	Provv. 132, f. 352^r Miss. II Canc. 1, f. 75^v ACA, Ancoratge 34 and 35, unp.
Sept./Oct.	Two great galleys sailed for Flanders and England	*Conductor*: Francesco di Nerone	Miss. II Canc. 1, f. 114^v Consoli del Mare IV, 3, f. 1

Sluys (5 Feb. 1443) Southampton (7 Mar.–20 Apr.)	*Captain:* Simone 'Venisa' *Patrons:* Bartolomeo di Niccolò Martelli Leonardo Mannelli	Consoli del Mare V, f. 42v MAP V, 431 and 435 PRO, KR Customs 141/25 PRO, Accounts various, Foreign merchants, 128/31, mm. 32 and 36
Oct.	One great galley sailed for Catalonia and Sicily Barcelona (16 Oct.) Majorca Barcelona (9 Nov.) Porto Pisano (Dec.) Sicily	*Conductor and patron:* Giovanni di Piero Bandini de' Baroncelli	Watson, 'Structure of the Florentine Galley Trade', ii, pp. 342–3 Ruddock, *Southampton*, p. 192 Miss. II Canc. 1, f. 146r Consoli del Mare V, f. 1r ACA, Ancoratge 38 and 39, unp.
1443 Apr.	Two great galleys sailed for Catalonia and Sicily on double voyage	*Conductor:* Andrea di Lotteringo della Stufa *Patrons:* Niccolò Cerretani Ludovico Gucci	Provv. 133, f. 251r Miss. II Canc. 1, ff. 161v and 178r Ibid. 2, f. 10r Consoli del Mare V, f. 2v
Nov.	Two great galleys sailed for Flanders and England; returned 4 June 1444 Aiguesmortes (20 Nov.) Cadiz (14 Dec.) Sluys (4 Jan. 1444) Southampton (16 Feb.–9 Apr.)	*Conductor:* Niccolò Buti *Patrons:* Giuliano di Niccolò Ridolfi Giovenco della Stufa	Miss. II Canc. 2, f. 31v Consoli del Mare III, f. 74r-v Ibid. V, ff. 35r-38v MAP V, 525 and 469 MAP VII, 445 MAP CXLVIII, 13 PRO, KR Customs 140/62 PRO, KR Memoranda 220, recorda, Easter, r. 10. <hr>Watson, op. cit. i, pp. 1077–9, and ii, pp. 336–9 Gras, *Early English Customs System*, pp. 642–5.

Date	Details of fleet and known ports of call	Officers	Sources
1443 Dec.	One great galley about to sail for Sicily	*Patron:* Antonio di Lorenzo della Stufa	Miss. II Canc. 2, f. 55ᵛ
1444 Mar.	One great galley about to sail for Catalonia	*Patron:* Leonardo Mannelli	Miss. II Canc. 2, ff. 67ᵛ and 71ʳ
?	One great galley sailed for Constantinople	*Patron:* Giovanni Tosinghi	Provv. 134, f. 164ʳ; Ammirato, *Famiglie nobili fiorentine*, pp. 71 and 74; Müller, *Documenti*, p. 284
May	One long galley sent to rescue galley of Giovanni Bandini	*Patron:* Giovanni di Simone Vespucci	Miss. II Canc. 2, ff. 93ᵛ and 102ʳ
Aug./Sept.	One great galley about to sail for Catalonia and Sicily		Miss. II Canc. 2, f. 108ᵛ
Oct./Nov.	Two great galleys sailed for Flanders and England; Sluys; Southampton	*Conductors:* Luca Firidolfi da Panzano, Niccolò Ridolfi; *Patron:* Orlandino Orlandini	Miss. I Canc. 36, ff. 56–57; Miss. II Canc. 2, ff. 104ʳ, 130ᵛ–131ʳ; Consoli del Mare III, f. 74ʳ⁻ᵛ; MAP CXLVIII, 13; C. Carnesecchi, 'Un fiorentino del secolo XV e le sue ricordanze domestiche', *ASI*, 5th ser., iv, 1889, p. 12
1445 12 June	Two great galleys sailed for Alexandria; returned 4 Apr. 1446; Naples (17 June); Palermo (21 June); Tunis (29 June–22 Aug.); Alexandria (17 Sept.–2 Dec.); Rhodes (7–9 Dec.); Candia (11–24 Dec.)	*Captain:* Giovenco della Stufa; *Patron:* Rosso Ridolfi	*Quaderuccio di Luigi Vettori, passim*; Provv. 136, f. 183ᵛ; Tratte 225 (*bis*) f. 39; Balle 26, ff. 53ʳ–54ʳ and 94ᵛ–95ᵛ; Miss. I Canc. 36, ff. 101–2; Consoli del Mare III, f. 71ʳ.

Date	Itinerary	Personnel	References
July	Syracuse (17–28 Jan. 1446) Tunis (25 Feb.–23 Mar.) Palermo (24–27 Mar.)		
	One great galley sailed for Sicily and Catalonia Sicily Porto Pisano (Sept.) Barcelona (16 Oct.) Valencia Barcelona (9 Nov.)	*Patron:* Giuliano di Niccolò Ridolfi	Provv. 136, f. 183ᵛ ACA, Ancoratge 44 and 45, unp.
Oct.	Two great galleys sailed for Flanders and England; returned 31 July 1446 Southampton	*Conductors:* Benintendi Pucci Niccolò Nasi *Captain:* Francesco di Cambi Orlandi	Provv. 136, f. 183ᵛ Tratte 225 (*bis*), f. 39 Tratte 67, f. 19 Miss. I Canc. 36, f. 137
1446 June–July M	One great galley sailed for Catalonia Majorca Barcelona (5 Aug.)	*Patron:* Antonio della Stufa	ACA, Ancoratge 53, unp.
?	Two great galleys sailed for Flanders and England	*Captain:* Giuliano di Niccolò Ridolfi	Provv. 137, ff. 168ᵛ–169ᵛ Tratte 225 (*bis*), f. 39
1447 June	One great galley sailed for Catalonia Valencia Barcelona (13 July)	*Patron:* Niccolò di Giovanni Nasi	Tratte 80, f. 440 ACA, Ancoratge 61, unp.
Nov.	Two great galleys sailed for Flanders and England; returned 16 June 1448 Barcelona (28 Nov.) Southampton (18 Apr.–8 May 1448)	*Captain:* Bartolomeo di Niccolò Martelli *Patrons:* Stefano di Taddeo Ambrogi Antonio Giraldi	Tratte 225 (*bis*), f. 39 Consoli del Mare III, ff. 80ᵛ–81ʳ PRO, KR Customs 141/29 MAP XVII, 55 Watson, op. cit. ii, pp. 344–5 Gilliodts van Severen, op. cit. i, pp. 683 and 692

Date	Details of fleet and known ports of call	Officers	Sources
1448	Two long and four great galleys sent to relief of Piombino	Captain: Bernardo Ventura	See above, pp. 106–7.
1449–54			
1455 July/Aug.	One great galley sailed for Cataionia (and Barbary?) Valencia (18 Aug.) Almeria	Patron: Giovenco della Stufa	ARV, Guiatges 705, unp.
Sept.	Two great galleys sailed for Flanders and England Southampton (5–25 Apr. 1456)	Captain: Bartolomeo di Niccolò Martelli Patron: Lorenzo Strozzi	Tratte 81, f. 117 Consoli del Mare III, f. 110ᵛ MAP V, 969 SPCB 1455–6, ff. 39ʳ–43ᵛ. Ruddock, op. cit., pp. 207–8
1456 Apr.	Two great galleys about to sail for Alexandria; returned 9 Sept.	Patron: Angelo di Nerone Dietisalvi Neroni	Tratte 81, f. 124
?	One great galley prepared to sail to Levant	Conductor: Arte della Lana	ASF, Arte della Lana 53, f. 96
Sept.	Two great galleys about to sail for Flanders and England	Captain: Alessandro d'Antonio del Vigna	Tratte 81, f. 117[1]
Oct.	One great galley about to sail for West Barbary and Sicily	Patron: Bartolomeo di Puccio Pucci	Tratte 81, f. 124 Heers, Piacamiglio, p. 137
1457 May/June	One great galley sailed for West Barbary and Sicily Valencia (20 June) Almeria	Patron: Jacopo di Giovanni Nasi	Tratte 81, f. 124 ARV, Guiatges 705, unp. Pardessus, *Lois maritimes*, iv, p. 594

[1] See above, p. 92.

Date		Officers	Sources
?	Galleys prepared to sail to Levant, but probably never sailed	*Patron:* Jacopo di Piero Guicciardini	Tratte 81, f. 124 Miss. I Canc. 41, ff. 20r and 53r Consoli del Mare III, f. 115v
1458 Sept./Oct.	Two great galleys sailed for Constantinople	*Captain:* Francesco di Paolo Vettori *Patrons:* Angelo di Nerone Dietisalvi Neroni Bernardo di Tommaso Corbinelli	Provv. 149, ff. 22v and 126r Tratte 81, ff. 117 and 124 Miss. I Canc. 42, f. 58v Consoli del Mare III, f. 115r
Sept./Oct.	One great galley sailed for West Barbary Genoa (Oct.) Cadiz Tunis	*Patron:* Bongianno Gianfigliazzi	Provv. 149, f. 126r
?	Two great galleys sailed for Sicily and Catalonia Savona		Heers, *Piacamiglio*, pp. 185 and 232 Mazzi, 'Carte di Benedetto Dei', p. 137
			Heers, 'Royaume de Grenade', pp. 110–11
Nov./Dec.	Two great galleys and one long galley sailed for Flanders and England Savona (18 Dec.) Valencia (24 Jan.) Cadiz Sluys Southampton (4 Sept.–3 Nov. 1459)	*Captain:* Alessandro d'Antonio del Vigna *Patrons:* Francesco Tedaldi Niccolò Bembi	Provv. 149, f. 126r Miss. I Canc. 42, f. 110v MAP IX, 341 MAP XCIX, 33 SPCB 1459–60, ff. 1–2. ARV, Guiatges 705, unp.
			Heers, *Piacamiglio*, pp. 256 and 267
1459 Mar.	One great galley about to sail for Catalonia	*Patron:* Cosimo d'Antonio Masi	Balle 29, ff. 70v and 106v Tratte 81, f. 124 MAP VI, 372 and 374
?	One great galley sailed for Sicily Palermo (Aug.)	*Patron:* Bongianno Gianfigliazzi	
Aug.	Two great galleys sailed for Constantinople and the Black Sea; returned mid-summer 1460	*Conductor:* Luca di Buonaccorso Pitti *Captain:* Filippo di Filippo Tornabuoni	Tratte 81, ff. 117 and 124 Miss. I Canc. 43, f. 43r MAP VI, 372, 374, 377, and 399 MAP IX, 464

Date	Details of fleet and known ports of call	Officers	Sources
1459 Aug.	Gaeta (19 Aug.) Palermo Constantinople (28 Sept.)	*Patrons:* Paolo di Piero degli Albizzi Bartolomeo di Puccio Pucci	
Oct.	Two great galleys sailed for Flanders and England London Isle of Wight (25–26 Aug. 1460)	*Conductors:* Jacopo d'Andrea Pazzi Averardo d'Alamanno Salviati *Captain:* Niccolò di Matteo Cerretani *Patrons:* Ristoro d'Antonio Serristori Carlo di Jacopo Guasconi	Tratte 81, ff. 117 and 124 MAP XVII, 259 SPCB 1459–60
Nov.	One great galley sailed for Catalonia and Barbary Valencia (7 Dec.) Tunis		ARV, Guiatges 705, unp.
1460 Feb./Mar.	Two great galleys sailed for Constantinople Constantinople (May)	*Captain:* Francesco di Paolo Vettori *Patrons:* Agostino del Nero Bernardo Corbinelli	Consoli del Mare III, f. 127ʳ Pagnini, *Della decima*, ii, p. 253
Apr.	Two great galleys sailed for Barbary	*Conductor:* Andrea di Lotteringo della Stufa *Captain:* Giuliano di Niccolò Ridolfi *Patrons:* Frosino d'Andrea Lau Bongianno di Bongianni Gianfigliazzi *Ambassador:* Angelo di Guglielmo Spini	Provv. 151, f. 1ʳ Tratte 81, ff. 117 and 124 Amari, *Diplomi arabi*, app. p. 28
July–Aug.	Two great galleys about to sail for Constantinople	*Conductor:* Angelo di Nerone Dietisalvi Neroni	Tratte 81, ff. 117 and 124 MAP XCVII, 129

Date	Voyage	Officers	References
Sept.	Two great galleys sailed for Flanders and England Southampton (?) Cadiz (2 July 1461)	*Captain:* Jacopo di Niccolò Sacchetti *Patrons:* Angelo Dietisalvi Neroni Piero di Francesco Corsellini	Provv. 151, f. 40ᵛ Tratte 81, ff. 117 and 124 MAP X, 93 and 211 MAP CI, 61 Quinn and Ruddock, *Port Books*, ii, pp. xxx and xxxviii–xxxix
1461 ?	Two great galleys sailed for Barbary; returned 3 Oct. Seville (July)	*Captain:* Guglielmo di Cardinale Rucellai *Patrons:* Jacopo d'Angelo Acciaiuoli Ruggiero di Tommaso Minerbetti *Conductor:* Andrea di Lotteringo della Stufa *Captain:* Angelo di Guglielmo Spini *Patrons:* Recco d'Uguccione Capponi Piero di Lutozzo Nasi	Tratte 81, ff. 117 and 124 Miss. I Canc. 42, f. 121 MAP X, 211 MAP LXVIII, 47 MAP CXXXVII, 106 Amari, op. cit., app. p. 32
May	Two great galleys about to sail for Catalonia	*Conductor:* Niccolò di Giovanni Bini *Captain:* Luigi di Buonacorso Pitti	Provv. 151, f. 374ʳ Tratte 81, f. 117 ASP, Contratti 280, f. 201
Sept.	Two great galleys sailed for Constantinople Gaeta (9 Sept.) Palermo (13 Sept.)	*Conductor:* Bartolomeo di Niccolò Martelli *Captain:* Filippo di Francesco Tornabuoni *Patrons:* Bartolomeo Martelli Giovenco di Lorenzo della Stufa	Provv. 153, f. 119ʳ Tratte 81, ff. 117 and 124 Miss. I Canc. 43, f. 174ʳ MAP CXXXVIII, 467
Sept./Oct.	Three great galleys sailed for Flanders and England Sluys London	*Conductor:* Antonio di Luca degli Albizzi *Captain:* Bongianno di Bongianni Gianfigliazzi	Provv. 152, ff. 119ʳ and 297ʳ Tratte 81, ff. 117 and 124 Consoli del Mare III, ff. 145ᵛ–146ʳ and 149

Date	Details of fleet and known ports of call	Officers	Sources
1461 Sept./Oct.		*Patrons:* Antonio di Luca degli Albizzi Giovanni di Manni Temperani	MAP X, 429 MAP CI, 61
Dec.	Two long galleys prepared to meet returning Levant galleys	*Captain:* Filippo di Giovanni Bonsignori *Patrons:* Paolo di Giovanni Machiavelli Piero di Niccolò Piaciti	Provv. 152, f. 198v Miss. I Canc. 43, f. 174r
1462 Aug.	Three great galleys sailed for Constantinople; returned 5 Feb. 1463 Constantinople Trebizond Caffa	*Conductors:* Antonio and Bartolomeo di Niccolò Martelli *Captain:* Giuliano di Niccolò Ridolfi *Patrons:* Giovanni di Niccolò Martelli Ludovico d'Antonio Masi Vanni di Francesco Strozzi	Provv. 152, ff. 284v–286v Provv. 153, ff. 1r and 99v Tratte 81, ff. 117 and 124 MAP X, 290 and 351 *Cronaca di Benedetto Dei*, ff. 54v–55r
Oct.	Three great galleys sailed for Flanders and England Valencia (6 Nov.) Almeria Sluys (18 Feb. 1463) Southampton (11 Mar.)	*Conductors:* Antonio and Bartolomeo di Niccolò Martelli *Captain:* Jacopo di Piero Guicciardini *Patrons:* Francesco di Niccolò Martelli Giovenco di Lorenzo della Stufa	Provv. 152, ff. 284v–286v Provv. 153, ff. 148r and 150r Tratte 81, ff. 117 and 124 Consoli del Mare III, ff. 156r–v and 162v–163r MAP X, 297, 481 ARV, Guiatges 705, unp.
1463 Feb./Mar.	One great galley sailed for Barbary: returned end of April	*Patron:* Piero di Giuliano Vespucci	Provv. 153, ff. 210v and 252v Tratte 81, f. 124 Miss. I Canc. 44. ff. 63v and 79r
Mar./Apr.	Two great galleys sailed for Catalonia and Sicily	*Conductors:* Zenobio Biliotti Piero Neretti	Provv. 153, f. 252v Provv. 154, f. 96v Tratte 81, ff. 117 and 124

	Valencia (20–27 Apr.) Majorca Collioure Aiguesmortes Porto Pisano (9 May) Sicily (Aug.)	*Captain:* Giovanni di Taddeo dell' Antella *Patrons:* Zenobio di Sandro Biliotti Jacopo di Giovanni Nasi	Miss. I Canc. 44, ff. 79^r and 87^r Consoli del Mare III, f. 157^v MAP VII, 60 and 64 Arch. di Stato, Palermo, Notaio Giacomo Comito (1462–3)
Oct.	Three great galleys about to sail for Levant Rhodes	*Conductors:* Antonio and Bartolomeo di Niccolò Martelli *Captain:* Luigi di Buonacorso Pitti *Patrons:* Giovanni di Niccolò Martelli Urbano Caetani	Provv. 153, f. 134^v Provv. 154, ff. 111^r and 335^r Tratte 81, ff. 117 and 124 Miss. I Canc. 44, f. 111^v Sig. X, VIII, 77, f. 57 *Cronaca di Benedetto Dei*, f. 61
Nov.	Three great galleys sailed for Flanders and England; returned Aug. 1464 (Ridolfi's and Ambrogi's galley lost) Valencia (29 Nov.) Sluys (?–30 Apr. 1464) Southampton (1 May–11 June) Portovenere	*Conductor:* Angelo di Nerone Dietisalvi Neroni *Captain:* Giuliano di Niccolò Ridolfi *Patrons:* Angelo Dietisalvi Stefano di Taddeo Ambrogi Piero di Lutozzo Nasi	Provv. 153, f. 228^v Provv. 155, f. 1^r Provv. 156, f. 12^r Tratte 81, ff. 117 and 124 Miss. I Canc. 44, f. 165^r Consoli del Mare VII, ff. 42^r–44^v. MAP XII, 327, 330, and 382 MAP LXXII, 444 PRO, KR Customs 142/3 ARV, Guiatges 705, unp. —— Watson, op. cit. ii, pp. 346–7 Quinn and Ruddock, *Port Books*, ii, pp. 210–11 *Ricordi storici di Rinuccini*, p. xciii
1464 Apr.	Two great galleys sailed for Catalonia and Sicily; returned Jan. 1465 Marseilles (19 June) Porto Pisano (June–Oct.) Sicily (Nov.)	*Conductors:* Antonio and Bartolomeo di Niccolò Martelli *Captain:* Bernardo di Piero Vespucci *Patrons:* Piero di Giuliano Vespucci Bernardo di Baldassare Bonsi	Provv. 154, f. 335^r Provv. 155, ff. 106^r, 170^v, and 218^v Tratte 81, ff. 117 and 124 Consoli del Mare III, f. 168^r —— Baratier and Reynaud, *Commerce de* *Marseille*, p. 465

Date	Details of fleet and known ports of call	Officers	Sources
1464 ?	One great galley sailed for Genoa with grain	*Patron:* Bartolomeo di Matteo Cerretani	Provv. 155, f. 44ᵛ MAP XVI, 146
1465 Mar.	Three great galleys sailed for Flanders and England; returned 16 June 1466 Civitavecchia Valencia (4 Apr.) Sluys (27 Oct.–Feb. 1466) Sandwich (7 Feb. 1466) Sluys (Mar.–28 Apr.)	*Captain:* Francesco di Paolo Vettori (Died on voyage) *Patrons:* Niccolò Bini (died on voyage) Agostino di Sandro Biliotti (Agnolo Buondelmonte and Simone Nori appointed as replacements)	Provv. 155, ff. 118ᵛ and 203ʳ Miss. I Canc. 45, f. 49ᵛ Consoli del Mare VI, f. 1ᵛ Consoli del Mare VII, ff. 41ᵛ and 65 MAP XII, 306, 314, 371, 376, and 393 MAP XIV, 78 MAP XVI, 182 and 184 ARV Guiatges 795, unp.
			Calendar of Patent Rolls (1461–7), pp. 517–18
23 Mar.	One great galley about to sail for Barbary; returned 23 June	*Patron:* Strozza di Marcello Strozzi	Provv. 155, f. 218ᵛ Tratte 81, f. 124 Consoli del Mare VII, f. 61ʳᵛ
May	Three great galleys sailed for Catalonia–Syria–Catalonia; returned 6 May 1466 Catalonia (June) Porto Pisano (12 July–29 Aug.) Chios Rhodes Cyprus Beirut (Alexandria) Catalonia Porto Pisano (25 Jan.–14 Feb. 1466) Catalonia	*Conductor:* Antonio di Niccolò Martelli *Captain:* Ruggiero di Tommaso Minerbetti then: Bernardo Corsi *Patrons:* Francesco di Giovanni Benci Piero di Francesco Corsellini Niccolò d'Ugolino Martelli	Provv. 155, ff. 60ᵛ, 83ʳ, 84ʳ, 227ʳ, and 245ʳ Provv. 156, ff. 26ʳ, 29ʳ, and 90ʳ Tratte 81, ff. 117 and 124 Consoli del Mare VII, ff. 41ᵛ, 42ᵛ, 45ʳ, 61ʳᵛ and 64ᵛ
July	Two great galleys sailed for Catalonia	*Conductor:* Domenico di Giovanni Benci	Provv. 155, ff. 60ᵛ and 144ʳ Provv. 156, f. 87ʳ

Date	Voyage	Officers	References
1466 Mar.	One great galley sailed for Barbary; returned 14 June	*Captain:* Ruggiero di Tommaso Minerbetti *Patrons:* Zenobio di Sandro Biliotti Piero di Lutozzo Nasi	Tratte 81, ff. 117 and 124
May	One great galley sailed for Catalonia Barcelona	*Patron:* Amerigo di Giovanni Benci	Consoli del Mare VII, f. 44^v
May	Two great galleys sailed for Levant; returned 12 Sept.	*Patron:* Piero di Giuliano Vespucci	A. Gallo, *Commentarius, RIS,* xxiii, i, int. p. xviii.
		Conductors and patrons: Antonio Altoviti Domenico Fagiuoli *Captain:* Bernardo di Simone del Nero	Provv. 156, f. 270^v Provv. 157, f. 101^r Balle 30, f. 15 Tratte 81, ff. 117 and 124 Consoli del Mare III, f. 176^v Consoli del Mare VII, ff. 44^v, 47^r and 67^v
16 June	Two great galleys sailed for Sicily–Catalonia–Sicily; returned Jan. 1467 Sicily Porto Pisano (13 July) Catalonia Marseilles Porto Pisano (24 Sept.) Sicily	*Captain:* Piero di Lutozzo Nasi *Patrons:* Zenobio di Sandro Biliotti Averardo di Bernardo de' Medici	Provv. 157, f. 201^r Provv. 158, f. 14^v Tratte 81, ff. 117 and 124 Consoli del Mare III, ff. 172^v and 178^v Consoli del Mare VII, ff. 45^v and 65^r. Balle 30, f. 69 MAP XXII, 121
18 Aug.	Two great galleys sailed for Flanders and England; returned 7 May 1467 Civitavecchia (24 Aug.) Southampton (30 Jan.–? 1467)	*Conductor:* Bongianno Gianfigliazzi *Captain:* Ludovico d'Adouardo Acciaiuoli *Patrons:* Bartolomeo di Matteo Cerretani Niccolò di Carlo Federighi	Tratte 81, ff. 117 and 124 Consoli del Mare VII, ff. 64 and 67 MAP XX, 177 and 225 ASR, Camerale III, Tolfa 2378, *Allumiere,* f. 14A

Date	Details of fleet and known ports of call	Officers	Sources
1467 12 Mar.	One great galley sailed for Catalonia and Sicily; returned 7 July Catalonia Porto Pisano (30 May) Sicily	*Conductor*: Zenobio di Sandro Biliotti *Patron*: Agostino di Sandro Biliotti	Consoli del Mare III, f. 189ᵛ Consoli del Mare VII, ff. 70ʳ–72ᵛ MAP XXII, 121
?	The *Ferrandina* sailed for Constantinople; returned 7 Dec. Chios Rhodes Constantinople Messina (4–7 Nov.)	*Patron*: Piero di Giuliano Vespucci	Consoli del Mare VII, f. 73ʳ MAP XX, 351 Mazzi, 'Carte di Benedetto Dei', p. 140
23 Oct.	Two great galleys sailed for Flanders and England; returned 10 Sept. 1468 Marseilles Valencia (19 Dec.) Almeria Cadiz (?–28 Feb. 1468) Sluys (26 Apr.–May) Southampton	*Conductor*: Antonio di Niccolò Martelli *Captain*: Giorgio di Niccolò Ridolfi *Patrons*: Cosimo d'Antonio Masi Baldassare di Rosso Montebuoni	Provv. 158, f. 127ʳ Consoli del Mare III, f. 190ᵛ Consoli del Mare VII, ff. 70ᵛ–74ʳ MAP XX, 394 ARV, Guiatges 707, unp. Edler de Roover, 'Voyage de Girolame Strozzi', pp. 118–19
Dec.	*Ferrandina* sailed for western Mediterranean Savona Marseilles	*Patron*: Piero di Giuliano Vespucci	MAP CXXVII, 234
1468 Mar.	One great galley sailed for Catalonia and Sicily; returned 1 Aug. Catalonia Porto Pisano (14 June) Sicily	*Conductor and patron*: Piero di Francesco Corsellini	Provv. 158, f. 171ᵛ Tratte 81, f. 124 Consoli del Mare VII, ff. 72ᵛ and 73ʳ MAP CXXVII, 234

Date	Voyage	Personnel	References
July/Aug.	*Ferrandina* sailed for Flanders and England / Civitavecchia (29 July)		ASR Camerale III, Tolfa 2378, *Allumiere*, f. 19A
?	Two Medici galleys sailed for Flanders and England; returned 31 May 1469 / London (Jan. 1469) / Sluys / Tunis / Sicily	*Patrons:* Francesco Tedaldi, Antonio di Niccolò Popoleschi	MAP XII, 307, 308 / MAP XVI, 332 / MAP XX, 503 / MAP XXIII, 252
27 Dec.	Two great galleys sailed for Levant / Rhodes (June 1469)	*Conductors:* Antonio Altoviti, Domenico Fagiuoli; *Captain:* Bernardo di Simone del Nero; *Patron:* Antonio Altoviti, Vanni di Francesco Strozzi	Provv. 158, ff. 27r and 70v / Provv. 159, ff. 109v, 146v and 216v / Provv. 163, f. 129v / Consoli del Mare III, f. 195r / Consoli del Mare VII, ff. 55r–57v
1469 11 Mar.	One great galley sailed for Catalonia and Sicily; returned 19 July / Port-de-Bouc (10 Apr.) / Porto Pisano (12 May) / Sicily (June)	*Conductor:* Pierfilippo di Gianozzo Pandolfini; *Patron:* Agostino di Sandro Biliotti	Consoli del are VII, f. 74r–v / MAP XVII, 698 / Reynaud, 'Port-de-Bouc', p. 156
?	Two galleys prepared to sail for Levant	*Conductor:* Giovanni di Piero Benizi; *Captain:* Lorenzo di Piero Davanzati	Provv. 159, f. 109v / Tratte 81, f. 117 / Consoli del Mare VII, ff. 51 and 74v / *Cronaca di Benedetto Dei*, f. 39v
Nov.	Two Medici galleys sailed for Flanders and England / Civitavecchia (17 Oct.) / Port-de-Bouc (24 Nov.) / Sluys	*Patrons:* Francesco Sermattei, Antonio Popoleschi (Francesco Tedaldi)	MAP IV, 501 / MAP XVII 465 / MAP LXXXIV, 27, f. 56 / MAP CIII, 94 / *Cronaca di Benedetto Dei*, f. 39v / ASR, Camerale III, Tolfa 2378,

Date	Details of fleet and known ports of call	Officers	Sources
1469 Nov.	Southampton (22 June–12 Sept.) Sluys (?–1 Dec.) Southampton (12 Dec.)		*Altumiere*, f. 20A PRO, Early Chancery Proceedings 31/80 SPCB 1469–70 and 1470–1 _____ Quinn and Ruddock, *Port Books*, i, pp. 60–61 and 96–99 Reynaud, op. cit., pp. 156–7
1470 Mar.	Two great galleys sailed for Catalonia and Sicily Port-de-Bouc (16 Apr.) Catalonia Port-de-Bouc (21 May)	*Captain:* Niccolò di Matteo Cerretani	Provv. 160, f. 248ᵛ Tratte 81, f. 117 _____ Reynaud, op. cit., p. 156
Sept.	Two great galleys preparing to sail to Flanders and England Valencia (29 Oct.)?	*Captain:* Simone d'Amerigo Zati *Patrons:* Priore di Gianozzo Pandolfini Piero di Francesco Corsellini	Balìe 33, f. 98 Tratte 81, ff. 117 and 124 ARV, Guiatges 707, unp. _____ Reynaud, op. cit., p. 156
1471 Jan./Feb.	Two great galleys sailed for Catalonia (and Barbary) Port-de-Bouc (15 Feb.) Catalonia Port-de-Bouc (16 Apr.)		Reynaud, op. cit., p. 156
June	One great galley sailed for Sicily and Catalonia; returned 10 Nov. Sicily Porto Pisano (27 July) Catalonia	*Patron:* Alberto Villani	Provv. 162, f. 45ʳ MAP XXVII, 420, 447, and 501

Date	Voyage	Officers	References
July	*Ferrandina* sailed for Levant; returned June 1472 Candia Alexandria Constantinople	*Patron:* Francesco Benci	Miss. II Canc. 4, f. 67ᵛ MAP XXVII, 495 and 485 Selfridge 495, ff. 96 and 121
5 Aug.	Two Medici galleys sailed for Levant Messina Rhodes (5 Sept.) Chios (Oct.) (Alexandria)	*Captain:* Paolo di Giovanni Machiavelli *Patrons:* Sermattei and Popoleschi	MAP XXV, 109 MAP XXVII, 275, 297, 405, 435, 441, 478, 479, 485 *Cronaca di Benedetto Dei*, ff. 40ʳ⁻ᵛ
?	Two great galleys sailed for Flanders and England		*Cronaca di Benedetto Dei*, ff. 40ʳ⁻ᵛ
1472 Apr.	One great galley sailed for Catalonia and Sicily Port-de-Bouc (8 May) Catalonia Port-de-Bouc (1 July) Porto Pisano (9 July) Sicily		Miss. II Canc. 4, ff. 43ʳ and 71ᵛ Reynaud, op. cit., p. 156
July	Two great galleys about to sail for Constantinople Palermo Messina (15 Dec.) Constantinople	Lorenzo Davanzati and Niccolò Guasconi, both experienced galley officers, were with this fleet and the former was probably Captain	Provv. 163, f. 32ʳ MAP XXIV, 343 *Cronaca di Benedetto Dei*, f. 40ᵛ
26 Sept.	Two Medici galleys sailed for Flanders and England; one returned 27 Oct. 1473 Cadiz Sluys	*Patrons:* Sermattei and Popoleschi	Müller, *Documenti*, p. 217 Malipiero, 'Annali veneti', p. 86 Miss. II Canc. 6, f. 16ʳ MAP XXI, 387 MAP XXVIII, 346, 356, 478 MAP XXIX, 931 *Cronaca di Benedetto Dei*, f. 41ʳ Strozziana III, 127, ff. 81–90.

Date	Details of fleet and known ports of call	Officers	Sources
1472 Sept.	Southampton (29 Apr.–27 July 1473)		PRO, KR Customs 142/8
			For secondary sources, see above, p. 98
1473 May	One great galley sailed for Catalonia and Sicily; returned 3 Sept. Port-de-Bouc (18–22 May) Barcelona Valencia (3 June) Porto-de-Bouc (2 July) Porto Pisano (16 July) Palermo	Patron: Giovanni di Simone Tornabuoni	Provv. 163, f. 182v Provv. 164, f. 70v MAP XXI, 396 MAP XXIX, 314, 366, 509, and 709 Reynaud, op. cit., p. 156
?	Two great galleys prepared for Levant	Patron: Niccolò Guasconi	Provv. 166, f. 77v
Oct.	One great galley sailed for Catalonia; returned Jan. 1474 Porr-de-Bouc (16 Oct.)	Patron: Giovanni d'Antonio Pazzi	Provv. 164, ff. 70v and 110v Miss. II Canc. 6, f. 59r Reynaud, op. cit., p. 156
Nov.	*Ferrandina* returned from unspecified voyage		MAP XXIX, 1002 Cronaca di Benedetto Dei, f. 41r
1474 Mar.	One great galley sailed for Constantinople	Patron: Piero Attavanti	MAP XXX, 125 Cronaca di Benedetto Dei, f. 41v
Apr.	One great galley sailed for Catalonia and Sicily; returned 5 Sept. Port-de-Bouc (20 Apr.) Catalonia Port-de-Bouc (28 May) Porto Pisano (June) Sicily	Conductor: Francesco di Tommaso Sassetti Patron: Leonardo di Silvestro Spini	Provv. 165, f. 92v Tratte 81, f. 124 Miss. II Canc. 6, ff. 122v, 125v, and 159r MAP XXI, 527 Reynaud, op. cit., p. 156
Oct.	Same galley sailed again for Catalonia	Conductor: Francesco di Tommaso Sassetti	Provv. 165, f. 92v Miss. II Canc. 6, f. 159r

	Port-de-Bouc (21 Oct.)	*Patron:* Leonardo di Silvestro Spini	Reynaud, op. cit., p. 156
1475 Mar./Apr.	One great galley sailed for Catalonia Port-de-Bouc (7 Apr.)	*Conductor:* Simone di Filippo Tornabuoni	Provv. 166, f. 69v Tratte 82, f. 23
	Catalonia Port-de-Bouc (23 May)	*Patron:* Agostino di Giovanni Mannelli	Reynaud, op. cit., p. 156
July	Two great galleys prepared to sail for Levant	*Patrons:* Piero d'Antonio da Rabatta Giovanfrancesco di Francesco Ventura	MAP XXXIII, 206 Tratte 82, f. 23
1476 Apr.	One great galley sailed for Catalonia; returned 31 July Port-de-Bouc (6 May)	*Patron:* Pierfrancesco Tosinghi	Miss. I Canc. 47, f. 36r Provv. 167, f. 86v
?	*Ferrandina* sailed for Levant; returned April 1477		Reynaud, op. cit., p. 156 Provv. 168, ff. 10v and 51r *Cronaca di Benedetto Dei*, f. 42v
1477 Apr.	*Ferrandina* ready to sail again	*Patrons:* Paolo Machiavelli Bartolomeo Pucci	MAP XXXV, 408
July–Aug.	Two great galleys sailed for Catalonia		Provv. 168, f. 108v *Cronaca di Benedetto Dei*, f. 43r
Sept.	Two great galleys sailed for Levant	*Captain:* Lorenzo d'Angelo Carducci	Provv. 168, ff. 57v and 108r Miss. I Canc. 47, f. 64v *Cronaca di Benedetto Dei*, f. 43r
Oct.	Two great galleys sailed for Flanders and England; returned 8 Feb. 1479	*Captain:* Piero Nasi	Provv. 168, ff. 84, 109v, and 142r Miss. X Balia 4, f. 174 SPCB 1477–8
	Southampton (19 June–17 Aug. 1478)	*Patrons:* Amerigo di Simone Carnesecchi Giovansimone di Filippo Tornabuoni	
	Marseilles (15 Dec.–?)		Quinn and Ruddock, op. cit., pp. 129–136 Baratier and Reynaud, op. cit., p. 469

Date	Details of fleet and known ports of call	Officers	Sources
1478 ?	Two great galleys sailed for Catalonia and Barbary; returned May 1478	*Captain:* Zenobio di Sandro Biliotti *Patrons:* Piero di Francesco Corsellini Ottavanto di Lorenzo Ottavanti	Tratte 82, f. 23 Miss. X Balìa 4, f. 42
July	Same galleys sailed again for Catalonia and Barbary; returned 8 Feb. 1479 Valencia (27 July) Almeria Marseilles (Jan. 1479)	*Captain:* Zenobio Biliotti *Patrons:* Piero Corsellini Ottavanto Ottavanti	Provv. 168, f. 169r Provv. 169, f. 7v Miss. II Canc. 8, f. 45r Miss. X Balìa 4, f. 174 MAP XXVI, 198 MAP XXXVI, 35 and 146 MAP XCVII, 42
?	Two great galleys prepared for Levant	*Patrons:* Niccolò di Zenobio Guasconi Andrea di Niccolò Aleis	Tratte 82, f. 23

APPENDIX B

Weights and Measures

THIS is in no sense intended to be a complete survey of the various weights and measures in use in the Mediterranean area in the late Middle Ages. The enormous variety not only in the terms used but also in the values assigned to them is clearly revealed in the handbooks of Pegolotti, Uzzano, Chiarini, etc., and a complete study of the whole problem remains to be written. I have here only attempted a brief explanation of the terms encountered in the cargo lists of the Florentine galleys, and an evaluation, in so far as this is possible, of their statistical significance.

A clear distinction has to be drawn between the terms which signified actual weights and measures, and the terms which basically described types of package or container and only by custom came to imply an approximate weight. These latter I have called for convenience 'package terms'.

I. ACTUAL WEIGHTS

Libbra (pound)

  1 Florentine pound = 339½ grammes
  100 Florentine lb. = 74·8 English lb.

  ___

  1 Genoese lb. = 317 grammes
  1 Venetian light (*sottile*) lb. = 300 grammes
  1 Venetian heavy (*grosso*) lb. = 477 grammes.

Centinaio (hundredweight)

  1 hundredweight = 100 lb. of various denominations.
  This unit of weight was rather less used by the fifteenth century than the cantar.

Cantaro (cantar)

  1 cantar = usually 150 lb.
  1 cantar in Barbary, Majorca, and Valencia = 150 Florentine lb.
  1 cantar in Genoa = 150 Genoese lb. or 139 Florentine lb.
  1 cantar in Marseilles = 118 Florentine lb.
  1 cantar in Sicily = 236 Florentine lb.
  1 cantar in Cyprus and Rhodes = 660 Florentine lb.

2. PACKAGE TERMS

These fall broadly into two groups, those which represented a complete mule-load and those which represented half a mule-load. Hence the degree of standardization which is apparent. Naturally the sizes of the packages tended to be much more standardized when actually travelling by land, but even when loaded on ships, although frequently repacked at the port, they still had usually at some stage to be carried by mules and tended to conform to the same criteria. Also the size of a mule-load depended to a certain extent on the terrain which had to be crossed. In Genoa mule-loads tended to be rather smaller than in England.

Half loads

collo, pondo, farda (bale): used for Levant spices and usually of about the same weight, e.g. 90 kg.

balla (bale): used for cloth and other less valuable goods and usually weighed *c.* 225–50 Florentine lb., or 80–85 kg.

fardello (bundle): used particularly for silk and equalled about 80 kg.

cassa (case): used for loose goods such as sugar and some spices. The weight seems to have depended on the commodity, e.g.

  a case of sugar = 64–68 kg.
  a case of lac = 90 kg.
  a case of indigo = 110–14 kg.

Whole loads

carica: equivalent in Venice 135 kg.

soma: equivalent in Genoa 143 kg. Both these terms mean a load, but I have translated them as a large bale.

sporta: equivalent in Alexandria to 200–50 kg. and used for spices. This also, for want of a better term, I have translated as a large bale, and it may be that the explanation for this rather larger package and for the heavy cantar in use in the Levant lay in the use of camels rather than mules as pack animals.

costale and *ballone*: the former was used for wax and rice and equalled about 185 kg.; the latter equalled two bales and was used for cloth. These I have also translated as large bale in the cargo lists.

sacca (sack): used particularly for wool and its size depended on the type of wool, e.g.

  1 sack English wool = 364 English lb., or 485 Florentine lb.
  (2 pokes = 1 sack)
  1 sack Spanish wool = 275–300 Florentine lb.

3. Other terms which appear in these cargo lists are:

caratello: a small barrel of uncertain size.

terzaruolo: a small keg used for shipping tuna fish. This is a term for which I have found no equivalents, but the Genoese had a *mezzaruola* which equalled 2 Genoese barrels or 105 litres. From this it might follow that a *terzaruola* equalled 1⅛ barrels or *c.* 70 litres.

bogiolo: a special cask for mercury and equivalent to 60 kg.

fother: an English term used for bulk goods, particularly metals, and describing a cartload. It later became standardized at 19½ cwt. but its equivalent seems to have been more variable in the fifteenth century.

bota: originally a large wine container, but used in many parts of Europe as a measure of a ship's burden instead of the ton. There are many theories as to its exact equivalent but most probably it equalled 476 kg. or 10 Genoese cantars.

The most useful recent works on the subject of medieval weights and measures are: Florence Edler (De Roover), *Glossary of Medieval Terms of Business; Italian Series 1200–1600*, Cambridge (Mass.), 1934, and Heers, *Piccamiglio*, pp. 15–27. For a complete bibliography of older works on the subject, see Florence Edler-De Roover's valuable work.

The most useful discussion of the size of the *bota* is Melis, 'Werner Sombart e i problemi della navigazione', pp. 95-8.

SELECT BIBLIOGRAPHY

PUBLISHED SOURCES

AIAZZI, G. DEGLI (ed.), *Ricordi storici di Filippo di Cino Rinuccini dal 1282 al 1460 colla continuazione di Alamanno e Neri suoi figli fino al 1506*, Florence, 1840.

AMARI, M., *Diplomi arabi del R. Archivio di Stato Fiorentino*, Florence, 1863 (*Appendice*, Florence, 1867).

Archivio Mediceo avanti il Principato, ed. by Francesca Morandini and Arnaldo d'Addario, 4 vols., Rome, Ministero dell'Interno, 1951–64.

BONAINI, G., *Statuti inediti della città di Pisa*, Florence, 1870.

BONGI, SALVATORE (ed.), *Cronache di Giovanni Sercambi, Lucchese*; Fonti per la Storia d'Italia, vols. 19–21, 1890–2.

BORLANDI, FRANCO (ed.), *El libro di mercatantie e usanzi de' paesi del Chiarini*, Turin, 1936.

BRANCACCI, FELICE, see Catellacci, D.

Calendar of the Patent Rolls Preserved in the Public Record Office: Edward IV, 1461–1467, London, 1897.

Edward IV & Henry VI, 1467–77, London, 1900.

Calendar of State Papers and Manuscripts, relating to English Affairs, existing in the archives and collections of Venice . . ., vol. I, 1202–1509, ed. Rawdon Brown, London, 1864.

CAMBI, GIOVANNI, *Istorie fiorentine*, in *Delizie degli eruditi toscani* (ed. Fr. Ildefonso di San Luigi), Florence, 1770–89, vol. xx.

CAMERANI, G., *I documenti commerciali del fondo Mediceo*, Florence, 1951.

CATELLACCI, D. (ed.), 'Diario di Felice Brancacci ambasciatore con Carlo Federighi al Cairo per il Comune di Firenze (1422)', *ASI*, 4th ser., viii, 1881.

CHIARINI, see Borlandi, F.

CIAVARINI, C., *Statuti Anconitani del mare, del terzenale e della dogana, e patti con diverse nazioni*, Ancona, 1896.

COBB, H. S., *The Local Port Book of Southampton, 1439–40*, Southampton Record Society, V, Southampton, 1961.

CORAZZA, BARTOLOMEO DI MICHELE DEL, see Corazzini, G. O.

CORAZZINI, G. O., 'Diario fiorentino di Bartolomeo di Michele del Corazza, 1405–1438', *ASI*, 5th ser., xiv, 1894.

COTRUGLI-RAUGEO, BENEDETTO, *Della mercatura e del mercante perfetto*, Venezia, 1573.

DOEHAERD, R., and KERREMANS, C., *Les Relations commerciales entre Gênes, la Belgique et l'Outremont d'après les archives notariales génoises*, vol. iv, 1400–40, Rome–Brussels, 1952.

DOPP, PIERRE-HERMAIN, *Traité d'Emmanuel Peloti sur le passage en Terre-Sainte (1420)*, Publications de l'Université Lovanium de Léopoldville, Louvain–Paris, 1958.

DORINI, V., and BERTELÉ, T., *Il libro di conti di Giacomo Badoer*, Rome, 1956.

FABRI, FELIX, *The Book of the Wanderings of Brother Felix Fabri in Palestine and Arabia* (trans. Aubrey Stewart), Palgrave Pilgrims Text Society, London, 1892.

GACHARD, L.-P., *Collection de documents inédits concernant l'histoire de la Belgique*, vol. ii, Brussels, 1834.

GALLO, A., *Commentarius de Genuensium maritima classe in Barchenonenses expedita, Anno MCCCCLXVI, RIS*, xxiii. i, Città di Castello, 1910.

GILLIODTS VAN SEVEREN, LOUIS, *Cartulaire de l'ancienne estaple de Bruges, recueil de documents concernant le commerce intérieur et maritime, les relations internationales et l'histoire économique de cette ville*, vols. i and ii, Bruges, 1904-6.

GRASSETTO, FRANCESCO, 'Viaggio di Francesco Grassetto da Lonigo lungo le coste dalmate greco-venete ed italiche nell'anno 1511 e sequenti', *Monumenti storici pubblicati dalla R. Dep. Veneta di Storia Patria*, serie iv, misc. vol. iv, 5, Venice, 1887.

GRUNZWEIG, A., *Correspondance de la filiale de Bruges des Médici* (vol. i. Commission royale d'Histoire), Brussels, 1931.

—— 'Les fonds du Consulat de la Mer aux archives de l'État de Florence', *Bulletin de l'Institut historique belge de Rome*, x, 1930.

GUASTI, C. (ed.), *Commissioni di Rinaldo degli Albizzi per il Comune di Firenze, 1399-1433*, Florence, 1867-73.

HEERS, J., *Le Livre de comptes de Giovanni Piccamiglio, homme d'affaires génois, 1456-59*, Paris, 1959.

MALIPIERO, DOMENICO, 'Annali veneti dell'anno 1457 al 1500', (ed. F. Lungo and Augustino Sagredo), *ASI*, 1st ser., vii, 1843.

MARUFFI, GIOACCHINO, *Viaggio in Terra Santa di Roberto da Sanseverino*, Bologna, 1888.

MASI, GINO (ed.), *Statuti delle colonie fiorentine all'estero, secc. XV-XVI*, Milan, 1941.

MAS LATRIE, L. DE, *Traités de paix et de commerce concernants les relations des Chrétiens avec les Arabes de l'Afrique septentrionale au moyen âge*, Paris, 1866.

MORENI, DOMENICO, *Del viaggio in Terra Santa fatto e descritto da Ser Mariano da Siena nel secolo XV*, Florence, 1822.

MOROSINI, ANTONIO, *Chronique d'Antonio Morosini; extraits relatifs à l'histoire de France*, (ed. G. Lefèvre-Pontalis and L. Dorez), Paris, 1898-1902.

MÜLLER, J., *Documenti sulle relazioni della città toscane coll'Oriente cristiano e coi Turchi*, Florence, 1879.

NANI-MOCENIGO, F., 'Un itinerario marittimo medievale', *Nuovo Archivio Veneto*, N.S., xxi, 1911.

NEWETT, M. MARGARET, *Canon Pietro Casola's Pilgrimage to Jerusalem in the Year 1494*, Historical Series, Publications of the University of Manchester, Manchester, 1907.

PEGOLOTTI, FRANCESCO DI BALDUCCIO, *La pratica della mercatura* (ed. Allan Evans), Cambridge (Mass.), 1936.

PITTI, BUONACCORSO, *Cronica* (ed. Alberto Bacchi della Lega), Bologna, 1905.

POLIDORI, F. L. (ed.), 'Lettera di Raimondo Mannelli intorno alla battaglia navale combattuta tra Fiorentini e Veneziani confederati, e i Genovesi,' *ASI*, app. vol. i, 1843-4.

QUINN, D. B., and RUDDOCK, A. A., *The Port Books of Southampton, 1469–70*, Publications of the Southampton Record Society 37, Southampton, 1937–8.

RAMUSIO, G. B., *Secondo volume delle navigationi e viaggi . . .*, Venice, 1559; contains 'Il naufragio di Messer Pietro Querini portato per fortuna settanta gradi sotto la tramontana'.

RICHARDS, G. R. B., *Florentine Merchants in the Age of the Medici; Letters and Documents from the Selfridge Collection of Medici Manuscripts*, Cambridge (Mass.), 1932.

RINUCCINI, FILIPPO DI CINO, see Aiazzi, G.

RUCELLAI, GIOVANNI, *Zibaldone Quaresimale* (ed. A. Perosa), Studies of the Warburg Institute 24, London, 1960.

RYMER, THOMAS (ed.), *Foedera, conventiones, litterae et cuiuscumque generis acta publica inter reges Angliae et alios quosvis imperatores, reges, pontifices, principes, vel communitates*, vol. xii, London, 1704.

SANTINI, P. (ed.), *Documenti dell'antica costituzione di Firenze*, Florence, 1895.

SANUDO, M., *Vite dei dogi*, Muratori, vol. xxii, Milan, 1733.

SCARAMELLA, G. 'Notizie e statuti della dogana fiorentina nel secolo XV', *Studi storici*, v, 1896.

SERCAMBI, GIOVANNI, see Bongi, S.

STUDER, P. (ed.), *The Port Books of Southampton, 1427–30*, Southampton, 1913.

TWISS, SIR TRAVERS (ed. and trans.), *The Black Book of the Admiralty*, vol. iii, London, 1874; contains: 'The Charter of Oleroun of the Judgments of the Sea', 'The Good Customs of the Sea'.

UZZANO, GIOVANNI DI ANTONIO DA, *Pratica della mercatura, 1442, see* Pagnini, *Della decima*, vol. iv.

VIGO, P., *Statuti e provvisioni del castello e comune di Livorno, 1421–1581*, Leghorn, 1892.

—— 'Statuto inedito della dogana di Livorno del secolo XV', *Miscellanea livornese di storia e di erudizione*, ii, 1897.

SECONDARY AUTHORITIES

ALMAGIA, R., *Il primato di Firenze negli studi geografici durante i secoli XV e XVI*, Pavia, 1929.

AMMIRATO, SCIPIONE, *Delle famiglie nobili fiorentine*, Florence, 1615.

—— *Istorie fiorentine*, Florence, 1824–27.

ANDERSON, R. C., 'The Bursledon Ship', *Mariners' Mirror*, xx, 1934.

—— 'Italian Naval Architecture about 1445', ibid. xi, 1925.

—— 'Jal's Memoire no. 5 and the Manuscript *Fabbrica di Galere*', *Mariners' Mirror*, xxxi, 1945.

—— *Oared Fighting Ships*, London, 1962.

—— 'The Wreck in the Hamble River', *Antiquaries Journal*, xiv, 1934.

ARIAS, G., *I trattati commerciali della Repubblica Fiorentina*, Florence, 1901.

BABINGER, F., 'Lorenzo de' Medici e la corte ottomana', *ASI*, cxxi, 1963.

—— *Mahomet II, il Conquistatore, ed il suo tempo*, Turin, 1957.

BANCHI, L., 'I porti della Maremma senese durante la Repubblica', *ASI*, x–xii, 1869–70.

BARATIER, E., and REYNAUD, F., *Histoire du commerce de Marseilles*, vol. ii, Paris, 1951.

BARBOSA, ANTONIO, 'Novos subsidios para a história da ciencia náutica portuguesa da época dos descobrimentos', 1.ª *Congresso da História da Expanseo Portuguesa no Mundo*, Lisbon, 1938.

BARUCHELLO, M., *Livorno e il suo porto. Origini, caratteristiche e vicende dei traffici livornesi*, Leghorn, 1932.

BATTAGLINI, N., *Le costruzioni navali nell'estuario veneto*, Venice, 1870.

BAUTIER, R., 'Notes sur les sources de l'histoire économique médiévale dans les archives de Toscane', *Mélanges d'archéologie et d'histoire*, lviii, 1941–6.

BEAUJOUAN, GUY, and POULLE, EMANUEL, 'Les origines de la navigation astronomique aux XIVᵉ et XVᵉ siècles', *Iᵉʳ Colloque d'histoire maritime*.

BISCARO, G., 'Il banco Filippo Borromei e compagni di Londra, 1436–39', *Archivio storico lombardo*, xl, 1913.

BONFANTE, P., *Storia del commercio*, Turin, 1946.

BONOLIS, G., 'Sul commercio delle città adriatiche nell'alto Medio Evo', *Rivista internazionale di scienze sociali*, lvi, 1911.

—— 'Sulle maone genovesi e su una maona fiorentina sconosciuta', *Diritto commerciale*, xxv, 1907.

BORLANDI, F., 'Note per la storia della produzione e del commercio di una materia prima. Il guado nel Medio Evo', *Studi in onore di Gino Luzzatto*, Milan, 1949.

BORSARI, S., 'L'espansione economica fiorentina nell'Oriente cristiano sino alla metà del Trecento', *RSI*, lxx, 1958.

BOZZANO, LUCIO, *Antiche carte nautiche*, Rome, 1961.

BRAUDEL, FERDINAND, *La Méditerranée et le monde méditerranéen à l'époque de Philippe II*, Paris, 1949.

BYRNE, E. H. *Genoese Shipping in the Twelfth and Thirteenth Centuries*, Cambridge (Mass), 1930.

CADDEO, RINALDO, et al., *Storia marittima d'Italia dall'evo antico ai nostri giorni*, vol. i, Milan, 1942.

CAGGESE, ROMOLO, *Firenze dalla decadenza di Roma al Risorgimento d'Italia*, 3 vols., Florence, 1912–21.

—— *Storia del commercio*, Florence, 1922.

Cambridge Economic History of Europe
Vol. II, *Trade and Industry in the Middle Ages*, Cambridge, 1952.
Vol. III, *Economic Organisation and Policies in the Middle Ages*, Cambridge, 1961.

CAMMILLERI, D., *La legislazione marittima in Italia*, Leghorn, 1956.

CANESTRINI, G., 'Relazioni commerciali dei Fiorentini coi Portoghesi', *ASI*, app. vol. iii, 1846.

CANTINI, L., *Storia del commercio e navigazione dei Pisani*, 2 vols., Florence, 1797–8.

CAPMANY, A. de, *Memorias históricas sobre la marina de Barcelona*, 4 vols., Madrid, 1786–94.

CAPPONI, GINO, *Storia della Repubblica di Firenze*, 2 vols., Florence, 1875.

CARNESECCHI, C., 'Un Fiorentino del secolo XV e le sue ricordanze domestiche', *ASI*, 5th ser., iv, 1889.

CARRÈRE Y COLL, C., 'Le droit d'ancrage et le mouvement du port de Barcelone au milieu du XVᵉ siècle', *Estudios de historia moderna*, iii, 1953.

CARUS WILSON, E. M., and COLEMAN, O., *England's Export Trade, 1275–1547*, Oxford, 1963.

CESSI, R., ' "L'Officium de Navigantibus" ed i sistemi della politica commerciale di Venezia nel secolo XIV', *Nuovo archivio veneto*, xxxii, 1916.

—— 'Le relazioni commerciali fra Venezia e le Fiandre nel secolo XIV', ibid. xxvii, 1914.

—— 'Studi sulle maone medievali', *ASI*, lxxvii, 1919.

CIANO, C., 'Costruzioni navali a Portovenere nel Duecento', *Economia e storia*, vi, 1959.

CIASCA, R., *L'arte dei medici e speziali nella storia e nel commercio fiorentino dal secolo XII al secolo XV*, Florence, 1927.

CIPOLLA, C. M., 'Revisions in Economic History, XII: Trends in Italian Economic History in the Later Middle Ages', *Ec.H.R*, N.S., ii, 1949.

—— *Money, Prices and Civilisation in the Mediterranean World; Vth.–XVIIth. Centuries*, Princeton, 1956.

—— *I movimenti dei cambi in Italia dal secolo XII al XV*, Pavia, 1948.

—— 'In tema di trasporti medievali', *Bollettino storico pavese*, N.S., v, 1944.

COLL, JULIA, N., 'Aspectos del corso catalan y del commercio internacional en el siglo XV', *Estudios de historia moderna*, iv, 1954.

COLLIER, R., and BILLIOUD, J., *Histoire du commerce de Marseilles*, vol. iii, Paris, 1951.

Colloques d'histoire maritime, see Mollat, M.

CONIGLIO, G., 'Mercanti forestieri a Napoli attraverso gli anni del notaio Petruccio Pisano, 1465–66', *Samnium*, 1955.

CORONELLI, PADRE, *Atlante venete*, vol. i, Venice, 1690.

CORTESÃO, A., 'Nautical Science and the Renaissance', *Archives internationales d'histoire des Sciences*, ix, 1949.

CRESCENTIO ROMANO, BARTOLOMEO, *Nautica mediterranea . . . nella quale si muestra la fabrica delle galee . . . si manifesta l'error delle charte mediterranee . . . s'insegna l'arte del navigar . . . vi è el calendario nautico e un portolane di tutti i porti da stantiar vascelli ed i luoghi pericolosi di tutto il mare Mediterraneo*, Rome, 1607.

CRINO, S., 'Portolani, manoscritti e carte da navigare per la marina medicea', *Rivista marittima*, 1931–2.

DAINELLI, AMELIA, 'Niccolò da Uzzano nella vita politica dei suoi tempi', *ASI*, 7th ser., xvii, 1932.

D'ALBERTIS, E. A., *Le costruzioni navali e la navigazione al tempo di Colombo*, Genoa, 1893.

DEL TREPPO, M., 'Assicurazioni e commercio internazionale a Barcellona nel 1428–29', *RSI*, lxix–lxx, 1957–8 (two parts).

DELUMEAU, JEAN, *L'Alun de Rome; XVᵉ–XIXᵉ siècle*, Paris, 1962.

DEL VECCHIO, A., and CASANOVA, E., *Le rappresaglie nei comuni medievali e specialmente in Firenze*, Bologna, 1894.

DEROISY, A., 'Les routes terrestres des laines anglaises vers la Lombardie', *Revue du Nord*, xxv, 1939.

De Roover, Raymond, 'La balance commerciale entre les Pays-Bas et l'Italie au quinzième siècle', *RBPH*, xxxvii, 1959.
—— *Money, Banking and Credit in Medieval Bruges*, Cambridge (Mass.), 1948.
—— *The Rise and Decline of the Medici Bank*, Cambridge (Mass.), 1963.
Dizionario Biografico degli Italiani, Fondazione Treccani, Rome, 1960– .
Doeheard, R., 'Chiffres d'assurance à Gênes en 1427–28', *RBPH*, xxvii, 1949.
Doren, A., *Le arti fiorentine*, 2 vols., Florence, 1940.
—— 'Die florentiner Wollentuchindustrie', in *Studien aus der florentiner Wirtschaftsgeschichte*, vol. i, Stuttgart, 1901.
—— *Storia economica dell'Italia nel Medioevo*, Padua, 1937.
Dupont, A., *Les Relations commerciales entre les cités maritimes du Languedoc et les cités méditerranéennes d'Espagne et d'Italie*, Nîmes, 1942.
Edler-De Roover, Florence, *Glossary of Medieval Terms of Business, Italian Series 1200–1600*, Cambridge (Mass.), 1934.
—— 'A Prize of War; a Painting of Fifteenth Century Merchants', *Bulletin of Business Historical Society*, xix, 1945.
—— 'Le voyage de Girolame Strozzi de Pise à Bruges et retour à bord de la galère bourguignonne San Giorgio', *Handelingen van het Genootschap 'Société d'Émulation' te Brugge*, xci, 1954.
Fanfani, A. (ed.), *Città, mercanti, dottrine nell'economia europea dal IV al XVIII secolo; saggi in memoria di Gino Luzzatto*, Biblioteca della rivista *Economia e storia*, 11, Milan, 1964.
Fanucci, G. B., *Storia dei tre celebri popoli marittimi dell'Italia, veneziani, genovesi e pisani e delle loro navigazioni e commercio nei bassi secoli*, Leghorn, 1853–5.
Fasano Guarini, E., 'Au XVIe siècle; comment naviguent les galères', *Annales*, xvi, 1961.
Fiaschi, Ranieri, *Le magistrature pisane delle acque*, Pisa, 1939.
Fincati, L., *Le triremi*, Rome, 1881.
Fiumi, E., 'Fioritura e decadenza dell'economia fiorentina', *ASI*, cxv–cxvii, 1957–9.
Flenley, R., 'London and Foreign Merchants in the Reign of Henry VI', *EHR*, 5th ser., xxv, 1910.
Frati, Ludovico, 'Un viaggiatore fiorentino del 1400', *Intermezzo*, 10 Jan. 1890.
Garcie dit Ferrande, Pierre, *Le Grand Routier, pilotage et ancrage de mer . . .*, Rouen, 1584.
Garnier, Abbé, 'Galères et galéasses à la fin du moyen âge', *IIe Colloque d'histoire maritime*.
Ginori Conti, Piero, *Le magone della vena del ferro di Pisa e di Pietrasanta sotto la gestione di Piero de' Medici e comp. (1489–92)*, Florence, 1939.
Giuseppi, M. S., 'Alien Merchants in England in the Fifteenth Century', *Transactions of the Royal Historical Society*, n.s., ix, 1895.
Gras, N. S. B., *The Early English Customs System*, Cambridge (Mass.), 1918.
Grunzweig, Armand, 'La filiale de Bruges des Medici', *La Revue de la Banque*, xiii, 1948.
Guarnieri, G. G., *Il porto di Livorno e la sua funzione economica*, Pisa, 1931.
—— *Livorno marinara*, Leghorn, 1962.

GUARNIERI, G. G., *Il principato mediceo nella scienza del mare*, Pisa, 1963.

GUASTI, C., 'Raimondo Mannelli alla battaglia di Rapallo', *Archivio veneto*, x, 1875.

GUGLIELMOTTI, A., *Storia della marina pontificia nel Medioevo*, vols. i and ii, Rome, 1886.

HAMY, E.-T., *Études historiques et géographiques*, Paris, 1896.

HEERS, JACQUES, 'Le commerce des Basques en Méditerranée au XVᵉ siècle', *Bulletin hispanique*, lvii, 1955.

—— 'Il commercio nel Mediterraneo alla fine del secolo XIV e nei primi anni del XV', *ASI*, cxiii, 1955.

—— *Gênes au XVᵉ siècle; activité économique et problèmes sociales*, Paris, 1961.

—— 'Les Génois en Angleterre; La crise de 1458–66', *Studi in onore di Armando Sapori*, vol. ii, Milan, 1958.

—— 'Le prix de l'assurance maritime à la fin du moyen âge', *Revue d'histoire économique et sociale*, xxxvii, 1959.

—— 'Le royaume de Grenade et la politique marchande de Gênes en Occident, XVᵉ siècle', *Moyen Âge*, lxiii, 1957.

—— 'Types de navires et spécialisation des trafics en Méditerranée à la fin du Moyen Âge', *IIᵉ Colloque d'histoire maritime*.

HEERS, M.-L., 'Les Génois et le commerce de l'alun à la fin du Moyen Âge', *Revue d'histoire économique et sociale*, xxxii, 1954.

HERLIHY, D., *Pisa in the Early Renaissance: A Study in Urban Growth*, Yale, 1958.

HEYD, WILHELM, *Le colonie commerciali degli Italiani in Oriente nel Medioevo* (trans. G. Müller), 2 vols., Venice, 1866–8.

—— *Storia del commercio del Levante nel Medioevo*, Turin, 1913.

HEYWOOD, W., *History of Pisa*, Cambridge, 1921.

HOLMES, G. A., 'Florentine Merchants in England, 1346–1436', *Economic History Review*, lxxv, 1960.

—— 'The "Libel of English Policy"', ibid. lxxvi, 1961.

HOUTTE, J. VAN, 'Bruges et Anvers, marchés nationaux ou internationaux du XIVᵉ au XVIᵉ siècle', *Revue du Nord*, xxxiv, 1952.

JAL, A., *Archéologie navale*, Paris, 1840.

—— *Glossaire nautique*, Paris, 1848.

KREKIC, B., *Dubrovnik (Ragusa) et le Levant au Moyen Âge*, Paris, 1961.

KRETSCHMER, K., *Die italienischen Portolans des Mittelalters*, Berlin, 1909.

LANE, F. C., *Andrea Barbarigo, Merchant of Venice (1418–49)*, Baltimore, 1944.

—— 'Cargaisons de coton et règlementations médiévales contre la surcharge des navires', *Revue d'histoire économique et sociale*, xl, 1962.

—— 'Fleets and Fairs: the functions of the Venetian *muda*', *Studi in onore di Armando Sapori*, vol. ii, Milan, 1958.

—— 'La marine marchande et le trafic maritime de Vénise à travers les siècles', *IVᵉ Colloque d'histoire maritime*.

—— 'Mediterranean Spice Trade', *American Historical Review*, xlv, 1940.

—— 'Ritmo e rapidità di giro d'affari nel commercio veneziano del Quattrocento', *Studi in onore di Gino Luzzatto*, vol. i, Milan, 1950.

—— 'Venetian Merchant Galleys, 1300–34; Private and Communal Operation', *Speculum*, xxxviii, 1963.

Lane, F. C., 'Venetian Naval Architecture about 1550', *Mariners' Mirror*, xx, 1934.

—— 'Venetian Shipping during the Commercial Revolution', *American Historical Review*, xxxviii, 1933.

—— *Venetian Ships and Shipbuilders of the Renaissance*, Baltimore, 1934.

Lapeyre, H., *Une famille de marchands, les Ruiz*, Paris, 1956.

—— and Carande, R., *Relaciones comerciales en el Mediterraneo durante el siglo XVI*, Cagliari, 1957.

La Roérie, G., and Vivielle, J., *Navires et marins. De la rame à l'hélice*, 2 vols., Paris, 1930.

Laurent, H., *Un Grand Commerce d'exportation au Moyen Âge; la draperie des Pays-Bas en France et dans les pays méditerranéens, XIIᵉ–XVᵉ siècles*, Paris, 1935.

Levi, Cesare A., *Navi venete da codici, marini e dipinti*, Venice, 1892.

Liagre, L., 'Le commerce de l'alun en Flandre au Moyen Âge', *Moyen Âge*, lxi, 1955.

Litta, P., *Famiglie celebri italiane*, Milan, 1819–67.

Lopez, R. S., and Raymond, W., *Medieval Trade in the Mediterranean World*, London, 1955.

—— 'Quattrocento genovese', *RSI*, lxxv, 1963.

Luzzatto, Gino, 'Sull'attendibilità di alcune statistiche economiche medievali', *Studi di storia economica veneziana*.

—— *Economic History of Italy* (trans. P. J. Jones), London, 1961.

—— 'Navigazione di linea e navigazione libera nelle grandi città marinare del Medioevo', *Studi di storia economica veneziana*.

—— 'Per la storia delle costruzioni navali a Venezia nei secoli XV e XVI', ibid.

—— *Storia economica dell'età moderna e contemporanea*, vol. i, Padua, 1955.

—— *Storia economica d'Italia: il Medioevo*, Florence, 1963.

—— *Storia economica di Venezia dall'XI al XVI secolo*, Venice, 1961.

—— *Studi di storia economica veneziana*, Padua, 1954.

Magalotti, Cesare, 'Discorso sulle galere' (ed. A. Scribanti), *Rivista Marittima*, 1922.

Main, A., *Costa del Tirreno superiore e Porto Pisano*, Leghorn, 1888.

Mallett, M. E., 'Anglo-Florentine Commercial Relations, 1465–1491', *Economic History Review*, 2nd ser., xv, 1962.

—— 'The Sea Consuls of Florence in the Fifteenth Century', *Papers of the British School at Rome*, xxvii, 1959.

Mancini, A., 'Osservazioni sul Porto Pisano e sulle origini di Livorno', *Bollettino storico livornese*, i, 1937.

Mandich, Giulio, 'Forme associative e misure anticoncorrenziali nel commercio marittimo veneziano del secolo XV', *Rivista della Società*, vi, 1961.

Manfroni, Camillo, 'Cenni sugli ordinamenti delle marine italiane nel Medioevo', *Rivista marittima*, 1898.

—— 'La disciplina dei marinai veneziani nel XIV secolo', ibid., 1902.

—— *Storia della marina italiana dal trattato di Ninfeo alla caduta di Constantinopoli*, Leghorn, 1902.

—— *Storia della marina italiana dalla caduta di Constantinopoli alla battaglia di Lepanto*, Leghorn, 1897.

MARCOTTI, G., *Un mercante fiorentino e la sua famiglia nel secolo XV* (Giovanni Rucellai), Florence, 1881.

MARÉCHAL, JEAN, 'Le départ de Bruges des marchands étrangers (XVᵉ et XVIᵉ siècles)', *Annales de la Société d'émulation de Bruges*, lxxxviii, 1951.

MARENGO, E., 'Genova e Tunisi (1288–1505)', *ASLSP*, xxxii, 1901.

MARIANI, A., *Notizie della famiglia Portinari*, Florence, 1897.

MARTINES, LAURO, *The Social World of the Florentine Humanists*, London, 1963.

MARINESCU, C., 'Les affaires commerciales en Flandres d'Alphonse V d'Aragon, roi de Naples (1416–58)', *Revue historique*, ccxxi, 1959.

MARKS, L. F., 'The Financial Oligarchy in Florence under Lorenzo', *Italian Renaissance Studies* (ed. E. F. Jacob), London, 1960.

MARTEILHE, JEAN, *Mémoires d'un protestant condamné aux galères de France pour cause de religion* (English trans.), London, Folio Society, 1957.

MARTENS, MINA, 'Les maisons de Medici et de Bourgogne au XVᵉ siècle', *Moyen Âge*, lvi, 1950.

MASI, F., *Ragionamento sulla navigazione e commercio della Repubblica Pisana*, Pisa, 1797.

MAS LATRIE, L. DE, *Relations et commerce de l'Afrique septentrionale ou Magreb avec les nations chrétiennes au Moyen Âge*, Paris, 1886.

—— 'Relations commerciales de Florence et de la Sicile avec l'Afrique au moyen âge', *Bibliothèque de l'École des Chartes*, 4th ser., v, 1859.

MASSART, E., 'Le relazioni commerciali fra Pisa e la Provenza', *BSP*, iii, 1934.

—— 'Sui trattati di navigazione e di commercio della Repubblica Pisana', *BSP*, vii, 1938.

MAZZI, C., 'Le carte di Benedetto Dei nella Medicea Laurenziana', *Rivista delle biblioteche e degli archivi*, xxv, 1914.

MELIS, F., *Aspetti della vita economica medievale*, vol. i, Florence, 1962.

—— 'Malaga sul sentiero economico del XIV e XV secolo', *Economia e storia*, iii, 1956.

—— *Note di storia della Banca pisana nel Trecento*, Pisa, 1955.

—— 'Uno sguardo al mercato dei panni di lana a Pisa nella seconda metà del Trecento', *Economia e storia*, vi, 1959.

—— 'Werner Sombart e i problemi della navigazione nel medio evo', in *Opera di Werner Sombart nel centenario della nascita*, Milan, 1964.

MERCIAI, G., *Mutamenti avvenuti nella configurazione del littorale fra Pisa e Orbetello*, Pisa, 1910.

MITCHELL, R. J., *The Spring Voyage; the Jerusalem Pilgrimage of 1458*, London, 1964.

MOLLAT, MICHEL, *Travaux des Colloques internationaux d'histoire maritime:*
   Vol. I. *Le Navire et l'économie maritime du XVᵉ au XVIIIᵉ siècle*, Paris, 1957.
   Vol. II. *Le Navire et l'économie maritime du Moyen Âge au XVIIIᵉ siècle*, Paris, 1959.
   Vol. IV. *Les Sources de l'histoire maritime européenne du Moyen Âge au XVIIIᵉ siècle*, Paris, 1961.

—— JOHANSEN, P., POSTAN, M., SAPORI, A., VERLINDEN, C., 'L'économie européenne aux deux derniers siècles du Moyen Âge', *Relazioni del X Congresso Internazionale di Scienze Storiche*, iii, Rome, 1955.

MORCHIO, D., *Il marinaio italiano*, Genoa, 1879.

MORGAN, J. B., and PEBERDY, PHILIP, *Collected Essays on Southampton*, Southampton, 1961.

MOROZZI, F., *Dello stato antico e moderno del fiume d'Arno*, Florence, 1762.

NALDINI, L., 'La politica coloniale di Pisa nel Medioevo', *BSP*, viii, 1939.

NUDI, GIACINTO, *Storia urbanistica di Livorno*, Venice, 1959.

OPPENHEIM, M., *A History of the Administration of the Royal Navy and of Merchant Shipping in Relation to the Navy*, London, 1896.

ORIGO, IRIS, 'The Domestic Enemy: Eastern Slaves in Tuscany in the 14th & 15th Centuries', *Speculum*, xxx, 1955.

—— *The Merchant of Prato; Francesco di Marco Datini*, London, 1957.

PAGNINI, G. F., *Della decima e di varie altre gravezze imposte dal comune di Firenze*, 4 vols., Lucca, 1765.

PANDIANI, E., 'Il primo comando in mare di Andrea Doria con uno studio sulle galee genovesi', *ASLSP*, lxiv, 1935.

PANTERA, PANTERO, *Armata navale*, Rome, 1614.

PARDESSUS, J.-M., *Collection des lois maritimes antérieures au XVIIIe siècle*, 6 vols., Paris, 1828.

PARDI, G., 'Disegno della storia demografica di Livorno', *ASI*, 6th ser., xi, 1918.

PARRY, J. H., *The Age of Reconnaissance*, London, 1963.

PEDRESCHI, L., 'Pisa. Ricerche di geografia urbana', *Rivista geografica italiana*, lviii, 1951.

PELLI, G., *Ritratti ed elogi degli uomini illustri toscani*, vol. i, Lucca, 1771.

PERRAGALLO, P., *Cenni intorno alla colonia italiana in Portogallo nei secoli XIV, XV e XVI*, Genoa, 1907.

PERUZZI, S. L., *Storia del commercio e dei banchieri di Firenze in tutto il mondo conosciuto dal 1200 al 1345*, Florence, 1868.

PETINO, A., 'Aspetti del commercio marittimo della Sicilia nell'età aragonese', *Bollettino storico catanese*, xi–xii, 1946–7.

PIATTOLI, L., 'Le leggi fiorentine sull'assicurazione nel Medioevo', *ASI*, 7th ser. xviii, 1932.

PIATTOLI, R., 'Firenze e Genova al tramonto della libertà di Pisa', *Giornale storico e letterario della Liguria*, vi, 1930.

—— 'Il problema portuale di Firenze dall'ultima lotta con Gian Galeazzo Visconti alle prime trattative per l'acquisto di Pisa, 1402–1405', *Rivista storica degli archivi toscani*, ii, 1930.

PISANI, MARIA, *Un avventuriero del Quattrocento; la vita e le opere di Benedetto Dei*, Naples, 1923.

PODESTA, F., *Il porto di Genova* (with a section by G. Pessagno on 'Le navi'), Genoa, 1913.

PÖHLMANN, R., *Die Wirtschaftspolitik der florentiner Renaissance und das Prinzip der Verkehrsfreiheit*, Leipzig, 1878.

POWER, E., 'English Wool Trade in the Reign of Edward IV', *Cambridge Historical Journal*, ii, 1926.

—— and POSTAN, M., *Studies in English Trade in the Fifteenth Century*, London, 1933.

RAMSAY, P., 'Overseas Trade in the Reign of Henry VII', *Economic History Review*, 2nd ser., vi, 1953.

RENOUARD, Y., *Les Hommes d'affaires italiens au Moyen Âge*, Paris, 1950.

—— 'Les voies du communication entre pays de la Méditerranée et pays de l'Atlantiqu eau Moyen Âge: problèmes et hypothèses', *Mélanges d'histoire du moyen âge dédiées à la mémoire de Louis Halphen*, Paris, 1951.

—— 'La capacité du tonneau bordelais au Moyen Âge', *Annales du Midi*, 1953.

REPETTI, E., *Dizionario geografico, storico, fisico del a Toscana*, 6 vols., Florence, 1841.

REUMONT A. VON, 'Di alcune relazioni dei fiorentini colla città di Danziga,' *ASI*, 2nd ser., xiii, 1861.

REYNAUD, F., 'Le mouvement des navires et des marchandises à Port-de-Bouc à la fin du XVe siècle', *Revue d'histoire économique et sociale*, xxxiv, 2, 1956.

RICHMOND, C. F., 'The Keeping of the Seas during the Hundred Years War: 1422–40', *History*, xlix, 1964.

RIGOBON, M., 'Per la storia delle sedi umane nel Valdarno inferiore', *Atti del R. Ist. veneto di scienze, lettere ed arti*, 1920–1.

ROGERS, F. M., *The Travels of the Infante Don Pedro of Portugal*, Cambridge (Mass.), 1961.

ROMANO, R., 'Aspetti economici degli armamenti navali veneziani nel secolo XVI', *ASI*, lxvi, 1954.

RUDDOCK, A. A., 'Alien Hosting in Southampton in the Fifteenth Century', *Economic History Review*, xvi, 1946.

—— *Italian Merchants & Shipping in Southampton, 1270–1600*, Southampton, 1951.

—— 'The Method of Handling the Cargoes of Medieval Merchant Galleys', *Bulletin of Institute of Historical Research*, xix, 1942.

SACERDOTI, A., 'Note sulle galere da mercato veneziane nel XV secolo', *Bollettino dell' Istituto di storia della società e stato veneziano*, iv, 1962.

SAPORI, ARMANDO, *Le Marchand italien au moyen âge*, Paris, 1952.

—— *Studi di storia economica medievale*, 2 vols., 3rd ed., Florence, 1956.

—— 'La Banca Medici', *Studi*, ii.

—— 'I beni del commercio internazionale nel Medioevo', *Studi*, i.

—— 'Una fiera in Italia alla fine del Quattrocento (La fiera di Salerno del 1478)', *Studi*, i.

—— 'I primi viaggi di Levante e Ponente delle galere fiorentine', *ASI*, cxiv, 1956.

SARDELLA, P., 'Nouvelles et spéculations à Venise au début du XVIe siècle', *Cahiers des Annales*, i, 1949.

SAYOUS, A.-E., *Le Commerce des Européens à Tunis depuis le XIIe siècle jusqu'à la fin du XVIe*, Paris, 1929.

SCARAMELLA, G., 'Fortificazioni di Livorno durante la prima dominazione fiorentina', *Miscellanea livornese di storia e di erudizione*, i, 1894.

SCHANZ, G. VON, *Englische Handelspolitik gegen Ende des Mittelalters*, 2 vols., Leipzig, 1881.

SCHAUBE, A., 'Die Anfänge der venetianischen Galeerenfahrten nach der Nordsee', *Historische Zeitschrift*, 3rd ser., ci, 1908.

—— *Das Konsulat des Meeres in Pisa*, Leipzig, 1888.

Bibliography 191

SCHEVILL, FERDINAND, *History of Florence from the Founding of the City through the Renaissance*, New York, 1936.

SCHULTE, A., *Geschichte der großen Ravensburger Handelsgesellschaft*, 3 vols., Stuttgart and Berlin, 1923.

SILVA, P., 'Intorno all'industria e al commercio della lana in Pisa', *Studi storici*, xix, 1910.

—— 'Ordinamento interno e contrasti politici e sociali in Pisa sotto il dominio visconteo', ibid. xxi, 1913.

—— 'Pisa sotto Firenze dal 1406 al 1433', ibid. xviii, 1909–10.

—— 'Sulle relazioni commerciali fra Pisa e l'Aragona', *Bollettino pisano d'arte e di storia*, 1913.

—— 'L'ultimo trattato commerciale fra Pisa e Firenze', *Studi storici*, xvii, 1908.

—— 'Il governo di Piero Gambacorta e le sue relazioni col resto della Toscana e coi Visconti', *Annali della R. Scuola Normale Superiore di Pisa*, xxiii, 1912.

SILVESTRI, A., *Il commercio a Salerno nella seconda metà del Quattrocento*, Salerno, 1952.

SINGER, C. J., *The Earliest Chemical Industry: an Essay in the Historical Relations of Economics and Technology Illustrated from the Alum Trade*, London, 1948.

SOMBART, WERNER, *L'opera di Werner Sombart nel centenario della nascita*, Biblioteca della rivista Economia e storia, viii, Milan, 1963.

SOSSON, JEAN-PIERRE, 'Un compte inédit de construction de galères à Narbonne (1318–20)', *Bulletin de l'Institut historique belge de Rome*, xxxiv, 1962.

SOTTAS, J., *Les Messageries maritimes de Vénise au XIVᵉ et au XVᵉ siècles*, Paris, 1938.

SPADOLINI, E., 'Il portolano di G. Benincasa', *La Bibliofilia*, ix, 1907–8.

SPEZIALE, C., 'Navi medicee', *Dedalo*, xii, 1932.

TEIXEIRA DA MOTA, A., 'L'art de naviguer en Méditerranée du XIIIᵉ au XVIIᵉ siècle et la création de la navigation astronomique dans les oceans', *IIᵉ Colloque d'histoire maritime*.

TENENTI, A., and VIVANTI, C., 'Le film d'un grand système de navigation; les galères marchandes vénitiennes XIV–XVI siècles', *Annales*, xvi, 1961.

TESI, C., *Livorno dalla sua origine ai nostri tempi*, Leghorn, 1865.

THIRIET, F., 'Quelques observations sur le trafic des galères vénitiennes depuis les chiffres des "incanti" (XIVᵉ–XVᵉ siècles)', *Studi in onore di Amintore Fanfani*, iii, Milan, 1962.

—— *La Romanie vénitienne au Moyen Âge. Le développement et l'exploitation du domain colonial vénitien (XIIᵉ–XVᵉ siècles)*, Bibliothèque des Écoles françaises d'Athènes et de Rome, 193, Paris, 1959.

TONIOLO, A. R., *Le variazioni storiche del littorale toscano fra l'Arno e la Magra*, Milan, 1927.

TOSCANELLI, N., 'Il Quartiere di Kinseca e i ponti sull'Arno a Pisa nel Medioevo', *BSP*, iii, 1934–5.

TOZZETTI TARGIONE, *Relazioni di alcuni viaggi*, Florence, 1768.

TRASSELLI, C., 'Les sources d'archives pour l'histoire du trafic maritime en Sicile', *IVᵉ Colloque d'histoire maritime*.

—— *Frumento e panni inglesi nella Sicilia del secolo XV*, Palermo, 1955.

TRASSELLI, C., 'Mercato dei panni a Palermo nella prima metà del secolo XV', *Economia e storia*, iv, 1957.
—— 'La produzione e commercio dello zucchero in Sicilia dal XIII al XIX secolo', ibid. ii, 1955.

TUCCI, R. DI, 'Costruzione di galee genovesi durante il dogato di Leonardo Monvaldi', *Ad Alessandro Luzio — gli archivi di stato italiani*, i, Florence, 1933.

TUCCI, U., 'Le conseil des douze sur les navires vénitiens', *IIe Colloque d'histoire maritime*.
—— 'Sur la pratique vénitienne de la navigation au XVIe siècle', *Annales*, xiii, 1958.

UZIELLI, G., 'Voyage des navires florentines au moyen âge sur les côtes de la France, l'Espagne, la Tunisie, l'Algérie, l'Angleterre et les Flandres', *L'Intermédiaire des chercheurs et curieux*, 1904.

UZIELLI, G. B., *Mappamondi, carte nautiche e portolani del Medioevo e dei secoli delle grandi scoperte marittime*, Rome, 1875.

VASILIEV, A., 'Pero Tafur. A Spanish traveller of the 15th century and his visit to Constantinople, Trebisond and Italy', *Byzantion*, vii, 1932.

VEDOVATO, G., 'Note sui privilegi capitolari fiorentini del sec. XV', *ASI*, xcvii, 1939.
—— *L'ordinamento capitolare in Oriente nei privilegi toscani dei secoli XII–XV*, Florence, 1946.

VERLINDEN, C., 'La colonie italienne de Lisbonne et le développement de l'économie métropolitaine et coloniale portugaise', *Studi in onore di Armando Sapori*, ii, Milan, 1958.

VIGO, P., *Il Porto Pisano; la sua difesa, il suo governo, la sua interna amministrazione*, Rome, 1915.
—— 'Il Porto Pisano', *Rivista marittima*, 1896.
—— *Le Repubbliche di Genova e Firenze per il possesso di Livorno*, Leghorn, 1915.

VINGIANO, GIUSEPPE, *Galee e galeotti*, Rome, 1960.

VIVES, J. V., FERNANDES, L. S., and CARRÈRE, C., *La economía de los países de la Corona de Aragon en la Baja Edad Media*, Cagliari, 1957.

VIVOLI, G., *Annali di Livorno*, 4 vols., Leghorn, 1843.

WATSON, W. B., 'The Structure of the Florentine Galley Trade with Flanders and England in the Fifteenth Century', *RBPH*, xxxix–xl, 1961–2.

WIEL, ALETHEA, *The Navy of Venice*, London, 1910.

WOLFF, P., *Commerce et marchands de Toulouse, 1350–1450*, Paris, 1954.

YVER, GEORGES, *Le Commerce et les marchands dans l'Italie méridionale au XIIIe et au XIVe siècle*, Paris, 1903.

ZANELLI, A., *Le schiave orientali a Firenze nei secoli XIV e XV*, Florence, 1885.

ZIPPEL, G., 'L'allume di Tolfa e il suo commercio', *ASRSP*, xxx, 1907.

POSTSCRIPT. Since this book was finished two works of considerable importance to the subject have appeared:

LANE, F. C., *Navires et constructeurs à Vénise pendant la Renaissance*, (revised edition), Paris, 1965.

MOLLAT, M. (ed.), *Les grandes voies maritimes dans le monde, XVe–XIXe siècles, VIIe Colloque d'histoire maritime*, Paris, 1965.

PART TWO

The Diary of
Luca di Maso degli Albizzi
Captain of the Galleys to
Flanders and England

1429–1430

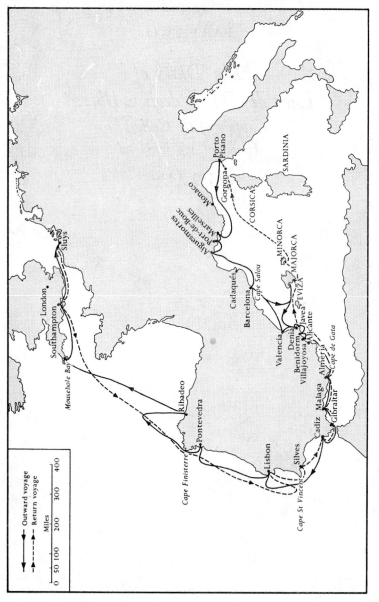

MAP I. Map of Western Europe, illustrating the voyage of the galleys of Luca di Maso degli Albizzi, 1429–30.

INTRODUCTION

Luca di Maso degli Albizzi

Public career. Luca was born in 1382 at a time when his father was already beginning to feel for the reins of power after the collapse of the popular régime established during the Ciompi rising.

Maso was for many years to be the leader of the oligarchic régime which turned back the Visconti threat, and, by expanding her frontiers and building up her wealth, led Florence to a new position of importance among the Italian states. Maso, despite his adulatory title of the 'Generous', was a tough and clever politician who seemed to be aiming at establishing his family as the permanent rulers of Florence. He was utterly ruthless with his rivals, and yet also knew the art of placating public opinion by well-timed financial and political concessions.

A part of Maso's policy was the careful education of his children to carry on after him, and Luca appears to have been brought up in the best courtly traditions of the time. Luca himself claimed that his father neglected the intellectual side of his education and that at the age of 19 he could only just read and write. The fault may perhaps be imputed more to adolescent laziness and preoccupation with sport and jousting, as it seems that Maso had a good deal of respect for spiritual things[1] and is unlikely to have been so much out of touch with the intellectual ferment of the time as to have deliberately discouraged his son's studies. Whatever the truth is and whether the subsequent studies were undertaken secretly or not, Luca began at a rather late stage to study the classics under the tutelage of Poggio Bracciolini. He later became one of the small group of Florentines which formed round Roberto de' Rossi, and among his companions at this stage were Cosimo de' Medici, Domenico Buoninsegni, Alessandro degli Alessandri, and Bartolo de' Tedaldi.[2]

However, we hear little more of Luca's humanistic leanings, although it was to him that Vespasiano da Bisticci was later to

[1] It was during the period of Maso's supremacy that Florence University took great strides forward as a centre of learning and became a vital influence in the rise of the humanists.

[2] Martines, *The Social World of the Florentine Humanists*, p. 256.

dedicate his 'Lives'. On his voyage to England Luca only took one book—a copy of St. Paul's epistles; a limited choice which perhaps reveals no great literary avidity if nothing else. He was, however, a prolific writer of diaries and personal memoirs many of which have survived and which we owe perhaps to his humanist training.[1]

But it was as a diplomat and statesman with a good deal of military and naval experience that Luca was to be best known. In 1403 he went on his first embassy with his father to Rome, and in the next year his diplomatic training was continued when he was attached to the embassy of Filippo Corsini to Genoa. In 1406 he fought in the campaign against Pisa and was one of the hostages given to Piero Gambacorta after his surrender of Pisa.

In 1410 Luca got his first maritime experience when he made a pilgrimage to the Holy Land which kept him away from Florence for over two years.[2] On his return he played the natural role of the younger brother of Rinaldo who had taken over the position of his father, and was sent as envoy to Perugia (1416), to Martin V in Mantua (1418) and Siena (1422). In those days ambassadors were still temporary appointments, sent to conduct specific negotiations, and Luca seems to have been very successful at this form of intermittent diplomacy.

In 1423 and 1424 he went to sea once more, first as commander of one of the new communal wool galleys on her trials off the coast of Provence, and then as special ambassador to the King of Aragon.[3] His mission on this occasion was to conclude a treaty with the Aragonese against Milan and her subject city Genoa. He succeeded in this and was himself Florentine commissary attached to the Infante's fleet in the campaign that followed. In 1425 his maritime experience was indirectly increased when he became Captain of Leghorn.

In 1427 he was a Prior, apparently for the first time; and later in the year he went to Hungary as envoy to the Emperor Sigismund.

[1] For details of ten of these diaries, see Marcello del Piazzo, *Signoria, Dieci di Balia, Otto di Pratica: inventario sommario. Quaderni della Rassegna degli Archivi di Stato*, i, Rome, 1960, pp. 7–10, 12, 13, 39–40. These diaries are the main sources for a biography of Luca, but for useful synopses see Litta, *Famiglie celebri*, s.v. Albizzi, table xviii, and *Dizionario Biografico degli Italiani*, Fondazione Treccani, Rome, 1960-, vol. ii.

[2] For further details of this pilgrimage see Guasti, *Le commissioni di Rinaldo degli Albizzi*, iii, pp. 674–6.

[3] See above, p. 38.

His last public responsibility before his voyage to the north was as one of the judges in the great tournament held in Piazza Santa Croce in April 1429. Thus in 1429 at the age of 47 he would seem to have been almost an ideal choice for Captain of the Galleys. He had travelled widely and was well accustomed to the hardships which travel at this time involved. In particular he had spent some time at sea and had commanded galleys at sea; this was a sort of experience which not many Florentines had at this time. Furthermore, he had considerable diplomatic experience which was very valuable for a galley captain who was also a travelling ambassador for Florence. Finally he had also military experience, and the upbringing and training which make a natural leader.

Luca's subsequent career can for our purposes be considered more briefly, although one cannot avoid some comment on what was perhaps the most crucial moment of his career, his decision to take the side of Cosimo de' Medici against his own brother Rinaldo in 1434. Luca has been generally blamed for his part in these events, and was described by Litta as 'uomo accortissimo, profondo simulatore' who accurately summed up the situation and turned against his family and his brother to further his own career. However, it should perhaps be pointed out that it would seem that Luca had not been very close to Rinaldo in recent years and indeed appears to have been always regarded by him with some suspicion. Is it coincidence that Luca had spent so much of his life out of Florence and only served in the *Signoria* once before 1434? Is it not a little surprising that between 1426 and 1433 there is only evidence of one letter passing between the brothers in the vast collection of Rinaldo's reports and letters published by Guasti?[1] Is it not perhaps slightly indicative that in his voyage to England Luca wrote four or five letters each to Niccolò di Gentile, his cousin, to Berto da Filicaia, and to his father-in-law, and two to Antonio Migliorotti and Bernardo Gherardi, but only one to his brother? A more detailed study than I can at present undertake would be needed to reveal the real relations between the two brothers, but the indications are that they were not very close. It is perhaps also interesting to note that most of Luca's correspondents at this time

[1] See Guasti, *Le commissioni di Rinaldo degli Albizzi*, iii, *passim*. In 1430 Luca declared himself as fiercely opposed to his brother's policy of declaring open war on Milan (ibid., p. 509).

were to reveal themselves as pro-Mediceans, including his cousins Niccolò di Luca and Niccolò di Gentile. He was in fact married to a Medici, but this is not particularly relevant as his father-in-law, Niccolà, was himself to take the side of Rinaldo in 1433, and came from the rival branch of the Medici family to that of Cosimo.

The fact remains that Luca had always held himself apart from internal politics, and had never figured amongst the leaders of the oligarchy. He had spent his life serving Florence, not trying to rule her, and it was as a servant of the *Signoria*, and commander of the infantry of the Comune that he played his part in the events of 1434.

He did indeed benefit from coming down clearly on the side of Cosimo and for the rest of his life was rather more active in internal politics than he had been previously. However, it was as a diplomat that he continued to render his greatest services to the Republic, going as envoy to Eugenius IV in Bologna and to Venice in 1436; to Francesco Sforza in 1437; to Genoa in 1440; to Venice in 1441; to Rome in 1445 and to Venice again in 1447 and 1449. He was Gonfalonier of Justice in 1442 and in 1449 was commissary-general with the Florentine army. He died in 1458 as Litta says 'mourned by Cosimo and detested by all lovers of liberty'.

Private life. Luca di Maso degli Albizzi was married twice; in 1410 he married Lisabetta di Niccolò de' Bardi who for many years remained childless. In 1418 Luca's illegitimate son Masetto was born and on him Luca lavished a good deal of affection and care. Masetto was destined for a career in the Church and at his death in 1467 he was a canon of Florence cathedral. In 1425 Lisabetta finally gave birth to a son Pier Francesco, but herself died a few days later. Pier Francesco died at the age of 23 after showing signs of becoming a considerable poet.

Luca took as his second wife Aurelia di Niccolà de' Medici whom he married in 1426 when she was 16. Niccolà di Vieri de' Medici was an erudite man, noted both in humanistic and in commercial circles. But he had seen control of the family mercantile interests pass from his father to his cousins Giovanni di Bicci, and later Cosimo. For some years the two branches of the Medici family had operated in competition but by the late 1420's Niccolà's fortunes were reaching a low ebb.[1] The Catasto returns of 1427 reveal that Luca was rather wealthier than his father-in-law;

[1] De Roover, *Medici Bank*, p. 37.

Niccolà, who in 1403 had together with his brother Cambio the third highest Prestanza assessment in the S. Giovanni quarter (and the fifth in all Florence), by 1427 ranked only 54th in the quarter when net capital was reckoned.[1] Luca with a net capital of nearly 8,000 florins ranked 35th in the same quarter. Luca's wealth lay entirely in real estate and in *Monte* holdings; besides his house in Piazza S. Piero Maggiore, he had a country house in Nipozzano and considerable holdings there and in S. Martino a Bibbiano, S. Niccolò a Vico, S. Jacopo a Frascoli, Montefalcone, Bientina, S. Miniato a Monte, and Castelfranco. In addition he had holdings to the value of 957 florins in the *Monte comune* and 308 florins in the *Monte* of Pisa. He appears to have had no commercial interests at all.[2]

Luca's marriage to Aurelia was immediately fruitful, and by the time that he left on his voyage she had already borne him two children and was carrying a third. Maso was born early in 1427, and Lisabetta, his first and only daughter, in 1428. While her husband was sailing home along the south coast of Spain, Aurelia bore her third child, Giovanbattista, born on 12 March 1430. Subsequently she was to have four more children, of whom Antonio, born in 1431, was to become a seaman like his father. One is tempted to think that Aurelia must have been both a good and fortunate mother, as all Luca's nine children survived into maturity, a rather unusual occurrence in those times. She survived her husband by seventeen years and died in 1475.

Luca's voyage and his diary. Luca was elected Captain of the Galleys in May 1429 and his nominee in the electoral council of consuls was Andrea di Giusto Coverelli, to whom he presumably paid the 10 florins laid down in the regulations.

This is one of the additional pieces of information about the voyage which can be gleaned from Luca's accounts which form the first part of the manuscript of the diary. These accounts also tell us of the equipment and furnishings which he took with him on the voyage. Apart from a supply of clothing and his armour he took eight cross-bows, a considerable quantity of bedding, his

---

[1] For some very useful lists of the leading assessments in the 1403 Prestanza and 1427 Catasto returns, see Martines, *Social World of the Florentine Humanists*, pp. 351–78.

[2] Catasto 58, ff. 80^r–92^r. Luca's estates were concentrated mainly in two areas, the Val di Sieve (Nipozzano, Bibbiano, Frascoli) and on the lower Arno round Castelfranco and Bientina.

pennant and flag, his copy of the Epistles of St. Paul, and a pair of slippers. It was laid down in the regulations that the Captain should fly his own flag on his galley, and Luca paid 28 florins for a new one to be made.

Also in these preliminary accounts appear reports of numerous purchases which Luca made, or were made for him, on the voyage. In Majorca he bought six small baskets; in Cadiz silk handkerchiefs; in Bruges and Southampton a considerable quantity of cloth of all types, candlesticks, brass bowls and jugs, and birettas for ecclesiastical friends. At one stage he even bought a monkey as a gift, and in Spain he bought some hair-nets for Aurelia.

A final interesting feature of the accounts are some records of observations of the height of the Pole Star at various points along the route. It is generally held that astronomical navigation was not used by Mediterranean sailors until the second half of the fifteenth century, and that an astrolabe had not yet been devised which could be used accurately on board a ship.[2] Certainly Luca's observations were very approximate and there is no indication that they were used in the navigation of the galleys, but they do indicate his interest in maritime matters. This interest is borne out by his familiarity with nautical terms and the care with which he describes the more technical aspects of the voyage.

The first and most striking impression on reading Luca's diary and his reports to the Sea Consuls is that he was an extremely conscientious official. Not only are his reports detailed and careful but also he seems to be almost exasperatingly anxious to do the right thing and to serve Florence to the best of his ability. We may find his letters repetitious in their constant reiterations of requests for instructions and support, but we cannot help but note the firm line which he takes with the Sea Consuls and his real determination to get his galleys back safely. He refused to be intimidated by Philip the Good when the latter wished to requisition the galleys, and yet says little in his letters to the Consuls about all the trouble he had had over this affair. He was also quick to seize the opportunity of opening negotiations for trade concessions in Portugal which was presented by his unscheduled stop in Lisbon. He seems

---

[1] A. Teixeira de Mota, 'L'art de naviguer en Mediterranée du XIIIe au XVIIIe siècle et la création de la navigation astronomique dans les oceans', *IIe Colloque d'histoire maritime*, Paris, 1958, *passim*, and A. Cortesão, 'Nautical Science and the Renaissance', *Archives internationaux d'Histoire des Sciences*, ix, 1949, pp. 1086-7

to have got on well with Soper and his English colleagues, and wherever he went he took a trained diplomat's interest in events around him.

The patrons and crews of the galleys

It is difficult to form an exact estimate of the size and the composition of the crews of Luca's two galleys, as at no time does Luca give any precise figures. He writes a good deal about his crews in his letters to the Sea Consuls from Sluys, but, as he had a very low opinion of the value of many of the men who had been signed on, he only takes account of the 'effectives'. Thus in his letters of 6 and 12 December (pp. 241–49) he tells us that the galleys had about 130 effective oarsmen each and 25 effective marines and senior sailors. On the other hand he says they needed 160 oarsmen and 50 others. This ideal figure of 210 was in fact about the standard complement of a Florentine galley,[1] and one wonders how far Luca's actual crews fell below this figure or whether he was writing off over fifty men in each galley as useless. The probability is that in view of Luca's harsh remarks about some of his men and the fact that he admits to 155 'effectives' per galley, his total strength (taking no account of desertions) fell not far short of the normal.

In order to have a better idea of what the normal complement of a Florentine galley was, and its various component parts, we must turn to two surviving records of the crews of other galleys. The first is the roll of the Alexandria galley of which Luigi Vettori was commissary in 1445, the second is the summary of the crew of the armed galley of which Benedetto Dei was commissary in 1471.[2] I have set the two side by side for purposes of comparison:

Luigi Vettori's great galley	*Benedetto Dei's long galley*
(Captain and his suite)	
Patron	Patron
Mate (*comito*)	Mate
2nd mate (*sotto comito*)	2nd mate
Commissary (*rassegna*)	Commissary
2 junior officers (*uomini di consiglio*)	2 junior officers
Carpenter (*maestro d'ascia*)	Carpenter
Caulker (*maestro calafato*)	Caulker

[1] See above, p. 29.
[2] *Quadernuccio di Luigi Vettori, passim*, and *Cronaca di Benedetto Dei*, f. 91ʳ.

Oar repairer (*maestro remolaio*)	(Doctor)
Purser (*scrivano*)	(Trumpeter)[1]
Assistant purser (*sotto scrivano*)	Purser
Master of the oarsmen (*aguzzino*)	4 helmsmen[2]
8 helmsmen (*nocchieri*)	50 marines
38 marines (*compagnoni*)	160 sailors and oarsmen
6 bow oarsmen (*prodieri*)	
6 2nd bow oarsmen (*secondieri*)	
6 stern oarsmen (*portolati*)	
6 2nd stern oarsmen (*secondieri*)[3]	
129 sailors and oarsmen	
211	225

Benedetto Dei's galley being an armed galley was slightly exceptional in that it carried fifty marines and a number of specialist sailors and officers, whereas on a merchant galley the number of men carried over and above the oarsmen totalled about fifty in all.

With these general figures in mind let us now return to Luca's galleys and some of the personalities on board.

Piero Vespucci's galley. The patron of this galley was almost certainly Piero di Simone Vespucci, as Luca at one point refers to him by mistake as Simone. Vespucci was a man of comparatively limited means, although his total wealth was not inconsiderable, amounting to 3,366 florins made up largely of real estate. But the bulk of this wealth was committed and his taxable capital came well below 1,000 florins. In addition to his lands he had a part share in a wholesale clothing firm run by Giovanni Altoviti.[4] There is no direct evidence that he had been to sea before although there was a Piero Vespucci who sailed to Sluys in 1395 and was a correspondent of Datini.[5] He had, however, been one of the Sea Consuls in 1426[6] and was a Prior in 1428. He was to be Sea Consul again in 1435 and in the following year he was chief tax collector in Pisa[7] (*provveditore delle gabelle*).

[1] These two do not appear in Vettori's list as they formed part of the Captain's suite when the Captain was travelling on the galley.

[2] By 1471 only four helmsmen were needed as the lateen rudders had been abandoned.

[3] These bow and stern oarsman were the most experienced of the ordinary sailors who rowed on the foremost and rearmost benches and assisted with the sails. For discussion of the equivalent ranks in the Venetian galleys, see Manfroni, 'Cenni sugli ordinamenti delle marine italiane', *passim*.   [4] Catasto 75, ff. 175ʳ–176ᵛ.

[5] F. Melis, *Aspetti della vita economica medievale*, Siena, 1962, tav. xii.

[6] Tratte 79, f. 95.   [7] Tratte 80, ff. 390 and 307.

Vespucci was married to Piera di Francesco Guiducci and had one son at this time, born in 1428. Presumably the connexion with the Guiducci family accounts for the fact that two young men of the family were serving amongst the officers on Vespucci's galley. The members of Vespucci's crew of whom we know the names were:

Niccolò di Lottieri—commissary
Andrea Marini—mate[1]
Guglielmo d'Asti—2nd mate
Antonio d'Andrea—3rd mate
Luciano da Portovenere—junior officer
Simone Guiducci, il Ghiozzo ⎫
Maso Aliotti ⎪
Rosso Guiducci ⎬ officers or marines
Taddeo da Piombino ⎪
Luca d'Antonio da Cortona ⎭
Bartolomeo di Bonifazio—promoted helmsman at the end of the voyage.

Bernardo Carnesecchi's galley. The patron of this galley was almost certainly Bernardo di Cristofano Carnesecchi, and if this assumption is correct, he was the only one of the three commanders who was an active merchant. He had been a partner in the firm of Vieri de' Medici & Co. in 1422, with particular interests in the Avignon branch of the firm.[2] A Bernardo Carnesecchi was reported as being active in Aiguesmortes and Montpellier in 1428, exporting cloths, silk, and honey to the East in Catalan shipping in partnership with Bernardo Ventura.[3] Certainly Carnesecchi claimed to know the governor of Aiguesmortes and was obviously very much at home there when the galleys passed through, and so it is likely that he was the same man. In this case and with this background it seems quite possible that Carnesecchi was one of the conductors of these galleys as well as being patron.

He was a comparatively wealthy man, having a house in the parish of St. Maria Maggiore in Florence, another house in Prato and a farm near Cascina. His net capital was rather smaller than Luca's in 1427 (6,241 florins), but he was vastly better off than

---

[1] After his return from this voyage Andrea Marini was put in charge of equipping the communal galleys in Pisa (MAP II, 345).
[2] Catasto 79, ff. 574ʳ–576ʳ.
[3] Del Treppo, 'Assicurazioni e commercio', ii, p. 51.

Vespucci. In 1427 he made no mention of a wife in his Catasto return, but he shared a house with his sister Ginevra and had two children aged 8 and 3½ respectively.

Apart from his merchant experience he had no connexion with the galley system before 1429, but he was Sea Consul twice in later years (1436 and 1446)[1] and in 1451 was Gonfalonier of Justice.

As Luca was not travelling on this galley we know very little about its crew. The commissary was Giusto di Lionardo and the mate was Gaddo who may have been the Gaddo da Livorno who was in command of a galleot at the battle of Rapallo in 1431. We also know that Carnesecchi's purser was a certain Giuliano.

The Diary

The diary of Luca di Maso degli Albizzi here published in part for the first time is to be found in the State Archives in Florence in the collection known as Signoria, Dieci di Balia, Otto di Pratica; Legazioni e commissarie, Missive e responsive, V, 1. This is a mixed collection of material which includes a number of Luca's diaries; this one came originally from the Strozzi archive.[2]

The diary is contained in a register of 128 pages entitled 'Quadernuccio di Luca di Messer Maso degli Albizzi capitano delle galere di Ponente del Comune di Firenze, del 27 agosto 1429 al 31 marzo 1430'. Its contents consists of:

folios 1–23 : 'Dare e avere del capitano delle galere.'
folios 45–46 : 'Ricordo de' di utili che steteno in Antona'
             (See pp. 278–80).
folios 47–50ᵛ : 'Ricordo de' nomi si daranno per la nocte.'
folios 51–114 :'Ricordo fatto per me Lucha di tutto il processo et
             viaggio . . . etc.'
folio 108 :   Lettera dei Consoli del Mare fiorentini a Luca degli
             Albizzi, del 10 gennaio 1429/30 (pp. 276–7).

Of the five sections which make up the manuscript, I have omitted two in this edition, and altered the order of the remaining three. The two parts omitted are the miscellaneous accounts which occupy the first 23 folios and the synopsis of the voyage on folios

---

[1] Tratte 80, f. 390.
[2] The importance of this manuscript was noted by Canestrini ('Relazioni commerciali coi Portoghesi', p. 98) who promised to publish it but never succeeded in doing so.

47–50. Luca's accounts are a muddled series of notes which indicate quite clearly that he had no business training. The items of interest which emerge from them have been mentioned in this introduction or in the footnotes, and for reasons of space I have thought it best not to publish this section. The synopsis of the voyage adds nothing to the complete narrative in the diary itself; it merely records the point which the galleys had reached each day. The only item of additional interest which emerges from this section is that there seems to have been a custom of dedicating each day at sea to a particular saint. The saints seem to have been chosen completely at random and bear no relationship to the liturgical calendar. A typical entry in this section reads: 'Santo Marco martedì nocte adì 14 a capo Gatto in Granata.'

I have also omitted two of the copies of Luca's letters to the Sea Consuls when they add nothing further to the narrative which precedes them. In these cases the omission is mentioned in the footnotes.

In preparing this diary for publication I have followed the normal rules current in Italy for the editing of manuscripts. I have modernized punctuation and capitalization; I have inserted the usual accents and apostrophes to indicate dropped letters, and respaced words which have been run together. But I have preserved the original spelling intact with notes of explanation when mispelling seems to obscure the meaning of the text. In addition I have adopted the following editorial conventions:

//   end of page in the manuscript.
[   ]   insertion of letter or letters by editor to clarify the text.
(   )   cancellation in the original text.
. . .   lacuna in the original text.

The following reference works have been used in the translation and clarification of the more obscure nautical and other terms found in this diary;

F. CORAZZINI, *Vocabolario nautico italiano*, Turin, 1900.
A. GUGLIELMOTTI, *Vocabolario marino e militare*, Rome, 1889.
A. JAL, *Glossaire nautique*, Paris, 1848.
B. REYNOLDS (ed.), *Cambridge Italian Dictionary*, vol. i, Cambridge, 1962.
NICOLÒ TOMMASEO and BERNARDO BELLINI, *Dizionario della lingua italiana*, Rome, 1865.
Vocabolario degli Accademici della Crusca, 4th ed., Florence, 1729–38.

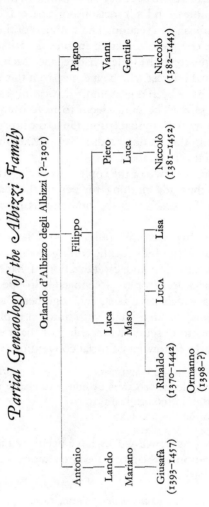

Partial Genealogy of the Albizzi Family

Orlando d'Albizzo degli Albizzi (?–1301)

The Narrative of the Voyage of the Galleys

RICORDO fatto per me Lucha di tutto il processo et viaggio ch'io 51^r
farò in sulle galee del comune che col nome di Dio debbano andare
in Fiandra et in Inghilterra per mercatantia, cioè galee ii grosse, per
partire di Porto Pisano in dì 1º di settenbre 1429, padroni Bernardo
Carnesecchi et Piero Vespucci, fatti et date le galee in sino adì . . . et
poi fatto io capitano adì . . . .
Partì' di Firenze col nome di Dio et di buona ventura adì 27
d'agosto, demo a mangiare a ora di vespro; et menai per miei con-
pagni Carlo di Nichola de' Medici, famigli et altri gl'infrascripti.[1]
Karlo di Nichola de' Medici.
(Lionardo Fighineldi tornossi a Firenze di 13 di settembre)
Ser Agnolo di Nolfo.
Mari dalla Cicogna.
Zanobi detto Magnino di Iohanni del Magno — rimissilo in
luogo di Lionardo.[2]
Puccino di Piero da Firenze in suo luogho.
Bentacordi di . . . da Firenze.
Curado di Giovanni tedescho per conpagnone.[3]

[1] The Captain's suite as laid down in the regulations consisted of a chaplain, a
barber-surgeon, two trumpeters, two servants, and four squires (Consoli del Mare V,
Capitoli dei capitani, c. 2). The latter were described as *compagnoni* as also were the
marines which the galleys carried, but presumably these four occupied a rather
different position from the other marines, being 'companions' of the Captain and
often young men of good family.

[2] These were presumably the four squires; Carlo di Nicoolà de' Medici was
Luca's brother-in-law, a very young man at this time but who was later to make his
mark in public affairs. Ser Agnolo di Nolfo came from Vicorato in the Mugello and
served as Captain's notary. He had been enrolled in the Guild of the Judges and
Notaries in 1420. One volume of his legal transactions is to be found in the notarial
archives of Florence, but it contains no entries for the period of this voyage (ASF,
Archivio Notarile ante-Cosimiano, A. 662). Of Mari dalla Cicogna and Zanobi di
Giovanni we know nothing, except that the latter seems to have been promoted
from the position of servant as a result of the sudden departure of Lionardo
Fighineldi. It is possible that one of these four was the surgeon who, at least by the
1440's, was a member of the Captain's suite.

[3] Luca in fact took three servants with him, one of whom, Curado di Giovanni of
Spires, was enrolled as a marine to comply with the regulations. Bentacordi was
brought from Florence by Luca and was paid 2¼ florins a month (Diary, f. 5^r),
whereas Puccino was taken on in Leghorn to fill the gap created by the promotion
of Zanobio and was paid 2 florins a month (Diary, f. 6^r).

208 *Luca di Maso degli Albizzi*

Ser Stefano di . . . dalla Pieve a Santo Stefano per capellano.[1]
La sera adì 27 albergamo a Empoli con Giusafà degli Albizzi che mi fè assai honore.[2]

Adì 28 d'agosto desinamo a Cascina e la sera venimo a Pisa, dove m'apresentai a' consoli et poi più a tardi venne Piero Vespucci padrone; Bernardo era a Pisa.

Piero di . . . di Spagna ⎫
Nerone di . . . corsicha ⎭ per trombetti

Curado di Iohanni da Spira mio famiglio stato fe' scrivere per conpagnone. //

51ᵛ Adì 29 d'agosto fu san Giovanni Dicollato et niente si fè[3] delle galee per reverentia.

Adì 30 demo sevo; et dietro a mangiare, si cominciò a mettere bancho, penossi alsino quasi tutto dì 31.[4]

Adì 31 sì cominciò a scrivere la ciurma et conpagnoni.

Adì 1° di settenbre mettemo in galea gran parte de' coredi et dì 2 die' danari.[5]

Adì 2 uscì de' ponti la galea di Bernardo et diessi danari a' conpagnoni e marinai.

Adì 3 si fornì quasi d'armare et uscì de' ponti la galea del capitano, ma nondimeno le manchava lanterne et l'artimone et altri fornimenti.[6]

---

[1] Ser Stefano, the chaplain, received 2½ florins a month for his services (Diary, f. 17ᵛ). His parish of S. Stefano may well have been S. Stefano ai Lupi, one of the parishes of Porto Pisano.

[2] Giusafà di Mariano degli Albizzi (1393–1457) was a distant cousin of Luca. He was a soldier of fortune who seems to have fought both for and against Florence. At this time he was engaged with Luca's brother Rinaldo in the taking of Volterra. (Litta, *Famiglie celebri*, s.v. Albizzi, table viii.)

[3] In the manuscript Luca uses the form *fe* both for *fei* ('I made', etc.) and for *fece* ('he made', etc.). To distinguish the two meanings I have adopted the normal convention of *fe'* for *fei*, and *fè* for *fece*.

[4] *sevo* or *sego*: tallow.

mettere banco was the normal expression for recruiting the crew of a ship. A table was set up by the patron and his mate, in this case probably in front of the palace of the Sea Consuls, and volunteers came forward to sign on.

[5] The regulations laid down that the crews should receive 2½ months' pay before leaving Porto Pisano, 2 months' pay at Sluys, and 2½ months' at Southampton; thus making the seven months which was the official duration of the western voyage (Consoli del Mare, IV, 4, *Capitoli dei conductori e patroni*, c. 2).

[6] *artimone* was the mainsail of a galley, although there was a larger sail for some ships known as the *bastardo*. The other sails used were:

terzaruolo: originally one-third the size of the mainsail and sometimes known as the *marabotto*;

pappafico: a small lateen sail hoisted high on the mast and used as a fair weather sail;

Adì 4 fu domenicha et desinamo co' consoli[1] io et padroni et fornissi d'armare et quasi di fare le preste a' marinai et conpagnoni.

Lunedì adì 5 stettono le galee fuori de' ponti et martedì adì 6 cominciarono ad andare verso la foce, et perchè l'aqua era pocha adurarono al 1/3 della via o circha.

Mercoledì adì 7 si fornirono lanterne nuove della galea capitana e l'artimone et mandoronsi a galea; e lle galee si tirarono insino al boschetto la sera et ivi adurarono. // Giovedì adì 8, il dì di Nostra Donna, le galeazze per forza d'argani 52ʳ et d'uomini si sdurarono et condusonsi a foce.[2]

Venerdì passata terza, adì 9, uscirono di foce et andarono a Porto Pisano alla torre del Magnano.[3]

Sabato mattina adì x di settenbre a levata di sole, mi parti' da Pisa et fu' a Livorno a desinare; et ordinai col capitano[4] che ciaschuno marinaio o conpagnone a ore 23 fussi alle galee et così misse bando sotto pena, et pena agli osti che ritenessino gl'uomini di galea da ora detta in là, acciò che le galee fussino meglio aconpagnate. A ora di vespro[5] vennono i padroni a Livorno et Andrea

cochina: a small square storm-sail sometimes known as the *trevo*;
mezzana: the sail for the mizzen mast.
All of these were lateen sails except for the *cochina*.

[1] The Sea Consuls at this time were Riccardo di Niccolò Sagni, Giuliano di Tommaso Martini, Andrea di Veri Rondinelli, Andrea di Giusto Coverelli, Nofri di Silvestro Cennini, and Maso di Filippo Neri (Tratte 79, ff. 95 sqq). Of these Coverelli is recorded as having died during his term of office. One of the Consuls in Pisa in Sept. 1429 was Andrea Rondinelli, and another was referred to by Luca as Bernardo (see below, p. 216). It is possible that Bernardo was Coverelli's replacement and his full name was never entered in the Tratte.

[2] These two galleys took three days to cover the 9 kilometres from the Ponte a Mare at Pisa to Foce d'Arno, the small fort and lighthouse at the mouth of the river.

[3] The Torre Magnano was one of three towers at the entrance to Porto Pisano. Round it there were twelve stone columns to which ships could moor.

[4] The Captain of Livorno at this time was probably Giovanni di Forese Salviati who had been appointed in Aug. 1429 (Tratte 67, f. 14).

[5] Luca and his companions used two methods of keeping the time during their voyage. By this date the division of the day into 24 hours of uniform length was general practice in Italy, and the day was reckoned to start from sunset. Hence, although Luca refers to the first or second hour 'of the night', he does not then speak of the first or second hour 'of the day' but instead by late afternoon has reached the 22nd or 23rd hour. In fact, during the day he tends to measure time by use of the liturgical hours which for his purpose were:

terza: three hours after sunrise (*mezza terza* came between sunrise and *terza*);
sesto (*mezzodì*): midday;
nona: the ninth hour, mid-afternoon;
vespro: one hour before sunset, the 23rd hour.

For discussion of the problems involved in medieval reckonings of time see Fasano

Marini di consentimento del suo padrone, mostrando per suoi fatti non potere fare di meno, andò a Pisa promettendogli di tornare a terza l'altro dì. Io dissi non gli davo nè toglievo licentia perchè anchora non ero capitano, che sopra sè andassi ma non di mia licentia. Tornamo a Livorno in casa Nieri spetiale, et parte di mia famiglia all'albergo del Capello.

Domenica adì 11 di settenbre vennono i consoli a desinare a Livorno e le galee si fornivano de' bisogni et molti galeotti et conpagnoni vennono et cominciarono a stare in galea. //

52ᵛ Martedì adì 13 montai in galea passata terza, con Andrea di Veri consolo, et facemo la rasegna delle galee et trovamole in punto secondo i capitoli. Diè loro il giuramento a tutti de' raconpagnare le galee et d'essere ubidiente al capitano et all'onore del comune di Firenze. Et oltre a cciò fe' bandire la pena del bestemiare et del giuocho etc.[1]

Fe' dipositare nelle mani del prete nostro della galea del capitano, cioè Ser Stefano, i fiorini 500 sugellati secondo disse avere veduti, et nelle mani di Giusto di Lionardo, rasegna della galea di Bernardo Carnesecchi, fiorini 500 secondo mi raportò Antonio da Malaventre che gli vide contare come mio mandato; poi che fu nocte.[2]

Mercoledì adì 14 stemo in porto per cattivo tenpo sino a ora di terza o circha; dipoi tornò il vento a sciloccho et mezzodì, et noi facemo vela al nome di Dio.[3]

Guarini, 'Comment naviguent les galères', pp. 280–3, and G. Bilfinger, *Die mittelalterlichen Uhren und die modernen Stunden*, Stuttgart, 1892.

[1] See above, p. 30, for an excerpt from the regulations on gambling and blaspheming.

[2] Here we see Luca following carefully the letter of the regulations: 'Anchora che a petitione del capitano chi conducerà com'è detto, sia tenuta e debba prima chelle galee partino di Porto Pisano dipositare fiorini 500 per galea, cioè nelle mani del prete che andrà in sulla galea capitana fiorini 500. Et cosi nelle mani di chi parrà al capitano in su l'altra galea fiorinin 500, denari sugellati. Excepto che al padrone non si possano dare o dipositare detti danari, et che'l detto capitano sia tenuto ricevere detti danari ogni volta si partino d'alcuno luogho dove avessino posto. Et in caso non vi trovasse detti danari o quegli vi dovessino essere, faccia il detto capitano rimectergli in ordine . . .' (Consoli del Mare V, *Capitoli dei capitani*, c. 24). *Fiorini suggellati* were florins that had been weighed, tested, and sealed in a purse as a guarantee of their true value.

It is not clear what position Antonio da Malaventre occupied on the galleys. He executed several commissions for Luca during the voyage, and was a Pisan who a few years later had a ship of his own.

[3] The eight primary winds were:

levante: east   *sciloccho (sciroccho)*: south-east

Giovedì al coricare del sole ci trovamo sopra Monacho circha miglia 20 larghi da terra col vento sciloccho et levante, adì 15.

Venerdì adì 16 a ora di nona o circha, col nome di Dio surgemo a Marsilia dove trovamo di fuori alle Ponude[1] Ciardullo de' Regno[2] con una galea et una galeotta armata // e aveva prese 3 navi che ve 53r n'era una di più che botti 800, ii di genovesi et la grande de' catalani, et dicevasi aveva guadagnati circha fiorini 50.000. Da Marsilia scripsi a' consoli la infrascripta lettera per aviso.

Magnifici patres et domini etc.[3] In questa ora giugnemo qui con prospero vento et a salvamento per la gratia di Dio, et diamo modo a scaricare le cose ci sono per qui et così caricare quello c'è da levare per tutto ogi, et come piacerà a Dio seguiremo nostro viaggio. Abbiamo trovato qui alle Ponude di Marsilia Certullo de' Regno con una gale[a] sottile et una galeotta armate et à prese ii navette di genovesi et con quelle à presa una nave catalana di Nantone di botti 900 o circha; et in su dette navi à guadagnato molta roba di catalani, genovesi et fiorentini in somma, secondo si dice, di più di fiorini 50000. Et così si sta con tutti in conserva. Per fretta dello spaccio nostro non vi posso avisare più particularmente. Nè altro per la presente. Racomandomi alla Magnificentia Vostra.

In porto di Marsilia adì 16 di settenbre a ora di nona o circha.

Sabato mattina adì 17 ci partimo da Marsilia con bonaccia, circha mezza terza, et riavemo una barcha di vini et altre cose conperate per le galee il dì dinanzi et non // l'avavamo potute trarre la sera per 53v

---

mezzodì (sometimes known as *ostro*): south
libeccio (sometimes known as *garbino*): south-west
ponente: west

maestro: north-west
tramontana: north
greco: north-east

[1] Île de Pomegues, about 5 miles south-west of Marseilles. This was a usual anchorage for ships and galleys calling briefly at Marseilles which was itself a harbour protected by chains. A number of editions of early portolans have been used to assist in the identification of the places mentioned in this diary; but the most valuable source for the subject is K. Kretschmer, *Die italienischen Portolans des Mittelalters*, Berlin, 1909, pp. 553–687.

[2] Apart from the fact that he was a Neapolitan pirate or naval condottiere, I can add nothing on 'Certullo'.

[3] Luca's diary also served as a letter-book into which were copied all the letters which he wrote to the Sea Consuls during his voyage. Some of these letters contain additional information which is not included in the text of the diary, while others merely repeat in different words the description of events which have already been mentioned. In the latter cases the letters have been omitted.

stupiacevolezze del governatore de' luogho che dubitava di frodi di certi arienti. Quando fumo sopra Boccholi[1] per ordine prima dato uscì dal porto il Savorino con iiii fardegli d'ariento della compagnia d'Andrea de' Pazzi con uno liuto armato et misse in galea per portare a Malicha.[2] Dipoi in sulle ore 22 si misse vento a libeccio, per che tornamo a surgere a Boccholi nel porto quasi a nocte.

Domenicha adì 18 a mezza nocte, cioè venendo la domenicha, ripartimo da Boccholi et navicamo tutto dì in bonaccia o con vento contrario; finalmente la sera surgemo sopra il capo della Spig[h]-etta[3] circha miglia x larghi da terra in passi 18 d'aqua.[4]

Lunedì adì 19 di settenbre a mezza terza o circha, ci partimo da detto luogho con vento contrario voltegiando per pigliare Aquamorta;[5] finalmente migliorò vento et surgemo in Aquamorta a ora di vespro o circha.

Smontarono i padroni in terra e gli scrivani per fornire le galee et charicare le mercatantie vi fussino, et dissono essere sicuri però che avevano // scripto innanzi et che il governatore de' luogho era molto loro amico. Dismontò con loro circha 20 persone di galea d'amendue le ciurme et non più. Mandai Piero spagnuolo, mio tronbetto, a bandire che chi volessi caricare s'aprestassi per tutto martedì adì 19 [*sic*: 20] però intendeva partire la sera se fia piacere di Dio. Adì 20 cominciamo a caricare a ora di terza, colle barche delle galee et con barche della terra.

Detto dì scripsi 1ª lettera ai consoli dello infrascripto tenore cioè;

Magnifici patres et domini miei etc. Adì 16 del presente da Marsilia scripsi alla Vostra Magnificentia quanto per insino allora

---

[1] Port-de-Bouc: now an insignificant fishing village but at this time the port for Martigues and the Rhone valley, and often preferred to Marseilles.

[2] *liuto* or *lintro*: a small river-boat. Andrea de' Pazzi & Co. was the leading Florentine firm in Marseilles at the time.

[3] Pointe de l'Espiguette which commands the entrance to the port of Aiguesmortes and lies about 8 miles south of the town.

[4] A *passo* was 3 *braccia* or about 5 feet 9 inches.

[5] Aiguesmortes: the port and town built by St. Louis as a base for his crusades. It has long since ceased to be a port and lies some miles from the coast. But although it is unlikely that the Mediterranean ever washed against its walls, it was possible for seagoing vessels to come right up to the town by means of canals through the dunes. By the fifteenth century the port was on the south side of the city at Étang de la Ville, but merchant shipping in transit frequently moored half-way along the canal at Digue de la Payade (see C. Lentheric, *Les Villes mortes du golfe de Lyons*, Paris, 1883, pp. 357–83, and C. H. Bothamley, 'The Walled Town of Aiguesmortes', *Archaeological Journal*, lxxiii, 1916).

acadeva et solo dimentichai scrivervi che Luigi Covoni vostro cittadino era suto preso in sulla nave di Nantone et per Certullo messo a remo in sulla sua galea.[1] Dipoi ieri a ora di vespro giugnemo qui, gratia di Dio, a salvamento et subito mandamo in terra a fare le robe preste per carichare, et così speriamo per tutto questo dì spacciarci di qui et questa nocte, se fia piacere di Dio, essere al nostro viaggio. Abbiamo pocho caricho, però che tra qui et Marsilia levereno [*sic*: leveremo] intorno di 200 capi // et non più. 54ᵛ Il tempo è stato assai bonaccevole, in forma che, durando, presto ci spacceremo da queste spiaggie di Catalognia. Ma secondo ch'io sento, la frutta non è anchora stag[i]onata, et dubito non sia cagione di farci perdere tenpo. Nè altro per la presente. Racomandomi alla Vostra Magnificentia. In Aquamorta adì 20 di settenbre 1429, a ora di nona o circha.

Lunedì detto adì 19 stettono i padroni in terra amendue et con loro più conpagnoni et albergarono.

Martedì adì 20 fe' fare la mostra a amendue le galee colla ciurma et conpagnoni armati, essendo in terra i padroni.[2] Dipoi a terza cominciaron a venire le robe alla marina et carichamo ciò che fu rechato. Et io avevo fatto bandire allo spagnuolo mio trolbetto [*sic*: trombetto] et dato termine a caricare tutto detto dì, et così fatto sonare a racolta a vespro. I padroni tornaro a galea a ora di vespro et dissono aspettavano molte altre robe il dì seguente, per che deliberai aspettare tutto dì 21, perchè il termine dato da' consoli enne [*sic*: ne è] 2 dì utili.[3] //

Mercholedì mattina fe' 1ª multa a Bernardo Carnesecchi padrone 55ʳ della galea conserva a ore 12 o circha di fiorini 200, la metà al comune di Firenze l'altra metà a' consoli del mare, in caso che a ora

---

[1] Luigi d'Antonio Covoni was a merchant with interests in Spain. He had taken a considerable interest in the galleys, having been conductor and patron of one of the first galleys to go to Catalonia in 1424. He also travelled at least part of the way with Salamone Strozzi's fleet to Flanders and England in 1425/6.

[2] According to the regulations the Captain or his notary had to inspect the galleys and their crews at least once a fortnight. On these inspections he would frequently be accompanied by the commissary of each galley who was also entitled to make additional inspections whenever he wished (Consoli del Mare V, *Capitoli de' capitani*, c. 13 and IV, 3, *Capitoli dei rassegnatori*, c. 1).

[3] In the regulations concerning stopping-places laid down in 1442 and 1443 there was no mention of Aiguesmortes at all, but in 1446 and again in 1462 two days was the permitted stopping time in this port. Three days was the maximum time allowed in any port on the route except for Sluys and Southampton.

20 detto dì non fussi tornato in galea, però che la sera dinanzi se n'era ito a dormire alla terra, diceva per spacciare i bisogni del noleggiare. Portò la polizza Nerone mio trombetto a diegl[i]ele in sua mano in Aquamorta, a ore 14½ o circha, presenti più testimoni. Di detta multa fu rogato Ser Agnolo di Nolfo mio cancelliere. El detto Bernardo come ubidiente tornò a tempo, et però gli fu cancellata detta multa.

Detto dì atendemo a carichare le robe che vennono alla marina insino a nocte et anchora parte della sera fu spiacevole barchegiare. Caricossi in tutto capi intorno di . . . . La sera medesima, circha a mezza nocte, ci levamo con vento a tramontana et con mare in prua, et navicamo tutto dì giovedì adì 22 perchè sempre abonacciò il vento e 'l mare. Il dì fè la mostra di tutta la galea Niccholò di Lottieri commissario de' consoli et ser Agnolo con lui.

Giovedì adì 22, a nocte, ci trovamo sopra Catachieri in Catalogna.[1] //

55ᵛ　Venerdì mattina adì 23 (ci trovamo a Barzalona), a nocte, ci trovamo sopra Branie.[2]

Sabato mattina adì 24 a ora di terza o circha, surgemo alla spiaggia di Barzalona dove surgono le navi, con vento a sciloccho e levante.[3] Smontò in terra Piero Vespucci padrone, Carlo et più altri di galea; era grosso mare et malamente si poteva andare o venire di terra. Smontati in terra, rinfreschò tanto di mare et di vento, che cci bisognò levare et non potemo mettere la barcha in galea. Ne' levare si ruppe la grippia del ferro marzocco e l'arghanello da prua et aramo tanto che fu presso non andamo atraverso in su una nave; pure, come piacque a Dio, ci schapulamo e lla barcha ch'era per poccha con un prodese nuovo et 1° huomo, si entrò sotto la galea e empiessi d'aqua. L'uomo, per gratia di Dio, montò in galea pe' remi. La barcha c'era tanto di brigha essendo piena, che non ci lasciava montare capo Vecchio, e 'l tempo era obscuro et già sera,

---

[1] Cadaqués: a small port in the province of Gerona, a few miles inside the Spanish frontier.

[2] Blanés: 40 miles north-east of Barcelona. Luca omitted to delete *mattina* when he crossed out this error over Barcelona.

[3] At this time Barcelona had no real harbour and although there were good moorings off the beach, it was recognized to be an extremely dangerous anchorage if the wind got up from the south or south-east (L. Bozzano, *Antiche carte nautiche*, Rome, 1961, portolano, p. 5). It was in 1438 that work began on an artificial harbour and the famous anchorage dues were imposed to pay for the improvements (Carrère, 'Le droit d'ancrage', p. 74).

sicchè ci convenne tagliare il capo de' prodese e lasciarla andare a traverso. Et così la galea conserva lasciò amendue i ferri in aqua perchè si ruppono le grippie.[1] //

Tutta nocte stemo in mare a seccho,[2] con molto mare et tenpo per 56ʳ insino a giorno. A giorno pigliamo la volta di Sulo,[3] dove surgemo a vespro o circha domenicha adì 25, et di quindi scripsi a Piero Vespucci a Barzalona et mandamo Antonio da Malaventre e 'l maestro d'ascia e avisa' lo del ferro nostro lasciato con 1ᵃ agumina [*sic*: gomena] nuova, et così della barcha, a cciò facessi ricoverare dette cose e se lla barcha non si ritrovassi, che se ne procacciassi 1ᵃ altra; et simile l'avisai come la galea conserva lasciò due ferri perchè si ruppono le grippie, et che anche facessi levare i suoi ferri, et oltre a cciò perchè facessi fare 1° carro per le nostre antente [*sic*: antenne] perchè era magagnato il nostro che levamo da Pisa nuovo.[4] Et avisa' lo come Luciano l'aveva trovato nella tarsina di Barzalona, e 'l maestro d'ascia mandai per che lo facessi.[5]

Lunedì mattina adì 26 Malaventre scontrò a Tarragona il padrone et gl'altri della nostra galea ch'erano rimasi a Barzalona, che venivano a ritrovarci a Sulo. Diegli la lettera et tornò adietro il padrone a Barzalona con alchuni, et gli altri ne vennono la sera a Sulo in galea, et così Carlo e gl'altri miei, e tutto lunedì stemo a Sulo. La nocte a mezza nocte ci levamo per andare a Barzalona et pocho fumo in mare che trovamo vento contrario et tornamo pure a Sulo la nocte. //

Martedì 27 di settenbre stemo a Sulo dove eravamo tornati la 56ᵛ nocte; passata la seconda guardia ci partimo da Sulo[6], et navicamo per tornare a Barzalona mercholedì adì 28 tutto dì, e trovamoci a

---

[1] The *ferro marzocco* was the second of three anchors carried by a galley and weighed about 550 lb. It appears that in this case the galleys had slipped their anchor cables (*gomene*) at the onset of bad weather and then they broke their anchor buoy ropes (*grippie*) when trying to recover the anchors.

[2] *a secco*: to drift before the wind without sails.

[3] Cape Salou: just below Tarragona on the Catalan coast. This cape provided the only protection from an east or south-east wind on the whole coast.

[4] The *antenna* was the lateen yard of the main mast which was made of two pieces bound together. The lower and heavier part of the yard was the *carro* and the upper part the *penna*.

[5] This was Luciano da Portovenere, one of the *consiglieri* or officers on Luca's galley.

[6] There were three watches (*guardie*) for the day and three for the night. Similarly, the crews were divided into three *quartieri* and whatever rowing had to be done was usually done by only a third of the oarsmen at a time.

nocte presso a capo Vecchio. A mezza nocte surgemo alla spiaggia di Barzalona in bonaccia.

Mercholedì adì 29, a levare del sole, mandai in terra il tronbetto spagnuolo a notificare che chi voleva carichare alchuna cosa, caricassi per tutto il dì; e mandai per la barcha in terra et pel ferro, ch'erano ritrovati et raconci. Et scripsi una lettera a' consoli dell'infrascripto tenore, cioè:

Magnifici domini et patres mei etc. Da Marsilia et d'Aquamorta scripsi alla Magnificentia Vostra quanto per fino alora era seguito. Dipoi giugnemo qui sabato mattina a terza o circha, adì 24, et mandato in terra Piero Vespucci et altri per lo spaccio nostro, si misse tanto tenpo a sciloccho che non fu possibile tenerci in su' ferri, ma con grande pericolo et faticha ci levamo circa ora di vespro et lasciamo qui uno ferro et la bargha della nostra galea convenne si 57ʳ lasciassi. Et per rispetto della grippia et dell'arghanello // che si ruppono fu presso che non andamo atraverso a una nave. Pure, gratia di Dio, scapulamo et così intervenne alla galea conserva, che lasciò ii ferri in aqua per difetto delle grippie et portò pericholo non piccholo. Questo vi scrivo perchè voi Bernardo et Andrea ch'eravate a Pisa, intendiate quanto pericolo si porta per uno cattivo capo, che Dio sa quanto è agevole a questi vostri provveditori da Pisa a confortare e starsi al coperto. Noi siamo si magri di[1] capi ch'io penso che questi padroni n'arrano spesa non picchola. Levati di qui sabato, coremo a Sulo et per fino a ieri non è stato tenpo da tornare in qua; pure, gratia di Dio, tornamo questa nocte qui e attendiamo a scaricare e allo spaccio, e se fia piacere di Dio, spero per tutto oggi spacciare almeno la galea per Maiolicha. Per infino a ora abbiamo trovati pochi noli, et questi padroni a mio parere fanno bene loro debito e vostro honore per insino a qui. Altro non acade. Racomandomi alla Magnificentia Vostra. A Barzalona adì 29 di settenbre a ora di terza o circha, 1429.

Detto dì riavemo in galea il nostro ferro e lla barcha raconcia et 1ª antenna comperata per lo carro, fiorini 43 d'Araona. //
57ᵛ   Giovedì adì 29 di settenbre, il dì di Santo Michele, tutto dì attendemo a caricare et scaricare; et la sera avisai Bernardo Carnesecchi, ch'aveva ire a Valenza, che quivi non aveva a stare più che uno dì e a Valenza tre e così avisai Gaddo suo gomino [*sic*:

[1] *si magri di*: so short of.

còmito],[1] et fessene scriptura per ser Agnolo, et avisai che aspettassino a Sciabbia[2] e così facemo noi. Et a mezza nocte o circha feci vela colla galea dov'era per ire a Maioricha, lasciando a Barzalona la conserva che anchora non era spacciata. Navicamo tutto venerdì adì 30, con vento scharso e con grosso mare; la nocte ci trovamo sopra Tortosa in mare circha miglia 30 et fuori di nostro camino per vento scarso. Et così navicamo quella nocte, che migliorò tempo, et tutto l'altro dì, sabato adì 1° d'octobre, et a nocte ci trovamo sopra Maioricha, all'isola circha miglia 15.

Domenicha mattina, a ora di terza o circha, surgemo nel porto di Maioricha col prodese alla seccha del molo, et subito mandamo per salvocondotto; voleva[n]lo dare a parole, in fine, non volendomene fidare, me lo dierono in scripto, ma penai a 'verlo per insino a ora // di vespro o circha. Allora mandai in terra Piero 58ʳ tronbetto et fe' notificare che chi voleva carichare aveva tenpo insino tutto dì seguente a ora di vespro, adì 3. Dismontò Piero Vespucci et più altri per ordinare il carichare, et così molti marinai et conpagnoni per fornire de' bisogni loro.

Lunedì adì 3 facemo dipignere il giglio nell'artimone in su una poppa di nave vinitiana; dipinse Lanzino.[3] Et facemo fare il carro per la nostra antenna ch'era cattivo, di quella antenna si conperò a Barzalona, riuscì sottiletto; il vecchio lasciamo ivi a santa Caterina, et Piero ordinò se ne facessi ritratto o mandassi a Pisa; perchè mancho il dì non si potè legare in terra, facemolo venire in galea a sera, et tanto lavorarono che circha ore 3 di nocte fu legato et collato. El dì tutto dì si carichò per fino a nocte a ore 2 o circha, ma cominciossi a carichare presso a vespro, perchè non erano i merchanti d'acordo de' noli col padrone. Caricossi datteri, melaghetta, cannella, grana, acciaio et rame in tutto capi . . . circha fiorini 400 di nolo; et tornò in galea il padrone a ore 4 di nocte o circha, essendo da me molto sollecitato. Passata la seconda guardia

---

[1] On the Florentine galleys the *comito* was the first mate whereas in some other Italian fleets of the period the commander of a galley was described as *comito* and not *padrone* (see Manfroni, 'Cenni sugli ordinamenti delle marine italiane', p. 46₁)

[2] Javea: a favourite port of call for the Florentine galleys because of the famous raisins, the pasas de Valencia, which are grown in the area. These raisins, the *frulla* to which Luca refers elsewhere, were dried in the vineyards themselves.

[3] *giglio*: the Florentine lily. This was a new mainsail which they had received at the last moment in Pisa, and so there had not been time to paint the Florentine emblem on it.

58ᵛ ripartimo con tenpo scharso et navichamo // martedì tutto dì, adì
4 d'octobre, per essere a Sciabbia e lla sera ci trovamo a ore 22 o
circha alla Dragonara,¹ et perchè era vento per prua surgemo ivi et
pigliamo aqua et legne la sera.

Detto dì fe' fare la rasegna di tutti gl'uomini di galea a ser
Agnolo et al commessario, et trovamo era manchato solo uno
galeotto rimaso a Maiolicha. La nocte a mezza nocte ci partimo
dalla Dragonara et navichamo con vento scarso tutto mercholedì
adì 5 d'octobre, e lla nocte ci trovamo in mare asai quasi sopra
l'Alfux.²

Giovedì adì 6 navichamo con vento in prua insino a sera; a nocte
ci trovamo tra Panischola e Valenza, et in sulla sera si misse vento
al tereno et navichamo tutta nocte con prospero vento. La mattina
veniente, cioè venerdì adì 7, al'alba del dì, entramo nel porto di
Sciabbia et quivi surgemo, et sentimo la conserva essere a Denia;
mandamo là uno et perch'ell'era spacciata et caricha quanto più
poteva ne venne a Sciabbia circha a ore 20 detto dì. Et stemo a
Sciabbia insino a mezza nocte passata, et facemo fornire la ciurma
et conpagnoni e lla conpagna di vino et d'altre cose, et sentimo che
resto del nostro caricho per la galea Vespuccia era a Bendormi,
59ʳ et però ci levamo // sabato adì 8, per innanzi dì forse 3 ore, con bonaccia, per essere a Bendormi. Ci partimo da Sciabbia et avemo
i batti,³ sicchè la sera surgemo a Carpina,⁴ presso a x miglia a
Benedormi.

La mattina al'alba, domenica adì 9 d'ottobre, surgemo a Benedormi et fe' fare la rasegna alla galea conserva : manchò iiii huomini
di remo. Caricamo parecchi barchate di zibibbibbo [*sic* : zibibbo];
poi gli uomini de' luogho, per amore della domenicha, non vollono
più caricare et però ci conviene stare la nocte.

Lunedì al'alba cominciamo a caricare e a terza o circha, adì 10,
avemo caricato quello che v'era, intorno di 400 cantara di zibibbibbo; e subito facemo vela et a nona o circha surgemo a Villa
Gioiosa, et messe in terra le barche attendemo a caricare. Detto dì
in detto luogho facemo frustare Lucha d'Antonio da Cortona, conpagnone di galea, perchè a Sciabbia aveva furata una tazza d'ariento.

---

¹ Dragonera : a small island off the western tip of Majorca.
² Puerto de los Alfaques.
³ *imbatti*, *venti d'imbatto* : onshore breezes, particularly common in summer when
the heat causes the air over the land to rise.   ⁴ Calpe.

Fu frustato da' marinai et condana' lo a rimanere in terra et se mai fussi trovato in su fuste di fiorentini, gli fussi mozzo l'orecchie ritto. Et tutto per processo et sententia rogato ser Agnolo. Di detto luogho, detto dì, scripsi a' consoli del mare nell'infrascripto modo. // Magnifici patres et domini mei etc.[1] Da Barzalona adì 29 del 59ᵛ passato scripsi alla Magnifica Vostra Signoria quanto per insino alora era acaduto d'avisare di nostro viaggio. Dipoi la nocte medesima parti' colla galea Vespuccia, nella quale navicho, et lasciate la conserva alo spaccio di Barzalona et di Valenza me n'andai a Maiolicha et di quivi tornamo a Sciabbia colla gratia di Dio, insino adì 7 del presente, al'alba del giorno. Et quivi senti' la galea essere a Denia, che anchora non era venuta a Sciabbia come eravamo rimasi, per non essere spacciata prima. Mandai subito uno fante propio e la sera al vespro giunse, spacciata da Valenza et da Denia et caricha insino a' puntelletti[2] per modo che niente più può caricare. Noi abbiamo per insino a questo dì circha mezzo caricho per tutte le schale et qui oggi spero enpieremo i' resto quanto la galea potrà levare. Sicchè, gratia di Dio, le galee aranno loro dovere per l'andare in là, e ànno auti di begli partiti; ma perchè credettono trovare qui di loro frutte circha 3000 cantari, non vollono a Barzalona pigliare partito // di carichare del'altrui, poi giunti qui 60ʳ trovamo la frutta non essere anchora fatta oltre alle 2/3, sicchè et [*sic*: è] pure stato mestiere[3] che tolgano dell'altrui, et non dimeno a soldi 3½ il cantaro di nolo di Fiandra. Spero caricare qui per tutto oggi ciò che si potrà e quello potranno portare le galee, se'l tempo ci terrà, et poi sareno [*sic*: saremo] a nostro viaggio se fia piacere di Dio. Penso ci converrà tocchare alla Cantera[4] et a Cartagena, perchè là sono certe grane di buono nolo: se caricho mancherà, leveremo quelle, sichè potete in tutto stimare le galee essere bene et ragionevolmente cariche et con noli condecenti secondo l'altre che sono ite; così piaccia a Dio prestarci buona ventura nel presto tornare. Racomandomi alla Magnificentia Vostra. Fatta a Villa Gioiosa adì 10 d'octobre, a ora di vespro o circha, 1429.

Scripsi in questo effetto ma con variate parole, perchè non trascripse ser Agnolo.

[1] For a translation of part of this letter and comments on it, see pp. 134–5.
[2] *puntelletti*: deck supports.
[3] *mestiere*: here used in the Dantesque sense of need, necessity.
[4] Alicante: here as at Barcelona there was no natural harbour, just a beach with a good anchorage.

Giunti a Villa Gioiosa, subito andarono in terra le barche et
cominciamo a carichare, et caricamo insino a nocte, e lla sera ci
60ᵛ trovamo quasi caricha la galea nostra che pocho o niente // le
manchava, pure perchè pareva alquanto più leggiere che lla conserva, contra volere quasi de' consiglieri et gomiti, consenti' si
mettessi anchora 200 cantari et così tra la no[cte] e lla mattina
seguente, si carichò intorno di cantari 240.

Adì 11 martedì d'octobre, veduta la nostra galea per amendue i
gomiti et per i nostri huomini di consiglio, volendo il padrone
carichare la galea più, dissono constretti da saramento in verità la
galea essere soprafatta più che 200 cantari et tutti gli intendenti
dicevano non doversi carichare et che lla conserva era assai più
leggiere. Il perchè fattone rogato ser Agnolo, fe' tornare a terra
barche ch'erano venute per carichare, et col nome di Dio ci partimo
con vento in prua, a ora di nona o circha.

Et quando fumo alungati circha 10 miglia, dicendo Simone [*sic*:
Piero] Vespucci che alla Cantera erano circha 40 balle di grana et
pregando de' levarle, dissi essere contento d'andare là se lla conserva le volessi levare, ch'era più leggiere di noi. Parlarono insieme
i padroni et in niuno modo Bernardo volle consentire di caricare se
61ʳ non la metà, se noi levavamo i' resto. // Per che, veduto quanto
eravamo più carichi di loro et che a loro pareva avere ass[a]i et
così in verità anche a me pareva, diliberamo se 'l tenpo il patissi,
d'andare di lungo sanza più impacciare la galea. Et prima, la sera
dinanzi, più volte Andrea Marino et io avavamo detto a Piero di
carichare i sopradetti 200 cantari et non più et ch'egli guatassi
quale era più utile, o carichare frutte o serbare il luogho per la grana
sopradetta : sempre rispuose volere prima la frutta perch'era loro.
Il perchè caricha la frutta, non pareva da carichare più d'alchuna
cosa, et così ci partimo et navicamo tutto quello dì e lla nocte
seguente con vento scarso.

Mercholedì adì 12 si misse vento a levante, et la sera a nocte
ci trovamo sopra Cartagena in Spagna.

Giovedì adì 13 navichamo con vento scarso; la sera ci trovamo a
capo di Lenzuoli[1] in Granata, presso a capo Gatto[2] a circha miglia
x, et quivi surgemo per vento in prua.

---

[1] This is possibly the Cape Genovesi which is mentioned in some of the portolans.
[2] Cape de Gata: one of the most notable landmarks on this stretch of coast.

Venerdì adì 14 prodegiamo quasi tutto dì con mare in bonaccia;[1]
la sera surgemo alla Lena d'Almeria[2] per vento a libeccio.

Sabato innanzi dì ci partimo di detto // luogho adì 15 et navi- **61ᵛ**
chamo circa 20 miglia; poi, per vento a ponente et libeccio, ci convenne tornare al detto luogho della Lena donde eravamo partiti et
quivi surgemo quasi a nocte.

Domenicha innanzi dì ci partimo, adì 16, da detto luogho per
andare in Almeria per rinfreschamento che c'era presso a miglia
15 o circa;[3] et circha mezzo camino ci messe vento a levante, per
che ci convenne mutare proposito et con faticha montamo il capo
della Lena et trovamo grosso mare per prua. Navichamo tutto dì
con vento scarso et fuori di camino et con faticha alla galea
perch'era troppo caricha.

Lunedì adì 17 innanzi dì si misse vento al nostro et noi ci trovamo in mare; navichamo tutto dì et la nocte et martedì insino a
nona.

Martedì adì 18, il dì di Santo Lucha, tra nona et vespro ciugnemo
[*sic*: giungemo] a Malicha[4] avendo grande bisogno d'aqua et
d'altri rinfreschamenti, et quivi surgemo etc. Et io scripsi una
lettera a' consoli per Franciosino nello infrascripto modo.

Magnifici patres et domini mei etc. Da Villa Gioiosa insino adì
8 di questa scripsi abastanza alla Magnificentia Vostra. Dipoi quivi
caricamo le galee ciò che portare potevano di frutta et convenne
lasciare di migliori partiti per rispetto della frutta che avevano //
questi della maona et quella ch'avevamo promessa d'altri, et pure **62ʳ**
comprendo che per insino a qui, queste galee hanno di nolo da

---

[1] *prodeggiare*: to sail into the wind or to tack repeatedly.

[2] Llanos d'Almería: a galley anchorage about 10 miles west of Almería where
there was protection from the east wind. In this case they were faced with a south-
west breeze which forced them to heave to despite their determination to press on
with all speed.

[3] The galleys had now spent five days battling along the south coast of Spain
without putting into port, so that it was decided to go back to Almería for provisions.
However, when the wind turned in their favour they sailed on westwards for a
further two days before eventually putting into Malaga for supplies. Therefore the
galleys seem to have been capable of sailing for a week before they were forced
to seek port and fresh provisions.

[4] Malaga.

fiorini 5500 in 6000 secondo posso conprendere.¹ Qui giugnemo circha a vespro, et spero scarichereno [*sic*: scaricheremo] quello abbiamo per qui subito et levereno [*sic*: leveremo] aqua e altri rinfreschamenti, et spero questa nocte sareno a nostro viaggio che Dio il conceda salvo et presto.

Questo regno di Granata è tutto in arme peròche uno re, che questo ch'è oggi cacciò pocho tempo fa, è entrato in questo regno da pocho in qua e ànne rubellato grande parte, et al presente è in Granata e tiene la terra, et l'altro re la fortezza, sicchè i mercatanti sono in molto sospetto et paura.² Nè altro per questa. Racomandomi alla Magnifica Vostra Signoria. Fatta a Malicha in Granata adì 18 d'octobre 1429.

La sera medesima, circha ore 3 di nocte, con vento al tereno ci partimo di Malicha et navichamo quella nocte et tutto l'altro dì. Detto dì misse il Ghiozzo³ in galea cantari 40 di frutta.

Mercholedì adì 19 nocte, circha ore 4, surgemo al monte Iubeltaro⁴ per aspectare la corente dal nostro. La nocte venne la febre a Andrea Marino nostro gomito, per che soprastemo insino a giorno.

Giovedì adì 20, circha a nona, surgemo a Tariffo perchè s'era
62ᵛ messo vento a ponente // et per levare rinfreschamento, però che a Malicha non avevamo levato il bisogno in tutto per lo presto partire. Mandamo in terra et pocho rinfreschamento potemo avere perchè que' della terra non si fidavano della nostra ciurma et non volevano entrassino se non pochi per volta et sopravenendo la

---

¹ The indications both in this letter and the previous one are that the bulk of the space on the galleys was booked ahead before they left Pisa, either by the conductor's partners (the *magona*) or other interested merchants. This would suggest that even the goods loaded in Spain were largely handled by Florentines at this time.

² Luca reported on contemporary events in Granada both on his outward and on his return journey. The king who had been expelled and had now returned was Muhammad VIII, El Izquierdo, or al Ayzar (the left handed). He succeeded his father Jusuf III in 1417 and was overthrown in 1427 by a popular rising and by a relative of uncertain status who established himself as Muhammad IX. Muhammad IX, known as El Chico or al Sagius, has been variously described as cousin, uncle, and son of Muhammad VIII, although the theory that he was the son is probably the best documented. Luca had his own theory about the relationship as will be seen when he describes the affair in more detail on his return journey.

³ *Ghiozzo* (simpleton) was the nickname of Simone Guiducci, one of the young Florentines of good family travelling with the galleys.

⁴ Gibraltar.

nocte pocho avemo di rinfreschamento. Alla mezza nocte partimo di detto luogho, et perchè Andrea Marino era pure malato, feci gomito in suo luogho per tanto che fussi sano, Antonio d'Andrea d'acordo col padrone. Uscimi de' luogho et pocho fuori del porto trovamo il vento in prua, per che surgemo forse uno miglio da ponente a Tariffi.

Venerdì mattina adì 21 d'octobre ci partimo da detto luogho con vento scarso e navichamo tutto dì voltegiando; la sera surgemo tra Tariffi et Trafichata[1] forse miglia x larghi da Tariffi, et così stemo tutta nocte.

Sabato mattina al'alba del dì, essendo rinforzato il mare e 'l vento nostro contrario, parendoci non stare bene in detto luogho tornamo indietro a Tariffi et quivi surgemo con asai di tenpo; et circha ora di nona, crescendo il mare e 'l vento rinfreschava et ne' luogho faceva fortuna assai perch' era paragho,[2] ci levamo con assai faticha et pericolo non potendo girare la galea per essere troppo caricha et scademo assai, convenne pigliare volta contraria. Aiutocci l'essere stati larghi et tornamo indietro alla Zizara[3] // presso al monte 63r Giubeltaro, et per non potere barcheggiare lasciamo in terra a Tariffi Simone Guiducci, Maso Aliotti et tre marinai i quelli erano iti per fornire la galea. Dipoi a ore 2 di nocte o circha, i sopradetti ci vennono a ritrovare alla Zizera con uno schifo di Tariffo.

Domenicha adì 23, passata terza, ci partimo dalla Zizera per andare a nostro viaggio. Come fumo al capo, trovamo vento et mare contrario, e però surgemo a capo di Canpo et quivi pigliamo aqua e legno le galee. La mattina fe' fare la mostra alla galea conserva.

Lunedì adì 24 d'octobre innanzi dì 2 ore o circha, ci partimo da Canpo con vento a scilocco, et surgemo circha a ora di vespro a Cadisi in Spagna; et giunti alla boccha del porto, manchò il vento et missesi vento a libeccio nostro contrario, ma fu utile a entrare nel porto. Et giunti, mandai in terra Nerone tronbetto et fe' notificare a ciascuno che volessi caricare, caricassi per tutto dì, et Andrea Marini et Gaddo andarono per torre i pedoti. Tolsono per la nostra

---

[1] Trafalgar.

[2] *paragho, pareggio*: a stretch of sea close to land (see below, p. 230, for another meaning). The portolans confirm that the sheltered anchorage at Tariffa was very small.

[3] Algeciras.

galea Iohanni Martini et Iohanni Gratia di Chitana biscaini, et per
la conserva Iohanni Gratia da Villa Bitrosa bischaino.[1]

Martedì adì 25 fu grosso mare et non si potè scarichare se non a
nocte, et e pedoti non vollono venire a galea dicendo non essere
tenpo. ‖

63ᵛ Mercholedì mattina adì 26 fornimo di scarichare quello che v'era,
che circha cantara 400 avavamo tra amendue le galee. E pedoti
vennono a galea circa mezza terza, e subito feci loro vedere le galee
et così agli altri intendenti, per vedere come restavano cariche; tutti
s'acordarono che lla galea conserva si poteva passare, ma che in
sulla nostra era di superchio più che 500 cantari, et in tutto i pedoti
negavano doversi passare il mare di Spagna così caricho. Fe'
chiamare i padroni et dissi loro che a me pareva che 'l nostro so-
prapiù pigliassi la conserva, tanto che le galee restassino a uno segno
del pari, e se questo non piacessi loro, ch'io voleva aleggiare [*sic*:
allegerire] la galea al pari del'altra e lle robe lasciassino in terra.
Fuvi molto che dire et molte parole strane; in fine, per consiglio de'
pedoti, del gomito et degl'uomini di consiglio, et vedute prima le
galee et fatte bene bilanciare a chi intendeva, feci scaricare 175
cantari di zibibbo et circha 40 pezzi d'assi da stiva[2] della galea nostra
64ʳ et mandai in sulla conserva, et per meno scandolo ‖ rimanendo
nondimeno la nostra galea più caricha che lla conserva. Parendoci
assai sospirate diliberai partire et così, circha ora di vespro, partimo con bonaccia et ser Agnolo fu rogato de' consigli ci renderono
i pedoti et gli ufficiali di galea perchè senpre apaia il vero.[3]

Navichamo insino a nocte, che poco s'aquistava per il vento
ch'era scarso. La nocte si misse buono tenpo dal nostro, et navicamo
tutta nocte e l'altro dì con vento prospero et bonacievole.

[1] The home towns of these pilots were Cutaria or Guetaria, and Villaviciosa, both
on the north coast of Spain. It was essential for Mediterranean galleys to take on
pilots when they entered the Atlantic, not only because their own sailors did not
know the coasts, but also because sailing conditions as a whole were totally different
beyond the Straits of Gibraltar.

[2] *assi da stiva*: loading planks. These were presumably boards used to divide up
and stabilize the cargo.

[3] This is an interesting indication of the rather delicate position of the Captain in
command of a fleet in which his subordinates owed allegiance to different masters
and to different interests from himself. He had to have a considerable weight of
expert opinion behind him before he ventured to interfere in the commercial side of
the voyage.

Giovedì a nocte adì 27 ci trovamo presso al capo di santo Vincenti a circha x miglia; et circha ore 3 di nocte, passato il capo di x miglia o circa, si misse vento in prua per che, essendo bonacevole, surgemo et stemo insino a giorno. Detto dì fe' fare la mostra alla galea nostra et manchò uno marinaio.

Venerdì mattina ci partimo di detto luogho, adì 28, con vento a levante et navicamo insino a vespro, dipoi si misse vento a ponente a noi scarso. Navicamo tutta la nocte, e lla mattina rinfrescò mare e vento assai, per che deliberarono i pedoti pigliare porto perchè 'l vento era traversia della costa di Portogallo dove ci trovavamo. E però facemo vela verso Lisbona.

Sabato adì 29 d'octobre, circha ora di terza, entramo nel porto di Lisbona con molto mare et vento, et surgemo a Rastrello,[1] presso alla terra // a 4 miglia circha. Et subito mandai in terra ser Agnolo 64ᵛ e 'l Ghiozzo con lettere di credentia alo 'nfante Pedro credendo vi fussi.[2] Et giunti alla terra, trovarono non v'era, per che gli avisai vicitassino la Maestà Reale et proferessino etc. et così ferono. Esso Re molto benignamente gli vide et profersesi per ogni cosa fussi di bisogno alle galee, et la sera medesima mandò Antonio Marabotti a me per sua parte a proferermi che se io voleva andare alla terra colle galee,[3] che lle faceva franche d'ogni gabella, costume o anchoraggio, et così ciascuna persona d'esse potessi dismontare liberamente per ogni cosa, con arme et sanza come ci paressi. Dipoi l'altro dì, domenica adì 30, mandò uno cavaliere per sua parte a vicitarne et proferere per rispetto de' nostri signori. Fugli risposto a honore del comune, et poi lo richiesi che gli piacessi, veduta la fe' et divotione che fiorentini portavano alla Reale Maestà et a' figl[i]uoli, pregare i' re per parte della comunità di Firenze che gli piacessi per sua

---

[1] Estoril, 4 miles down the Tagus from Lisbon itself.

[2] The Infante Don Pedro, a younger son of John I, had visited Florence in 1428 during the course of his European travels. He had made a considerable impression in Florentine society; 'un costumatissimo e valoroso cavaliere, e il più leggiadro, e il più bello della persona, che mai fosse uscito di Spagna' (Ammirato, *Istorie fiorentine*, vol. vii, pp. 81–82). In addition he had a considerable investment in the *Monte*, and it was natural that Luca, who had probably met him in the previous year, should make his first approach to him (see also Rogers, *The Travels of the Infante Don Pedro*, pp. 50–52).

[3] Antonio Marabotti, who is not mentioned in Perragallo's survey of Italians active in Portugal (P. Perragallo, *Cenni intorno alla colonia italiana in Portogallo nei secoli XIV, XV e XVI*, Genoa, 1907), was reported in Lisbon by Uzzano in 1424 (Pagnini, *Della decima*, iv, p. 176).

benignità dare a queste galee et al'altre che in futuro venissono ne'
65ʳ suoi // porti libertà et immunità come ànno quelle de' vinitiani,
mostrandogli che questo era utile della sua terra, a llui honore et
fama con guadagno, e sarebbe conperare la nostra comunità etc.
Mostrò quello cavaliere che gli piacessi et che ne parlerebbe collo
re et farebbemi risposta. Il detto caval[i]ere era governatore della
camera de' re et delle sue pechunie, aveva nome messer Piero
Consalvo de Lisbona, actore delle facende de' re ch'è uno huficio.[1]
La sera mi mandò a dire per Antonio Marabotti ch'aveva fatta la
mia anbasciata et che l'altre mattine mi farebbe risposta grata etc.

Lunedì adì 31 d'octobre tornò il detto cavaliere et fè risposta
che a re piaceva quello gl'era per me stato domandato et che
bisogna essere in consigli[o] per farlo et in caso che noi non
partissimo presto, lo farebbe, et dove noi partissimo ch'io lasciassi
a chi lo ricordassi et che farebbe suo consiglio et farebbe cosa
grata etc. Per che lasciai la commessione a Antonio Marabotti
et a Bartolomeo di . . . da Firenze mercatanti.[2] La sera mandò il
re a presentare le galee per reverentia del comune, cioè iiii buoi,
x porci morti, iiii botti di vino, 8 zane di mele et molto pane cotto.
65ᵛ E padroni mandarono a donare // a lui per quegli medesimi
in mio nome con molte schuse, come s'usa, uno pondo di
datteri di lb. 400 o più, ii caretgli di razese di riviera,[3] lb. 5 di
zafferano, 25 marzolini lucardesi begli[4] et 25 mazzi di finocchio
dolce, dicendo tutto essere cose di loro paese salvo i datteri di
Maioricha. Levò la conserva 1ᵃ balia della figliuola del detto re

---

[1] Don Piero Consalvo de Lisboa, chief minister and treasurer to John I at this
time.

[2] Bartolomeo da Firenze or Bartolomeo Florentin was the name given to Bartolo-
meo Marchionne, the wealthy Florentine merchant, who in the later years of the
century had a considerable share in financing the Portuguese voyages of discovery.
However, reference to a Bartolomeo di Firenze has already been noted in 1443 in
connexion with a five-year monopoly of Portuguese coral fisheries granted to
Bartolomeo and Jean Forbin of Marseilles (C. Verlinden, 'La colonie italienne de
Lisbonne et le développement de l'économie métropolitaine et coloniale portugaise',
Studi in onore di Armando Sapori, ii, p. 621). This has led historians to suspect that there
were two Florentine residents in Lisbon who went by this name, and Luca's refer-
ence to Bartolomeo in 1429 must make this suspicion a certainty. Whether the earlier
Bartolomeo was a relative, possibly even father, of the more famous Bartolomeo
Marchionne is still uncertain, but it does seem quite likely (see Perragallo, *Colonia
italiana in Portogallo*, p. 417).

[3] *razese* is a type of wine produced on the Ligurian coast.

[4] Lucardo is near Montespertoli in Tuscany. These cheeses were famous throughout Italy and derived their name from the fact that they were made in March.

ch'era ita a marito al duca di Borgogna circha dì 15 innanzi, per portarla a Bruggia con 5 persone.[1]

Martedì adì 1° di novenbre, il dì d'Ognisanti, circha terza, tornarono i pedoti in galea et parendo il tenpo abonacciato co' remi i' mano et colla corrente uscimo di porto et trovamoci la sera sopra capo di Casche[2] con faticha, et navichamo tutta nocte e l'altro dì, adì 2, fu il dì de' morti, con grande afanno di mare et di vento et colla cochina il più del tempo e chollati.[3]

Giovedì adì 3 ingrosando il mare e 'l vento, trovandoci sopra Baiona e 'l vento facendo segno di saltare a ponente et vedemo la galea conserva ronpere il temone baonese,[4] deliberamo d'andare in porto a Baiona, all'isola de' Romito.[5] Et quando fumo ivi, presto tornò il vento verso il porto per modo non parve da potervi montare et però ci calamo // in uno porto in Galitia, che 66ʳ ssi chiama Ponteveteri, circha ora di vespro, dove trovamo ii balenieri armati di corso e altri legni.[6] Et la galea conserva aveva rotto la feminella del temone baionese et rocto uno temone latino,[7] e suo fornimenti aveva bisogno d'aconciare; e lla nostra galea aveva fatta molto aqua per le lacte [*sic*: lati] pe' colpi del mare,

---

[1] Luca and his galleys were to be closely involved in this voyage of the Infanta Isabella to Burgundy; see below, pp. 231-5.

[2] Cascaes.

[3] The *cochina* was the small, square storm-sail.

[4] The *timone baionese* or *bavonescho* was the name given to the single rudder hung on the stern post which was gradually replacing the two side or lateen rudders of earlier times (in fact Luca's galleys had lateen rudders as well, as did those illustrated in the *Fabbrica di galere*). This new type of rudder is thought to have first appeared in the north, and was later introduced to the Mediterranean by Bayonese sailors (R. C. Anderson, *Oared Fighting Ships*, London, 1962, pp. 59-60).

[5] I have not been able to identify the island of Romito but it was probably close to Bayonne.

[6] This was Pontevedra, a good sheltered port at the head of a long inlet which forms the mouth of the river Lérez.
The balinger (*baleniere*) was a small light sloop the exact details of which are unknown. It is usually thought that it had both oars and sail, but Luca's galleys by using oars were able to escape from three balingers in Pontevedra. This coast was in fact a noted haunt of pirates, and in 1431 Pietro Querini on his voyage to the north (see G. B. Ramusio, *Secondo volume delle navigationi e viaggi . . .*, Venice, 1559) went right out as far as the Canary Islands after leaving Lisbon in an attempt to bypass the coasts of Castille. In the event he got lost and eventually had to return to Lisbon. There is evidence of the Florentine galleys doing the same thing, and indeed Albizzi tried to keep well out but the westerly winds frustrated him.

[7] *feminella*: rudder gudgeon.

anche era bisogno di conciare, et però deliberamo di raconciare
tutto prima ci partissimo di detto luogho. E lla sera medesima
mandai alla terra per salvacondocto Giuliano di . . . scrivano
della conserva et Maso Aliotti.

Venerdì adì 4 tornaro dalla terra i sopradetti et dissono che
gl'uomini della terra avevano mandato all'arciveschovo di santo
Iacomo loro signore a notificargli delle galee et che non ci farebbono ofensione se da lui non venisse, nè salvacondotto ci darebbono sanza sua saputa.[1] Apresso dissono che uno padrone di
nave ch'era di detto luogho ch'aveva nome Albero Crudo, et uno
altro ch'à nome Piero Falcone, le quali erano in detto porto, l'una
di botti 500 l'altra di 400 di portata, gl'avevano detto che per
66ᵛ rispetto // di quegli balenieri tenevano alla terra i temoni e le vele
delle navi per paura che no' lle furassino loro et che sanza fallo a noi
bisognava guardare da loro però che gl'avevano uno baleniere a
Baiona et uno a Bugea[2] et che avevano mandati per loro et ch'era
tutta genti di male afare. Mostrarono che i balenieri pocho curavamo se lle loro navi non ci impaciassino; rispuosono che non ci
farebbono se non bene, salvo quando l'arciveschovo mandassi a
comandare altro et ch'eglino conoscevano l'arciveschovo povero
per che sanza fallo tenevano che noi non aremo salvacondotto et
che noi c'ingegnassimo di partire più presto potessimo. Et questo
fu a ora di vespro e 'l tempo fu per modo che in niuno modo ci
potavamo partire, ma atendemo a stare a buona guardia tutto dì et
tutta la nocte apresso, et continuo i nostri schifi la nocte stettono
intorno alle navi e a' balenieri per vedere quello facevano. L'altra
67ʳ mattina, // sabato adì 5 di novenbre, non potendo partire per tenpo
et pure avendo alchuni sentori che i balenieri erano in cattivo
pensiero, diliberamo di fare pruova d'uscire e levamoci colla
corente, con vento asai in prua. Et quando fumo alargati forse uno
miglio, venne uno schifo da terra e rechò certi huficiali della terra
e altri, i quali ci rechavano salvacondotto da parte dell'arciveschovo
loro signore, secondo dicevano; et che però non avevano auta risposta da lui, et che voleva che noi fussimo bene trattati et sicuri, et
datoci ogni rinfreschamento pe' nostri denari. Facemo loro honore

---

[1] The Archbishop of St. James of Compostella at this time was Lope de Mendoza
(1386–1445).
[2] In his letter describing these events (p. 243) Luca refers to other balingers at
Mongia (Mugia) and it may be that he means the same place here.

et ringratiamo come si conveniva, acettando la sicurtà et che in caso che'l te[n]po non ci lasciassi ire a nostra via, noi torneremo et useremo il porto et la terra sicuramente etc. Partiti eglino, facemo forza d'uscire bene 2 ore et esendo già nona et non potendo uscire del detto golfo, ch'è lungho circha 15 miglia insino al capo, et parendoci essere sicuri perchè de' balenieri pocho curavamo se lla terra e lle navi non ci offendessino, tornamo in porto per aconciare ‖ le galee et pigliare rinfreschamento. Et giunti, mandai Giuliano et 67ᵛ Maso Aliotti sopradetti per spiare nuove alla terra et alle navi. Et quando furono alle navi trovarono che padroni d'esse erano venuti dalla terra insieme col capitano de' balenieri da Ribadeo, chiamato Comesi Frescho, e rechate le loro vele e temoni et gente asai; et parlando con uno di loro Giuliano, esso gli fè cenno che venivano per ofenderci et che noi ci partissimo, però bisognava ubidire il loro signore. Et secondo sentimo, loro dicevano in sulle galee essere robe di catalani et con questa schusa le volevano rubare.¹ Et in questo tempo venne il baleniere ch'era a Baiona, per che subito tornò Giuliano sanza andare alla terra, et date queste novelle et vedute le navi mettersi a punto, auto consiglio da' nostri, si diliberò riprovare il levarci, però eravamo sopra vento alle nave forse uno tratto di balestro. Et così subito facemo, sanza avere spatio di levare barche o schifi, solo colla speranza de' remi. I balenieri come ci vidono levare, ci ferono vela dietro ‖ tutti e tre et 68ʳ così amendue le navi voltegiando per lo golfo per entrarci sopra vento. Ma nostro signore Idio ci fè gratia chè tenpo abonacciò un pocho perchè i remi avanzavamo loro alchuna cosa. Et così armati gl'uomini di capo e lle galee fornite da battaglia, salvo la ciurma in camicia, vogamo per insino a nocte, che poco avavamo aquistato. Fatta nocte, mettemo le nostre barche et schifi in galea et alargando un pocho il vento, facemo vela. Et arivati presso al capo, non pareva poterne uscire sanza voltegiare, et balenieri erano asai più destri di noi per che dubitando non ci sopragiugnessino al capo, prendemo uno consiglio del pedoto della galea conserva, che cci menò tra certe isole et schogli dove niuno degli altri pedoti nè che fussi in sulle galee, era mai passato, et con grande tremore ci mettemo a quello partito; pure il lume era della luna, et scapulamo

¹ In 1429–30 Castile was at war with Aragon and twenty galleys, thirty large nefs, five balingers, and one carrack were armed in Seville for an attack on Majorca and Minorca (Cesareo Fernández-Duro, *La marina de Castilla*, Madrid, 1894, p. 188). Luca refers to these preparations in his letters later, and the seizure of Catalan goods by Castilian shipping was a normal side-effect of such a war.

tutto; e 'l vento si misse frescho et noi pigliamo la volta di mare tutta quella nocte. La mattina ci trovamo sopra il capo di Fini-
68ᵛ busterre circha 20 miglia et non avavamo // alchuna vista nè di navi nè di balenieri, parendoci per la gratia di Dio essere scapulati di grande pericolo. Essendo vento frescho a ponente et grosso mare, parendo a molti buono l'andare a porto, pure per fugire il pericolo de' balenieri et anche d'altri corsali che stimavamo fussino in paese, pigliamo la volta di mare col nome di Dio et navichamo tutto dì domenicha e la nocte apresso [al]la volta di Fiandra, domenicha adì 6. Lunedì mattina adì 7, ci trovamo quasi a mezzo il pareggio[1] et il vento ci tornò al maestro e 'l mare grosso, per che anchora per lo meglio ci convende [*sic*: convenne] pigliare la via di Galizia. Et tutti credevano gl'intendenti essere in mare sopra il capo Finisterre almeno migl[i]a 200 la via d'Inghilterra, et nel pigliare il partito assai v'era chi voleva fare la volta di Brettagna gredendo [*sic*: credendo] essere in mare a camino quanto è detto. Presa adunque la volta di Galizia, credendo tornare alle Cologne,[2] et navichamo tutto dì e la nocte apresso con terzeruolo, il quale si stracciò tutto et noi col pappaficho il dì; e lla nocte, raconcio il terzeruolo, il
69ʳ mettemo però che 'l // mare era molto grosso, et così navichamo insino a giorno, avendo la nocte auta vista di 5 fanali di navigli a tratta di balestro, il perchè spegnemmo tutti i nostri lumi, et così la conserva, e alargamoci da essi. La mattina vedemo erano 5 navi et trovamoci presso a 3 o 4 miglia sottovento; imaginamo fussino navi di Portogallo che menavano la figliuola delo loro re al ducha di Borgogna per donna; pure per molto tempo non potemo parlare loro.[3]

Martedì mattina stimavamo essere larghi da terra sopra il capo 100 miglia, chi meno diceva, venimo la volta di terra insino a mezzo dì sanza niente potere vedere perchè era frescho. A mezzo dì avemo vista di terra contro alla credenza di ciaschuno et tutti dicevano essere le Cologne, et poi acostandoci insino a ore 23, penamo a riconoscere ch'era Ribadeo più che miglia 100 di sotto verso Bischaia, et quivi entramo con faticha perchè stretta entrata. Trovamo 2 navi di bischaini che cci mandarono le barche et feronci grande aiuto, et così entramo dentro come piacque a Dio,
69ᵛ et insino a ore 2 di nocte penamo a trovegiare[4] et // a ormegiarsi.

---

[1] *pareggio*: in this case a stretch of dangerous sea as in French *les parages*.
[2] Corunna.   [3] See below, p. 231.
[4] *trovegiare*: probably the same as *prodeggiare* in the sense of tack repeatedly.

Et fu grande gratia di Dio perchè era buono luogho et trovamoci statati 100 miglia contro al giudicio di tutti i più intendenti, che se per aventura il tempo non fussi rischiarato per modo avessimo auto vista della terra, ciaschuno era in pensiero di navicare la nocte seguente almeno miglia 50 o 60, et noi ci saremo trovati in terra a traverso. Di tutto sia lodato Idio.

Mercholedì mattina adì 9 di novenbre vennono in galea i padroni vischaini delle navi, et feronci grande proferte. Avevano 2 navi di circa botti 400 l'una; l'uno aveva nome Iohan Ferando il padrone di Montesso, e l'altro Martino Gales vischaino, di botti 600. Facemo loro honore di collatione et facemo donare loro, per l'aiuto ci ferono le loro barche al'entrare del porto, fiorini 20 d'Araona. Et facemo con loro conserva, però che sentimo che gl'uomini della terra ci volevano offendere et avevano richiesti detti padroni per avere le loro navi, et presi la fede loro in sulla mia galea molto alegramente. Nondimeno stavano [*sic*: stavamo] con sospetto, considerata la natura de' vischaini. Et // oltre a cciò, era venuto in 70ʳ galea la mattina 1° che diceva essere chugino del'uno de' padroni ch'aveva nome Piero Ruis, e diceva che messer Agnolo Aciaiuoli, capitano di 3 galee sottili di fiorentini, gli aveva presa una sua nave per la guerra di Genova[1] et facevagli grande danno et ch'era stato a Firenze et non aveva auta la menda; e bene che cortesemente parlassi, pregandoci di favore per avere risposte, nondimeno ne faceva sospetto assai a noi.

Detto dì, circha ora di nona, entrarono nel porto 5 navi de' re di Portogallo, ch'erano quelle vedemo in mare la nocte dinanzi: portavano la figliola per mogl[i]e al ducha di Borgogna e avevano a venire alle Schiuse et dicevano avere smarite 9 altre navi di loro conserva,[2] e parveci ventura per nostra sicurtà, et subito mandai

---

[1] The war with Milan and Genoa lasted intermittently from 1422–6, and there are references to Florentine galleys joining the Aragonese fleet against the Genoese in 1425 and 1426 (see above p. 105).

[2] The story of the marriage of the Infanta Isabella to Philip the Good and of the voyage to Flanders has attracted a good deal of attention, not only because it was one of the more important dynastic matches of the century, but also because Jan Van Eyck was a member of the Burgundian embassy which carried through the negotiations. Van Eyck was Groom of the Bedchamber to Philip and was commissioned on this occasion to execute a portrait of Isabella which was sent back to Flanders in February 1429 for the Duke's approval; the picture has not survived. Isabella's fleet of fourteen ships had finally left the Tagus on 17 Oct. but had been quickly dispersed by storms off the coast of Galicia. Four ships including that of the Infanta sought shelter in Vivero where they were soon joined by a fifth, and the

Bernardo Carnesecchi colle barche armate incontro et andò a proferere alla donna et allo 'nfante don Ferando suo fratello et capitano dell'armata,[1] per parte de nostri signori et di me, le galee etc., et offerere la nostra compagnia, la quale mostrarono 70ᵛ avere cara e accetta et profersono a noi etc. ∥ La quale cosa a noi parve grande nostra sicurtà, veduto che'l tempo era cattivo da non si potere partire, parendoci che senza fallo non ci lascerebbono offendere ad altri.

Giovedì mattina disinarono con noi i padroni bischaini sopradetti in sulla galea Vespuccia, adì 10.

Venerdì adì 11 di novenbre, il dì di santo Martino, desinamo il padrone ed io con Bernardo Carnesecchi in sulla sua galea. Dipoi dietro a' desinare, parendo a' padroni e a' gomiti ch'io dovessi andare a parlare alla duchessa e allo 'nfante don Ferando suo fratello, per più sicurtà delle nostre galee per ogni caso che potessi occorere, deliberai seguire loro consigl[i]o et maximamente veduto il tempo molto contrario a noi et dubitando di non avere a soprastare più dì. Et però fe' armare amendue le barche delle galee et con amendue i padroni andamo alla nave dov'era la duchessa e lo 'nfante nel detto porto, apreso a uno prodese. Et prima fumo alla donna et per parte de' magnifici nostri signori proferemo noi e lle galee a' suoi servigi, ricordando l'amicitia che i nostri signori 71ʳ tenevano col padre et anchora per la reverentia portavano ∥ al suo marito futuro, ducha di Borgogna. Rispose gratiosamente come si richiedeva, rimettendoci nondimeno al suo fratello, il

reduced fleet set out once more on 6 Nov. to attempt the passage of the Bay of Biscay. But on 9 Nov. they were forced to seek shelter in Ribadeo where they found the Florentine galleys.

The principal source for these events is L. P. Gachard, *Collection de documents inédits concernant l'histoire de la Belgique*, Brussels, 1834, ii, pp. 63–91, but see also: Morosini, *Chronique*, iii, pp. 236–55; Joaquim de Vasconcelos (ed.), 'Voyage de Jehan Van Eyck, 1428–30', *Revista di Guimarães*, xiv, 1897; Baronesse Amaury de Lagrange, 'Itinéraire d'Isabelle de Portugal Duchesse de Bourgogne et Comtesse de Flandres', *Annales du Comité flamand de France*, xlii, 1938; Leo van Puyveld, 'De reis van Jan van Eyck naar Portugal', *Verslagen en Mededelingen det Koninklijke Vlaamse Academie voor Taal- en Letterkunde*, 1940; J. Cardoso Goncalves, 'O casamento de Isabel de Portugal com Filipe o Bon, Duque de Borgonha, e o fundação da ordem militar do Tosão de Ouro', *Arqueologia e História*, ix, 1930.

[1] Isabella was accompanied on her voyage by her brother Don Fernando, who commanded the Portuguese fleet, the Count d'Ourém her nephew, and more than 2,000 followers (Morosini, iii, p. 242, puts the following at 3,000). Don Fernando was the youngest son of John I, and was to die in prison in Fez in 1443 as a hostage of the Moors.

quale era in altra camera. Et giunti a lui, usate le medesime parole et
più che noi avavamo a fare il medesimo viaggio di loro et per
referentia del serenissimo re di Portogallo suo padre credendo fare
honore suo et piacere de' nostri signori, noi fareno [*sic*: faremo]
loro compagnia quanto il tempo patirà, avendo nondimeno
riguardo che altro tenpo bisognava alle galee che alle navi, et
altra marineria richiedeva l'una che l'altra, et così per ogni caso
noi ricoreremo a loro e loro navi, come se fussino propie de'
fiorentini. Acettarono l'oferte et versa vice profersono a noi
simile in generale etc. Il dì medesimo parlò con noi uno schudiere
di quello cavaliere che aveva fatto il parentado et dièci intentione
che quello aveva volontà di passare in sulle galee nostre et smontare
di nave et pagare il dovere etc.[1] Fugli risposto che eravamo presti
a ogni comandamento della duchessa ricevere nelle galee tutti
quegli ci fussi possibile etc. //

Sabato adì 12 di novenbre stemo in detto porto di Ribadeo con 71ᵛ
molto mal tempo, et tutto dì avemo a ormegiarci per rispetto delle
navi asai e 'l porto picholo, che rotavano in su' nostri ormeggi.

Domenicha adì 13 stemo in detto luogho per detto tenpo e fessi la rasegna : mancharono asai, ch'erano in terra per lo maltenpo.

Lunedì adì 14 et martedì adì 15 et mercholedì adì 16 stemo pure
in detto porto di Ribadeo per tenpo contrario, e lle 2 navi vi-
schaine ch'avevano andare in Galitia uscirono di porto detto dì
perchè il tempo fece vista di farsi buono. Et le navi di Portogallo et
noi ci mettemo in punto, credendo partire; il tenpo pure si ruppe,
le navi tornaro dentro al porto la sera, perchè trovorono in mare
altri tenpi che non parevano in porto.

Detto dì, mercholedì adì 16, die' il saramento a tutti quegli
ch'erano in terra d'amendue le galee et fe' gli apuntare per le gior-
nate ch'erano dormiti in terra. Et più trovai circha 12 ch'avevano
giuochato a zara in sulla galea conserva et condana' gli in fiorino
uno per uno, et missi in ferri alchuno che più era stato in terra
de' conpagnoni disubidienti. //

[1] The Burgundian embassy which was sent to negotiate for the hand of Isabella
was led by Monsieur 'Jehan', Seigneur de Roubais et de Herzelles, councillor and
first chamberlain to the Duke. It was he who stood as proxy for his master at the
betrothal ceremony in Lisbon on 25 July 1429. When he eventually came aboard the
galleys Luca referred to him as Monsignor de Rubesse; it appears that he had been
very sick during the journey up from Lisbon and presumably hoped that the
galleys would give him a smoother passage (Gachard, op. cit. ii, p. 78).

72ʳ　Mercholedì detto adì 16, essendosi fugiti a detto Ribadeo circha 5 de' nostri galeotti, et quasi tutti del tereno di Firenze, credo per non potere il disagio del freddo et del'aqua in galea chè quasi senpre pioveva, Bernardo et Piero padroni mi parlarono pregando ch'io fussi contento che lla ciurma potessi più largamente scendere, alegando che per certo, avendo più larghezza, se ne fugirebbe meno. Io alegai loro il caso di Ponteveteri, et mostrai loro che 'l disagio era quello gli faceva fugire, non la stretteza di tenergli in galea, et che per mio consiglio veduto il modo tenuto di chi andava in terra, che a me non pareva lasciargli dismontare infino che fusimo passati in Inghilterra et che gl'erano forniti del vivere. Nondimeno che se essi credessino pure tenergli meglio per quella forma, facessino quello paressi loro più hutile, ma ch'io gli avisava che come fussimo in luogho da potere avere huomini, io vore' rimettessino quegli manchassino. Rimasono pure volere provare la larghezza alla giurma, et io il consenti' mostrando loro nondimeno ch'era più pericoloso. Et chosì seguitamo alchuno dì con 72ᵛ larghezza. // E parendo che le galee rimanessino per ogni caso molte sole, mettemo regola che ogni dì andassi in terra una squadra di conpagnoni, cioè uno quartiere, et così uno quartiere di marinai, partendosi a sorte. Et così stemo insino adì 23 di novenbre in detto porto, per vento cattivo et traversia.

Mercholedì adì 23, vedendo che'l tempo stava pure tristo et dubitando del molto soprastare avendo rispetto a' pericoli de' corsali per assicurarci meglio delle navi, mandai i padroni alo 'nfante et alla duchessa et fe' domandare con cortesi parole se noi potevamo fare conto d'essere difesi da loro in ogni caso come noi stavamo a fidanza, disposti a mettere per loro le nostre galee a ogni pericolo in loro favore et difesa. La duchessa rispuose che così voleva et ch'era la sua intentione, ma pure che s'avessi risposta dalo 'nfante suo fratello. Lo 'nfante rispuose di buona aria, ma pure 73ʳ si riserbò volere parlare // co' suoi padroni et poi ci farebbe risposta precisa. La nocte si cominciò a mutare tenpo et mettersi vendi [*sic*: venti] a sciloccho e levante, il perchè credendo partire il dì seguente di buonora.

Giovedì mattina adì 24 mandai i padroni per la risposta, per intendere quello avessimo a fare o nello andare o nello stare. Parlarono alla duchessa, et in tutto disse era disposta in nostra difesa se 'l bisogno fussi mettere la sua armata, et che così ci aveva mandato rispondendo lo 'nfante per Giovanni di . . . . Et stando in queste parole, venne detto Giovanni et quello medesimo fermò, presente la duchessa, et rispondendo lo perchè non era venuto a rispondere la sera dinanzi, si schusò perch'era di nocte quando lo 'nfante gli commisse. Il perchè auto rispetto se 'l tempo fussi traverso come già era stato 3 volte et bisognando tornare ne' porti de' re di Spagna rispetto a' balenieri armati et nondimeno pe' paesani et simile sentendo che in Bretagna aveva più balenieri et navi di corsali, per più salvamento || parve a' padroni et a' gomiti et gli 73ᵛ altri di consiglio, che migliore partito fussi stare in conserva colle navi persino che Dio ci dessi gratia di trovarci in canale.[1] Et così rispondemo d'acettare la compagnia delle navi et per loro mettere le nostre galee a ogni difesa mentre fussimo con loro. Racogl[i]emo subito tutta la gente in galea e così le navi credendo partire, et in sulla nona saltò il vento a grecho per che bisognò rimanere. Il dì venne in galea monsignore di Rubesse anbasciatore del ducha di Borgogna con circha 12 persone, il quale aveva fatto il maritaggio della duchessa, et dismontò di nave et venne per passare in sulle galee per più sua sicurtà.

Venerdì mattina adì 25 il dì di Santa Katerina benedetta, a levare di sole, col nome di Dio uscimo di Ribadeo con vento buono a valle,[2] in conserva || con tutte le sopradette 5 navi. Navichamo tutto quello 74ʳ dì e lla nocte et sabato adì 26 et tutta la nocte in conserva.

Domenicha mattina adì 27, parendoci perdere molto tempo colle navi, domandamo licentia, credendo passare avanti per essere a Antona et poi, perchè il vento rinfrescò, ci tenemo pure con loro tutto quello dì et tutto lunedì adì 28 e la nocte in sino mezza nocte. Alora, cioè a mezza nocte o circha, le navi si tirarono più al grecho et i nostri pedoti, parendo essere loro in Bretagna, si tirarono verso tramontana, et scandigliarono più volte, credevano essere sempre in Bretagna dentro da Uscenti.[3] Pure a ore 7½ di nocte o circha

---

[1] Once again one is struck by the care with which the Captain had to exercise his authority. Here after making three requests for a mutual defensive agreement with the Portuguese fleet, when his request is at last accepted by the Portuguese, he himself only confirms the arrangement after prolonged consultation with all his advisers. Commitments of this sort were obviously not undertaken lightly, and Luca was not going to be made the scapegoat for risking a fight on behalf of Portuguese ships which might damage the trading prospects of the voyage.

[2] *a valle*: 'Le vent d'aval est, par rapport à une coté, le vent du large' (A. Jal, *Glossaire nautique*). The word used in this sense does not appear in any of the Italian maritime dictionaries, but its use by Luca, particularly on p. 254, indicates that it meant an onshore wind which made it difficult to leave harbour.

[3] Ushant.

scandigliarono et perchè il fondo parve meno circha 15 passi e lla sonda più in canale, alora preso[no] la via per grecho, et così navichamo per insino a ore 2 presso al'alba.[1] Allora Nerone corso, mio trombetto, andò in coverta o a caso o per sospetto, guardando intorno, vide terra, essendo schuro et pioveva. Disse lo al gobito [*sic*: comito], allora più altri procurando s'avidono ch'eravamo in terra. Volendo ire a orza ci pareva terra et a poggia ‖ pure terra,[2] et così quasi da 3 bande, per che non sapiendo che fare, calamo et surgemo per aspettare il giorno, però che quasi tutti et spetialmente i pedoti dicevano essere in Brettagna nel canale de' Mulini tra Saina et Uscenti.[3] Aiutocci Nostro Signore Idio chè senpre fu bonaccia. El surgitoio era buono e 'l fondo di passi 25 o circha, pure stemo così insino a giorno chiaro, con grande pensiero et paura, parendo quasi a tutti essere perduti, credendo essere a Uscenti. La galea conserva c'era di dietro et vennendo colle vele, le facemo più volte segno; domandocci quello che voleva dire il nostro rumore; gridamole per modo c'intese ch'eravamo in terra, alora s'avide et surse anchora lei.

Martedì mattina adì 29, come l'alba cominciò a' parire, scorgemo la terra ch'era alla quale eravamo stati a miglia 2 o meno, et vedemoci ingolfati per modo non potevamo uscire colle vele, et subito si fè turbo et cominciò di nuovo ‖ a piovere, per modo perdemo ogni vista. Allora molti dicevano pure essere in Brettagna a U-scenti, alchuni dicevano essere al'isola d'Inghilterra, che v'era di battito di circha 150 miglia. Infine stemo tanto che rischiarò e fessi dì chiaro et veduta la terra molti dissono ch'era Inghilterra, et tutti s'acordarono ch'era il capo di Gomestieri in canale, dentro a nostro camino, et che eravamo presso a Palamua, mostrando l'isola verde e altri segni.[4] Io veduto eravamo a soquadro[5] di terra se tenpo ci sforzassi, dissi al gomito:—Conoscete voi bene il porto et voi altri tutti?—s'acordarono di sì, et ch'era presso a miglia x o

[1] The pilots of the Florentine galleys obviously made the very common mistake of misjudging the distance which they had travelled across the Bay of Biscay, and continued to sail northwards long after they should have turned north-eastwards into the Channel.

[2] *orza*: windward; *poggia*: leeward. *Orza* was in fact the tackle controlling the heel of the lateen yard, while the *poggia* was that controlling the fore end.

[3] Île de Molène and Île de Sein are both small islands off the coast of Brittany.

[4] Capo di Gomestieri was Goodstart or Startpoint. The 'green island' was, according to the portolans, one of the landmarks to look for when approaching Plymouth (Palamua) from the south-east.

[5] *a soqquadro*: in danger, hence dangerously close to land in this case.

circha :—Ora, dissi, in nome di Dio menateci là, però ch'io non intendo, se altro tenpo fussi, trovarmi qui.—Parve a molti buono consiglio et alora ci levamo, et facemo la volta di ponente. Et quando fumo presso al porto, secondo loro, e noi ci trovamo in uno golfo che mai più niuno di nostre galee v'era stato et non riconobbono niuno ‖ luogo intorno a detto golfo. Fuvi molti che 75ᵛ dissono :—Noi siamo fuori dal'isola et non siamo in canale—, ma i luoghi non conoscevano, et così i pedotti come gli altri. Erano in quello golfo molte barche di pescatori i quali, per levare bandiere o per amattare,¹ niuna si fidava di venire a noi. El vento ci rinfreschava adosso et di quello golfo non vedevamo potere uscire con quello vento, nè surgitoio o porto non sapevano [*sic*: sapevamo]. Allora fe' gittare lo schifo lo schifo [*sic*] in mare et mandai 2 che sapevano un pocho d'inghilese alle barche. Allora s'asicurarono, et tornò lo schifo con 2 huomini de' luogho et 2 de' nostri lasciarono per stadighi,² et da loro fummo avisati ch'eravamo al'isola d'Inghilterra, da lato di fuori, presso al golfo di Bristo, et che quello golfo si chiamava golfo di Musuofolo et che quello monticello che noi diciavamo l'isola verde era il monte di Santo Michele che loro chiamano monte Vai in Cornovaglia³ et dissono ci darebbono buono luogho ivi dendro pe' tenpi ch'erano et chosì ‖ a lloro ci lasciamo 76ʳ menare ivi presso a circha 7 miglia in luogo coperto da tutt' i venti salvo da sciloccho. Et parendo a tutti essere in buono luogho rispetto al dubbio auto, colla gratia di Dio surgemo passato mezzo dì. Allora vennono molte barche alle galee et molti montarono e facemo loro honore di vino che bevevano per sacrificio, però che in quello paese non se ne ricogl[i]e et pochi v'erano che mai avessino vedute galee in quello luogho. Mandamo in terra, levamo aqua et carne et polli, ringratiando Idio de' luogho dove ci aveva conservati, chè in verità a grande soquadro fumo et pericolo. Di tutto sia ringratiato Idio.

Mercholedì stemo in detto luogho per vento a sciloccho e mezzodì, che ci tenne impegnati et scrivemo ad Antona⁴ di nostra venuta per terra, acciò che mercatanti da Londra e da Bruggia sentissono, se per aventura il tenpo ci tenessi. Et io scripsi una

---

¹ *amattare*: to signal for help.   ² *stadighi*: hostages.
³ It is something of an exaggeration to describe Mousehole Bay as being in the Bristol Channel, but that was obviously where Luca's galleys found themselves.
⁴ Southampton.

238 *Luca di Maso degli Albizzi*

lettera a Bruggia a Antonio del Lapeggia[1] et manda' la a Pagolo Moregli[2] a Antona et che lla mandassi a Bruggia. L'effetto della lettera era ch'egli avisassi a Firenze, cioè detto Antonio, come io et tutti quegli ch'erano mecho stavamo bene, gratia di Dio, et che mandassi la lettera a casa. //

76ᵛ Anchora fò ricordo che lunedì adì 28 di novenbre essendo nel golfo di Spagna già presso che a Uscenti, a nostro parere, ci giunse una caracha genovese di botti 800 o circha, che veniva da Sibilia, et disseci avere trovata la galea di Priore sopra Lisbona[3] insino adì 21 del mese, et disse avere auta la nocte di santa Katerina adì 25 grande fortuna sopra Galitia, per modo aveva rotte et fracassate vele et sartie etc. La detta nocte noi stemo in mare in grande bonaccia et pure sopra Galitia, credo ne fussi cagione il capo di Finisterra, che si dovè trovare tra noi et loro. Come si fussi, grande gratia fu da Dio che nel medesimo mare altri avessi grande fortuna et noi grande bonaccia.[4] Anchora la sera avemo vista di iiii altre navi che venivano la nostra via, ma non avemo lingua di loro. La nave genovescha ci si proferse molto in ogni nostro bisogno. Aveva nome il padrone .... Ringratiamola e proferemo di converso. //

77ʳ Mercholedì detto adì 30, il dì di Santo Andrea, fe' fare la mostra alla galea nostra: manchò 7 huomini di remo, de' quali 6 s'erano fugati a Ribadeo et quasi tutti di quello di Firenze e di Pisa.

Giovedì mattina [a] ore 3 innanzi dì o circha, adì 1º di dicenbre, si misse vento a tereno et noi ci levamo col nome di Dio del golfo di Losuolo sopradetto, dove avevamo sentito le galee vinitiane essere a Palamua,[5] et venimo al capo di Lucerta[6] per andare in

---

[1] Antonio del Lapeggia de' Bardi was an employee of Gualterotto de' Bardi & Co., of Bruges, one of the largest Florentine firms in the city. He acted as Luca's financier when the galleys eventually reached Sluys, as Luca was carrying letters of credit issued by Simone del Lapeggia in Florence (Diary, f. 12ʳ).

[2] Paolo Morelli was for a long time the leading Florentine factor in Southampton and was also Consul. He handled the goods of many Italian trading companies but seems to have done little trading on his own account (Ruddock, *Southampton*, pp. 98–102).

[3] This was the private galley of Priore di Marioto (see above, p. 84). Luca makes further references to this galley on his return voyage (see below, p. 266).

[4] Luca discovered later that the two Biscayan ships, which had presumably left Ribadeo bound southwards at much the same time as he left for the north, were also wrecked in the storms on St. Catherine's Day.

[5] A Venetian fleet on its homeward voyage left Plymouth on 4 Dec. The Captain was Stefano Contarini and the patrons Domenico Buono, Giorgio Bembo, Daniele Pasqualigo, and Giacomo Barbarigo. They arrived in Venice on 25 Feb. 1430 (Morosini, *Chronique*, iii, pp. 2–3 and 256–7). [6] The Lizard.

detto porto di Palamua, se fussi possibile. Il tenpo ci tornò al davanti scarso e lla corente essendo presso al capo, per che insino a terza stemo con grande afanno co' remi in mano a prodeggiare, et niente ci pareva avanzare. Pure, come a Dio piacque, il vento s'alargò per modo montamo il capo et mettemoci in canale, deliberando d'andare di lungo se 'l tempo tenessi. Et così passamo quel di Palamua et navicamo tutta nocte, et venerdì mattina adì 2 di dicenbre ci trovamo sopra Artemua[1] et sentimo la nocte da una barcha di pescha//tori che lo 'nfante di Portogallo colle sue 77ᵛ navi era in Palamua.[2] Navichamo tutto quello dì e lla nocte con vento mezzodì et sciloccho.

Sabato mattina adì 3 ci trovamo sopra l'isola di Vicche,[3] e 'l vento tornò a sciloccho e levante, per che ci convenne mutare proposito et tornamo in porto presso ad Antona circha 8 miglia, in sul'isola di Vicche che ssi chiama Calzadores.[4] Giunti, mandai a fare la rasegna alla galea conserva; trovossi meno 3 conpagnoni e due marinai, ch'erano rimasi in terra a Musuolo. Mandamo uno sc[h]ifo a Antona per avere aviso da' mercatanti, et prima che lo schifo fussi là, venne da Antona Pagolo Morelli con più giovani fiorentini, perchè avevano auto vista delle galee et avisaronci come i nostri carichi si mettevano a punto in Antona et che già ve n'era grande parte; et con queste buone novelle si stettono la nocte in galea. Trovamo in detto porto parte // delle navi di Portogallo 78ʳ smarite e l'altre erano ite su in Fiandra. Trovamo quivi 2 famigli di Bernardo, rimasi in terra a Lisbona per portare il presente a' re et dissono come Lucha Bue che rimase per suoi fatti, era in su una nave a Artamua che nne veniva. Stemo tutta nocte in porto, e lla mattina levato il sole di pocho, ci partimo per essere a nostro viaggio, lasciando quivi per ordinare la stiva i maestri d'ascia e Rosso Guiducci per ordinare e bisogni. Avemo buono vento dal nostro insino pocho passata terza, poi cominciò a rinfrescare e saltò a libeccio et da libeccio a mezzodì et in pocha d'ora si fè tanto mare et vento che pareva una marmuglia[5] molto più che mai avessimo

---

[1] Dartmouth.

[2] Isabella and her brother were apparently given a warm welcome in Plymouth where they arrived on 29 Nov. The Treasurer was authorized to lend her £100 for her expenses in England (Rymer, *Foedera*, x, p. 436).

[3] Isle of Wight.

[4] Calzadores (sometimes Calge Cesore) was Calshot Castle; the anchorage itself was off the sandbanks at the end of Calshot Spit.

[5] *marmaglia* (*marmuglia*): confusion, disturbance; the word with reference to

trovato in tutto il viaggio. Et con questo si fè scuro et piov[v]e assai, e 'l vento rinfreschava et la nocte adosso et pocho da potere corere. Mettemo il terzeruolo et poi il pappafico, il quale per tenpo si stracciò; allora, essendo di nocte, mettemo la cochina. Durò la fortuna sì terribile che ciaschuno dubitava la galea non poteva stare ‖ 78ᵛ in sul'aqua per lo grande travaglio, anzi ogni cosa ch'era di sotto si percoteva insieme et coreva sotto vento. Pochi huomini stavano in coverta in piè per lo vento et mare; i marosi passavano la coverta dal'una banda al'altra ch'era una schurità, et infra gli altri venne uno maroso per poppa che misse molta aqua in poppa, per forma che più d'una soma ne venne per la porta nella camera di poppa. Allora Bentacordi ch'era afannato per lo mare et turbato si giaceva tutto stordito, si levò gridando ad alte boci [*sic*: voci] misericordia, come colui che pensava la galea avere ferito in terra et d'essere rotto. Gli altri tutti se ne risono et ripresollo, ma in verità niuno ve n'era sì gagliardo nelle parole che'l cuore no' gli tremassi. Durò il tenpo asprissimo insino a ore ii di nocte o circha a 3; allora si schiarò un pocho et vedemo dove eravamo, però che la luna 79ʳ luceva. Trovamoci ‖ il capo di Belceppo¹ circha miglia x, che cci fu assai sicurtà però che era quello capo che più entra in mare et di che più si dubitava. Atendemo a fare le vele pichole, cioè la cocchina che pocho se ne mostrava, per andare meno via. Infine chome piacque a Dio, il vento cominciò a calmare et a tornare da mezzodì a libeccio et poi a ponente et a maestro, e'l mare a bonnacciare perchè la corente gli tornò contro, per forma che a ore 8 di nocte o circha ci parve tutti essere rasicurati, e per la gratia di Dio innanzi giorno fummo in bonaccia et trovamoci presso alo stretto, al'alba del dì, circha 20 miglia. Allora mettemo il terzeruolo et quasi a mezza terza surgemo a capo Dobla² per dare parte a lo nocte et pigliare la colla per ire ale Schiuse se Dio il concedessi.³ Et così stemo insino a ore 5 di nocte, poi ci levamo con fresco vento a mezzodì et navichamo insino a ore xi o circha di nocte, che stimavamo essere innanzi miglia 60, et surgemo per aspettare il dì.

Martedì adì 6 di dicembre, il dì di Santo Niccholò mattina al'alba, ci trovamo sopra Ostendi, surti in mare presso alle Schiuse a circha 79ᵛ miglia 30. Facemo vela et pigliamo ‖ uno pedoto peschatore. El

the sea seems to have passed out of use, and today the usual sense is rabble, i.e confusion of people.

¹ Beachy Head.   ² Dover, e.g. the Downs.

³ *cola* (*colla*): a wind that holds firm; hence *pigliare la colla* presumably means to catch the prevailing wind.

vento rinfreschava continuo, in modo che 'l terzeruolo schiattò da lato del carro più di x ferze et rupesi il gratile.[1] A noi pareva essere inpacciati perchè pappafico era rocto la nocte dinanzi; convenne pigliare l'artimone et legare il poggiale e llo spigone, et così ci convenne governare con assai pericolo, colpa de' cattivi corredi,[2] tanto che a ora di nona passata surgemo alla boccha del porto delle Schiuse, avendo prima nondimeno toccho al'entrata de' banchi col timone perchè l'aque erano basse. E lla galea conserva anchora stracciò il suo terzeruolo et bisognò pigliassi l'artimone, et così ci conducemo bestemiando ciaschuno chi sì male in ordine ci aveva mandati. Giunti che fumo, sentimo chome per tutto il paese si teneva che lla duchessa e l'altre navi di Portogallo ch'erano rimase adietro, fussino perdute, per che si fè grande alegrezza delle nuove di loro salvamento, e monsignore // di Rubesse ch'era in 80ʳ sulla nostra galea, dismontò in terra, e 'l padrone andò con lui pe' salvacondotti et ser Agnolo. Et io scripsi una lettera a' consoli dello infrascripto tenore.

Magnifici signori consoli etc. L'ultima che scripsi alla Magnificentia Vostra fu da Malicha insino adì 18 d'octobre, e avisa' vi di ciò che per insino a quivi era seguito; nè poi non abiamo toccho il luogo da stimare che le lettere giugnessino prima che di qui. Ora col nome di Dio essendo giunti a salvamento, è necessario che voi sentiate de' nostri processi sì per provedere a' ritorno e anchora, se altre galee mandassi com' era ordinato al gennaio, voi siate avisati di quello che per chi no' llo pruova, non può sapere nè credere.[3] Di poi che scripsi per insino al capo di santo Vincentio navichamo presti et con bonacce, dove giugnemo adì 27 d'octobre al fare di quella luna, et credendo passare con quella colla ci mettemo in mare gran via.[4] La traversia si misse, per che coremo a Lisbona, dove per reverentia de' nostri signori il re di Portogallo ci fè grande honore e presentò le galee di vini, carne, pane, e altre cose, et padroni anchora sodisferono a' loro honore. Fe' chiedere per

---

[1] *gratile*: bolt rope.

[2] *poggiale*: the dipping line, attached to the fore end of the lateen yard.

spigone: any extension of a mast or yard; in modern parlance the studding sail yard.

[3] In a *provvisione* of 27 May 1429 it had been ordered that in future two fleets of two galleys each should sail each year for Flanders and England (Provv. 120, f. 155ʳ). Luca's fleet was the first to sail under the new arrangement, and another two-galley fleet was due to leave on 1 Feb. 1430. Luca's remark suggests that the idea of two fleets was already being discussed in Jan. 1429.

[4] There is a Tuscan proverb: 'Al fare della luna in mare, al tondo in terra.' Sailors said that the new moon was a less risky time to be at sea than at the full moon.

80ᵛ parte de' nostri signori ∥ le franchigie per le galee e legni nostri, com'ànno i vinitiani. Mandomi a rispondere che liberamente andassi dove voleva colle galee, et che per quelle ch'hanno a venire bisognava con ordine, a che darebbe effetto se troppo tosto non ci partissimo, et se noi partissimo, ch'io lasciassi chi gliele ricordassi et farebbelo. Et così commissi a Antonio Marabotti et a Bartolomeo da Firenze che stanno quivi, lo ricordassino, et simile a lo 'nfante Pietro che fu costà, quando tornassi, che allora non era in paese. Avisovene per che se vi paressi scrivere a quello re, et a' detti mercatanti mandassi le lettere, sono certo arete le franchigie che vi saranno hutili et honorevoli. Partimoci de' luogho la mattina d'Ognisanti et cacciamoci in mare molto più che prima; infine la traversia ci ributtò et tornamo a Ponteveteri in Galitia, la conserva con ii timoni rotti et noi gottando a 3 sentine. Et giunti là così rotti, trovamo 2 balenieri armati di corsali et due navi, l'una di 600 l'altra di 400 botti, de' luogho. Surgemo per non potere ire

81ʳ altrove, et mandamo alla terra per salvacondotto et si∥curtà. Rispuosono quegli della terra che manderebbono all'arcivescovo di santo Jacopo, ch'era loro signore, e che sanza sua parola non ci farebbono detto salvacondotto. Eravi presso a circha miglia 30. La medesima sera fumo avisati da' padroni delle navi che quegli balenieri avevano mandato per ii di loro conserva et richiesti loro, e che sanza fallo ci offenderebbono potendo, et ch'eglino avevano anchora mandato al'arcivescovo il quale era povero, et che dubitavano non consentissi. Rispondemo che de' balenieri pocho churavamo s'eglino ci tenessino amicitia; dissono ci sarebbono amici se l'arciveschovo non comandassi il contradio. Parveci stare con pericolo, perchè partire non potevamo, et balenieri non potevamo offendere per la stretta comessione abiamo. Stemo tutto quello dì, e 'l altro dì venne uno de' 2 balenieri per chui avevano mandato, et noi facemo forza di levarci ma non si poteva. Intanto quegli della terra malvagiamente ci mandarono certi loro huficiali, i quali per parte dell'arciveschovo loro signore ci asicurarono et proferso[no] aiuto et vettovaglie etc. Fucci necessario ritornare in

81ᵛ detto porto et giunti che fumo, vedemo le navi et bale∥nieri mettersi in punto per ofenderci et uno de' padroni delle navi ci mandò ad avisare et tutti gl'uomini ch'erano in quello luogho montavano con battegli in sulle navi e balenieri. Allora, veduto il tradimento, ci levamo prodegiando contro al vento e lla corente, e per ventura il vento calmò alquanto, per modo che pigliamo speranza ne' remi. I balenieri ch'erano 3 e amendue le navi ci ferono vela adosso con molti battegli de' paesani. Noi ci trovamo a vento 1ª tratta di balestro, mettemoci in ordine a battaglia non abandonando però i remi. Era già ora di vespro, sicchè tosto si fè nocte et noi avavamo a montare circha miglia 20. Fucci ventura che uno pedoto disse sapere una via tra isole, che niuno altro di nostre galee sapeva. Aventuramoci, veduto il pericolo delle navi, e gratia di Dio uscimo di quelle isole con grande sospetto; et bene che 'l vento non fussi molto buono, pure per fugire dinanzi a' corsali ci mettemo in mare et navicamo passato mezzo il golfo a nostro credere. Dipoi la medesima traversia ci asaltò e stracciamo vele, e colla galea ch'asai // aqua faceva, tornamo la volta di Galitia, 82ʳ volendo prima stare al pericolo degl'uomini che del mare. Trovamo in mare 5 grosse navi di Portogallo, le quali n'avevano smarite per tenpo altre 9; eravi su lo 'nfante don Ferrando di Portogallo et una sua sirocchia che menava a marito al ducha di Borgogna. Tornamo indietro a uno luogho che si chiama Ribadeo, donde erano i balenieri che cci caciavano, et quivi trovamo ii navi bischaine, di botti 400 l'una, et pigliamo da' padroni fede di conserva per paura degli uomini della terra, i quali sentimo gli avevano richiesti per ofenderci, dicendo le nostre galee avere robe di catalani nimici de' loro re. Et più vi trovamo uno Piero Ruissi bischaino, cugino del'uno de' 2 padroni delle navi, il quale si venne a dolere che quando Messer Agnolo Aciaiuoli fu capitano delle galee sottili, gli prese una sua nave et tolsegli molta roba, secondo suo dire, e diceva essere venuto a Firenze e nonn avere trovata giustitia, et parlava però cortesemente ma noi ne pigliamo sospetto asai. Come piacque a Dio, il dì medesimo le navi di Portogallo arivorono al detto // porto, per che ritrovata l'amicitia 82ᵛ de' nostri signori, facemo conserva et promissono di difenderci da ogni persona et così noi loro.

Et quivi sentimo da uomini ch'erano stati in su' balenieri, però che'l capitano d'essi era di Ribadeo, che tutta la nocte ci avevano seguiti, non credendo che no' sapessono uscire per altra via che per la generale, e che l'arciveschovo di santo Jacopo era venuto in persona con gente assai a piè e a cavallo, et tutti si disperavano dell' avere indugiato tanto a fare la 'npresa contra noi. Ma che gli erano iiii balenieri a Mongia[1] adunati con intentione di seguirci insino in Inghilterra e sanza fallo, se non per paura delle navi con chi

[1] Mugia, near Cape Finisterre.

eravamo, ci sarebbono venuti a trovare quivi. Et oltre a cciò
sentimo che quegli padroni bischaini che ci avevamo data la loro
fede erano d'acordo con quegli di Ribadeo di manomettere le
galee sotto pretesto avessino robe di catalani, ma eravamo sì
forti per la conpagnia delle navi, che ciaschuno lasciò il suo mal
proposito. Forse non sarebbe male che lla Signoria scrivessi a' re
di Castiglia dogl[i] endosi di questo, però che balenieri e navi erano
di sue terre e ll'arciveschovo è suo huomo.[1]

Ci stemo in quello porto tutta quella luna, che furono intorno
di 16 dì. E dipoi, il dì di Santa Katerina, come piacque a Dio ci partimo insieme colle navi e allo spelagare i nostri pedoti presono
grande erore, però che credendosi essere in Brettagna ci trovamo
una nocte in terra a 2 miglia al'isola d'Inghilterra di fuori, presso al
golfo di Bristo, a uno luogho che si chiamo golfo di Losuolo, dove
niuno di nostre galee era mai stato. Aiutocci Idio ch'era bonaccia
morta, pure vi stemo ii dì et venimo ad Antona adì 3 di questo,
dove vennono più fiorentini a noi al porto e dissono il nostro
caricho in grande parte essere in ordine. Lasciamo quivi maestri
d'ascia e altri per ordinare la stiva, et venimo a nostra via et siamo
stati in tanta tormenta et pericoli insino qui ch'è suto asai. Non c'è
rimasa nè vela nè sartia che non sia rotta più d'una volta, et questo
dì abiamo spezati ciaschuna galea il suo terzeruolo, e lla passata ǁ
83ʳ nocte noi spezamo il pappaficho; pure, per gratia di Dio et del
beato messer santo Niccholò[2] circha ora di vespro giugnemo qui
a salvamento, et tutte le navi sono rimase, crediamo, al'isola
d'Inghilterra. Sentimo da una caracha che la galea di Priore si trovò
sopra Lisbona adì 21 del passato.

Ora, signori miei, v'ò scripto sì lungho processo come di sopra
ò detto, perchè sapiate che per tutte le terre de' re di Spagna i vostri
legni saranno malsicuri, così da paesani, potendo, come da' corsali,
che grande quantità se ne truova, et però bisogna ci si proveggha et
masimamente perchè nel nostro ritorno i corsali saranno tutti
fuori, et simile molte galee sottili et balenieri et navi che s'armano
in Sibilia per la guerra de' catalani, et dura il tereno di Spagna da
Cartagena insino in Inghilterra, che non trovate luogho per voi
sicuro salvo Portogallo. Et granfatto sarebbe che lle nostre galee
non convengano portegiare, et simile i catalani armerano et tutti
inbercio. Al fatto di queste galee, a me parebbe d'armarle meglio

---

[1] The consuls later reported that they had asked that this be done.
[2] St. Nicholas of Bari was, of course, the patron saint of sailors.

che non sono et mettere ad avaria,[1] però che bene che questi padroni abbiano il numero che ànno a tenere, che per insino a qui non credo ci ∥ manchi x persone tra 'mendue le galee. Chi si trovò a 83ᵛ Pisa per l'uficio vostro aprovò loro molto disutili et fanciugli et non pratichi, in modo non gli posso canbiare pel saramento dato loro et servigio non pena. Parebbemi necessario che a ognuno di queste galee s'agiugnessi 20 huomini di remo, però vogano 130 o in quel torno al presente, et x conpagnoni di balestro, però che non c'è per galea oltre a 25 tra uficiali et conpagnoni da starne a fidanza, perchè non sono pratichi nè al'arco nè al balestro.[2] Io ne ragionai a' giovani ch'erano ad Antona et scripsi al consolo[3] con intentione che se'l consolo et padroni voranno, come dicono i miei capitoli di farlo, trovai la brigata diretta ala spesa; non so che si voranno fare i loro maestri. Il perchè a me pareva dovervi ricordare che a vostro honore voi mandassi uno fante a comandare che così si faccia, per salvamanto del vostro honore et delle galee, il quale fante ci sarà a tempo perchè non veggha ci po∥siamo spacciare tra 84ʳ di qui et dal'isola che non sia presso che tutto genaio. Apresso vi ricordo che l'altre galee non vengano nè armate nè guarnite di coredi come noi, che quanto Dio perdoni a chi chosì ci mandò che grande villania è stata che qui in su queste galee non à nè vele nè sartie che marce non sieno. Et bene che noi ce n'avedessino [*sic*: avedissimo], per non essere tenuti spiacevoli abiamo portato questo pericolo et non stimando tanta fortuna di tenpo. Anchora con fede vi ricordo che alla nostra tornata trovando simili balenieri ne' porti o in mare, a nostro salvamento ci converebbe cominciare prima a loro acciò non si adunassino, però che avendo presi e due balenieri chome pareva a ciaschuno intendente, potavamo stare senza dubio e sicuramente se ne potavamo valere, ma in su' ca∥pitoli a me fatti parlano in modo che a noi non ci posiamo valere 84ᵛ contro ad alchuno che non ci cominci a dare. Et per tanto, considerato questo pericolo passato et quegli potebbono seguire, pareva a chi intende che voi ci dovessi alargare un pocho la commessione, acciò che noi ci possiamo valere con questi corsali come fanno i genovesi et vinitiani et non perdersi così vilmente. Are' che dire assai; solo vi ricordo a questa parte che vinitiani non s'asicurano a

[1] *avaria*: the general average. When additional expenses were incurred by the galleys, the merchants were sometimes called upon to pay in proportion to the value of their goods loaded on the galleys.

[2] See above, p. 201, for discussion of the size of Albizzi's crews.

[3] This would be the Florentine consul in London, Alessandro Ferrantini.

mandarci meno di iiii galee, alle quali non mancha uno remo, tutte armate di lungho a 3 a 3, et oltre i conpagnoni di balestro portano 60 archi pe' terzeruoli loro et molte spade e altre armadure per la ciurma, et si ànno altra riputatione che noi altri da essere riguardati.[1] De', per Dio, non ne vogliamo sapere più di loro, però che questi 85ʳ mari et paesi sono d'altra natura che nostri.[2] // Almeno, se queste galee saranno armate et che abiamo un pocho di larghezza contro a questi corsali, chi ci vorrà bisognerà che sudi. Avisandovi che di loro fedi o salvocondotti non si può stare a fidanza niuna et allora fidano quando vogliano pigliare. È stata tanta la piova e'l maltempo, che per disagio abiamo circha x marinai che ci sono fugiti et quasi tutti di vostro contado o di Pisa. Et quegli sanza mancho faremo rimettere qui se se ne troverrà, che in verità questi padroni fanno asai loro honore quando si può, e sono bene pentuti degl'uomini che a richiesta altrui ànno menati disutili, ma lasciare non gli possono e servigio non se ne aspetta a' bisogni. Non dicho più, se non che io mi racomando a voi et pregovi mi faciate risposta et avisate di quanto volete si segua intorno a questi ricordi. A' comandi vostri, ale Schiuse il dì 6 di dicembre 1429.

Adì 7 et dì 8 stemo fuori del porto francho per tenpo et corenti, et avemo fortuna grande di vento ma del mare eravamo coperti, pure avemo asai disagio senza pericolo, però rompemo de' remi e altre cose per lo strignerci con altri legni. //

85ᵛ   Adì 9 di dicembre, venerdì mattina, colla corente ci trovegiamo dentro dalle Schiuse alle palate tra due castelli. Fessi publicare la franchigia che ànno i fiorentini pe' loro legni et poi scaricamo tutto tra quello dì et la nocte apresso. Le lettere ch'io scripsi a' consoli mi scripse Piero Vespucci da Bruggia averle mandate per uno fante con vantaggio, che doveva infra dì 19 essere a Firenze.[3] Con dette lettere scripsi agl'infrascripti; una lettera a madonna B et al'Orelia, comune,[4]

---

[1] *a 3 a 3*: this presumably meant with a full complement of oarsmen; e.g. all the benches occupied by three men. The Florentines never seem to have armed their outside rank of oarsmen (*terzaruoli*) with cross-bows; they used a kind of pike instead.

[2] The letter originally concluded here, but Luca deleted his usual formal valediction and continued the letter as an afterthought.

[3] In fact this letter took a month to reach Florence, being received by the Sea Consuls on 7 Jan. 1430.

[4] Madonna B. was Luca's mother Bartolomea di Andrea di Segnino Baldesi who

una lettera a Niccholò di Gentile e a Berto, comune,[1]
una a Ormanno di messer R.[2]
una lettera a Bernardo Gherardi[3]
una lettera a Antonio Migl[i]orotti[4]
una lettera a Nichola de' Medici[5]

Adì 10 et dì 11 stemo pure in detto luogho.

Sabato nocte adì 10 essendo il gomito in terra et quasi tutti gl'uficiali, che pochi huomini erano in galea, si misse uno vento frescho a maestro, per modo che l'anchora arò et noi ci acostamo per forza in terra, per che manchando la marea rimanemo adurati et per modo ala banda, che in galea non si poteva stare; anda' mene la nocte al'altra galea e mandai per lo gomito, e come crebbe la marea ci sduramo e ormeggiamo megli[o]. Quella mattina desinò con noi il consolo de' fiorentini e lla moglie et una figliastra e altri; chiamasi Iacopo Oricellari dale Schiuse,[6] et fecci dimesticha cortesia. //

Adì 12 di dicembre scripsi dalle Schiuse questa lettera a' consoli 86ʳ
dello infrascripto tenore.[7]

Magnifici domini etc. Adì 6 di questo vi scripsi una lettera, avisandovi de' nostri passi da Malicha in qua, cioè del malvagio tenpo auto et de' nostri cattivi coredi, che Dio sa che non c'è vela che più d'una volta non abiamo stracciate. Apresso fusti avisati come a Ponteveteri in Galitia dell'arciveschovo di santo Iacopo et sotto sua fidanza et ordine, tre balenieri et due navi grosse ci vollono pigliare di sua volontà et favore, dicendo noi avere robe de catalani nimici del loro re; et però per questa pocho resta a dire, se non ricordarvi del provedimento nel tornare, chè come v'è per me stato scripto, alla primavera saranno fuori molti balenieri et navi et galee armate che s'armano in Sibilia per la guerra de'

had been a widow since 1417. Orelia was his second wife whom he had married in 1426 (not in 1438 as reported by Litta).

[1] Niccolò di Gentile degli Albizzi was a distant cousin. He had been a Prior in 1421 and was to be Gonfalonier of Justice in 1437. Berto di Francesco da Filicaia (a later letter reveals that this was the Berto referred to) had been Gonfalonier of Justice at the time when Luca's galleys departed. Why these two should have been sent a common letter is not clear.

[2] The recipient of this letter was Ormanno di Messer Rinaldo, Luca's nephew.

[3] Bernardo di Bartolomeo Gherardi was one of the most influential members of the pro-Medici party. He was Gonfalonier of Justice no less than five times.

[4] Antonio di Piero Migliorotti, a lesser-known figure but also of the pro-Medici faction.

[5] Niccolà di Vieri de' Medici, Luca's father-in-law.

[6] Jacopo Rucellai, Florentine consul in Sluys.

[7] For a translation of part of this letter see pp. 59–60.

catalani, e'l simile si deve credere faranno i catalani co' loro navilii. Et sapete che queste sono due nationi atte a torre la roba dove la possono trovare, et queste galee sono tenute più ricche ancora che non sono et ànno l'entrata di dire ciaschuno di volere certificarsi se noi abbiamo roba di loro nemici. Il perchè a volere salvare il vostro 86ᵛ honore et ∥ queste galee, è sommamente necessario a mio parere d'armarle bene nella tornata, però che, perchè i padroni abbiano il numero loro, le galee non sono armate nè si può loro dire armino più. La cagione è che chi si trovò a Pisa, aprovò loro molti disutili et marinai et conpagnoni, et bisognò fussino scripti, volessino i padroni o no. Buona parte altri vi furono scripti per amicitia et anche in piacere de' padroni e a richiesta di molti cittadini, et a tutti fu dato saramento del tornare colle galee. Il perchè, al fare del conto, queste galee ànno 130 remi o circha che vogano, et intorno di 25 tra uficiali et conpagnoni che fanno le fationi et sono hutili;[1] de' resto non è da fare conto in mare se non per logorare il bischotto, et di quello pocho quando il mare ingrossa. Et però potete vedere come siamo armati. Vorebbono queste galee 50 conpagnoni utili et 160 remi per una, che vogassono; pure, ricordandovelo con reverentia, almeno 20 huomini di remo e x conpagnoni per galea 87ʳ a me parebbe che ∥ si dovessino crescere, veduti i pericoli ci sono, et mettere ad avaria delle robe. Et così sarebbe mia intentione se a' merchatanti da Londra parrà; ma perchè ànno pure la sicurtà e gli asicuratori non sono qua, credo non voranno fare la spesa. Et per tanto, volendo sodisfare al debito mio, non posso fare di meno ch'io non ve lo ricordi di nuovo et ch'io non vi prieghi che vi piaccia, se così pare a voi hutile, di mandare presto uno fante propio a comandare che così si faccia o altrimenti come meglio vi pare, e lla spesa potete mettere alla mercatantia e agli assicuratori e altri parte in chui benificio si fa. Et per Dio, non vi fate beffe di questo, però che'l territorio de' re di Spagna è più di 1500 miglia, ed è gran fatto che non si convengha porteggiare ne' suoi porti et queste colle di qua mi pare che se ne vanno tutto uno lunare e stassi più ch'altri non vorebbe. Lo schampo delle galee è d'essere bene armate, et spetialmente di remi per potere entrare et uscire de' porti. Queste sono buone galee et se fussino bene armate et bene coredate, per Dio, elle farebbono vergogna a galee sottili e sarebbe 87ᵛ grande sicurtà. Oltre a cciò pareva a ∥ tutti questi intendenti che noi ci alargassi un pocho la commessione, per modo che trovando

---

[1] *fanno le fationi*: carry out their duties.

corsali a noi sospetti, noi ce ne potessimo asicurare et non aspettare che si facciano grossi et poi ci vengano a trovare, che quanto io per me non vore' vergogna et ogni cosa sono disposto a fare perchè queste galee tornino a salvamento. Et pertanto piacciavi ordinare in modo che facendo per bene, non fussi auto per male, chè sanza mancho a noi non conviene più tanto aspettare a volerci salvare quanto abiano [*sic* : abiamo] fatto per sospetto di voi. Comprendo che qui non sia da carichare robe di fiorentini o poche. Le galee abbiamo dischariche; sarebbeci robe di catalani, et queste non pare a' padroni nè a me da caricarle, per levare la cagione agli spagnuoli e per non avere a porteggiare in Catalognia; pure ci pare, e spetialmente perchè sentiamo che in Inghilterra et [*sic* : è] per noi più che caricho. La duchessa e lle navi ch'erano con lei sono anchora venute, salvo una che dice lasciò le conserve ‖ al'isola. Mettesi in 88ʳ punto tutto questo paese a feste per la sua venuta e 'l ducha di Borgogna è venuto a Bruggia a questi dì aspettando la donna di dì in dì. Crediamo spacciarci presto, et quando il tempo il patirà, essere ad Antona et se fia piacere di Dio, di là partire prima ch'escha genaio. Non so che più dire, se non ricordarvi abiate buono riguardo a l'altre galee che vengono et noi non dimentichate et non l'abiate a beffa perchè troveranno fuori molti cattivi catalani e spagnuoli al tenpo. Racomandomi alla Magnificentia Vostra. Fatto ale Schiuse adì 12 di dicenbre 1429.

A detto dì scripsi l'infrascripte lettere a Firenze et manda'le con la sopradetta legate.

1ª comune a Madonna B e al'Orelia.
1ª a Mona Lisa mia sirocchia.¹
1ª lettera a Nicchola de' Medici.
1ª lettera a Niccholò di Lucha² ⎱ degli Albizzi
1ª lettera a Niccholò di Gentile ⎰
1ª lettera a Antonio Migl[i]orotti.

Martedì adì 13 ⎫ di dicembre stemo pure alle Schiuse et la sera
Mercholedì adì 14 ⎪ tornò Piero Vespucci per comandamento
Giovedì adì 15 ⎬ fatto insino adì 10, rogato Ser Agnolo, a'
Venerdì adì 16 ⎭ padroni, a pena di fiorini 200. Subito mandò

---

¹ Luca's sister Lisa married Biagio di Piero Guasconi, and after his death she entered a convent.
² Niccolò di Luca degli Albizzi was another distant cousin of Luca's and like him came down on the side of the Medici in the struggles of the next few years.

per lui monsignore di Rubesse e richieselo che fussi mecho da parte del ducha di Borgogna, et che voleva che noi andassimo in 88ᵛ Inghilterra colle galee ‖ per la donna sua ch'era là rimasa colle navi. Scusa'mi per l'obrigho de' capitoli et pe' comandamenti de' miei signori, mandando a lui il detto Piero e ser Agnolo co' capitoli. Rimase che noi ci pensassimo et che la sera mandassimo al capitano del castello la risposta, però ch' egl' era signore et pe' suoi danari doveva essere servito etc.

Sabato adì 17 mandai Piero Vespucci al capitano della terra la risposta nel medesimo effetto, colle più cortesi parole che a me fu possibile. Disse voleva parlare a me et così m'acozzai con lui in barcha presso alla riva. Lui molto strettamente richiese per parte della ducha me e lle galee. Io in tutto mostrai non potere servire, rispetto a comandamenti de' miei signori et al saramento preso et al danno estremo delle galee. Disse molte cose et che'l signore ne scriverebbe a' miei signori etc., et che considerato il caso, m'arebbono per schusato. Io stetti neluno proposito colle risposte ci erano da mostrare in fine, et disse che'l ducha era signore et aveva brevilegio di potere sforzare ogni legno che fussi ne' suoi porti maximamente pagando. A questo rispuosi che se io fussi sforzato 89ʳ mi converebbe fare com'io potessi, ma che ‖ io non credevo che'l ducha ci sforzassi micha col suo salvocondotto. Disse s'io gli dire' altro. Rispuosi che no' perchè non poteva.—Se ttu sarai sforzato ara'tu la schusa?—S'io sarò sforzato, non potrò più, ma non sarà honore di chi lo farè et a me fia grande dispiacere—. Disse scriverebbe questo a Bruggia al ducha, et che voleva che Piero andassi là egli colla lettera et fussi con monsignore di Rubesse. Alora diè licentia a Piero che andassi et portassi i capitoli e schusassisi quanto si poteva, et simile portassi il salvocondotto però che questa era cosa da fare grande danno alla maona et disagio a noi et portavasi pericolo di non perderne la gratia de' nostri signori di Firenze. Et scripsi a Antonio di Francesco da Volterra che pe' Boromei a Bruggia era consolo de' fiorentini[1] del fatto, pregandolo fussi con gli altri fiorentini et insieme co' padroni pigliassi la schusa nostra quanto fussi possibile, et così andò.

Lunedì adì 19 di dicenbre tornò Piero da Bruggia et disse era

---

[1] Antonio di Francesco da Volterra was manager of the firm of Galeazzo Borromei & Co. of Bruges, one of the largest Italian firms in Bruges at this time. He was also a partner in the London branch which traded under the name of Galeazzo Borromei and Antonio da Volterra & Co.

stato con monsignore di Rubesse egli et tutta la natione de'
fiorentini in su' caso nostro, et in effetto in niuno modo aveva potuto
avere licentia ma 'spresso comandamento che nne venissi et che ‖
eglino ed io mectessimo in punto le galee ad andare come tenpo 89ᵛ
fussi et che lui sarebbe l'altro dì alle Schiuse per montare. Vennono
al salvamento delle galee: a questo disse si rimettessi in lui et
che'l ducha voleva che lle galee fussino salve del loro danno; nè
più ne potè avere.¹

Martedì adì 20 venne monsignore di Rubesse, e padroni andaro
a lui et stette nel medesimo proposito; infine i padroni pigliando
schusa, volle venire a me in galea insieme col capitano delle
Schiuse et col balio del mare. Et auti lunghi ragionamenti, in tutto
disse bisognava andare et che da parte del ducha, sotto pena etc.,
così comandava a me e a' padroni. Bernardo era in terra malato.
Rispuosi in su' capitoli et forma ch'avevo da' miei signori, et ch'io
non poteva ubidire senza disubidire a' signori miei. Disse che conveniva che così fussi et che'l ducha poteva iustamente pe' suoi
danari adoperare i navili che ssi trovavano ‖ ne' suoi porti. Allora 90ʳ
dissi che lle galee poteva prendere come era di suo volere, ma ch'io
per me voleva rimanere in terra et così me ne tornerò per terra a'
miei signori, però ch'io non voleva per mio comandamento et
volontà disfare i conductori delle galee et padroni et disubidere a'
miei signori, mostrando i grandi inconvenienti ne potevano seguire
alle galee e 'l danno oltre alla spesa, che non credeva si salvassino
e fiorini 3000 il mese tra le spese et fruttamento di coredi e fuste.
Allora disse che farebbono i padroni bene contenti di loro salvamento et darebbe la promessa loro di Filippo Alberti:² a questi
asentì P. Vespucci et andonne in terra con lui per provedere forma
et fare e patti. Et io allora dissi che quanto al'utile e danno de'
padroni et galee stava a loro et a me l'observanza giusta posse de'
capitoli. Et di tutto fu rogato ser Agnolo che v'era presente, e così
se n'andarono in terra et Piero con loro. Dipoi a nocte tornò Piero
molto turbato perchè niente avevano voluto patteggiare ‖ ma in 90ᵛ
tutto volevano si rimettessi in detto monsignore di Rubesse, et
così mi disse che voleva che noi scrivessimo a Firenze però che'l
ducha scriverebbe a' nostri signori del bisogno suo, et perchè

---

¹ *salvamento* in this sense implied financial compensation.
² Filippo Alberti had been a Papal collector and banker in the north for many
years, and it was presumably felt that his wealth would be an impeccable guarantee
(see G. A. Holmes, 'Florentine Merchants in England, 1346–1436', *Economic History
Review*, lxxvi, 1961, pp. 197–206).

aveva arestate le galee; et Bernardo, secondo Piero, in tutto gli pareva meno pericolo rimettersi in loro. Rispuosi che a me non pareva et ch'io per me prima dismontere' in terra che consentire il loro danno, salvo se di loro buona volontà et d'acordo non fussino del salvamento delle galee. Et così rimanemo di provare l'altro dì di fermarci a cosa certa se meglio non si poteva. Dal consolo di Bruggia ebbi lettera che in niuno modo si poteva fuggire questa andata et che a lui et agli altri fiorentini pareva di farla con buona cera poi che così era, però che in tutto era diliberato che lle galee andassino.[1] El tempo era pessimo et così stato poi che giugnemo alle Schiuse, nè era possibile a uscire del porto per andare 91ʳ in alchuna parte, e nostri huomini // erano in terra, parte alle Schiuse e parte a Bruggia, per forma che a ogni posta del ducha stavano gl'uomini e lle galee. Et simile ci pareva che se noi fussimo in Inghilterra, questo medesimo ci temerebbe, però che lla sirocchia del ducha è moglie del ducha . . . zio de' re che governa l'isola,[2] e lla donna del ducha, figliuola de' re di Portogallo, che questi inghilesi davano [*sic*: amano?], sicchè ci vedevamo a molto stretto partito e pericoloso.

Mercholedì adì 21 andò Piero Vespucci in terra et acozzossi con Bernardo e con lo consolo de' fiorentini per provare di vedere quello si potessi fare dell'andata. Il dì tutto dì monsignore di Rubesse stette a stufa et a' suoi agi, et non poterono parlare con lui. L'altro dì, cioè giovedì adì 22, ritornò et furono al ducha et detto del nostro fatto, che a noi bisognava sapere quello ci dava il mese et che 'l tenpo s'intendessi dal dì che faciavamo vela insino alla tornata, et tanto più quanto potessimo rifare vela per andare in Inghilterra, et che altrimenti non ci potavamo salvare. Le parole furono molte; 91ᵛ infine non poterono avere se non che volevano salvare le galee // et che del salvamento d'esse darebbono per sicurtà Filippo degli Alberti. Et così tornarono a galea et pareva a Bernardo Carnesecchi che meglio fussi a starsi alla fede loro che a rompersi, stimando

---

[1] Luca's position in this whole affair was perhaps strengthened by the fact that the regulations prevented him from leaving the galleys. Thus the Burgundians had either to approach him through the patrons, or else make the effort to go out and see him. Nevertheless, he was fighting a losing battle and once again his difficulties partly arose from his comparatively weak position with regard to his own patrons. As he himself admitted, it was the responsibility of the patrons to consider the financial and commercial aspects of the voyage, whereas he had to confine himself to seeing that the regulations were obeyed.

[2] Philip the Good's sister Anne was married to John, Duke of Bedford, regent for Henry VI.

che in ogni modo bisognerebbe andare. Et anchora a Jacopo Rucellai dale Schiuse, nostro consolo, pareva da non si rompere, allegando che veduti i tenpi che regnavano, che sanza fallo la donna verebbe prima che tenpo si mettessi dal nostro; ma se pure tenpo si mettessi al loro volere essere chiari. A Piero et a me pareva pericoloso lo 'ndugiare, perchè loro non potessino dire che noi gli avessimo tenuti di parole se tenpo si mettessi. Et però facemo una scripta delle spese delle galee che tra spese et danno di coredi era di fiorini 3186 adì 23 che così batteva.[1] Et sabato adì 24 andò Piero con essa per darla a monsignore di Rubesse et dirgli la facessi vedere, et che questo bisognava a noi per lo tenpo perdessimo in loro servigio, stando in capitale, et che cci facessi promette[re] a Filippo degli Alberti come ci aveva promesso et non si indu-// giassi al dì che lla bigia si mettessi,[2] per non perdere tenpo, et che 92ʳ mandassi per Filippo acciò si facessi la promessa. Il consolo et Bernardo non si acordarono con Piero, ma pareva loro d'aspettare per amore del'aque vive,[3] tutto dì 25, et poi dargli la scripta. Et così rimanemo, parendo a me et a Piero pericoloso se lla donna non venissi, et dubitando che non avessino parlato più largho che a me non dicevano.

Domenicha adì 25 di dicenbre, il dì della Pasqua della Natività, a ora di nona o circha, venne la donna del ducha con parecchi navi, 3 delle sue et altre 3 di gente di passo o circha, che con lei s'erano messe in conserva. Di che fu fatto grande allegrezza alle Schiuse, et noi maximamente ne facemo alegrezza, parendoci essere liberi da grande afanno, però che l'andare per lei ci pareva di molto tenpo et pericolo, d'avere et di persone. Et di 16 navi che furono al partire di Lisbona co' llei non se ne condusse altro che 3,[4] l'altre vennono prima dispersi salvo una ne ruppe a Palamua, et quella di madama ebbe danno // ma non molto in su una seccha, tanto mutò 92ᵛ

---

[1] This was presumably 3,186 florins per month. It was reckoned to cost 35 florins a day or about 1,000 florins a month to keep a galley at sea but this did not include any estimate for depreciation of equipment, etc.

[2] *bigia*: usually north wind but there is an indication from Luca's use of the word that it also meant the opposite to *a valle*, i.e. offshore wind. Both to leave Sluys and to leave Southampton, the galleys required the *bigia* which, in view of the very different positions of the two ports, would seem to indicate a variable wind.

[3] *acque vive*: spring tides.

[4] Luca had already twice reported the original size of the Portuguese fleet as being fourteen ships, and this number is confirmed by Gachard (p. 77). Pancrazio Giustiniani, whose letters from Bruges are quoted by Morosini, put the number of ships at twenty, but this was certainly an exaggeration.

nave. Et bene che in uno medesimo dì con dette navi giugnessimo
al'isola d'Inghilterra noi a losuolo, di fuori dell'isola, ed ellino a
Palamua nell'isola a suo cammino, nondimeno noi giugnemo adì
6 e ellino adì 25 di dicenbre, sicchè Idio ci fè molto di gratia però
che per infino detto dì poi che fumo in porto, non fu ora di buono
tenpo, senpre tenpi a valle o traversie fortunevoli, sanza mai
restare di piovere, Idio lodato di tutto. Fumo spaciati delle mercatantie insino adì 20, da potere partire con amendue le galee se'l
tenpo il patisse; stemo nel canale dele Schiuse tra' due castelli,
insino adì 2 di gennaio, lunedì, per maltenpo. Lunedì adì 2 di
gennaio, essendo abonaciato ma pure vento a valle, diliberamo
tirarci fuori rispetto alle ciurme, per aspettare vento in galea, et
così facemo et tiramoci la mattina fuori delle palate, con quegli
huomini si poterono avere, essendo già stati dì 27 a'spettare tenpo.
Et detto dì scripsi a Firenze a' consoli la 'nfrascripta lettera
sottoscripta ne' dì 3 et manda' la a Bruggia al consolo.[1] ||

93ʳ–93ᵛ

Et più scripsi le 'nfrascripte lettere, e legate insieme le mandai
a Bruggia per Bernardo Carnesecchi, che le dessi a Antonio di
Francesco da Volterra, consolo de' fiorentini; scripsi le mandassi
a Firenze per lo primo egli fa pe' Boromei:

1ª lettera a Madonna B. comune et all'Orelia.
1ª lettera a Nicholò di Gentile et a Berto da Filicaia.
1ª lettera a Nicchola de' Medici.

Martedì adì 3 di gennaio, parendoci essere male a punto de' pedoti
94ʳ rispetto a casi ocorsi, togl[i]e//mo uno bischaino ch'aveva nome
Iohanni Artisti, il quale ci fu lodato sommamente. Detto dì andò
Bernardo a Bruggia, non parendo tenpo da doversi levare, overo
il dì dinanzi a nocte, per certi suoi bisogni, secondo disse. Fe'gli
comandamento tornassi, sotto pena del mio arbitrio, mercholedì
mattina, o prima se tenpo si mettessi, et funne rogato ser Agnolo.
Martedì mattina adì 3 s'abonacciò et con grande sicurtà di tenpo
si cominciò alitare bigia, per che subito mandamo in terra e tra
quello dì et mercholedì adì 4 racogl[i]emo tutti quegli che non
volevano rimanere. Ma'l vento non stava fermo, per che niuno
navilio usciva di porto, et così stemo senza lasciare dismontare

---

[1] This letter has in fact been omitted as it contributes nothing new to the narrative.
Luca recapitulates his remarks about the need to enlarge the crews of the galleys,
and summarizes, surprisingly briefly, the controversy with Philip the Good and his
advisers over his threat to requisition the galleys.

niuno in terra, in punto di tutto, tutto dì giovedì adì 5 di gennaio.
Et perchè il tenpo era molto fresco et cheto, sanza freddo niuno,
s'asicurava che fussi bigia e anche non stava ferma; et così aspet-
tamo la gratia di Dio insino a venerdì mattina.

Giovedì adì 4 fe' fare le rasegne delle galee, et trovossi meno alla
galea Vespuccia huomini di remo ... et conpagnoni ...; e lla galea
conserva ebbe meno huomini ... di remo et conpagnoni. ... //

Venerdì mattina adì 6 di gennaio e il dì di Befania, levato il sole   94ᵛ
di una ora o più, col nome di Dio facemo vela alle Schiuse, con
vento a grecho et tramontana, et surgemo ad Antona dinanzi alla
terra sabato seguente adì 7 a ore 21 o circha. Et la sera medesima
dismontamo et anda'ne al'albergo aparecchiato per me,[1] et quivi
cenamo la sera insieme co' padroni et ordinamo che lla mattina
seguente i padroni andassino a Londra a sollecitare il caricho, et ser
Agnolo con loro a protestare il manifesto e altre cose a' mercatanti
secondo la forma de' capitoli.[2] Et io scripsi la sera una lettera a'
consoli dell'infrascripto tenore, cioè.[3]

95ʳ–95ᵛ

Tornamo in casa Guigl[i]elmo Aure et madonna Agnese
a Antona.[4] Domenicha mattina adì 8 andarono i padroni a Londra
amendue, ser Agnolo con loro, per essere co' mercatanti.

Lunedì adì 9, il mere d'Antona insieme col suo consiglio mi

[1] It was usual and indeed obligatory for the captains and patrons of the galleys
to be accommodated in the houses of leading Southampton citizens, who were to
a certain extent responsible for them. It does in fact seem that Luca, after an initial
night or two at the inn, did move in with William Soper. See also A. A. Ruddock,
'Alien Hosting in Southampton in the Fifteenth Century', *Economic History Review*,
xvi, 1946.

[2] 'Ancora che infra dieci dì dal dì saranno giunte le galee in Antona, il consolo
de' mercatanti et sottoposti alla nostra comunità che saranno al tempo in Inghilterra,
debbano avere dato il manifesto e la nota delle robe che vogliono et promettono di
carichare in su dette galee' (Consoli del Mare V, *Capitoli dei capitani*, c. 6).

[3] This letter has also been omitted as Luca only reports his arrival at Southampton,
and the fact that not all the cargo has yet arrived as the merchants were holding some
back in order to take full advantage of the last few days.

[4] He must mean William Soper as he refers to him and Madonna Agnese elsewhere.
Soper was one of the most influential figures in Southampton, being a wealthy
merchant and shipowner. He had been mayor of the city twice and was Member of
Parliament for Southampton many times between 1413 and 1449. He was in fact
the sitting member at this time, and was also chief customs officer for many years
(Ruddock, *Southampton*, p. 193, and B. C. Turner, 'Southampton as a Naval Centre,
1414–1458', *Collected Essays on Southampton*, ed. J. B. Morgan and Philip Peberdy,
Southampton, 1961, p. 42). For Soper's activities as Keeper of the King's Ships,
see p. 258. On his departure Luca gave Madonna Agnese a small basket, one of six
which he had bought in Majorca (Diary, f. 19ᵛ).

volle parlare in una chiesa,[1] et quivi volle rimanere d'acordo mecho come gl'uomini di nostre galee s'avessino a governare, et questo con molta carità et discretione a mio parere. E prima volle ch'essi non portassino arme da offendere, salvo gl'uficiali di galee et che non andassino di nocte senza lume da ore 8 in là, cherano 3 ore di nocte al modo nostro, e che niuno montassi in sulle mura della terra, nè niuno danificassi gli orti o altre cose, sotto le pene de' loro ordini. Et chosì feci notificare per Piero trombetto in sulle galee martedì adì 10, e lle galee erano allo schalo per carichare quello che c'era colla schala in sul carichatoio. //

96ʳ   Domenicha adì 15 di gennaio tornarono i padroni et ser Agnolo da Londra et recharono il manifesto, et io avevo protestato per ser Stefano mio capellano adì 14 a Pagolo Morelli chome gli argani erano in punto sulle gallee per stivare a posta de' mercatanti, et dopo la venuta de' padroni rimanemo di cominciare a charichare lunedì adì 16.

Lunedì adì 16 di gennaio, circha a ora di vespro, s'ebbono i costumieri, che prima non si poterono avere, et pesarono 390[2] poche di lana di nostro caricho, le quali si carichò in su 3 battelli et misonsi allato alle galee, però che già era nocte e diliberarono i gomiti di non cominciare il dì a stivare perchè era il dì di santo Giovanni Dicollato.[3] El dì seguente adì 17 era santo Antonio e però diliberarono fare coprire dette lane et averle in punto col nome di Dio, per mercholedì adì 18. Et così si ferono coprire dette lane colle tende de' marinai et colle vele de' dette battelli. La nocte si fè' maltenpo et piovve circa la metà della nocte, per che passò le

96ᵛ   tende et la più parte della lana si bagnò, per che fu necessario // che martedì adì 17, il dì di santo Antonio, le dette lane tornassino in terra per asciugarsi, et così fè' fare Pagolo Morelli. Stivasene parte in sulle galee et in su uno de' detti batti ch'erano mancho molli.[4]

---

[1] The Mayor of Southampton at this time was John Seldon (Studer, *Port Books*, p. 117).

[2] The detailed description of the loading (pp. 278-80) reports 290 pokes of wool weighed on the first day.

[3] The Feast of the Decapitation of St. John is celebrated on 29 Aug. as Luca himself tells us early in the diary. Why he should now be celebrating it again is extremely obscure, as although it is accepted that 29 Aug. was more probably the date of the translation of the remains of St. John rather than of the actual execution which is supposed to have taken place before Easter; there seems to be no tradition for an additional celebration on 16 Jan. (*Dictionnaire d'Archéologie chrétienne et de liturgie*, vii, Paris, 1927, p. 2170).

[4] Once again there is a slight discrepancy between this general account and the

Mercholedì mattina adì 18 di gennaio, col nome di Dio, si cominciò
a stivare cogli argani le lane ch'erano in galee asciutte, finiti a
punto i x dì dal dì giugnemo, et la mattina di buonora cominciato
le prime andane.¹ Per ser Agnolo protestai a' padroni, gomiti,
sottogomiti, nocchieri, huomini di consiglio et scrivani il modo
della stiva cio è tanto et tanto et una per [una], a pena di fiorini 500
per uno et della restitutione del danno delle galee, come ne' capitoli
si contiene. Aveva auta sconcie parole la sera dinanzi Bernardo
Carnesecchi con Andrea Marini, con villane parole, perchè
essendo rimasi di cominciare a stivare adì 18, la sera Andrea aveva
cominciato a mettere a barccia² certi sacchi per essere meglio in
punto la mattina. Et Gaddo³ diceva a Bernardo, secondo con-‖
prendo, questo riputarsi in vergogna che prima di lui cominciassi, 97ʳ
et così per una gara di niente, non essendo io a galea, il detto
Bernardo ebbe dette parole pocho considerate con Andrea detto,
di che cortesemente poi lo ripresi lui et Gaddo, mostrando il
pericolo si portava per niente etc.

Mercholedì adì 18 di gennaio, fu il primo dì che l'argano cominciò
a lavorare et piovve tutto dì, sicchè non si potè stivare una andana
per galea, perchè le lane erano bagnate et non si potevano avere per
la piova. Le lane che Gaddo aveva tratte di galea et poste in sul
batto, si convennono rechare in terra, et fu assai che dire tra lui et
Pagolo Morelli, perchè diceva Pagolo erano più molli che l'altre
ch'erano venuto dentro et per difetto di detto Gaddo et ch'egli
protesterebbe etc.⁴ Detto dì scripsi a' consoli una lettera dell'infrascripto tenore.

Magnifici Signori consoli etc. Il dì 7 del presente, per la via di
Londra, scripsi alla Magnificentia Vostra la nostra venuta qui a
salvamento, gratia di Dio. Et adì 8 andarono i padroni a Londra per

more detailed account of the loading on pp. 278–80. The latter reports that a part of
the wool was already on board the galleys before the rain and was better protected.

¹ *andana*: a row or column, in this case of bales. It could perhaps mean a layer,
but the extremely shallow draught of the galleys would not permit many layers of
bales which weighed over 350 lb. each. It seems more likely that the wool cargo was
stored in rows, with perhaps each row divided from the next with boards (*assi di
stiva*). For details of the loading of medieval galleys see A. A. Ruddock, 'The
Method of Handling the Cargoes of Medieval Merchant Galleys', *Bulletin of the
Institute of Historical Research*, xix, 1942.

² *barccia*: probably meaning *barca*, a small boat.

³ Gaddo was the mate on Carnesecchi's galley.

⁴ It seems in fact that the wool which was in the third boat after the rain had in
fact been taken out of Carnesecchi's galley by Gaddo.

essere d'acordo co' mercatanti et io sono stato a sollecitare i gomiti pe' bisogni delle galee et stive et concimi. Ora i padroni sono tornati d'acordo co' mercatanti, et ieri, gratia di Dio, si cominciò a 97ᵛ stivare cogli argani. El caricho è qui quasi tutto, // et così abbiamo il manifesto, che spero tra quello che è qui e alchuna particella ci resta a venire, aranno queste galee, salvo non ci inpaccia, intorno di pocche 1200 et balloni di panni 60 in 80; et se 'l tenpo ci lascierà, spero presto aremo stivato, ma la piova è grande et non ci lascia lavorare, per che se non ci acconciassi il tenpo, ci torebbe assai. Idio ce lo dia buono et presto, però che se 'l tenpo il patirà, spero per la gratia di Dio presto saremo a camino per ritorno. Per più lettere dalla Schiuse fusti avisati de' provedimenti pareva a noi di qui da fare per più sicurtà delle galee et honore vostro. Non so quello n'arete diliberato; attendiano vostre risposte. Questi mercatanti di qui in niuno modo vogliono fare alchuno provedimento nè spesa: avisone la Vostra Signoria per che tutto vi sia noto, alla quale mi racomando umilmente. A' comandi vostri. In Antona adì 19 di gennaio 1429. Dipoi partimo da Pisa niuna lettera nè aviso abiamo auto dalla Signoria Vostra.

Detto dì scripsi le infrascripte lettere et manda'le a D. Villani a Londra,[1] con quella di sopra, che lle mandassi a Firenze:

una lettera a madonna B. et all'Orelia, comune.

una lettera comune a Berto da Filichaia et a Niccholò di Gentile.

una lettera a Bernardo Gherardi.

una a Pagolo da Ghiacceto[2] adì 22 o circha, che andò con quelle di sopra. //

98ʳ Martedì adì 31 di gennaio andai con Guglielmo Supper costumiere d'Antona a vedere le navi grandi de' re d'Inghilterra, che sono in Anbra presso ad Antona miglia iiii o circha.[3] La maggiore dice-

---

[1] Domenico Villani was still one of the leading Florentine merchants in London in the late 1430's (Biscaro, 'Banco di Filippo Borromei', p. 61).

[2] This was probably Paolo di Zanobio Ghiacceto who was to become Gonfalonier of Justice in 1439.

[3] After the death of Henry V the fleet which he had built up for his French campaigns was allowed to run down. In 1423 William Soper, who had had a part in building some of the ships, was made Keeper of the King's ships with instructions to sell them off. By 1429 only four of the great ships remained and these were laid up at Bursledon on the Hamble, never to see active service again. These were the *Grace Dieu, Trinity Royal, Holigost*, and the *Jesus*. See M. Oppenheim, *A History of the Administration of the Royal Navy and of Merchant Shipping in Relation to the Navy*, London, 1896, pp. 11–15 and 22–23, Turner, 'Southampton as a Naval Centre', pp. 42–47, C. F. Richmond, 'The Keeping of the Seas during the Hundred Years War: 1422–40', *History*, xlix, 1964.

vano era di portata di botti 3000 et chi di più di 3300, et in verità mai vidi sì grande edificio et sì bello. Fe' misurare l'albero in sulla prima coverta: volgeva braccia 11 0 circha, alto braccia 102, dal ballatoio da prua al'aqua braccia 26, et dichono che quando navicha s'alza altro coridoio sopra esso; lungha braccia 92 0 circha, largha braccia 50 0 circha. Et apresso a quella, aveva una nave di botti 1600 et una di 1200 0 circha.[1] Desinamo in su detta nave et feronci grandissimo honore il detto Super et conpagni suoi.

Giovedì adì 2 di febraio il dì di santa Maria Candellaia,[2] andamo io et padroni a' luogho del detto Super dal'altra parte del porto, lungi qualche 3 miglia, tra per aqua et per terra, et vennono gli altri 2 costumieri, che l'uno à nome Iohanis Stivelda e l'altro Roberto Arsaelse, conteruolo che tiene i loro conti quasi come notaio. Fecci uno riccho desinare nella sua casa ch'era a lato a uno boscho ci[n]tta di fossi pieni d'aqua con molti cceveri [sic: cervi?].[3] //

Aveva in casa assai valletti e cavagli et molti cani, perchè era 98ᵛ presso alla foresta. Desinato che avemo, con buona cera et molta cortesia ci menò alla foresta dove trovamo molti cerbi et danii

---

[1] The first of these ships was probably the *Grace Dieu*, and it is therefore interesting to compare Luca's measurements with those reported by R. C. Anderson after his examination of the wreck in the *Hamble* in 1934 (see R. C. Anderson, 'The Bursledon Ship', *Mariners' Mirror*, xx, 1934, and 'The Wreck in the Hamble River', *Antiquaries' Journal*, xiv, 1934). Anderson came to the conclusion that this wreck was the *Grace Dieu*, thus setting aside the curious theories which had prevailed about it since the nineteenth century (it had been variously described as a Viking ship and a nineteenth-century merchantman!). The measurements of the original ship he estimated to be about 125 feet in the keel, 200 feet stem to stern, and 48 feet wide. From these dimensions Anderson estimated the tonnage to have been c. 1,400 tons, and this agrees with one of the contemporary figures for the *Grace Dieu*, which Oppenheim had previously rejected as impossible. Luca's 3,000 *botti* is also about 1,400 tons, and in addition he reports a stem to stern measurement of *c.* 177 feet and a width of 96 feet. This last dimension is very curious and, if it is to be accepted, indicates a most unusual ship which in fact as we know never got to sea. The other two ships which Luca saw were presumably the *Holigost* (760 tons; 1,600 *botti*) and the *Trinity Royal* (540 tons; 1,200 *botti*). This must have been the moment at which the *Jesus* was towed away to Southampton. Of the three ships which Luca saw, the *Grace Dieu* was burnt in 1439 and the other two were broken up.

[2] Sta. Maria Candellaia is the Feast of the Purification of the Blessed Virgin.

[3] Soper was a considerable landowner and had, amongst other possessions, an estate to the west of the Watergate. The Watergate itself he obtained in 1439 as his office on a 120-year lease for an annual payment of one red rose (Wallis Chapman, *Black Book of Southampton*, i, p. 118 n.). Of the other two customs officials 'Stivelda' was certainly John Asshefeld whose name appears in the accounts for this period along with that of Soper (Studer, *Port Books*, p. vi); 'Arsaelse' is rather more obscure, but there were two local officials whose names could conceivably be twisted into this form. One was Robert Aylward who was steward 1430–1, and a leading citizen of the town; the other was Robert Florys, water bailiff and collector of the custom.

[*sic* : daini]. Parte di noi a cavallo, gli altri tutti a piè, pigliamo uno cervo giovane et uno danio. Il cerbio prese uno cane che m'era stato donato. Tornamo a casa sua a ore 22 o circha, quivi facemo collatione più volte. Poi volle udissimo il vespro in sua casa, c'aveva il capellano e lla capeletta ordinata; et così ci fè tutte quelle cortesie et dimestichezze che dire si potessi, non volendo ci partissimo. Infine passate l'ore 24 già nocte, montamo in sulle nostre barche et tornamo ad Antona col cerbio et col danio, chè lasciare non gli potemo.

Adì 5 di febraio, domenicha dietro desinare, diliberai d'andare a vedere Londra. Montai a cavallo con 5 cavagli insieme con Giorgio Luchi et con Totto Machiavelli et loro conpagnia,[1] e lla sera albergamo a una villa si chiama || Dilforte migli[a] 15 di lungi d'Antona.[2]

Lunedì adì 6 desinamo a Farnan, e la sera aloggiamo a Ghilforte[3] migli[a] 23 più oltre, verso Londra.

Martedì adì 7 desinamo a Chinchistona[4] e giugnemo a Londra a vespro, et dismontai in casa Ubertino de' Bardi con Giorgio di Niccholò di Lucha che governa la conpagnia. Et tutto quello dì et mercholedì et giovedì apresso, adì 8 e dì 9 di febraio, atesi a vedere tutte le cose notabili di Londra. Et ordinai che ll'armadura che s'era portata per donare al ducha di Concestrie si mandassi, ch'era in casa il consolo et no' ll'aveva mandata anchora,[5] et simile che'l salvocondotto s'avessi per le galee, che anchora non era publicato. Et ricevetti grande honore da tutti i fiorentini, et maxime dal detto Giorgio, da Totto Machiavelli et da Domenico Villani. El collettore del papa, messer Giovanni degli Obbizi,[6] non si potrebbe dire quanto cortesemente m'onorò per rispetto del comune,

---

[1] Giorgio Luchi was presumably Giorgio di Niccolò da Lucca who was London manager of the firm of Ubertino de' Bardi. Totto di Buoninsegna Machiavelli was a partner with Ubertino de' Bardi in the same, or possibly another, firm of which the headquarters was in London. Both merchants had been in England for some years. See Holmes, 'Florentine Merchants in England', pp. 204–5, and De Roover, *Medici Bank*, pp. 209–29, 318, and 470 n. 5.

[2] Probably Alresford.   [3] Guildford.   [4] Kingston.

[5] The *ducha di Concestrie* was presumably the Duke of Gloucester, Protector during the minority of Henry VI.

[6] Giovanni Obbizzi was known in English records as Master John Obbizis or Opizis of Lucca. He was Papal Chaplain and auditor, and collector of the papal tenth in England and Ireland. He also held the title of Papal Nuncio, and served as envoy not only for Eugenius IV but also on occasions for Henry VI (see *Calendar of Entries in the Papal Registers relating to Great Britain and Ireland—Papal Letters*, vol. viii, London, 1909, *passim*).

99ʳ

convitandomi etc. Ma a me parve di non vi soprastare nè d'acettare conviti; et così avendo vedute le cose notabili v'erano, mi parti' venerdì mattina, adì 10, et venimo a desinare a Chinchistona e albergho // a Farnam. Sabato adì 11 desinamo a Dilforte et giugnemo 99ᵛ a vespro ad Antona. Trovai che'l dì dinanzi, cioè adì 10, erano fornite di stivare le lane, che furono al peso della costuma saccha circha 580, e levati gli argani et arborate le galee per mettere balloni et altre cose. E chosì sabato detto, adì 11, cominciarono a carichare balloni et a rimettere in galea i nostri fornimenti et coredi. Et avemo caricho tutt'i balloni et altre merchatantie ch'erano ad Antona, che furono balloni circha . . ., et le cose rechate di Fiandra ricarichate, ch'erano per circha balloni 24 di mercie e altre cose d'involture, per tutto giovedì adì 16 di febraio.

Venerdì adì 17 et sabato adì 18, demo il sevo et atesesi a spacciare i ccocchetti¹ et mettere in galea i nostri fornimenti et vettovagl[i]e. Et mandai la grida che per tutta domenicha adì 19 ciaschuno fussi in galea co' suoi arnesi e robe. Sabato sera ad octe [*sic* : nocte], dopo dette cose et diliberationi fatte, venne una lettera dal consolo di Londra che scrivevano i consoli del mare da Firenze, a me fatta adì 9 // di gennaio,² i quali rispondono alla lettera a lloro scripta dalle 100ʳ Schiuse adì 6 di dicenbre, et comettomi per detta lettera che io debba torre 20 marinai et 10 conpagnoni per galea a spese delle mercatantie, come scrivevo. Et Zanobi del Cavallaro mi disse per parte del detto consolo ch'egli ragunerebbe i mercatanti et che subito mi manderebbe di loro diliberatione perchè, secondo diceva in sua lettera, i consoli gli scrivevano comandando ci dessino detti huomini, ma lui voleva consigliarsi cogli altri mercatanti.

Io, veduta la lettera che comandava che così si facessi, subito fu' co' padroni et rimasi d'acordo si cerchassi degl'uomini. Commissi a' gomiti che cerchassino, et così a Pagolo Morelli consolo et a più altri della Linghuadocci, con intentione di torre tutti gli uomini si potevano per insino in detta somma, e fare presto acciò non si perdessi tenpo perchè la bigia era bella.

Domenicha adì 19 si mutò tenpo e tornò vento a valle, sicchè cci levò la speranza del così subito partire. Nondimeno atendemo a sollecitare et a mettere in galea hu[o]mini et cose, che assai pena

¹ *cocchetti*: cockets. These were the officially stamped customs receipts issued by the customs officials to indicate that all goods on a ship had been duly entered and the necessary duty paid.

² See pp. 276–7 for this letter which is to be found loosely inserted in the manuscript of the diary.

100ᵛ fu a riavere la ciurma perchè tutti voleva//no di nuovo denari et sì tutti avevano aute paghe 7, convenivasi a ciaschuno prestare di nuovo a chi fiorino 1 a chi 2 et a chi una paga.[1]

Lunedì adì 20 mettemo in galea i remi et gran parte della ciurma et fornimenti che manchavano, et a reverentia di Dio si fè dire una messa cantando et 12 piane. Et dette le messe, si fè uno bello convito in casa dove stava a' costumieri della villa et al mere, con 6 de' più honorati della terra, et pure il tenpo era tristo.

Martedì adì 21 mandai i trombetti a racorre per la terra di buonora, acciò che ognuno si riducessi in galea. Dipoi fummo insieme con Polo[2] et Zanobi del Cavallaro ed io, et in tutto mi dissono non potere avere huomini inghilesi perchè non si volevano partire per pocho tenpo, et comessione non c'era da potere dare loro soldo di là poi. Il perchè scripsi una lettera a Alexandro Ferrantini,[3] consolo, et prima la sugellassi, la lessi a' sopradetti et commissi la mandassi Zanobi per propio fante, in questo effetto, chome noi non trovavamo huomini in Antona però v'era pocha

101ʳ gente et non volevano venire se non col mo//do detto et gl'inghilesi anchora volevano licentia, bene se ne trovava alchuni che tutti gli torre' huomi[ni] fuori del'isola, et quegli ch'avessino oltre al numero delle galee, che nne fare' chiaro Zanobi e Polo mettere a loro conto. E veduto ad Antona non si trovavano gli uomi[ni], che a me pareva che per hubidire a' consoli gli togliessino a Londra come gl'uomini di remo, insino in 40, et recassino gli archi sicchè al bisogno gli potessino adoperare alo remo et con l'archo. Avisandogli che per la moltitudine ch'è a Londra, ero certo gli arebbono, volendo, et ch'io non avendogli da loro et no' gli trovando qui, gli pigliere' dove gli potessi trovare per ubidire a' consoli etc. Et scripsi che detta lettera legessi alla natione, et presto rispondessi di loro intentione, et che bene ch'esso disperava montare in galea colle ciurme, nondimeno il tempo s'era messo cattivo, per forma speravo arebbono tenpo da mandargli etc. La lettera andò a ore 8 o circha la mattina adì 21 di febraio.

---

[1] In Southampton the last 2½ months' pay was due, so presumably by the time the galleys were about to leave many of the crews were short of money. As they probably used most of their money to buy their seaman's venture, on which they could realize profits before, or at, the end of the voyage, it was not unduly risky to lend a little for this purpose.　　　　　　　　　　　　　　　　　[2] Paolo Morelli.

[3] Alessandro Ferrantini was manager of the Alberti company in London until 1436 (Holmes, 'Florentine Merchants in England', p. 195) and one of the leading figures in the controversy over payments for wool which resulted in the imposition of the 1448 reprisal.

Mercholedì adì 22 di febraio // il tempo fè vista dirizzarsi per noi, 101ᵛ
il perchè mandai a ricorre le genti pe' tronbetti et scripsi a' consoli
la 'nfrascripta lettera.

Magnifici Signori Consoli etc. Dipoi che di costà partimo non
avemo vostre lettere se non solamente una vostra che avemo adì
18 di questo, fatta adì 9 del passato, risposta alle nostre dalle
Schiuse, per la quale ci avisate et commettete di torre gl'uomi[ni]
vi scripsi, per salvamento delle galee, et che soldi vadano ad avaria
e lle spese di boccha a' padroni, et così sono d'acordo co' padroni.
Il consolo da Londra anchora mi scrive che mercatanti sono contenti d'ubidire a' vostri comandamenti et ch'io gli tolgha.

Ma questa terra è povera d'uomini et oltre a cciò gl'inghilesi non
vogliono venire sanza promessa d'avere soldo costì; et anchora,
perchè lo re s'aparecchia a passare in Francia, non si possono avere
sanza licentia.¹ Abbiamo tolti et toremo per lo remo tedeschi et
fiaminghi che cci sono, il più // si potrà, et per insino nel numero 102ʳ
scrivete; se si troveranno, che credo di no, poremo a conto de'
mercatanti, rimettendo prima a punto le galee insino alla debita
quantità. Se il consolo da Londra avessi voluto fare davero, avrebbe
presi là gl'uomini et mandati qui, però che ivi è una moltitudine
infinita di genti forestieri et anche del paese; pure io gli ò scripto
per propio fante già è 2 dì, la carestia ci è d'uomini, et veduto che
conpagnoni di balestro non si truovano in questi paesi se non per
ventura, ch'egli ci mandi insino in 40 huomini di remo et faccia che
ciaschuno rechi l'archo suo, però che ciaschuno sa adoperare
l'archo di qua e 'l vogare s'insegna presto; et se licentia bisogna al
trargli, di là si conviene avere. Et così, se gli manda, sareno [*sic*:
saremo] forniti bene, che llo attendereno [*sic*: attenderemo]
insino che'l tenpo si metta dal nostro, però che come si mettessi,
non pare a niuno nè uficiali nè // mercatante di perderlo, però che 102ᵛ
qui le bigie si mettono molto di rado. Le galee, gratia di Dio, sono
di tutto spacciate et cariche, et questo dì crediamo avere i ccocchetti
et montare tutti in galea, se fia piacere di Dio. El tenpo al presente
à buona vista, et se terrà, sareno [*sic*: saremo] alla vela questa nocte,
se piacerà a Dio, con tutti quegli si potranno avere d'agiunti. Et in
caso non ci potessimo partire, aspetteremo quegli da Londra, se di
là si potessino avere, aspettando fornirci di conpagnoni dove ne
potreno trovare, et così pare a questi padroni e gomiti e a chi c'è

---

¹ It was in 1430 that Henry VI went to France for his coronation, and all available
shipping was assembled to transport his following.

pe' mercatanti et consolo da Londra, e al consolo di qui et a me pare il migliore partito. Et col nome di Dio c'ingegnereno [*sic*: c'ingegneremo] di venire più avisati che fia possibile, per ogni rispetto.

E si [*sic*: Si è] detto qui che'l signore di Luccha à tolto a soldo 5 galee catalane; ma perchè da voi niente n'abiamo, non crediamo 103ʳ sia vero.¹ Pure se così fussi, possendone avere // aviso sarebbe utile. Et almeno fate rinovare uno ricordo ch'io lasciai a Pisa a Andrea di Veri Rondinelli e al conpagno, di certi segni che alla Gorgona² ci fussino fatti alla tornata, di che noi n'abiamo la copia et se cci sarà fatto come rimanemo d'acordo, asai sareno [*sic*: saremo] avisati, se meglio non si potessi. La Vostra Signoria sa bene il pericolo si porterebbe costà ne' nostri mari et spetialmente a Livorno, se cose nuove aparissino et noi no' llo sapessimo. Sicchè, per Dio, provedete a casi secondo che ocoressino, come si conviene. Qui a noi, per infino a questo punto, c'è stata fatta optima conpagnia e siamo stati bene veduti et trattati, et presto spaccio [avremo?] gratia di Dio. Così piaccia a lui darci presto ritorno con salvamento. Nè più per questa. Racomandomi a la Signoria Vostra. In Antona, adì 22 di febraio 1429. Scripsi con essa lettera le 'nfrascripte:

1ª a madonna B. et al'Aurelia,
1ª a Nicchola de' Medici,
1ª a messer Rinaldo mio fratello,³
1ª a Niccholò di Gentile.

Dirizza' dette lettere a Domenico Villani a Londra che lle mandassi. //

103ᵛ Dipoi detto dì tolsi huomini xi per la nostra galea et 4 per la conserva, che credevo mancassino, et desinamo; et il dì, circha ora di vespro, montai in galea col nome di Dio co' ccocchetti, e con noi venne il cercatore e spacciò tutto.⁴ Ma per la marea manchata non ci potemo levare, et simile per molti de' nostri ch'erano in terra. Tornò il padrone in terra per mandare gl'uomini e io rimasi in galea, levati dal caio dove caricamo et surti dinanzi alla grua della costuma a mezzo canale.

---

¹ In fact it was true and Luca was not unnaturally furious when he discovered that he had not been warned.

² Gorgona: a small fortified island belonging to Florence about 20 miles from Porto Pisano.

³ Rinaldo di Maso degli Albizzi. This is the first and only letter which Luca wrote to his brother, whereas other correspondents received four or five from him.

⁴ *cercatore*: the customs' searcher.

Giovedì mattina adì 23, il dì di Berlingaccio,[1] parendoci la
bigia ferma racogl[i]emo tutta nostra gente in galea, salvo alchuni
fuggiti, et col nome di Dio, parendo a tutti di non aspettare altro,
con circha 20 huomini tolti per lo remo che manchavano al numero
de' padroni, sanza poterne avere più, colla marea piena, passato
mezzo dì, facemo vela con vento biagia cioè tramontana. La nocte
ci trovamo sopra il capo di Brullano.[2]

Venerdì adì 24, a terza o circha, ci trovamo sopra Puamua [*sic*:
Palamua] et capo di // Gomestieri d'Inghilterra, et col nome di Dio   104ʳ
pigliamo la volta di Spagna con tenpo prospero ed era il dì di santo
Mattias.

Sabato adì 25 et domenicha adì 26, navichamo e a nona avemo
la vista di terra et trovamoci presso al capo di Finisterre in Spagna.
La sera di nocte, cioè domenicha adì 26 et la nocte, passamo il capo
detto; rompemo il terzeruolo.

Lunedì mattina adì 27, ci trovamo sopra Baiona con mare et vento
[in] bonaccia, et trovamo caldo dove prima avavamo auto grande
freddo; parevasi essere nella state [*sic*: estate].

Martedì adì 28, il dì carnasciale[3], navicamo in bonaccia, con venti
dal tereno e con i batti, e lla sera ci trovamo presso alle Berlinghe.[4]
Detto dì fe' fare la mostra a nostra galea, e fatto conto de' fugiti et
de' rimessi, manchò solo 1° huomo di remo a tutto il numero.

Mercholedì adì 1° di marzo ci trovamo tutto dì in calma sopra
Lisbona, et fu il primo dì di quaresima, e lla sera ci trovamo passato
il capo di Picceri[5] con bonaccia, et così navicamo insino alla terza
guardia; dipoi si mutò tenpo et missesi vento la [*sic*: da] levante et
poi da scilocco et sciloccho et mezzodì.

Giovedì mattina adì 2, ci trovamo con venti sopradetti presso al
capo di santo Vincentio a miglia 50 o circha, larghi in mare molto,
per che veduto il tempo contradio a noi di non potere ire al // capo   104ᵛ
et forte dubitavamo di tornare in Galitia, pigliamo la volta di
Lisbona, dove con faticha, perchè il vento era scarso, entramo et
surgemo di nocte a Rastrello. Et subito mandamo a Lisbona, per

---

[1] *Berlingaccio* is Tuscan for the last Thursday of Carnivale.
[2] Portland Bill.   [3] Shrove Tuesday (Carnival).
[4] 'La Berlingue est une montagne grosse, haute et ronde dessus, et droite devers la
mers, et au pied d'elle, y a deux ferraillons, et en terre d'elle y a abri et l'entré devers
l'est est la meilleure et auras abri dessus de siroest d'oest et de noroest' (Pierre Garcie
dit 'Ferrande', *Le Grand Routier*, Rouen, 1584, p. 63). The island of Berlengo is about
five miles off the coast of Portugal and 50 miles north of the mouth of the Tagus.
[5] Cape Espichel 15 miles south of the estuary of the Tagus.

rinfreschamento et per nuove, lo scrivano et Maso Aliotti. Sentimo da una nave alamanna che entrava in porto quando noi, come la nave di Priore caricha d'aringhe era stata presa da Consalvo Corero, la quale si menava per Matteo di ser Antonio in nome di Gian Grillotto da Bruggia.[1]

Venerdì adì 3 la mattina, tornarono i detti mandati con nuove et dissono i' re nella corte nè alcuno de' figl[i]uoli essere nella città ma fuori, di lungha più che miglia 60. Venne Bartolomeo di . . . da Firenze a galea et a lui lessi la lettera de' consoli et inpuosi parlassi quando potessi, per parte de' nostri signori, a' re et allo 'nfante Pietro per impetrare la gratia già domandata per le galee. Et disse che'l fante anchora non era arrivato colle lettere della Signoria a' re nè a loro, come a me avevano scripto i consoli.

Fe' la mostra della conserva detto dì, e ebbe il conto. Sabato adì 4 et domenicha adì 5 di marzo, stemo in detto porto per tenpo, et 105ʳ vero è che la dome//nicha mattina avemo pensiero di levarci et mandamo pe' pedoti ch'erano in terra et tanto penarono a venire che lla marea passò et anche il tenpo era molto fresco. Pure ci levamo dal detto Rastrello, avendo preso rinfreschamento d'aqua et d'altre cose, et venimo la sera a surgere in boccha del porto dentro alle secche de Cacioppi,[2] per essere la mattina, se tenpo fussi, più in nostra levata et per che i pedoti non dismontassino in terra. Trovamo quivi la nave dell'aringhe sopradetta surta, et venne a noi Matteo di ser Antonio padrone, et disse avere perdute solo le robe de' catalani et non quelle de' fiorentini e d'altri, et pocho danno mostrò avere auto, salvo perdimento di tenpo. Però s'era partito dalle Schiuse insino adì 6 di gennaio il dì che noi et quivi si trovava con noi ch'eravamo stati in Antona alla stiva dì 46. Detto dì, circha ore 22, si misse vento a ponente e maestro, il perchè i pedoti della conserva mandorono a dire che a lloro pareva d'uscire del porto. Per che avemo a consiglio i nostri pedoti cioè Giovanni Martini et Iohani Artisti, Andrea Marini gomito, Guiglielmo d'Asti sotto gomito, Antonio d'Andrea et Luciano da Portovenere 105ᵛ consiglieri et più altri va//lenti nocchieri et marinai. Et udite le ragioni ch'erano loro asegnate se ne ferono beffe, però che lla marea era già straccha et ivi a 2 ore doveva tornare contro, e lle secche durano asai de Cacioppi et pareva loro che troppo fussi pericoloso

[1] This is presumably Priore Marioto's galley again although it is now referred to as *nave*.

[2] *Cachopo* is the Portuguese word for reef from which these shoals at the mouth of the Tagus took their name.

trovarsi di nocte sopra quelle secche se 'l vento calmassi o si mutassi, aspettando la marea per prua. Il perchè intanto dilibera-rono tutti d'acordo di non si dovere partire insino al giorno, et io ne fe' rogato ser Agnolo per ogni cagione et acorda' mi a quello medesimo per più salvamento. La sera medesima, dopo sole tra-montò, si levò Tadeo[1] sopradetto colla sua nave d'aringhe et uscì di porto a sua via, di che fu parlato come di gente sanza ragione di navicare, per lo pericolo a che si mettevano.

Lunedì mattina adì 6 di marzo, al'alba del dì, uscimo di detto porto con bonaccia, dipoi a ora di terza passata si misse vento a ponente et maestro dal nostro, et navichamo tutto dì e la nocte apresso. Et martedì mattina adì 7, ci trovamo sopra il capo di santo Vincentio. El vento si fè contradio per che tutto il dì e lla nocte voltegiamo in mare per non perdere il capo. //

Lunedì detto adì 6 fe' ragione de' carichi delle galee et trova' gli 106ʳ nello infrascripto modo, cioè la somma di tutte et ii le galee cariche in Antona d'Inghilterra e alle Schiuse.

Pocche 1028 di lana, rechate a pocche alchune saccha.

Balloni 63 di panni.

Carategli, ballette, fardegli, tra berette, stagni lavorati et pani e altre cose, in tutto capi 54.

Stimo involture per balloni 17.

Stagni et pionbi per savora, pezzi 281, di peso circha lb. 160,000.

Tutto per Porto Pisano.

E più balloni vi di panni di genovesi per a Calisi e Malicha, caricamo in detto luogho.

E più caricamo alle Schiuse per Porto Pisano, ballette, balloni, carategli et fardegli, in tutto capi 42 di pani, mercie e altre cose.

Stimo d'involture per balloni 24.[2]

Credo monti il nolo, andando a salvamento per la gratia di Dio, intorno di fiorini 10,000; nè più si poteva caricare, perchè le galee erano stivate quanto era possibile, però che asai panni di genovesi areno levati et d'altri, avendo auto da caricare, ma tutto era pieno. //

Mercholedì adì 8 ci trovamo la mattina essere assai scaduti per 106ᵛ lo volteggiare della nocte, e'l vento rinfreschava da levante e sciloccho per che per lo meglio deliberamo entrare nel porto di

---

[1] Meaning Matteo presumably.
[2] See p. 138 for translation of this cargo list and the English customs account record of the same cargo.

Silvi de' re di Portogallo, tra santo Vincentio et il capo di santa
Maria, porto di barsia e di marea, dove con molto pericolo s'en-
trava.¹ Stemo surti alla boccha del porto circha ore ii, per aspettare
che 'lla marea montassi; poi entramo a ora di nona, gratia di Dio,
a salvamento. Et senza fallo, essendo entrati quando giugnemo,
eravamo perduti per la pocha aqua.

Et quivi trovamo che lle due navi trovate in Ribadeo al'andare
in Fiandra, amendue avevano rotto il dì di santa Katerina, et
anchora v'era di loro huomini ch'avevano ricolto legname et
altre cose. Entrati dentro il porto era bonissimo, ma l'entrate
pessime.

Tutto detto dì avemo vista della nave dell'aringhe di sopra
nominate, et volteggiò sopra detto porto, ma per la male entrata
non si calò, secondo ci parve. Stemo in detto porto di Silvis tutto
giovedì adì 9 e lla nocte apresso, per tenpo contradio. //

107ʳ Venerdì adì 10 di marzo, a ora di nona passata, essendo l'aqua
piene, uscimo di Silvis con bonaccia, et col nome di Dio pigliamo
la via dì Cadisi. La sera circa ore 23 avemo vista di ii galee sottili da
levante et nel fare della nocte si trovarono con noi. Domandarono
che galee noi eravamo et noi loro, senpre colle balestre cariche et
in punto da zuffa. Loro non volevano dire chi fussino nè noi prima
di loro, nè essi levavano bandiere nè noi. Infine dissono e[sse]re
galee di Castiglia, et allora rispondemo essere di Firenze.

Domandaro di nuove noi et noi loro. Noi sempre seguimo
nostro viaggio, e loro si tornarono la via di terra et chosì a una ora
di nocte o circha ci partimo l'uno dal'altro. Avemo vista di ii navi
in mare le quali stimavamo essere la nave dell'aringhe e una de'
vinitiani ch'era stata a Lisbona con noi, et chosì dicemo alle galee
sottili che cci domandarono che navi quelle erano, che l'una era
107ᵛ fiorentina l'altra vinitiana. Nel detto porto di Silvis trova//mo le
mandrole [*sic*: mandorle] grosse da mangiare et le vigne che già
mostravano l'uve, e 'l caldo come di mezza state, di che avemo asai
admiratione che in sì pochi dì partiti d'Inghilterra, dov'era il cuore
del verno, c'eravamo trovati nella state con tanto dolci tempi et
caldi dì, che tutta la ciurma si confortava. Navicamo tutta nocte a

¹ 'Silvis è porto di marea e achostati dalla banda da Levante presso all'altare
un prodese e vai dentro fino alla punta dell'arena e ivi surge' (Portolan Parma-
Magliabecchi, in Kretschmer, *Die italienischen Portolans*, p. 279). Silvi was the capital
of the Algarve province of Portugal, which, incidentally, is usually thought to have
given its name to the Florentine *panni garbi* which were originally made from wool
from this area.

nostro viaggio, et sabato mattina adì 11 di marzo, ci trovamo sopra il capo di santa Maria et a ore 22 o circha, surgemo a Cadisi, fuori del porto, che si dice a' Porci.[1] Perchè 'l tenpo era frescho et buono per noi, per non ci i[n]pegnare mandamo i pedoti in terra et ii mercatanti genovesi per avere lingua se volevano ivi le loro robe o a Malicha, chè così avevano pattegiato,[2] et con loro mandai Tadeo di Pionbino per che subito tornassi indietro colla barcha et non si lasciassi tenere a parole. Et così fè, per che la sera, tramonto il sole, tornò colla barcha et co' mercatanti. Et subito facemo vela et navichamo tutta nocte con vento prospero, et la mattina domenicha adì 12, a levata di sole, ci trovamo dentro allo stretto, sopra il monte Giubelta//ro in Granata, et rivedemo le dette ii navi 108ʳ per poppa a noi circha miglia 15. El vento era ponente et libeccio, a noi prospero e bonaccievole, et così navichamo insino a ore 22 o circha, et surgemo a Malicha, dove scarichamo uno mercatante genovese con certi baloni di rami et stagni, et non trovando niente da carichare per la cattiva dispositione del paese, a una ora di nocte fumo spacciati per partire, che pocho rinfreschamento pigliamo. Ma il vento cambiò et tornò a levante, per che stemo insino a mezza nocte; allora essendo bonaccia, col nome di Dio ci partimo tirandoci in mare a remi perchè il tenpo alitava pure da levante et scilocho. Trovamo che Malicha s'era ribellata dallo re che ubidiva all'andare che facemo in Fiandra, et ubidì al'altro re venuto di Tunisi, et così si diceva che aveva fatto Granata et tutto il paese et che el detto re s'era ridocto in Anbra, forte castello et mirabile in Granata, con più di 500 uomini, et quivi era asediato.[3] Et già per cava quegli fuori gli aveva//no tolta l'aqua per sotterra, ronpen- 108ᵛ dogli la vena del pozzo, per che pocho si sperava si potessi tenere. Et i detti re, quello che al presente era asediato era nipote del'altro, et a lui in verità pare s'aparteneva i' regno, ma essendo rimaso fanciullo alla morte del padre, il zio aveva occupato i' regno. Il perchè, circha tre anni passati, questo garzone aveva ritolto i'

---

[1] Las Puercas of Cadiz are two sandbanks on the right hand going up to the harbour which were a common anchorage for ships passing through.

[2] Both Cadiz and Malaga were favourite markets of the Genoese for the sale of English cloth (Heers, 'Royaume de Grenade', p. 116).

[3] By this time the end of Muhammad IX's usurpation was in sight. He was besieged in the great fortress of the Alhambra at Granada, and soon after Luca's galleys had passed, he was betrayed by his remaining followers and executed. See J. A. Condé, *History of the Dominion of the Arabs in Spain*, London, 1855, vol. iii, pp. 309–15. There seems to be no substance for Luca's theory that Muhammad IX was the rightful heir whose throne had been usurped by his wicked uncle.

regno al zio e lui cacciato del paese, il quale se n'andò a' re di Tunisi et da lui aveva aute navi et galee, et in quegli dì che noi passamo era venuto in Almeria et quivi smontato in terra et col favore de' paesani ripreso il regno come di sopra si dice.

Navichamo quella nocte et tutto dì lunedì adì 13 con bonaccia, e al tardi collo batto, sicchè la sera ci trovamo passato Mileccha et Stravigna.[1] In Malicha trovamo de' baccelli già duri et erbaggi come fussi del mese di maggio. Et tutti i galeotti vogavano in camicia per lo caldo grande.

Martedì mattina ci trovamo sopra capo Gatto, pure in Granata, 109ʳ e 'l vento saltò a grecho et ∥ levante, a noi contradio. Ma perch'era asai bonaccia di mare, voltegiamo tutto dì insino a ore 22 o circha; allora rinfreschando il vento, facemo la via del capo detto, per dare parte alla nocte, dove giugnemo a una ora di nocte o circha. Et giunti al capo, trovamo una nave la quale per sospetto di noi prese la volta di mare, e 'l vento si mostrò da ponente; il perchè diliberamo non surgere et stemo a seccho, di fuori del capo, per vedere se 'l vento si fermava insino a ore 4 di nocte o circha. Di poi facemo vela co' pocho vento et bonaccia, e la mattina ci trovamo sopra Bera,[2] in Granata, cioè mercholedì adì 15 di marzo, et navicamo tutto dì con bonaccia et pocho di vento a noi contradio. La sera ci trovamo presso a Cartagena a circha miglia 30; la mattina ci trovamo sopra capo di Palo e sopra Cartagena.

Giovedì mattina, con pocho vento e contradio a noi, ma mare [in] bonaccia, ci trovamo sopra Cartagena, et avendo bisogno d'aqua si diliberava d'andarvi per rinfreschamento d'aqua et di vino, chè più non aveva la ciurma, et altre cose. Non parve a quegli dell'altra galea per sospetto et maxime perche ii navi uscirono del 109ᵛ porto al'alba ∥ del dì. Et ricordandoci quello c'era stato fatto a Ponteveteri et che Cartagena era de' re di Spagna, diliberamo patire disagio et andare di lungho, et così tutto dì navicamo con venti contradi l'una volta e l'altra, perchè era mare [in] bonaccia. La sera ci trovamo sopra Guardamare[3] preso alla Cantera in Catalognia de' re di Raona [*sic*: Aragona]. La nocte navichamo con venti contradii et bonaccievoli et pocho avanzamo; pure la mattina, cioè venerdì mattina adì 17 di marzo, ci trovamo sopra la Cantera, ma perchè il

---

[1] Almuñécar and Salobreña.

[2] Bera was probably Vera which now is some distance from the sea but perhaps gave its name to a small coast settlement.

[3] Guardamer del Segura, 20 miles south-west of Alicante.

vento era dal tereno non potemo aterare ivi nè a Villagioiosa nè a
Bendormi, et disagio avavamo asai d'aqua noi e lle ciurme, et vino
pocho e lla ciurma niente. Per che diliberamo pigliare a Sciabbia o a
Denia, et così facemo perchè rinfreschandosi il vento a ora di nona,
da libeccio e ponente, ce ne venimo a Sciabbia a ore 22 o circha, et
subito mettemo in terra le barche et gli sc[h]ifi, per aqua et per vino.
Et stando ad aspettare l'aqua con molti huomini ch'erano in terra,
circha a sera [a] nocte entrò in // detto porto una galea sottile di 110ᴿ
messer Bernardo di Gabriera et volle sapere nuove et a noi ne disse;[1]
et sentimo erano in quegli mari 7 galee sottili armate, che stavano
per la guerra degli spagnuoli. Sollecitamo quanto si poteva, per
non ci avere a trovare con loro, che dissono erano a Denia 2 o 3
altre galee, et quella si levò a nocte mostrando d'andare là. A ora
4 di nocte riavemo in galea le barche et gl'uomini coll'aqua et con
botti 2 di vino o circha, et subito facemo vela et uscimo di detto
porto con buono vento a nostro camino, et col nome di Dio
pigliamo la volta di Maiolicha.

Detto dì, sopra Villagioiosa, esendo in bonaccia, la mattina fe'
leggere le condanagioni ordinate de' fuggiti et d'altri. In detto
luogho trovamo le mandrolle già sì dure, che non se ne mangiave più.

Sabato mattina adì 18 di marzo, ci trovamo sopra l'isola di
Evizza e'l vento tornò alo scilocco, per modo non potemo passare
tra Ievizza et Maioricha come volavamo; convenneci entra//re 110ᵛ
dentro, perchè el vento ci saltò al davanti, a grecho et levante,
come era prosimo al'isola. Per che, veduto con detti tenpi non
potere andare di fuori nè pigliare l'isola, parve al nostro comito
et agl'uomini di consiglio et così al padrone che se'l tenpo il
concedessi, che noi andassimo dentro, non potendo ire di fuori,
più tosto che tornare a Sciabbia o a altro luogho di Catalogna, per
rispetto delle galee sottili armate che v'erano.[2] Feci domandare
l'altra galea per messer Luciano da Portoveneri. Rispuosegli il
gomito per parte del padrone, e disse che così ancora pareva a loro;
et così la sera rimanemo di fare secondo che'l tempo ne dicessi la
nocte. Et trovamnoci atraverso del'is[ol]a di Maioricha presso a

[1] Cabrera (Gabriera) is a small island off Majorca—so Bernardo must have been
an Aragonese subject.
[2] In this context by *dentro* Luca means to the north-west or landward side of
Majorca, whereas *fuori* was the south side. He planned to sail, eventually succeed-
ing, along the south coast, presumably to avoid being blown towards Catalonia.
Both Cape Biancho and Cape de Salinas to which he refers are on this south coast
of the island.

miglia 15 o circha la sera a nocte. La nocte si misse vento a grecho e levante a noi in prua, ma bonaccievole, per che ci fu necessario tornare a l'isola di Maioricha alla Dragonara. Entramo di fuori 111ʳ dell'isola la mattina ch'era bonaccia e levamo aqua per la conpa‖gna, e 'l vento saltò a mezzodì circa a terza.

Domenicha mattina adì 19, ci trovamo alla Dragonara di Maiolicha et pigliamo la volta di fuori per rispetto delle lelde,[1] vedendo non potere passare sanza essere conosciuti. Il vento ch'era a mezzodì c'era scarso, pure insino a sera navichamo tirandoci innanzi. La sera il vento tornò a noi per prua, et noi surgemo al'isola tra capo Biancho et capo delle Saline, a uno miglia o circha in terra, per aspettare quello il tenpo facessi, perchè allora era bonaccievole et chiaro. La nocte calmò, sicchè ci levamo col venticciuolo dalla terra e lla mattina, cioè lunedì mattina adì 20, ci trovamo a capo delle Saline e 'l vento tornò a levante, a noi contradio, per che non potendo prodegiarlo perch'era frescho, circha ora di nona pigliamo la volta di mare et po' tornamo in terra credendo pigliare Portopetro, ma non potemo et per non tornare adietro entramo in una cala si chiama cala Fichiera,[2] luogho molto stretto ma assai buono, 111ᵛ dove trovamo assai paesani che stavano ‖ alla guardia che corsali o loro nimici non dismontassino per fare terazzaneria et anchora traevano non sapiendo che galee si fussino. Il luogho era molto salvaticho, ma mandamo alla villa per avere rinfreschamento, lungi più che 2 miglia; quivi non si trovava altro che legne, aqua non c'era. Il dì tutto dì et così il dì dinanzi, avevamo vedute ii grosse navi volteggiare sopra l'isola di Gabriera tra l'isola et Maioricha, ma non potemo sapere che navi fussino. Stimavassi fussino di corso, perchè gl'uomini di cala Fichiera ci dissono ch'avevano volteggiato così iiii dì et credevano fussino di male afare. Detto dì fe' fare la rasegna alla galea conserva: trovo aveva suo conto.

Martedì et mercholedì adì 22 di marzo, per tenpo contradio da levante et grosso mare, stemo pure in detto luogho di cala Fichiera et quivi con molto disagio per lo mare che v'entrava grosso; e' 112 luogho era stretto ch'apena vi si capeva, e 'l mare ribolliva in modo che essendo ormegiati in 4, con prodesi in terra, d'o‖gni banda avavamo sospette, per forma che x prodesi avavamo in terra.[3]

---

[1] *lelde*: Dr. Corti has suggested that the *lelda* was an Aragonese levy on shipping.

[2] Cala Figuera and Porto Petro are close together on the south coast of Majorca.

[3] *ormeggiare in quattro*: a technical term meaning to anchor with two hawsers and two anchors out in the same direction or at a very acute angle to each other. This method of mooring was sometimes referred to as *a barba di gatto*.

Tanto mare vi si rivolgeva, che tutto il porto bolliva, e' luogho era sì stretto che bisognava stare l'una galea per poppa al'altra. Pigliamo aqua a stento, perch'era di lungi circha miglia 3 in 4, e bisognava conperarla. Altro rinfreschamento pocho potemo avere per le ville ch'erano di lungi.

Giovedì mattina adì 23 di marzo, essendo abonacciato, uscimo di detto luogho di cala Fichiera per pigliare uno porto presso a miglia 4, che ssi chiama porto Petro. Quando fumo ivi, si misse inbatto da libeccio, per che andamo di lungho, e lla sera a nocte ci trovamo sopra Cittadella di Minoricha.[1] Et perchè la nocte doveva fare la luna et anche perchè il vento calmò e 'l tenpo era caricho, alchuni volevano ire in porto, pure ci atenemo a chi disse di stare in mare. La nocte a ore ii di nocte o circha, si misse vento frescho da grecho et tramontana, nostro contradio, che ssi dice ‖ in quegli 112ᵛ meri nerbonese,[2] per che ci bisognò volteggiare insino a giorno. A levare del sole, veduto il vento stare a suo segno frescho, pigliamo la volta di Cittadella di Minoricha, et col nome di Dio surgemo nel suo porto innanzi nona. Quivi demo largho alla ciurma si fornissi, perch'era buono luogho et buona terra, et presesi molto rinfreschamento per le conpagne et pe' marinai, di vino, pane, erbaggio e altre cose; et così venderono nella terra molte loro cose,[3] cioè, venerdì adì 24 di marzo. E lla sera a nocte, avemo ognuno in galea quantunque degli ubriachi asai, per aspettare i ltenpo la nocte da levarci. E la nocte medesima, circha mezza nocte, si misse venticciuolo a libeccio et mezzodì, et noi uscimo del porto col nome di Dio.

Sabato adì 25 di marzo, il dì di Nostra Donna,[4] navichamo tutto dì per la gratia di Dio con vento prospero; la sera a nocte ci trovamo circha miglia 100 in mare de' Lione da Cittadella di Minoricha. ‖

Domenicha adì 26 di marzo 1430 navicamo tutto dì et così la 113ʳ nocte dinanzi, con prospero vento, quasi tutto dì, salvo in sulla nona avemo molte mutationi. La sera stimamo essere in mare larghi da Minorcha miglia 260 o circha et dal'isola d'Ieri intorno

---

[1] Ciudadela.

[2] The wind from Narbonne.

[3] The custom of medieval seamen carrying out small trading operations on their own account, known as the seaman's venture, was accepted by all the maritime regulations of the time. The Florentine regulations placed severe limits on the amount of space allowed to each of the galley crews for his belongings and his 'venture', but they nevertheless make it apparent that the custom was accepted.

[4] Lady Day, 25 March, was the first day of the year by Florentine reckoning.

di 80 o 90.[1] Et detto dì facemo podestà Simone Guiducci detto Ghiozzo,[2] et consigliere Luciano da Portovenere, Bartolomeo da Bonifacio nocchiere, et il Cervelliera di . . . prodiere. Et navichamo tutto dì e lla nocte apresso con buono vento. Et lunedì mattina adì 27 di marzo 1430 ci trovamo sopra Calvi di Corsicha con buono vento et frescho da libeccio, et giugnemo alla Gorgona circha ore 20 et quivi facemo i segni ordinati co' consoli nella partita per avere aviso, come era ordinato, facendo i fumi e traendo le bonbarde. Ci acostamo insino sotto la fortezza, per forma ci potevano bene vedere et conoscere. Niuno segno o risposta ci fu fatta, per che passamo di lungho; et per la gratia di Dio, tra le 22 et 23 ore, entramo in Porto Pisano et per la pocha aqua aduramo 2 volte. ‖

113ᵛ Uscici incontro Mariano da Piombino con una galea sottile armate et Papi Tedaldi con una galeotta di 22 banchi et uno brigantino che padroneggiava Petruccio da Turpia.[3] Da loro sentimo come il signore di Luccha aveva a soldo 4 galee catalane, per che maggiore admiratione ebbi come i consoli non ci avevano fatto sentire alla Gorgona d'aviso, come ero d'acordo rimaso con loro. Questo dicho perchè pocho pare prezzino le loro galee poi che l'ànno mandate, nè più se ne ricordano quando per inavertentia lasciano adietro tanto aviso et sì utile, per niente di spesa.[4] Ringratia Idio che per sua pietà et misericordia che ci condusse a salvamento da Antona a Porto Pisano in 32 dì, di che sempre sia lodato et rin-gratiato. La nocte stetti in galea, et martedì adì 28 vennono i consoli et a ora di nona fu' licentiato. Dismontai in terra et andai a visitare Nostra Donna piena di gratia.[5]

---

[1] Île d'Hyères.

[2] *Podestà* was not a rank ever mentioned in the galley regulations but presumably he was responsible for discipline.

[3] The war with Lucca had started and so the harbour guard had been strengthened and was on the alert. Mariano da Piombino was a minor naval *condottiere* who in 1431 was patron of one of the Genoese galleys at the battle of Rapallo (Polidori, 'Lettera di Raimondo Mannelli', p. 145). Papi Tedaldi became one of the better-known Florentine galley commanders; he commanded one of the Florentine galleys in the same battle, and later sailed as patron in two galley fleets to England and Flanders.

[4] This was one of the unfortunate effects of the rotation of Sea Consuls. Promises and commitments made by one group were possibly entirely unknown to and fre-quently neglected by the next. Even the notaries were changed every year and so there was no real administrative continuity.

[5] By visiting S. Maria 'in pleno gratiae' in Leghorn, Luca was fulfilling the first of a number of vows he had made before leaving on the voyage. Other churches in which he had vowed to offer candles on his safe return were S. Maria a Rigoli,

Mercholedì adì 29 andai a Pisa e qui alberghai.

Giovedì adì 30 a Montelupo.

Venerdì adì 31 di marzo, per la gratia di Dio a Firenze et fu fornito il viaggio, lodato Idio, e 'l dì medesimo mi rapresentai a' consoli. E martedì adì 4 aprile 1430 incamerai le condanagioni di viaggio.

Adì 2 di giugno fu' libero del sindacato.[1]

SS. Annunziata in Florence, S. Giovanni Gualberti in Vallombrosa, and S. Romualdo in Camaldoli (Diary, f. 8ᵛ).

[1] In the meantime the Consuls would have been auditing the accounts of the voyage, and hearing any complaints about the conduct of the expedition by Luca and the patrons. Before this had been done none of them could be completely released from their responsibilities.

Letter to Luca di *Maso* degli *Albizzi* from the Sea Consuls

Nobili et Egregio viro Luce Masi de Albizis de Florentia [civi] Flor. [h]onorabili capitaneo ghalearum, etc.

Spectabilis et egregie vir etc. Adì 7 di questo ricevemo tua lettera fatta alle Schiuse adì 6 di dicembre, la quale ci diè non piccola consolatione et allegreza, veduto che per la Iddio gratia siate giunti a salvamento. Et veduto quello scrivi dello honore ricevuto dal re di Portoghallo, ci è somma letitia, et bene comprendiamo dal canto delle ghalee si fece in modo che l'onore del comune non rimase adietro, di che e te et i padroni sommamente commendiamo.

Et al fatto scrivi della franchigia ne' suoi porti come ànno i vinitiani, ci piace molto si sia chiesta. Et perchè ad effecto si conduca, abbiamo adoperato co' nostri Magnifici Signori che lla loro Signoria ne scrive una lettera alla Mtà del re, suplicando detta franchigia et ringratiandolo dello honore fattovi. Et noi ancora ne scriviamo ad Antonio Marabotti e Bartolomeo da Firenze che sollecitino, ringratiandoli di quello ànno fatto.[1] Et però alla tornata, se potrete, a Lisbona di nuovo la chiedete che speriamo l'arete.

Al fatto scrivi de' 3 balenieri et delle 2 navi et dell'arciveschovo di san Iacopo, et quanto villanamente contro di voi si sono portati, ci duole. Et tutto abbiamo fatto noto a' nostri Magnifici Signori e a' loro collegii, et per loro s'è deliberata lettera al re di Castiglia la quale mandiamo per uno fante proprio et così quella del re di Portogallo, nella quale i nostri Signori si dolgono delle iniurie ricevute et per l'avenire preghano il re voglia provedere che ingiuria non vi sia fatto pe' suoi sottoposti.

Et alla commessione chiedi s'allarghi in case essendosi volessi essere offeso, a questo rispondiamo che abbiamo avutone il consiglio di valenti et buoni mercatanti, non pare loro nè anche

[1] The *Signoria* wrote to the King of Portugal along these lines on 9 Jan. 1430 (Miss. I Canc. 32, f. 167). See also Canestrini, 'Relazioni commerciali coi Portoghesi', pp. 98–99.

a nnoi per non recare a chasa nuova inimicitia, et per più altri rispecti. I fiorentini ànno i capelli troppo lunghi, non è ancora tenpo.

Al fatto d'aggiungere 20 marinai et 10 conpagnoni per galea, rispondiamo essere contenti et così vogliamo et commandiamo si facci et vada ad avaria delle mercatantie, salvo che lle spese del vivere, le quali vogliamo, e così è ragionevole, vadino a spese de' padroni. Ma abbia advertenza togliate tali huomini che siano pratichi, atti et experti e benivoli del nostro comune e da tenerne buono servigio. Et in conclusione, tu se' in sul fatto et se' persona prudente et discreta; provedi e fa' in modo che debitamente ne meriti essere commendato. Nè altro per questa. Parati ad bene-placita tua. Florentie, die x mensis januarii 1429.

Consules Maris }
Comunis Florentie }

Account of the loading of the galleys in Southampton

45ʳ Ricordo de' dì utili che staremo ad Antona.[1]

Giugnemo ad Antona adì 7 di gennaio in sabato a ora di vespro o circha; adì 8 fu domenicha et adì 15. Lunedì adì 16 di gennaio avemo in punto gli argani delle galee per stivare et protestato al consolo essere a sua petitione. Detto [dì] si cominciò a pesare tardi, a ora di vespro o circha; pesossi poche 290, missonsi in su tre batti et parte in galea, ma niente la sera si potè stivare per l'ora tarda. La notte piov[v]e tutta notte e l'altro dì, per modo si bagnarono la più parte delle lane et fu Santo Antonio adì 17. Di questi di sopra, dì 3 disutili per le feste.

1. Mercoledì adì 18 fu il primo dì si conta alla stiva, passati i x dalla nostra giunta, per lo manifesto et mettere a punto gli argani. Il dì si stivò la lana ch'era asciutta in galee, che non fornì la prima andana, sicchè non si potè lavorare da terza in là.

2. Giovedì adì 19 il dì 2°, piov[v]e tutto dì e era piovuta la nocte dinanzi, sicchè niente si potè fare.

3. Venerdì adì 20 fu parte da lavorare et pesossi la sera 50 poche di Totto.[2] Piov[v]e per modo si lavorò pocho. ½ dì stimo utile.

4. Sabato adì 21, piov[v]e tutto dì, pure si stivò le nane [*sic*: lane] ch'erano in galea e di quelle del primo dì ch'erano rasciutte, e lavorassi tutto il dì.

5. Domenicha adì 22 per la festa niente si fè e piov[v]e tutto dì insino a nocte.

[1] This detailed account of the loading of the galleys in Southampton was obviously written by Luca with the regulations concerning the loading time-table in mind. Every day of the forty-five days allowed is accounted for, and in fact he succeeded in keeping to the time-table despite rain and holidays. The regulations actually laid down that 'i padroni debbano tenere dopo i detti dieci di [the first ten days set aside for unloading and preparing the manifest], xx dì l'argano et ricevere et stivare le robe sieno date loro mentre durarano detti xx dì. Et poi per altri x dì sequenti che sieno in tutto dì quaranta, detti mercatanti debbano avere dato et carico in galea tutti i panni, mercie et altri mercatantia et cose volessino in su quelle caricare. Et passati i detti XL dì, fra cinque di poi sequenti, debbano avere spacciato ogni loro roba e cose avessino carico d'ogni costume o vero gabella e d'ogni altro impaccio avessino in modo che nessuna cosa per loro resta a fare' (Consoli del Mare V, *Capitoli dei capitani*, c. 6).　　　[2] Totto Machiavelli.

6. Lunedì adì 23 non piov[v]e; stivossi tutto dì, salvo la galea Vespuccia, perchè marinai volevano denari, non si poterono avere tutti nè tutto dì. Dì 3 utili stimo i sopradetti 6.

7. Martedì adì 24 piov[v]e la mattina, pure, perch'era lana in 45ᵛ galea, si lavorò tutto dì.

8. Mercholedì adì 25 fu buono tenpo et dì utili, manchò parte per non avere i costumieri.

9. Giovedì adì 26 si lavorò tutto dì et pesossi pocche 140 di Totto per rata.

10. Venerdì adì 27 lavorossi tutto dì.

11. Sabato adì 28 di gennaio si lavorò tutto dì, conpiessi la prua di stivare andane 6, mutossi gli arghani et pesossi pocche 49 per lunedì, avemone 25.

12. Domenicha adì 29 per la festa non si lavorò e fu buon tenpo.

13. Lunedì adì 30 di gennaio fu buon tenpo; lavorossi et pesossi pocche 72, d'elle ebbene la nostra 40.

14. Martedì adì 31 di gennaio fu buon tenpo; pesossi 42 pocche per galea, in tutto 84.

15. Mercholedì adì 1° di febraio fu buon tenpo.

16. Giovedì adì 2 fu Santa Maria Candelaia, per la festa niente si fè.

17. Venerdì adì 3 di febraio pioveggginò quasi tutto dì et non si potè pesare, ma lavorassi il forte lane di galea.

18. Sabato adì 4 si pesò pocche 40 alla galea capitana et 30 alla conserva, in tutto 70; piov[v]e grande parte del dì.

19. Domenicha adì 5 per la festa niente si fè.

20. Lunedì adì 6 di febraio piov[v]e parte; erano lane in galea, lavorossi.

21. Martedì adì 7 fu buon tenpo.

22. Mercholedì adì 8 fu buon tenpo.

23. Giovedì adì 9 fu buon tenpo.

24. Venerdì adì 10 fu buon tenpo; stivossi insino a vespro 46ʳ poi s'arborò et levossi l'argano perch'erano stivate le lane.

25. Sabato adì 11 cominciorono a stivare baloni et missonci l'antenna nostra.

26. Domenicha adì 12 per la festa niente si fè.

27. Lunedì adì 13 fu buon tenpo; a' balloni.

28. Martedì adì 14 di febraio, buon tenpo; balloni.

29. Mercholedì adì 15, buon tenpo.

30. Giovedì adì 16, buon tenpo et fornissi di caricare ciò ch'era in Antona.

Somma insino a qui dì 40 contenti, de' quali v'ero[no] disutili 11 cioè

7 domeniche
1 Santo Antonio
1 Santa Maria Candellaia   Somma i dì disutili dì xi.
2 per piova

Restano gl'utili dì 29 insino adì 16 di febraio.

2. Venerdì adì 17 et sabato adì 18 fu buon tenpo.

Domenicha adì 19 per la festa niente si fè.

2. Lunedì adì 20 fu buon tenpo. Martedì adì 21.

1. Mercholedì adì 22 montai in galea col nome di Dio, spacciati di tutto.

1. Giovedì adì 23 di febraio, circha ora di nona, col nome di Dio facemo vela.

APPENDIX C

The Rhythm of Sailing of the Florentine Galleys

IN 1961 E. Fasano Guarini produced a very interesting study of three Venetian galley itineraries of the sixteenth century.[1] From an analysis of these itineraries Mlle Fasano Guarini was able to arrive at a number of conclusions regarding the rhythm of sailing of these galleys. In the first place she was able to conclude that on these voyages only slightly over a third of the time was spent actually navigating either with sail or oars. The remaining two-thirds of the time was either reckoned as lost due to bad weather, or spent at anchor reprovisioning, resting the crew, or in port for other purposes. For two of the voyages it was also possible to divide the period of navigation according to the method of propulsion used (e.g. oars, sails, or both). From this computation it emerged that the ratio of time spent using oars alone to that spent using sails alone was about 5 to 7.

I have attempted to carry out the same sort of calculation of the rhythm of sailing of Luca di Maso degli Albizzi's galleys, bearing in mind at the same time that these were great galleys as opposed to the long galleys and 'bastard' galleys which Mlle Fasano Guarini was studying. The effect of this difference was considerable; in the first place the great galleys relied on sail far more than the long galleys; secondly, and partly as a result of this, they required fewer stops for rests, but more for trade; thirdly they were less affected by bad weather.

In my calculations I have not attempted to distinguish between trade stops and stops for reprovisioning. The two frequently co-incided and I have regarded all such stops as legitimate for this type of galley. On the other hand I have tried to distinguish the stops and hold-ups caused by bad weather. When bad weather prevented departure after a stop for trade, I have allowed only the stopping time laid down in the regulations for each port as legitimate, or twenty-four hours if it was a trading stop unspecified in the regulations. If, however, departure was delayed after a simple reprovisioning stop, I have allowed only the initial twelve hours as legitimate, and thereafter have considered the time as lost due to bad weather. On occasions the galleys

---

[1] Fasano Guarini, 'Comment naviguent les galères', *passim*. See above, pp. 31–33, for a larger discussion of the rhythm of sailing of great galleys.

were also forced to retrace their steps or heave to, entirely because of adverse weather conditions, and on such occasions I have attempted to assess the length of time lost.

Finally there is insufficient information in Luca's diary to be able to distinguish sailing time from rowing time, but it is possible to say that these galleys were very rarely rowed for long periods.

The result of these calculations is therefore:

1. Outward voyage: Porto Pisano (14 Sept.) — Marseilles — Aigues-mortes — Barcelona — Majorca — Javea — Gibraltar — Cadiz — Lisbon — Pontevedra — Ribadeo — Sluys (6 Dec.).

Navigation time	776½ hours	38·88%
Provisioning and trade stops	470½ hours	23·57%
Bad weather delays	750 hours	37·55%
	1,997 hours	100%

(83 days and 5 hours)

2. Return voyage: Southampton (23 Feb.) — Lisbon — Silvis — Cadiz — Majorca — Porto Pisano (27 March).

Navigation time	532½ hours	68·6%
Provisioning and trade stops	74 hours	9·8%
Bad weather delays	166 hours	21·6%
	772½ hours	100%

(32 days and 4½ hours)

On the outward voyage this basic rhythm differed little from that of the sixteenth-century Venetian galleys except that trade stops took the place of rest stops. However, on the return voyage when little trade was done the whole picture changed completely. This second pattern perhaps gives us a truer impression of the voyage of a medieval great galley when no external circumstances (trade, military commitments, sight-seeing, etc.) dictated the course of the voyage.

MAP 2. Map of Europe and the Mediterranean
and the route

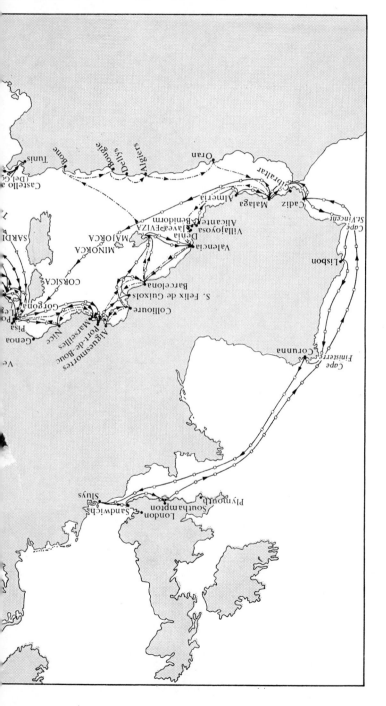

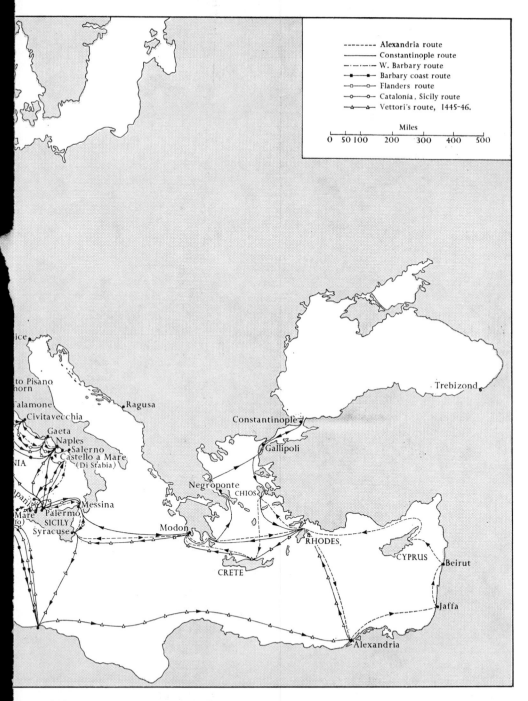

Alexandria route
Constantinople route
W. Barbary route
Barbary coast route
Flanders route
Catalonia, Sicily route
Vettori's route, 1445-46.

Trebizond

ice

to Pisano
horn

alamone
Ragusa

Civitavecchia

Gaeta
Naples
Salerno
Castello a Mare
(Di Stabia)

NIA

Constantinople

Gallipoli

Negroponte
CHIOS

Messina
Mare
fo)
Palermo
SICILY
Syracuse

Modon

RHODES

CYPRUS
Beirut

CRETE

Jaffa

Alexandria

n, illustrating the routes of the Florentine galleys as laid down in 1447,
of Luigi Vettori's galleys in 1445-46.

INDEX

Index

291

PRINTED IN GREAT BRITAIN
AT THE UNIVERSITY PRESS, OXFORD
BY VIVIAN RIDLER
PRINTER TO THE UNIVERSITY